Thinkin

Second Edition

Gary R. Kirby

Jeffery R. Goodpaster

Prentice Hall
Upper Saddle River, NJ 07458

Library of Congress Cataloging-in-Publication Data

Kirby, Gary.
  Thinking / Gary Kirby, Jeffery R. Goodpaster. — 2nd ed.
    p. cm.
  Includes bibliographical references and index.
  ISBN 0-13-081443-1
  1. Thought and thinking. I. Goodpaster, Jeffery R. II. Title.
BF441.K49 1999
153.4′2—dc21
                                                          98-6236
                                                            CIP

Editorial/production supervision: *Harriet Tellem*
Acquisitions editor: *Karita France*
Manufacturing buyer: *Tricia Kenny*
Cover design: *Kiwi Design*
Editorial assistant: *Jennifer Ackerman*

This book was set in 11/13 Garamond by BookMasters, Inc. and was printed and bound by Courier, Westford. The cover was printed by Phoenix Color Corp.

©1999, 1995 by Prentice-Hall, Inc.
Upper Saddle River, New Jersey 07458

Printed in the United States of America
10 9 8 7 6 5 4 3

ISBN 0-13-081443-1

Prentice-Hall International (UK) Limited, *London*
Prentice-Hall of Australia Pty. Limited, *Sydney*
Prentice-Hall Canada Inc., *Toronto*
Prentice-Hall Hispanoamericana, S.A., *Mexico*
Prentice-Hall of India Private Limited, *New Delhi*
Prentice-Hall of Japan, Inc., *Tokyo*
Pearson Education Asia Pte. Ltd., *Singapore*
Editora Prentice-Hall do Brasil, Ltda., *Rio de Janeiro*

Contents

PREFACE   **xxi**

CHAPTER 1   WHAT IS THINKING?   **1**

Our Cultural Legacy   1

Why Think?   2

Thinking Activity 1.1:
Things More Important Than Thinking   2

   Thoughts Richer Than Gold   3

   Thinking as Possibility   4

   Thoughts Accumulate   4

   Life Without Thinking   4

What Is Thinking?   5

   The Mystery   5

   Toward a Definition: Thinking as Communicating   5

Communicating: The Mirror of Thought   6

Box: The Centrality of Thinking   6

Thinking as Writing: Clarity, Exactness, Awareness, Richness   7

Thinking Activity 1.2:
Thinking, Sensing, Writing   8

Thinking as Dialogue: Validation and Insight   9

Misthinking   10

Summary   10

Thinking Challenges   11

CHAPTER 2   PERSONAL BARRIERS   **13**

Enculturation   13

Sources of Enculturation   14

Box: Some Common American Beliefs   15

Box: Religion and Enculturation   15

Thinking Activity 2.1:
Our Own Enculturation   16

Self-Concept   19

Thinking Activity 2.2:
The Idea of Self   20

Thinking Activity 2.3:
Letting Go   21

Ego Defenses   22

Denial   22

Projection   22

Rationalization   23

Self-Serving Biases   24

Box: Other Attribution Errors   25

Box: Self-Serving Biases?   25

Thinking Activity 2.4:
Owning Up to Our Dark Side   26

The Role of Expectations and Schemata   27

Emotional Influences   29

Anger   29

Passion   31

Depression   32

Thinking Activity 2.5:
Five Thinking Errors   35

Striving for Cognitive Consistency   36

Stress   38

Box: Signs and Symptoms of Stress   39

Stress Management   40

Summary   42

Barrier Challenges   42

CHAPTER 3   SENSING   **44**

Sensual Beginnings   44

The Power of Our Senses   45

The Deception of Our Senses   45

Thinking Activity 3.1:
Ideas: Innate or Learned?   46

Thinking Activity 3.2:
Our Personal Sense Deceptions   47

Sharpening Our Senses   48

Thinking Activity 3.3:
Seeing Anew   49

Powerful Listening   49
  The Paradox of Powerful Listening   49
  How to Listen   50

Thinking Activity 3.4:
Developing an Action Plan   52

Summary   53

Sensing and Thinking Challenges   53

CHAPTER 4   BRAIN AND MEMORY   **56**

The Mystery   56

Thinking and Our Brain   57

Thinking Activity 4.1:
An Exercise in Mental Discipline   58
  Food and Drugs   58
  Sleep   61

Thinking Activity 4.2:
Critical Reading Before We Sleep   61
  Our Thinking Potential   62

Box: Brain and Mind   64

Thinking and Memory   65
  The Changing Nature of Memory   66

Thinking Activity 4.3:
Memories of Childhood   66

   Forgetting 68

Box: Recall vs. Recognition   69

   Why We Forget 69

   How to Improve Memory 70

Thinking Activity 4.4:
Using Mnemonics   71

Summary   73

Brain and Memory Challenges   73

CHAPTER 5   LANGUAGE: OUR THINKING MEDIUM   76

Thinking Activity 5.1:
Language and Thinking   77

Language and Our Mind   77

   The Universalizing Power of Language 78

   The Structuring Power of Language 78

Language and Society   79

Thinking Activity 5.2:
A Brief Mind Sketch   80

The Metaphorical Power of Language   82

   What Is a Metaphor? 82

Metaphorical Models Control Thinking,   82

Box: Language, Lawyers, and Lawmakers   84

The Limitations of Language   84

The Power of English   85

   Word Meanings 85

Thinking Activity 5.3:
The Language in Our Mind   86

Thinking Activity 5.4:
Identifying Our Flame Words   88

   Word Order Creates Meaning 89

   The Power Parts: Noun and Verb 90

   Thinking and the Context 90

   Clarity 91

Box: Clearly Embarrassing   91

The Pitfalls of English   91

   Generalizations and Abstractions 91

Box: High Specificity   92

   Wordiness 92

   Redundancies 92

   Illogicalities 93

   Clichés 93

Summary   94

Language Challenges   94

CHAPTER 6   FEELING   97

Feelings and Thinking   97

Cultural Context   98

   Business 98

   Church 98

   Family 99

The Force Behind Our Thoughts   99

   Beneath the Rational Surface 99

   The Importance of Tone 100

Thinking Activity 6.1:
Feelings Beneath Our Thoughts   100

Generating Speech   101

Generating Writing   102

   The Inspiration Method   102

   The Recollection Method   103

   The Conscious Selection Method   103

Feelings Toward Topic and Audience   103

Thinking Activity 6.2:
Evoking Emotions   104

Summary   104

Thinking/Feeling Challenges   105

CHAPTER 7   CREATIVE THINKING   **107**

What Is Creativity   108

Metaphorical Thinking   108

Thinking Activity 7.1:
Making Metaphors   109

Kinds of Creative Thinking   110

Who Can Think Creatively?   110

Thinking Activity 7.2:
Poetic Impressions   111

Conditions and Limitations of Creativity   111

Beginning to Create   112

   Brainstorming   112

   Starbursting   112

Coaxing Creativity   114

    Step 1: Desire   114

    Step 2: Knowledge and Skills   114

    Step 3: Edisonian Effort   114

Thinking Activity 7.3:
Prepcreation   115

    Step 4: Fermentation and Insight   116

    Step 5: Evaluation   117

Summary   117

Box: Leonardo da Vinci   117

Creative Thinking Challenges   117

CHAPTER 8 ORGANIZING   **119**

Origins of Order   119

Natural/Mental Orders   120

    Topical Order   120

    Analogical Order   120

    Chronological Order   120

    Causal Order   121

Thinking Activity 8.1:
Other Natural Orders?   121

Thinking Activity 8.2:
The Order of the Elements   121

Mental Orders   122

Thinking Activity 8.3:
Other Mental Orders   123

    Clarity and Memory   124

Steps in Organizing   124

Clustering   125

Analyzing   126

Thinking Activity 8.4:
Analyzing the Clusters   126

Prioritizing   127

Using the Orders   127

Thinking Activity 8.5:
Creating a Seminal Structural Analogy   130

Curtain Call   131

Summary   131

Organizing Challenges   132

CHAPTER 9   LOGICAL THINKING   **134**

DEDUCTIVE THINKING: THE SYLLOGISM   134

Categorical Syllogisms   135

Three Kinds of Propositions   137

Four Figures   138

Thinking Activity 9.1:
Drawing the Conclusion   138

Thinking Activity 9.2:
Finding Terms and Figures   139

Validity of Categorical Syllogisms   141

Thinking Activity 9.3:
Identifying Valid Categorical Syllogisms   142

Thinking Activity 9.4:
Using Venn Diagrams   142

Enthymemes and Syllogisms in Everyday Life   147

Thinking Activity 9.5:
Finding Multiple Syllogisms and False Premises   150

Soft Deductions   151

Thinking Activity 9.6:
Challenging Soft Deductions   154

Reasoning Errors in Categorical Syllogisms   154

Undistributed Middle   *154*

Illicit Process   *156*

Thinking Activity 9.7:
Finding Undistributed Terms   159

The Four-Terms Fallacy   *159*

Equivocation   *160*

Box: The Importance of Agreed Meaning   161

Rules for the Categorical Syllogism   162

Thinking Activity 9.8:
Identifying Invalid Syllogisms   163

Hypothetical Syllogisms   163

Reasoning Errors in Hypothetical Syllogisms   *165*

Disjunctive Syllogisms   167

Reasoning Error in the Disjunctive Syllogism   *168*

Valid Conversions   168

Thinking Activity 9.9:
Writing Valid Conversions   171

Informal Deductive Fallacies   171

The Fallacy of Division   *171*

Circular Reasoning   172

The Either/Or Fallacy   172

Thinking Activity 9.10:
Identifying the Either/Or Fallacy   173

Box: Reductio ad Absurdum   174

INDUCTIVE THINKING   175

Thinking Activity 9.11:
Distinguishing Between Inductive and Deductive
Arguments   178

Thinking Activity 9.12:
Considering Past Errors   178

Analogical Argument   179

Box: Chuang Tzu's Analogies   180

Thinking Activity 9.13:
Using Analogies   181

Causation   181

Thinking Activity 9.14:
Thinking About Causation   182

Informal Inductive Fallacies   182

Hasty Generalization   182

Post Hoc Ergo Propter Hoc   183

Extravagant Hypothesis   184

False Analogy   185

The Fallacy of Composition   185

Slippery Slope   186

Other Reasoning Fallacies   187

Appeal to Authority   187

Appeal to Tradition   188

Bandwagon Appeal   189

Appeal to Ignorance   189

Summary   190

Logic Challenges   191

CHAPTER 10   SCIENTIFIC THINKING   **193**

The Scientific Method   193

Observation   193

Hypothesis   193

Experimentation   195

Verification   195

Science and Other Ways of Knowing   196

Box: Copernicus and Galileo   197

The Empirical Nature of Science   198

Erroneous Operational Definitions   198

Operational Debates   199

The Limits of Science   199

Thinking Activity 10.1:
Creating Operational Definitions   200

Thinking Activity 10.2:
The Domain of Science   201

Science and the Understanding of Human Nature   201

Determinism as Foundation   202

Human Beings and Determinism   202

Box: Determinism and Probability   205

Proving a Theory   205

Controlled Experiments   207

Correlational Designs   208

Significance   211

Box: Sizable Effects   213

Experimenter Bias   213

Box: Placebo Effect   215

Box: Cases of Fraud   216

The Survey   216

Case Studies   220

Box: Pseudoscience   221

Summary   222

Scientific Thinking Challenges   223

CHAPTER 11   PERSUASIVE THINKING   226

What Is Persuasion?   226

The Ethics of Persuasion   227

Thinking About What Moves Us   227

Box: Confucius, Christ, and Kant   228

Knowledge   228

Objectivity and Honesty   228

Biases   228

Likability   229

Motivation and Purpose   229

The Rational Appeal   229

The Emotional Appeal: The Root Elements   230

Thinking About What Moves Our Audience   231

Demographics   232

Thinking Activity 11.1:
A Demographic Analysis   232

Values and Needs   232

Thinking Activity 11.2:
Identifying Values and Needs   233

Adjusting Our Goals   234

Organizing for Persuasion   234

Thinking Activity 11.3:
Motivation Mountain   235

Step 1: Establishing Credibility   236

Step 2: Acknowledging the Audience's Position   236

Thinking Activity 11.4:
Recognizing the Other Side   237

Step 3: Constructing Our Rationale   238

Step 4: Transplanting the Root Elements   238

Step 5: Asking for the Response   238

Defending Ourselves Against Deceitful
Persuasion   239

Manipulative Tactics   239

Thinking Activity 11.5:
Your Vulnerability to Fear Appeals   243

Erroneous Attacks   244

Abuse of Language   246

Summary   247

Persuasion Challenges   248

CHAPTER 12   PROBLEM SOLVING   **251**

Defining the Problem   252
  Discovering Causes   253
  Problems Without a Cause   254

Removing Barriers   254
  The Myth of Perfection   254
  The Myth of Genius   255

Generating Solutions   255
  Gathering Information   255

Thinking Activity 12.1:
Identifying Problem Components   257

Box: Creating a Healthy Communication Climate   258

Creative Thinking   259

Thinking Activity 12.2:
Functional Fixedness   260

Selecting Solutions   260
  Preliminary Evaluation   260

Box: Chaotic Systems   262
  Pros and Cons   262

Box: Rejections on Minor Grounds   263

Thinking Activity 12.3:
Weighing Pros and Cons   264
  Subgoal Analysis   264
  Trial and Error   265
  Working Backwards   265
  Problem-Solving Tips   266

Evaluating Solutions   267

Summary   267

Problem-Solving Challenges   268

CHAPTER 13   EVALUATING   **270**

The Necessity to Test Thinking   271

The Crucible of Critical Dialogue   271

Thinking Activity 13.1:
Using Dialogue   272

Critical Monologue   272

The Elegance of Simplicity   272

The Flattery of Imitation and Development   273

The Power of Predictability   273

Perspective, Balance, and Completeness   274

The Test of Time   274

Thinking Activity 13.2:
Does Time Always Test True?   275

Testing Against Our Thinking Bases   275

Personal Barriers   275

Perceptions and Memory   275

Language   276

Feelings   276

Creativity Check   276

Organization   277

Logic Check   277

Thinking Activity 13.3:
Our Tone Toward Our Thinking   277

Summary   277

Validating Challenges   278

CHAPTER 14   **DECISION AND ACTION**   **280**

Why Act?   280

Decision   281

    Difficulties in Deciding   282

    How to Decide   284

Box: Changing Criteria: Putting on the Gloves   286

Thinking Activity 14.1:
Feelings and Decisions   286

Thinking Activity 14.2:
Role Playing   287

    When to Decide   287

    The Deciding Moment   288

Action   288

After Action   289

Thinking Activity 14.3:
An Action Plan for Improving Thinking   289

Summary   290

Decision and Action Challenges   290

CHAPTER 15   **THE CHALLENGE TO GO ON THINKING**   **292**

APPENDIX   **PROPOSITIONAL LOGIC**   **295**

           REFERENCES   **298**

           INDEX   **303**

Preface

We are but thinking reeds, but because we know, we are superior to the universe. Thought constitutes our greatness.

—*PASCAL*

THE CHALLENGE

This is a book about our thinking. If we begin to think more actively, some stunning changes are possible: we can know ourselves better, we can have more options in life, we can distinguish fact from fiction and hype from hope, we can begin to think more decisively as we choose liferoads to walk down, and we can become more persuasive as we listen and talk to our fellow thinkers.

We often define ourselves by our actions. In a way, we are what we do, but perhaps more than we realize, we are *what we think*. For instance, if people pretend to like someone whom they hate, is it their hateful thinking or their false acting (or both) that really represents what they are? "Whether a thought is spoken or not, it is the real thing and has power" (Herbert, 1987, p. 257).

We want you, the reader, to *use* this book, to challenge your mind, to strengthen your thinking ability. Says Dr. Arnold Scheible, director of the Brain Research Institute at UCLA, "If you decrease input you decrease structure. The brain is just like a muscle—use it or lose it."

We have used our brain to explore the universe, and the sciences of physics and astronomy are now firmly established. But exploring our brain will be more difficult. The neurosciences are still at an early stage, even though knowledge of the brain has leapt exponentially. We have already identified many of the neurotransmitters that control neural activity, and our ability to look inside the brain has progressed from anatomy to EEG to CAT to MRI to PET. Still, unlike the DNA code in genetics, the brain code has not been deciphered. If we use physics as a measure, brain research is still at the pre-Newtonian stage of knowledge.

Complicating this puzzle is our brain's enormous intricacy: Over a trillion cells compose it; 100 billion of them are neurons devoted to our thinking process. Each of these, on the average, reaches out to make thousands and thousands of other contacts. If we could walk along this marvelous labyrinth, the number of different journeys we could take may exceed the number of atoms in the universe! The neurons cannot communicate to quite that extent, but the number of real, potential pathways in the brain is still absolutely unimaginable! With such tremendous complexity, can our thinking brain even begin to comprehend itself?

And that, perhaps, is the greatest obstacle of all: we are attempting to know our mind *with* our mind. That is like a pair of pliers trying to grasp itself. How can the instrument of thinking grasp itself? While this obstacle may seem theoretically insurmountable, practically we do experience the ability to reflect on our thought; and in an attempt to escape from this cyclic conundrum, we will frequently stress communicating our thinking in writing and in dialogue so that we can objectively analyze the results of our thinking. One of the best ways to understand what is in our mind is by what comes out of it: our expressed thinking.

THE INTERDISCIPLINARY CHALLENGE

This book is not pitched towards a specific discipline: students of all disciplines think. No one area of research or academic discipline owns a monopoly on thinking: the more we share our knowledge the better thinking we can do. In this text we have begun at our classical wellspring of thought, and we have drawn ideas on thinking from every subsequent period of history from the philosophers, the poets, the scientists, the psychologists, the linguists, and more recently the neuroscientists.

Teachers of philosophy will find a large chapter on logic replete with syllogisms and fallacies, and will see contributions throughout this text from Parmenides, Heraclitus, Plato, Aristotle, Seneca, Marcus Aurelius, Ockham, Anselm, Aquinas, Montaigne, Pascal, Descartes, Bacon, Locke, Hume, Kant, Schopenhauer, Dewey, Russell, and Wittgenstein.

English teachers will find that our definition of thinking focuses on the expressed thought of writing: writing is called the mirror of our mind. Most of the chapters are directly applicable to writing. For instance, "Language" heightens word awareness, deepens knowledge about crafting a structure, and stresses clarity and brevity, thus assisting expository writing. "Sensing and Listening" helps the writer perceive more acutely and describe more vividly; thus it demonstrates the descriptive paper. "Feeling" helps writers infuse pulse and tone into their writing. "Creative Thinking," which addresses the beginning point of discovery that incorporates classical topics and invention, helps writers solve the fundamental hurdle of saying something strong and original. "Organizing" supports writing a research paper by demonstrating what all good writing needs: a clean structure. "Persuasive Thinking" presents powerful methods to move other minds that can be used in writing a persuasive paper. All of these chapters have been successfully used in writing classes, and there are over three hundred thinking challenges which can be given as writing assignments.

Science teachers will find a full chapter on scientific thinking as well as chapters dealing with each step of the scientific method: observation correlates with the chapter on sensing, hypothesis with creativity, experimentation with action, and validation with evaluation. Additionally, there are references to neuro-research, to the chaos theory, and to giants such as Galileo, Newton, Darwin, Mendeleev, Einstein, and Watson and Crick.

Psychology teachers will find that we deal with the whole person, addressing the cognitive, behavioral, and affective dimensions. The chapter "Personal Barriers" covers important cultural and psychological barriers to clear thinking. "Brain and Memory" addresses the neurological basis of thinking, the effects of drugs, and some characteristics of memory and forgetting. The chapter "Scientific Thinking" examines controlled experiments, correlational studies, surveys, case studies, and the assumptions of the scientific method. In addition, throughout this text we draw upon psychological research and such psychological thinkers as Freud, Jung, James, Skinner, and Maslow.

CHAPTER ARRANGEMENT: THINKING BASES

Thinking is a whole and cannot be chopped into chapters. Yet because we need some way to reflect upon and understand what is going on in our mind, we have organized this book according to "thinking bases," places to anchor and check a "part" of our thinking. Some of the major bases, or thinking platforms, are sensing, feeling, language, creating, organizing, logical thinking, judging, deciding, and acting. All of these bases interrelate and most of our thinking involves many of these fundamental bases.

Although the chapters on these bases are arranged somewhat "chronologically" from the original perception to the final result of thinking (decision and action), our thinking can begin at any point and jump to any other point. Rarely do we move systematically from one base to the next; sometimes we start with our memory and not with our senses. Except for repetition, each of our thinking acts is unique, just as each of us is unique. Pardon us then, this artificial, analytical act of chopping thinking into chapters.

THINKING SUPPORTS: PRACTICAL AND PERSONAL

To actively engage, enlarge, and enrich your thinking, to help you adapt and personalize the chapter concepts, and to provide meaningful in-class and out-of-class assignments, we have placed over three hundred thinking challenges throughout the book, arranged into three kinds:

1. At the end of each chapter there are over a dozen thinking challenges, most of which can be easily used for group discussions, a journal entry, a personal reflection essay, a research paper, or a class presentation.
2. Within each chapter there are major thinking activities to help students practice or apply a particular aspect of thinking. These, too, can be used in multiple ways.
3. Also inside each chapter are brisk ventures into thinking called "Think About It." These summons to think can also be used flexibly. All of the thinking supports in this book can greatly enliven a classroom.

In addition, the book contains selections from students and some highlighted material on great thinkers like Leonardo da Vinci or on systems of thought like *the chaos theory.* Each chapter has an introduction that weaves the coming sections together and a summary to reinforce and bring the concepts home.

As you read this text, we encourage you to pause and think often, to use this book as a beginning place to understand your thinking and to improve it, and then to go on to discover, create, and apply your thinking toward a richer life.

ASSUMPTIONS

While the fundamental epistemological and pedagogical assumptions that underlie this book will be discussed, a single statement can get us started: we believe that we can learn to think better with an honest effort at self-reflection and practice, tested and honed whenever possible in the dialogue of expressed thought.

We have presented one approach to understand and to sharpen thinking, and have attempted to avoid being dogmatic. The vast and largely unknown arena of the mind would be a foolish place in which to be dogmatic. We encourage you to think about the ideas in this book, to find the hidden assumptions, to challenge the stated positions, and most importantly, to adapt these thoughts into a better way of thinking for yourself.

THE SECOND EDITION

We have listened to teachers, reviewers, editors, colleagues, and students and have rewritten accordingly. We thank you all for your analyses, ideas, and support; especially we thank our students who have enjoyed and struggled with us towards better thinking.

Since good thinking is clear thinking, each sentence has been rechecked for clarity. With the student in mind, we have made the terminology friendlier while retaining accuracy. We have increased the number of thinking activities and challenges in most chapters, and we have added examples that are especially relevant to young adults thinking their way through the world.

Some of the more significant changes occur in the logic chapter. This chapter has been reorganized and expanded. To make the chapter more relevant to everyday logic, a section has been added on soft deductions, which applies the rigorous rules of logic to the world of probability. Substantial material on enthymemes and analogical argument have also been added. Finally, there are more thinking activities and many minor changes throughout. All of the logic material is presented in more manageable sections under clearer headings, which we hope will make the arduous act of logical thinking more accessible to the reader.

INSTRUCTOR'S MANUAL

An instructor's manual is available from Prentice Hall. This manual nearly doubles the amount of discussion topics and thinking activities in the text and gives motivating introductions, chapter goals, content overviews, lecture ideas, answers, and testing options.

ACKNOWLEDGMENTS

We are grateful for the assistance and positive support of many people. We would like to single out the following reviewers, each of whom has made this a better book:

Donald Porter, Department of Philosophy, College of San Mateo, San Mateo, CA

Beth M. Waggenspack, Department of Communication Studies, Virginia Polytechnic Institute and State University, Blacksburg, VA

Henry N. Carrier, Department of Liberal Arts, Brevard Community College, Cocoa, FL

Nicholas C. Kierniesky, Department of Psychology, Mount St. Mary's College, Emmitsburg, MD

Stephen Carey, Department of Psychology, Portland Community College, Portland, OR

Jon Stratton, Department of Philosophy, Walla Walla Community College, Walla Walla, WA

Thomas F. MacMillan, Departments of Philosophy and English, Mendocino College, Ukiah, CA

Keith Krasemann, Department of Philosophy, College of Du Page, Glen Ellyn, IL

Tom Morrow, Department of Communications, Richland Community College, Decatur, IL

Richard L. Wilson, Department of Philosophy and Religious Studies, Towson State University, Towson, MD

Daniel Wolne, Department of Philosophy, University of New Mexico, Albuquerque, NM

James W. Gustafson, Department of Philosophy, North Essex Community College, Haverhill, MA

Frederick J. O'Toole, Department of Philosophy, California Polytechnic State University, San Luis Obispo, CA

Especially, we would like to thank Sue Kosidowski who discovered us, Ted Bolen who acquired us, Karita France who advised us through the second edition, Jennifer Ackerman who assisted us, Harriet Tellem who produced the book, Chris Johnson who marketed the book, our colleagues who critiqued us, and our students who taught us, and mostly our wives and children for the sacrifices they made during this project.

Thinking

I don't know what I may seem to the world. But to myself I seem to have been only like a boy playing on the seashore and diverting myself in now and then to find a smoother pebble or prettier shell than ordinary, whilst the great ocean of truth lay all undiscovered before me.

—ISAAC NEWTON

1

What Is Thinking?

We are such stuff as thoughts are made on.

—*ADAPTED FROM SHAKESPEARE*

OUR CULTURAL LEGACY

In this book we encourage you to engage your mind and plunge into thinking. But first, let's meet some powerful thinkers who have preceded us.

Humans were speaking, and thus thinking, many millennia before the Sumerians, the Egyptians, and the Phoenicians learned to write their thoughts. The Greeks took their alphabet and burst forth into song, literature, philosophy, rhetoric, history, art, politics, and science. Corax of Syracuse, perhaps the first rhetorician, taught us how to use words to pierce into other minds. The sophists, skeptics, and cynics asked us to question everything, including our own questioning. Socrates probed and prodded the Athenians to think: "The unexamined life is not worth living," he said. And he threw down to us the ultimate gauntlet: "Know thyself." Plato was so caught up with Socrates and with the pure power of the mind that he thought we were born with ideas and that these innate ideas were as close as we could come to divinity. Plato's pupil, Aristotle, sharpened his senses to make impressive empirical observations that climbed toward first principles; then he honed his mind into the absolute logic of the syllogism that stepped inexorably, deductively downward.

The Roman rhetoricians Cicero, Tertullian, and Quintilian built massive structures of the mind and legal mentalities that rivaled Rome's architectural vastness.

The medieval thinkers, mental to a point that matched their ethereal goals, created mental structures mainly based on Plato, fortified with the logic of Aristotle. Aquinas, in his *Summa,* forged an unmatched mental creation that, if one grants his premises, still stands as an unassailable mountain of the mind. In contrast to much of this abstraction was the clean cut of Ockham's razor, slicing off unnecessary entities, and the welcome freshness of Anselm, who preempted Descartes by stating, "I doubt, therefore I know."

The Renaissance thinkers turned their minds and energies to earthly navigation, sidereal science, art, pleasure, and empire. Some of these thinkers, like Leonardo da Vinci, returned to the Greeks (Archimedes); some like Montaigne recovered rich ore in the Romans, sifted by the skepticism described on a medal around his neck: *Que sais je?* ("What do I know?").

Pascal called his whole book of aphorisms *Thoughts.* Descartes echoed Anselm—"I think, therefore I am"—and challenged our pride by telling us that "it is not enough to have a good mind. The main thing is to use it well" (*Les Discours,* Vol. 1). Those were the French rationalists.

No less rational, the British empiricists progressed from Locke's Aristotelian focus on the senses (the mind as a *tabula rasa*), to Berkeley's idea that we can be sure only of our perceptions to Hume's radical skepticism.

Hegel looked on all history as an idea unfolding, and Marx concretized and capitalized that idea.

Twentieth-century thinkers like Wittgenstein, Whorf, and Chomsky all enter the open, unfolding, and marvelous arena of the mind. They welcome us to come, enter with them, and think. . . .

WHY THINK?

Is anything more important than thinking? Is anything important that is not connected with thinking? STOP! Did you think about the first question before you read the second one? Our guess is that many of you kept reading; consequently, you may have missed a chance to think.

THINKING ACTIVITY 1.1
Things More Important Than Thinking

Let's start thinking now. Can you list anything more important than thinking?

1. _____

2. _____

(continued)

Thinking Activity 1.1 (continued)
Things More Important Than Thinking

   3. _____

   4. _____

What is on your list? How did you determine its value?

_____

Thoughts Richer Than Gold

Take a look at the following very different lists. Are the items on any one list more important than thinking?

List A	List B	List C
1. money	breathing	goodness
2. good job	eating	life
3. nice house	exercising	love
4. new car	mating	truth

Think about list A. Although money is high on the list of American dreams, it cannot be earned or spent without the ability to think. Imagine a chimpanzee (limited ability) or a mannequin (no ability) trying to earn money or even spend it. Thinking is often behind the making of money. Larry Ellison, one of computer software's financial giants, says: "I observe and I plan and I think and I strategize." (Ramo, 1997, p. 58) Clearly, the ability to think is more important than money, jobs, houses, or cars.

What about list B? Is breathing more important than thinking? At this point we need to think more sharply and define the word *important*. If *important* means a sequentially first or necessary condition for something else to exist, then breathing is more important than thinking, for without oxygen the thinking brain quickly dies. But if *important* means a higher order or value, then thinking is of a higher order than breathing because breathing "serves" the brain (which, by the way, uses a disproportionately large amount of the oxygen). Rarely, however, does the cerebral cortex "serve" breathing, such as when one is studying to be a respiratory therapist.

Another way to understand that thinking is of a higher order than breathing is to realize that many philosophers since Aristotle have defined humans as "thinking animals." In other words, horses and horseflies breathe, but thinking makes us human; if humans are of a higher order than animals, it is our thinking that makes us so. As a quality of a higher order, thinking is more important than eating, mating, or breathing.

And what do we think about list C? Are not goodness, life, love, and truth vast concepts of great importance? To weigh their importance against that of thinking would take many pages and much thought; but to judge quickly the worth of thinking, we can again ask the question, is anything important that is not connected with thinking?

If we have thought of anything, we have just used our thinking process; thus we have connected thinking to the item we thought of, regardless of how important the item is. Similarly, love, life, truth, and goodness are necessarily connected with thinking. We may be able to mate without much thinking, like two fireflies, but we cannot love without thinking. Thus we think as we live life.

Just how important is thinking in relation to life? Since we think largely with language, consider how Wittgenstein connects life and thinking: "The limits of my language are the limits of my life." Is this an accurate statement? Does language limit life so strictly? If so, does this limitation show the importance of language and thinking? We will meet this idea again in chapter 5, "Language: Our Thinking Medium."

Thinking as Possibility

Our life at this moment, as we read this book and make choices about our actions today, is strictly limited by how much we have learned and by the thinking patterns we have developed. We can only choose to do what we know; for example, we simply cannot search for a sunken treasure unless we know that it sank. And the more we know and the better we can think with our knowledge, the more successful we are likely to be. If we know that a Spanish galleon, laden with Inca gold, sank in the Caribbean, and if we can think about the route it might have followed, the ocean currents, and its last reported sighting, then we might find the gold. More importantly, by thinking we might find the gold in our own lives.

Thoughts Accumulate

Tennyson tells us that "we are a part of all that we have met." Likewise, we are also part of all that we have thought; to a degree, we have become what we have thought about, and who we will become is limited by how and what we think. If we reflected earlier about language limiting life, we probably realized that our thinking has set the boundaries for our past choices in life. We have chosen from what we have known and how we have been able to think about our knowledge.

Life Without Thinking

What if we acquired no new thoughts for the next ten years? Could we hold our jobs? What would we think about quarks and nanotechnology? How well would we talk to people?

If in the next ten years we choose to read many thoughtful books, will our mind be different? Will we be markedly different because of the books we read, the people we listen to, the thoughts we have, and the way we express those thoughts? Certainly, thoughts accumulate. We grow as we think, and thus we change our future ability to think.

Thoughts accumulate not just arithmetically but exponentially. Each thought has the potential to merge with others and create an enormous number of new thoughts; for instance, just forty-six items (your chromosomes) can be assembled into 25,852,010,000,000,000,000,000 combinations. With a six-thousand–word active vocabulary, imagine the creative combinations! In chapter 7, "Creative Thinking," we will learn how to form some of these combinations.

WHAT IS THINKING?

Right now you are thinking. Think about it. What *exactly* are you doing now? What is happening in your head as you think? Can you figure out how you have just processed these words into meaning? Simply put, how does your brain work?

The Mystery

Do not feel bad if you do not know the answer because neither do the experts. Humans have learned much about areas of the brain and neuroelectrochemical processes, but much is still to be discovered. We know more of the basic principles of the universe, of the atom, and of our bodies than we do of our brains. Newton drew the lines of forces connecting the earth to the stars, Einstein formulated the energy in matter, Watson and Crick cracked the genetic code, but the model for the brain has not yet been found. (Some possible models include *tabula rasa,* or blank tablet, memory grooves, a computer, a hologram, and recently the metaphor itself.) The brain remains a mystery.

Toward a Definition: Thinking as Communicating

If we do not understand the workings of the brain, if we cannot enter its inner sanctum and unfold its mystery, then how can we define thinking? One way to reach a definition is by observing the results of thinking as expressed in human communication. But what if some people claim that they do "thinking" that is totally internal and can never be externally communicated? We will not argue with them, but if they cannot talk about it or share it with us, their thinking cannot be useful to us. Therefore we can define thinking as *the activity of the brain that can potentially be communicated.* The media of communication are multiple: language (speaking, writing, signing, paralanguage, miming), images (blueprints, charts, symbols), art (drawing, painting, sculpting, modeling, architecture, music, dance), scientific formulas, and mathematics. All of these forms of communication have their special subtleties and strengths, but far and away the primary form of human communication is language; therefore, this book focuses on thinking as *the activity of the brain that can potentially be expressed in speaking or writing.*

The *potential* to express our thoughts includes, of course, the unexpressed thinking that is almost always in our heads: we plan the day and imagine scenarios; we worry through problems and search for solutions; we day dream; we discover, invent, and create systems; we enjoy reflecting on our ventures, and sometimes we redesign our failures. Unexpressed thinking is valuable, and we use it often before speaking or acting.

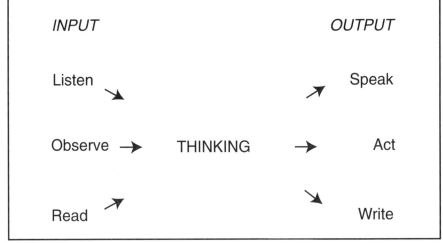

The Centrality of Thinking

You have only to look at the diagram below to see the importance of, the centrality of, thinking. Much of the stimuli around you enters your mind, you process it, or *think,* and then, if you choose, you respond.

INPUT   *OUTPUT*

Listen   Speak

Observe →   THINKING   →   Act

Read   Write

COMMUNICATING: THE MIRROR OF THOUGHT

How do we think about our thinking? That's not an easy question because we are caught in a circle: trying to know our mind with our mind is analogous to trying to see our eyes with our eyes. The eyes need a reflector such as a mirror or a still pond to see themselves. Similarly, to understand our thinking we need a mirror for our mind. Writing or talking can provide just such a mirror. Expressing our thoughts allows us to look at them more objectively; others, then, can share their ideas about our thinking, and so, ultimately, we can think better.

Writing records our thinking on a piece of paper so that we can then examine it. Try writing for sixty seconds as fast as you can on whatever comes to your mind without censoring any thought. In that way you will be able to externalize some of your thinking.

This externalization will probably not give us an exact replication of our thinking but will generate a cloudy mirror. The clouds will begin to clear if we repeat this activity often and learn to chart our thinking with our pen. Penning our thoughts is a challenge because the brain moves much faster than the pen, much faster than a "rapper" rapping 300 words per minute. The exact speed of the brain is not known, but let us guess that it is about 500 to 700 words per minute. Often the brain moves even faster because it does not think every word. Sometimes it leaps over phrases and whole groups of ideas to jump to almost instant insight.

We can also find out much about ourselves by looking for patterns in those sixty-second sketches: what are the *topics* that occupy our thoughts (people? things? money? work? home?) What is on our sixty-second list? How much *time* do we spend rehashing the past, processing the present, planning the future, or daydreaming about our fantasies? Placing a percentage alongside those time frames (past, present, future) might amaze us.

Attempt these sixty-second snapshots at different times and in different places to get other sketches of your mind. They will change greatly with your environment and your feelings.

Thinking as Writing: Clarity, Exactness, Awareness, Richness

> *Print allows you to hold another's mind in your hand*
>
> —*JAMES BURKE*

Writing does more than mirror our mind, it can clarify it, sharpen our thinking, and enrich our mind with an understanding that was not there before we wrote.

Clarity is a gift writing gives to our thinking. Although many of us can "think on our feet," few humans can continually think crystal clearly. Our brains rarely function continually at a high level of clarity. With writing we have a chance to achieve some of that clarity. We can put our thinking on paper and excise the ambiguity. This sentence, for instance, has been reworked until several readers approved of its clarity. And this clarity achieved in writing might even influence the type of person we are becoming: Francis Bacon tells us that writing makes an "exact" person.

Besides bringing clarity and exactness to our thinking, writing can intensify our physical and mental awareness. Just the attempt to describe what we are seeing, feeling, and thinking can allow us to see sharply, feel deeply, and think more clearly. Later we explore these areas more thoroughly, but a warm-up activity is given below.

Writing then, can mirror the mind, focus it into a state of clarity, and present new awarenesses. Beyond these gifts, writing offers another rich gift that is a paradox: when we pour water out of a glass we are emptying the glass, but when we pour thoughts out of our mind onto paper we are filling our mind. As we assemble those thoughts into a new written structure, we are writing a new combination of words that was not in our mind before we wrote it down; hence, this

---

THINKING ACTIVITY 1.2
Thinking, Sensing, Writing

Look around the room. In the first column quickly make a list of what you see.

1	2	3
————————————	————————————	————————————
————————————	————————————	————————————
————————————	————————————	————————————

Now in the second column make a list of what you *did not* see before. You can become aware of what you missed by looking *between* the items on your first list. If, for instance, your first item is a blackboard and your second item a student, notice what is between the blackboard and the student that you overlooked. Go ahead now and make a second list of overlooked items.

These two lists can tell you a lot about what kind of data you are putting into your mind. The first list might contain your usual observations, your usual "input" to your brain. The second list might contain items that you usually pass over. Now for the third list, try to see the most minute details of what you again overlooked. Try to see reflections of light, surface undulations, scratches and dents so small and so specific that they become hard to describe because there may not be exact words for them in our language. In the third column make a third list of small, sharp details that you see. To help you achieve this microscopic awareness, you may wish to peer into objects very close to you.

Has this third list helped you see new things? If you begin to record what you see, you will grow more alert and see what you never saw before. Try this looking activity in different places. And then attune yourself to your other senses of hearing, smell, touch, and taste. Respond with your feelings to what you sense. Finally, think about what you have sensed and felt. What does it mean?

---

powerful paradox: as we write something we create it both on the paper and in our mind. Thus, as we write we grow richer.

The poet Byron expresses this paradox in words that challenge our thinking:

'Tis to create, and in creating live
A being more intense, that we endow
With form our fancy, gaining as we give
The life we image.

Because writing is important as expressed thought, throughout this book you should take time to write out your thinking, especially when you wish clarification or feedback.

Thinking as Dialogue: Validation and Insight

Thought and speech are inseparable from each other.

—*CARDINAL JOHN HENRY NEWMAN*

We have seen that writing is a way to know, clarify, and enrich our thinking. Dialoguing is another way to attempt to know and understand our thinking. Dialoguing is simply talking with and listening to other people. They become the sounding boards, the graveyards, and the launching platforms of our thoughts. As we will see in a later chapter, dialoguing is crucial to test our thoughts.

While we talk (expressing our thoughts) we can watch what effect our words have on others. Do people wrinkle their foreheads and repeatedly ask us, "What do you mean?" Or do our words quickly and easily get our ideas across? Do people lose interest in what we are saying, or do our words have the power, precision, and logic to gain attention, to hold attention, and to convince others? Their reactions give us information that helps us to judge and adjust our thinking.

As we read these reactions of others we need to interpret them, but sometimes we get direct, focused comments from friends, students, or fellow learners who specifically critique our thinking as expressed in dialogue. One cautionary note concerning unrecorded dialogue is that it is gone as soon as it is spoken: "To base thought only on speech is to try nailing whispers to the wall" (Rosenthal, 1994). At the end of this chapter, some activities provide practice in critiquing dialogue.

Because human interaction is so important to our thinking, throughout this book we present activities that can be discussed, and we analyze the validity of dialogue in chapter 13, "Evaluating." Besides validating our thinking, dialoguing can stimulate our thinking. Our thoughts can resound and rebound with new shape and vigor from the thoughts of others. Our ideas can intermingle, cross-fertilize, and become the seeds for whole new species of thoughts. A single head is a lonely thinker; however, we can seek out classmates, friends, colleagues, and new acquaintances who can excite our mind.

MISTHINKING

The opposite of clear thinking is confusion, and it can lead to costly conclusions. A young American inventor appeared before Napoleon and offered him a means to defeat the British navy: a ship that could sail against the wind and waves and outmaneuver the British fleet. Napoleon scorned his offer, called the American a crackpot, and sent him away. That young man was Robert Fulton. Napoleon had just turned down the steamship.

Napoleon's thinking error was common to most of us: he was blinded by the past. In addition, he was blinded by his quick temper. Instead of opening his mind and asking "how," his imperial temper may have cost him the war. In chapter 2, "Personal Barriers," we will examine our personal thinking tendencies and barriers that could blind us from thinking clearly.

> **Think About It:** *We are not emperors, but we have mental blinders and habitual filters that block our thinking. Think for a moment about how we could make serious blunders. What are some of the topics we just will not listen to, the people whom we will not hear, the books we will not touch? How could our own thinking patterns lead us to costly conclusions?*

SUMMARY

We have thought about the enormous importance of our thinking and how it can greatly impact our future. We have even had the audacity to rate thinking as more important than money. Although much of thinking remains a mystery in the vast, unexplored realm of our brain, writing and speaking can provide an entry into our unknown selves. Writing can be a mirror of our thoughts, a mirror that can give us clarity, exactness, awareness, and richness. The opposite, cloudy thinking, can miss its mark and cost us dearly.

We have just begun to probe the mystery of thinking. In coming chapters we will look more deeply into our thinking patterns and the way our language, beliefs, and values influence those patterns. We will then look at some of our major thinking "bases": sensing, feeling, creating, organizing, reasoning, scientific thinking, persuading, and problem solving; finally, we will look at evaluation, decision, and action.

THINKING CHALLENGES

We have already suggested several thinking activities that can begin to help you to understand the thinking process. The following thinking challenges are designed to stimulate your thinking about issues related to this chapter. Your responses to the activities and questions that conclude each chapter might take various forms:

A simple reflection
A journal entry
A chat with a friend
A dialogue with a student
A class discussion
A group discussion
A formal paper
A research project
An individual or group presentation

1. How do you think differently from other people? Does your mind seem to move quickly or slowly. Do your thoughts come out in jumbles or clear steps? Are there certain times of the day that are better for certain types of thinking?

2. Write as you did for the 60-second snapshots of your thinking but for a longer time. Then look into your writings as the mirror of your mind. Gradually, see if you can wipe some of the fog off the glass and begin to get some understanding of what is in your mind.

3. Is Wittgenstein accurate when he says that "the limits of my language are the limits of my life"?

4. How might you think differently ten years from now according to the books you've read and the words you have written and spoken? What if you have not read any books?

5. Record a trip into your mind in any way you wish. You might try a stream-of-consciousness account like the novelist James Joyce, who often just lets the impressions of his mind pour out; you might make a list of associative thinking (for example black—white—snow—snowman—bully who knocked mine down . . .). Enter a fantasy, a daydream, or any kind of thinking. The point is to attempt to become more aware of what you think about and how you think.

6. Look around, in different places, and describe what you don't usually see or hear. Think about why you do not usually see those things. What does this tell you about the interests of your mind?

7. Talk with someone else, and attempt to read the reactions your words are having on that person. Judge your thinking processes accordingly.

8. How might your particular thinking patterns lead you into costly errors? For instance, do you quickly accept what you read or hear? Do appearances of things or feelings of others strongly sway you?

9. Have you ever approached a problem, thought it through, and reached a decision that worked well for you? What were the thinking steps you took to produce those satisfactory results?

10. Have you ever jumped too quickly to a conclusion? Why? Have you ever been "absolutely certain" and then discovered you were wrong? What had you overlooked in your thinking?

11. If, as Tennyson says, "I am a part of all that I have met," what are the main events, persons, and places that have formed you? How have they formed your mind?

12. Before we go further into this book, take some time to reflect upon the mystery of thinking. Ask yourself some questions that you would like to find answers to as you think through this book.

2

Personal Barriers

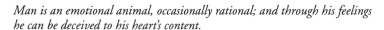

Man is an emotional animal, occasionally rational; and through his feelings he can be deceived to his heart's content.

—*WILL DURANT, MANSIONS OF PHILOSOPHY*

Who we are is how we think. Where and how we were raised may determine whether we are pessimists or optimists, conservatives or liberals, atheists or theists, idealists or realists. Our upbringing shapes our fears, which keep us from facing thoughts. It shapes our self-concept, which moves us to defend our thoughts. And it shapes our emotions, which can distort our thinking to an exceptional degree. In this and in other ways our psychological world, shaped by our exposure to cultural and genetic forces, often acts as a barrier to sound thinking. In this chapter we learn about these barriers so that we can diffuse some of their negative influence on our thinking. But this requires that we face ourselves honestly and completely, so that we can discover the personal factors that inhibit our thinking. Unless we face the fact of who we really are, we will not become the sound thinkers we are meant to be.

ENCULTURATION

Imagine for a moment that you have the genetic constitution you have now but were raised by parents in another country. Imagine how you would be different.

If you were raised in India, you would probably be of Hindu faith, worshipping Vishnu and Shiva. Or perhaps you would be of the Jain religion, revering animal life so much that you would never eat meat and would even sweep insects out of your house instead of killing them. If you were raised by parents in Iran, you would probably despise American capitalism. If you were a man in the Sambian tribe of New Guinea, you would likely engage in homosexual behavior until you were married. And if you were a woman in the Mbuti tribe in Africa, you would feel comfortable roaming your community in nothing but a loincloth. Even your taste preference is subject to cultural forces. In America, your favorite pizza topping might be sausage and mushroom, but in Japan it would probably be squid, in England tuna and corn, and in India pickled ginger! In sum, many of the values and preferences you have now, including religious ideas, sexual mores, and work ethic, were instilled in you since birth by your culture. This process, called *enculturation,* is going on continually, even now, no matter what your age. What does this have to do with thinking? Just this: the extent to which you are able to think critically about ideas that conflict with your basic attitudes and values is inversely related to the extent to which you are enculturated.

Sources of Enculturation

Enculturation has many different sources or influences. One of the major influences is the family in which we grow up. There we learn our religious beliefs, ethical standards, prejudices and stereotypes, eating habits, and worldview. The two great depth psychologists of the twentieth century, for example, Sigmund Freud and Carl Jung, both accused each other of being negatively influenced by their family background. Jung accused Freud of establishing a negative psychology because he was a Jew, while Freud accused Jung of being blinded by his strong religious background, which prevented him from accepting sexual maladjustment as the root cause of neurosis (Puner, 1947).

Another source of enculturation is our place of work. Here we may learn certain manners of behavior, dress code, professional ethics, and work attitude. The city in which we grow up can also be a strong source of enculturation. Some cities are known for wine and theater, others for beer and brats. Some cities tend to develop men with a lot of machismo, whereas others allow more tolerance for androgyny. In Milwaukee they may prefer Miller Beer, in Denver they may have a strong preference for Coors, and in Munich it may be Lowenbrau. Are the taste buds of citizens in these cities different? Or have the citizens *learned* to prefer one over the other? And what do you suppose the residents of Detroit think about Japanese automobiles? In the United States we can also find differences in enculturation between northerners and southerners. Southern males, for example, think differently about the use of violence in self-protection and honor (Nisbett and Cohen, 1996). In sum, how we think about masculinity, violence, food and drink, sex, God, and most other things is often a matter of enculturation. The more we examine these enculturation effects on ourselves, the more we can think more objectively, more independently, more clearly about various matters in the world.

Some Common American Beliefs

1. *It's okay to kill animals.* The Jains of India consider it sinful to kill even insects.

2. *It's morally wrong to go outside without clothing, no matter where you live.* Women in the Netherlands feel quite comfortable gardening in their back-yard topless. And many tribes in Africa, of course, go without clothing or wear very little of it.

3. *Intentionally deforming the body is sick.* It was once traditional in China to wrap the feet of young girls for years to keep the feet abnormally small. Such abnormality was considered a mark of beauty. And in some tribes in Africa, deforming the lips and ears, making them abnormally large, is also considered a mark of beauty. Perhaps deformation of the body is no longer considered "sick" by most Americans. Consider: In the United States most women, and some men, put holes in their ears; most males have the foreskin of their penis removed; and many thousands of women each year have surgery to enlarge their breasts. Maybe what is considered "sick" is only that deformation which is not done in one's own culture.

4. *There is only one God.* This monotheism is characteristic of Judaism, Islam, and Christianity. Most other religions are polytheistic.

5. *Jesus is God.* People of Jewish and Islamic faith would certainly disagree with this.

6. *The Christian Bible is the only holy book.* Of course, virtually every non-Christian would disagree with this. There are many great holy books. The Koran and the Bhagavad-Gita are two examples.

7. *Money is what makes the world go round.* The American obsession with money is catching fire throughout the world, but some cultures put less emphasis on it. Years ago, one Russian emigrant to the United States actually returned to Russia! His reason: we worship money like a god.

8. *Marrying for reasons other than love is immoral.* Throughout history and even today marriages are arranged for practical reasons: to strengthen family ties, for companionship, and for healthy offspring. Love grows later. In fact, people in some countries find our requirement of romantic love for marriage absurd.

Religion and Enculturation

Intellectually, religious emotions are not creative but conservative. They attach themselves readily to the current view of the world and consecrate it. They steep and dye intellectual fabrics in the seething vat of emotions.

—JOHN DEWEY, INFLUENCE OF DARWIN ON PHILOSOPHY

(continued)

Religion and Enculturation *(continued)*

Religion is one area in which it is easy to see the enculturation process and its effects on thinking. For example, most Americans are Christians, primarily because they were raised by Christian parents and not because of any choice they ever made about the matter. Most Christians have not objectively investigated alternative religions or looked extensively into the history of their own religion. Most are unaware, for example, that the stories of Buddha, like the stories of Jesus, portray him as the son of a virgin and that the Buddhist code of ethics is in some ways more strict than that of the Christian ten commandments. And most Christians are probably unaware of the extent to which their own Christian doctrine has been shaped by "mere mortals" over the last seventeen hundred years. Despite our moderate ignorance about our creed and those of others, most of us are certain that the beliefs of our faith are true, and the faith of others and their heroes is false. This we "know" without any investigation at all! Obviously our thoughts about religion are based more on feelings engendered by our faith and our culture than on critical thinking based upon knowledge. Therefore, we can see that resisting enculturation and its blinding influence becomes essential to critical thinking, for it allows people to step back from their conditioning to look at issues more objectively—issues such as abortion, proofs for God's existence, new roles for women, and so on.

THINKING ACTIVITY 2.1
Our Own Enculturation

Below is an exercise in enculturation. Answer honestly "yes" or "no" to the following questions. The purpose of this exercise is to examine the foundations of some of your thinking, not your conclusions, so don't be concerned with whether your answer is right or wrong. In some instances there is no general agreement on what the right answer should be.

_____   1. Do you believe that the democratic form of government is the best kind of government in the world?

        _____   a. Are you aware of the problems of democracy often cited by sociologists and people from nondemocratic countries?

        _____   b. Can you express the basic philosophy of alternative forms of government?

        _____   c. Can you cite any positive aspects of either communism or socialism?

(continued)

THINKING ACTIVITY 2.1 (continued)
Our Own Enculturation

_____   2. Do you believe that abortion is wrong in most or all cases?

_____   a. Do you have good arguments to support your belief?

_____   b. Do you know at what moment a human being comes into existence?

_____   c. Do you know at what moment a developing embryo has human rights?

_____   d. Do you know at what moment a developing fetus becomes conscious?

_____   e. Do you know at what moment a developing fetus is capable of experiencing pain?

_____   f. Can you cite any arguments used by pro-choice advocates to support abortion?

_____   g. Do you believe that a seed of an apple has the same value as an apple tree?

_____   3. Do you believe that capital punishment is justified for mass murderers?

_____   a. Do you know that capital punishment is a more expensive way to punish than life imprisonment because of the numerous and very expensive judicial appeals of the former?

_____   b. Have you seen any statistics that clearly show capital punishment to inhibit murder?

_____   4. Do you believe there is a God?

_____   a. Have you ever heard of an argument against this idea?

_____   b. Can you present an argument against this idea?

_____   5. Do you believe that it is moral to use animals for medical experiment to make life better for human beings?

_____   a. Do you believe that it would be moral for beings on another planet with intelligence superior to ours to use human beings as guinea pigs for the advancement of their alien culture?

_____   b. Have you ever seen experimental animals suffer in an experimental laboratory?

_____   c. Do you know that pigs are blowtorched under anesthesia, bunnies have their eyes sewed shut, and monkeys have their heads smashed to study the effects of burn treatment, cosmetics, and concussion, respectively?

_____   d. Have you ever read any argument against the use of animals in a laboratory?

_____   e. Can you cite such an argument now?

(continued)

THINKING ACTIVITY 2.1 (continued)
Our Own Enculturation

_____ 6. Do you believe that ESP is nonsense?

      _____ a. Have you read any studies by parapsychologists?

      _____ b. Do you believe that if we cannot explain something it does not exist?

_____ 7. Do you believe that humans are the most intelligent life forms in the universe?

      _____ a. Do you know that there are billions of galaxies, each with billions of stars, so that if just one in 10 billion stars has a planet with life, there would be billions of planets with life?

      _____ b. Do you know that human life emerged on this planet in about 4.5 billion years and that the universe is old enough for this evolutionary process to have happened three times in succession?

_____ 8. Do you believe that one racial group is innately superior to another?

      _____ a. Do you know that Japanese score slightly higher on intelligence tests than whites?

      _____ b. Do you know the extent to which the environment determines intelligence?

      _____ c. Do you know the amount of genetic similarity among racial groups?

_____ 9. Do you believe that America is the best country in the world?

      _____ a. Do you know that our infant mortality rate is higher than that of many other modern industrial countries?

      _____ b. Do you know that the United States has one of the highest rates of violent crime in the world?

      _____ c. Do you know that the top 10 percent of the U.S. population hold more than 67 percent of all wealth in the country, including 90 percent of stocks and bonds?

_____ 10. Do you believe that humans did not evolve from lower life forms but were created separately?

      _____ a. Have you ever read a book on the evidence for evolution?

      _____ b. Have you ever talked to a paleontologist, geologist, biochemist, or zoologist about evolution?

      _____ c. Are you aware of any of the following?

            Homologous structures
            Vestigial traces
            Fossil discoveries
            DNA similarities
            How our embryonic ontogeny recapitulates phylogeny

(continued)

THINKING ACTIVITY 2.1 (continued)
Our Own Enculturation

If you answered "yes" to the numbered questions above, but "no" to parts a, b, c, and so on, it *could* be that you have merely adopted your position through an enculturation process, that is, picked it up through your acquaintance with your peers, parents, religious community, and so on, instead of through careful reflection and the gathering of facts. A "yes" response to many of the questions above might be supported by sound reasoning and facts. The point is not to determine what is true about the issues but to illustrate the lack of both thinking and knowledge that tends to go into these beliefs.

SELF-CONCEPT

> *It happens over and over again. A company that is doing pretty well in a business it knows will take over another company and ruin it. . . . Why do companies make such big mistakes? One reason, I suggest, is ego. They want to show they are the biggest, smartest kids on the block. . . . When will these guys grow up?*
>
> —J. NEASE, "AT & T=NCR COMBO JUST DIDN'T COMPUTE"

Recognizing the extent of our enculturation lessens its effects and moves us closer to an open mind, which is essential to critical and creative thinking. But we must also deal with other barriers that inhibit sound thinking, one of which is self-concept.

Our self-concept is the way we view ourselves. It may be unhealthy if we see ourselves rather negatively as, for example, someone who is not very intelligent or very pretty; or it may be positive and healthy, as when we believe ourselves to be an attractive and worthwhile person. What goes into our idea of ourselves may include not only intelligence and attractiveness but a variety of other things: the sports team we favor, our grades in school, our home, friends, religion, state, country, car, political position, values, possessions, and so on. Thus, someone may view herself as an American, a "card-carrying Republican," a 49er fan, a conservative Catholic, an animal rights activist, an exceptionally beautiful person, and one who would never buy anything but a Mercedes. People vary in the degree to which they use their attributes, things, values, and affiliations to define themselves and form their self-concept. To some people these elements are central to the notion of self, such that they defend them as though they were defending themselves. Thus, we hear stories of people assaulting others because of some critical remark against their favorite football team, people killing others over a pair of athletic shoes, and wars between countries because of different religious beliefs. When these contingencies become so central to our notion of who we are, we are not likely to think critically about them. Instead, we respond emotionally and may engage in ego-defense mechanisms, self-serving biases, and other distortions to ensure ourselves that what we identify with, that is, what we think we are, is good.

THINKING ACTIVITY 2.2
The Idea of Self

What is our idea of self? Were we born with it? It seems not. Then have we made it our own creation? If so, have we done the right thing in creating it? Does the self truly exist? Or is it only the mind's idea? Whether our idea of self refers to a real or an illusory self, most will agree that we do spend a lot of time defending, maintaining, and creating that idea of self, as when we fight with others when they demean us, explain away a bad exam grade in order to appear more intelligent, or buy a new car to show off our wealth. According to the Buddhist Walpola Rahula,

> the idea of self . . . produces harmful thoughts of "me and mine," selfish desire, craving, attachment, hatred, ill-will, conceit, pride, egoism, and other defilements, impurities, and problems. It is the source of all troubles in the world from personal conflicts to wars between nations. In short, to this false view can be traced all the evil in the world. (1974, p. 51)

Do you agree with Rahula's statement? Is the idea of self this dangerous? Can you cite instances to support it? Can you cite reasons to disagree with this statement?

Pay special attention to the news for the next few days. To what extent can the "troubles in the world" be attributed to the idea of self?

What about troubles in your own personal life? Reflect on your recent arguments or moments of tension with others. To what extent was your thinking affected by your need to protect your self-concept?

Finally, as an exercise in "self," try to respond to others today and tomorrow without a sense of self, without protecting an ego. How difficult was it? What were the results?

THINKING ACTIVITY 2.3
Letting Go

If your idea of self can get in the way of your thinking, a good strategy to aid straight thinking is to practice letting go of those ideas you have of your self, whether true or false. Letting go means reducing as much as possible your identification with the constituents that you use to define your self. You can begin this letting go by listing the major ideas you have of your self on the lines below.

Activities you most like to do

_____
_____
_____
_____
_____

People and things you most enjoy

_____
_____
_____
_____

Traits you most admire about yourself

_____
_____
_____
_____

Now imagine that you are fifty years older. Which traits will be gone? Which people and things will have been replaced? Which activities will you no longer be doing? Most likely your idea of self today will not be your idea of self tomorrow, yet you will probably believe that you are the same person (Philosophers debate whether a person is actually the same or not over time). Should we, therefore, identify with those traits, activities, and loves to the point that it leads us to conceit, anger, defensiveness, and an inability to take constructive criticism when those cherished things are threatened? On the other hand, would it be acceptable to believe in something so much that you would die for it? Do you think it would be possible to let go of your idea of self and still act to defend some principle?

EGO DEFENSES

Ego defenses are psychological coping strategies that distort reality in order to protect ourselves from anxiety, guilt, and other bad feelings. Some of the more basic ones that impact on our thinking are denial, projection, and rationalization.

Denial

> *Experience with an alcoholic population suggests that certain individuals will deny to the point of dying.*
>
> —G. FORREST, DIAGNOSIS AND TREATMENT OF ALCOHOLISM

When we simply refuse to accept an unpleasant reality, we are using *denial*. What an unpleasant reality is varies from one person to another. For the alcoholic, it is his or her drinking problem. Thus, because of denial, many alcoholics are unable to think critically about their drinking behavior. Similarly, college students may deny that they are doing poorly in school, that they are lazy, or that their boyfriend or girlfriend really does not love them. By keeping these unpleasant realities from conscious awareness, we protect ourselves from a reality that is unpleasant, but we also inhibit our ability to think objectively about the situation and to make intelligent decisions for our own and others' best interests.

Projection

> *There I see the beam in my own eye as a mote in my brother's eye. It is right there because I am unconscious of the beam in my own eye.*
>
> —CARL JUNG, C. G. JUNG SPEAKING

Projection is the defense mechanism by which we see in others a part of ourselves that we cannot accept and do not recognize. We may believe others are hostile toward us when it is we who are hostile toward them. We may see in others our own incompetence and deceitfulness, which we are unable to accept in ourselves. We may see selfish motives in others, which are really the selfish motives in us which we do not consciously recognize. In short, we see others not as they are, but as *we* are. Our thinking about ourselves and others is therefore grossly distorted when we engage in projection. Like denial, this interferes with our ability to think critically about ourselves, others, and our social situations. Notice in the example below how a man's perception of others as crazy and his desire to hurt someone seem to be projections of his own inner reality.

INTERVIEWER: Well, how do you feel about all those things they are saying?

PATIENT: What do you mean, "feel"? (said with distrust). *They're crazy. They want to see me destroyed.*

INTERVIEWER: Oh, well, that's awful. It's scary to have people say crazy things about you. What would make them do that?

PATIENT: They're jealous of me, that I have my wife; they must be trying to get her from me.

INTERVIEWER: Well, of course, you're a proud man, and it must be difficult to have them talking about you like that. Now let's see if there's any way we can help you stay on top of things and keep in control. We can both agree that you're a strong man, and it's important not to let it weaken you.

PATIENT: Yes. I'm strong. *But I'm very worried that her family might make me do something crazy—like want to hurt someone.* (Vaillant and Perry, 1985, p. 965) [emphasis added]

Rationalization

> *The easiest person to deceive is one's self.*
>
> —*LORD LYTTON*

Of all the defense mechanisms, rationalization is perhaps the greatest inhibitor of clear thinking. Rationalization is distorted thinking that attempts to justify behavior motivated by self-interest or unacceptable drives. It serves to protect us from bad feelings by, for example, turning selfish motives into honorable ones. For example, the captain of the cruise ship *Oceanos,* which sank in the Indian Ocean, was asked why he left his ship in a lifeboat while hundreds of passengers were still on board. He replied that the order to abandon ship applies to everyone, and once the order is given it doesn't matter when the captain leaves. He also mentioned that he could control rescue operations better from the shore.

In essence, rationalization is lying to ourselves about the real reasons for our behaviors and feelings. It is essential that we believe in this lie for it to protect us; if we knew we were lying, it would do us no good. Many of us can recognize it during tax season:

> I prepare my taxes the way I do because of the way the government spends our money, you know—hundreds of dollars for a plain hammer and thousands of dollars for a toilet seat. It's our duty as U.S. citizens to put a stop to this nonsense. Maybe if we all held back a little Uncle Sam would get the message.

SELF-SERVING BIASES

Nothing is easier than self-deceit. For what each man wishes, that he also believes to be true.

—DEMOSTHENES

If our motives are good they do not need to be rationalized. But sometimes, in spite of our good motives, undesirable consequences occur, consequences that threaten our self-esteem. The actions of others can also threaten our self-esteem. Such ego-threatening situations can lead us to cognitive biases. These biases in our thinking and perception that serve to protect or elevate our self-esteem are called *self-serving biases*. As noted above, we do not always think about and perceive things as they are, for that would often mean looking at ourselves in an unpleasant light. Consequently, most people tend to see what they *need* to see and what they *want* to see in order to maintain or strengthen positive feelings about themselves (Maslow, 1954).

One aspect of the self-serving bias is the tendency to take credit for our successes and to blame our failures on external factors (Zuckerman, 1979; Bradley, 1978). For example, a student failing an exam might attribute her failure to an unfair test or an incompetent instructor rather than her poor study habits. And when politicians lose elections, they are likely to attribute their loss to negative campaigning by their opponent or a lack of funds necessary to get their message across rather than their own personality flaws or their own flawed political perspective.

Whereas we often attribute our failures to situational factors and our successes to personal ones, a second aspect of the self-serving bias is the tendency to make *opposite* attributions when judging the behavior of others that threatens our own self-esteem. When a student competitor in college gets a better grade than we do, we may find it threatening to our self-esteem and attribute it to luck or some privileged relationship with the instructor. Yet, when others *fail,* we may look to their character for an explanation and ascribe their failure to their incompetence, ignorance, or laziness.

The tendency to engage in ego defenses and self-serving biases should decrease as our psychological health increases. As a healthy person we are better able to own up to the totality of who and what we are, both positive and negative (Jung, 1969). When we can truly accept ourselves as we are with our faults, that is, when we can think of ourselves as worthwhile persons in spite of our failings, then we have less need to repress, deny, project, or make misattributions to protect ourselves. As healthier people we are less threatened by the successes of others and more able to tolerate our own failures; we own up to our mistakes and give credit to others. In sum, we think better for being better.

Other Attribution Errors

Our attributions about our own and others' behaviors are often wrong because they are biased by our need to protect our self-esteem. But they can also go wrong for other reasons. For example, if we saw a young man speeding by in a red convertible with a beautiful lady by his side we would probably attribute his behavior to immaturity and showing off. This is because of a tendency we have to attribute the behavior of others to their personal traits instead of to their situation. Oftentimes our internal attributions are wrong and the *situation* is the real force behind the behavior. In such instances we have committed the *fundamental attribution error.* In the example above the student is speeding to the hospital because his gorgeous wife is about to deliver a baby.

The *actor-observer bias* extends the fundamental attribution error one more step by stating that we tend to make internal attributions when observing the behavior of others but situational attributions when assessing our own behavior (except when examining our success). Thus, employees (observers) may attribute a manager's strict rules to the manager's rigid personality, whereas the manager (actor) explains the rules as necessary to deal with the stresses and pressures coming from her superiors. On the other hand, a manager (the observer now) may see her unproductive employees as lazy and unmotivated, whereas they (the actors) perceive their unproductive behavior as a natural consequence of working for an insensitive, authoritarian personality. The differences in attribution are probably rooted in differences in points of view: the actor is less aware of herself and more aware of the employees, while the employees are focused on the boss and are less focused on themselves. Fortunately, this bias can be minimized by having each side empathize with the other (Regan and Totten, 1975).

Think About It: Have you ever made an erroneous attribution for someone else's behavior? Have you ever been the victim of such an attribution?

Self-Serving Biases?

Self-serving biases are cognitive distortions that put us in a favorable position. The statements below come from the insurance forms of car-accident victims who were asked to summarize the accident. Are these self-serving biases or just grammatical mistakes?

1. A pedestrian hit me and went under my car.
2. As I approached the intersection a sign suddenly appeared in a place where no sign had ever appeared before.

(continued)

Self-Serving Biases? *(continued)*

3. My car was legally parked as it backed into the other vehicle.
4. The indirect cause of this accident was a little guy in a small car with a big mouth.
5. An invisible car came out of nowhere, struck my vehicle, and vanished.
6. The telephone pole was approaching. I was attempting to swerve out of the way, when it struck my front end.
7. I had been driving for forty years when I fell asleep at the wheel.
8. To avoid hitting the car in front of me, I struck the pedestrian.
9. The pedestrian had no idea which direction to run, so I ran over him.
10. I pulled away from the side of the road, glanced at my mother-in-law, and headed for the embankment.

THINKING ACTIVITY 2.4
Owning Up to Our Dark Side

We have seen how a failure to see and accept ourselves as we are can lead to thinking distortions as we rationalize, project, deny, and use self-serving biases. Therefore, it is worthwhile to look at the dark side of ourselves and accept it as part of who we are. So as not to walk away from such an exercise depressed and full of loathing about ourselves, it is important to write down our positive characteristics as well. At home in a private place, write down ten positive characteristics of your personality. Then, be honest with yourself and write down some of your less-positive characteristics that you have not really looked at before. To help you identify those dark elements, which the psychologist Carl Jung called the "shadow," reflect back on how you have reacted to criticism from others in the past and consider these statements by one of Jung's students, M.-L. von Franz:

> If you feel an overwhelming rage coming up in you when a friend reproaches you about a fault, you can be fairly sure that at this point you will find a part of your shadow, of which you are unconscious.
>
> It is particularly in contacts with people of the same sex that one stumbles over both one's own shadow and those of other people.
>
> When an individual makes an attempt to see his shadow, he becomes aware of (and often ashamed of) those qualities and impulses he denies in himself but can plainly see in other people—such things as egotism, mental laziness, and sloppiness; unreal fantasies, schemes, and plots; carelessness and cowardice; inordinate love of money and possessions—in short, all the little sins about which he might previously have told himself: "That doesn't matter; nobody will notice it, and in any case other people do it too." (Jung, 1964, pp. 168–69)

THE ROLE OF EXPECTATIONS AND SCHEMATA

> *Nan-in, a Japanese master during the Meiji era (1868–1912), received a university professor who came to inquire about Zen. Nan-in served tea. He poured his visitor's cup full, and then kept on pouring.*
>
> *The professor watched the overflow until he no longer could restrain himself. "It is overfull. No more will go in!"*
>
> *"Like this cup," Nan-in said, "you are full of your own opinions and speculations. How can I show you Zen unless you first empty your cup?"*
>
> —*N. SENZAKI AND P. REPS, "ZEN STORIES"*

Not only do we tend to think about the world according to what we want to see and what we need to see, we tend to think of it in terms of what we *expect* to see. We tend to perceive and think about others and situations in terms of the ideas we have already formed about them. These ideas are called *schema*. Often we distort the truth to make it fit into our existing schema, or we notice only those aspects of others' behavior or ideas which fit into our existing ideas about them. In other words, human beings are reluctant to change their perceptions and ideas to accommodate the facts (accommodation); instead, it is easier to fit our observations and thinking into our existing schemata (assimilation). If our prior experience with someone is that he is extremely selfish and we form an idea of him as "a selfish person," then we tend to see his actions as selfish. If he suggests a new policy at work to increase morale and productivity, we wonder about the selfish motives that must be underlying his new policy. Surely he cannot be interested in the well-being of others and the company's productivity.

Similarly, if a teacher believes that a student is not very bright, frequent questions from that student may be interpreted by the teacher as verification of the student's ignorance. On the other hand, if the teacher is told that a student is intelligent and highly motivated, the student's questions may be seen as reflecting that person's insight and motivation. Imagine what your reaction would be if you heard that a dictator was freeing some political prisoners and giving millions of dollars to the poor in his country. You would probably either discount the information as mere propaganda or question his motives, believing that he was trying to manipulate his people for some reason. His behavior would not likely cause you to change your perception of him from a ruthless dictator to a compassionate benefactor.

A good example of a schema that influences the way we perceive and think is the *stereotype*. Stereotypes are simplistic, biased views about members of a certain group. We learn stereotypes from a variety of sources. Sometimes we overgeneralize from our limited experience with members of a group. Often we learn our parents' stereotypes by listening and observing them, and we sometimes absorb stereotypes from our peers and the media. Whatever their source, stereotypes have a powerful effect on our thinking.

It is important to realize that stereotypes are inaccurate. They assume that groups are more homogeneous than they are. For some reason when it comes to *our* group we see the richness and diversity of its members, but when it comes to our perception of other groups, we assume that their members are all alike. On what basis can we possibly assume so? Certainly, similarities exist among group members but not to the degree that stereotypes imply.

Think About It: *An open mind is essential to critical thinking. But there is no easy recipe for acquiring an open mind, especially regarding prejudice. Negative thoughts toward a minority group may go, but negative feelings often linger on. Those feelings may lead us to continuing negative behaviors and attitudes toward a group.*

Although stereotypes in particular, and schemata in general, often distort our thinking, sometimes we do change our views of people and situations when we experience facts contradicting our schema. Some research suggests that this accommodation is most likely to occur when the new information is *moderately* discrepant with our schemata (Bochner and Insko, 1966). If an idea is very similar to our existing views, we are likely to minimize the difference and assimilate it into our existing schema, thus not modifying our views. Likewise, if the information is highly discrepant, it simply cannot fit into our schema and we reject it. For example, if typical Christians were exposed to arguments that Jesus never existed and that the entire New Testament is a myth, they would find this information very discrepant and would probably reject it without the least consideration. On the other hand, information that Jesus was unusually friendly with a political group whose intent was to overthrow the Romans might simply be assimilated into their schema of Jesus as a spiritual leader, who just happened to appeal to some political groups bent on overthrowing Roman rulers. Little or no change would be made in their concept of Jesus.

Moderately discrepant information, however, is too different to be easily assimilated and yet not so different that it must be rejected. Thus, if we are likely to change our views in the face of evidence, moderately discrepant information will most likely, but not necessarily, lead to that change. Can you imagine any real or fictitious revelation about Jesus that could be considered by most Christians as moderately discrepant with their views?

EMOTIONAL INFLUENCES

Emotions are an important mark of human experience. They are in part what separates humans from machines and the lower animals, for machines can compute but they can not experience joy. And animals may find themselves attached to others, but they do not love them. Emotions give our world taste and richness, joy and surprise, but also pain and sorrow. Emotions can affect and inspire thought, said William James, but he also said they can destroy it. Later in this book we look at how emotions can give birth to thinking, but for now our attention focuses on their inhibiting influence, on their capacity to bury, twist, and fragment the thinking process and take it to the depths of the irrational.

Anger

> *Why does my violence so silence reason and intelligence?*
>
> *—JEAN RACINE, PHAEDRA*

Both Plato and Aristotle believed that anger could be a "potentially constructive ally of reason" (Averill, 1982, p. 85), but both of them also recognized its destructive influences on rational thought. Some philosophers, like Seneca, considered it wholly without value:

> Seneca sees absolutely no value in anger. . . . No provocation justifies it, no situation permits it, and no benefit is gained by it. Once allowed, anger entirely consumes its possessor and renders dull his capacity for reasoning and sensible action. (Averill, 1982, p. 83)

Certainly anger and reason appear to most people to be the antithesis of each other; where one appears, the other seems to be absent. Anger has destroyed intimacy, thwarted good judgment, motivated senseless killings, inspired numerous wars, and probably burned more bridges in the career paths of men and women than any other single force. It also distorts our perception of a situation, colors our ability to think critically about it, and impairs our self-control.

The cause of anger may be a threat to something we hold dear. It may also be due to frustration, which is often caused by the blocking of a goal, or even by stress and hormonal changes in our bodies. No matter what the source, it is important not to make important decisions in the heat of anger, for good thinking does not prevail during such moments. Instead, we want to release the tension caused by the anger and strike out, hurt, or destroy.

The short-term goal of releasing tension can supersede and crush years of careful deliberation and planning as we say or do things we know we should not. The aspiring businesswoman ruins her career by berating her boss for making a poor decision, or a man angry at his fiancée's selfish behavior castigates her for all her personal faults and breaks off the engagement. Although anger may inspire great speeches, it often throws thinking in the backseat as our emotions take control.

Earlier we mentioned how previous knowledge, like stereotypes and other schemata, can distort our thinking. Feelings can also affect thinking in a similar way. For example, anger can not only overrule our thinking, but it can distort it so that we believe that what we are doing is justified and rational. For example, a parent may spank a child because of the parent's frustration with the child and need to release anger. The parent may then rationalize the aggression against the child by claiming that such punishment was necessary to teach the child appropriate behavior—in spite of the fact that psychologists have for years been saying that appropriate behavior can be taught by nonviolent methods and that such spanking can be harmful to the child. The parent does not acknowledge the real motivation for the behavior.

Dealing with Anger

If anger can lead to unthinking behavior or override our better judgment, we need to lessen its impact. We offer five suggestions.

First, *do not vent your anger:*

> The psychological rationales for ventilating anger do not stand up under experimental scrutiny. The weight of the evidence indicates precisely the opposite: expressing anger makes you angrier, solidifies an angry attitude, and establishes a hostile habit. If you keep quiet about momentary irritations and distract yourself with pleasant activity until your fury simmers down, chances are you will feel better, and feel better faster, than if you let yourself go in a shouting match. (Tavris, 1982, pp. 143–44)

Besides fueling the original anger, ventilating anger more often results in guilt, lowered self-esteem, mild depression, anxiety, embarrassment, and an exacerbation of the original conflict (Tavris, 1982; Averill, 1982). This is not to say that one should stew for days with unabated anger. If the anger does not eventually subside, although usually it does, an attempt should be made to calmly talk about the matter. Pick a time when the other person is not angry and will therefore be more likely to listen.

Second, *get advice* about your chosen course of action from others who are not angry. They may be able to give you a clearer perspective and prevent the sometimes disastrous consequences of decisions made under the influence of anger.

Third, *become assertive.* Anger is sometimes caused by continuous victimization. Being assertive means standing up for your rights in a nonaggressive manner that diminishes the potential for defensiveness in the other person. Unlike with anger, when one is assertive, one has self-control. Bear in mind, however, that it is irrational to believe that life should always treat us justly. In other words, don't overdo it.

Fourth, *learn to relax* and to practice other stress-management strategies. Reducing the stress in our lives and practicing relaxation exercises regularly can help us control the frequency of our anger.

Lastly, *don't get angry*. This may sound simplistic; however, when we consider that anger is rooted in the meaning we give to the events around us, as opposed to the events themselves, it is reasonable to try to alter that initial perception and prevent the anger from occurring altogether. Psychologists call this *cognitive restructuring* or *reappraisal*. For example, if we perceive that someone is trying to slight us in some way, we might ask ourselves if there is another reason for his behavior. It might be possible, for example, that he is unaware of the impact his behavior has on us. Empathy, identifying with the position of the other person, sometimes helps us to make these reappraisals. Or we might want to put things in proper perspective. For example, if we were counting on someone to mow the lawn for us today and he did not, we can ask ourselves how important it is that the lawn be mowed today as opposed to tomorrow.

Think About It: *Aristotle said, "But to be angry with the right person, to the right degree, at the right time, for the right purpose, and in the right way—this is not easy" (Nichomachean Ethics). This statement suggests that there is a place for anger. Even Jesus got angry: "And making a kind of whip of cords, he drove them all out of the temple, also the sheep and oxen, and he poured out the money of the changers and overturned the tables" (John 2:15). In what situations, if any, do you think anger is an appropriate response? What would be the right way to express it? Be careful that you do not rationalize your past behavior.*

Passion

> *Be it what it will, the ruling passion conquers reason still.*
>
> —*ALEXANDER POPE, MORAL ESSAYS*

William Penn defined passion as "a sort of fever in the mind, which ever leaves us weaker than it found us" (1906, p. 57). We define it more prosaically as the intense love of some person, thing, situation, or value. Most people have experienced it in romatic love, whence the statement "Love is blind." In love or wherever it is found, passion is able to unseat reason, and rational thought becomes "rationalized thought."

How many women regretably become pregnant because they surrender to "the heat of passion"? How many lives have been lost to the passion for the high of drugs, and how many good relationships to passion felt for someone else? When we love a person or thing, we do not see the dark side; we tend only to justify our desires. Romantic lovers, for example, idealize their partners and often find them without faults. Contrary opinions from friends and family are seen as motivated by jealousy or born of misunderstanding.

Our passion may be our religion, our food, or our drugs. It may be sports, the television, a person, a home, or a material object. Whatever the source, we tend to immerse ourselves in our object of passion, revel briefly in its taste, and only later, if ever, find our reason again.

Depression

When our object of passion is lost, we may find ourselves dysphoric or seriously depressed. This response is echoed in the story of Romeo and Juliet and the numerous young and old alike every year who commit suicide out of a deep sense of loss. But the loss of something dear to us is only one cause of depression. Other causes include biochemical factors, severe stress, a sense of hopelessness, lack of sunlight, and illogical thinking.

Of particular interest to us are the effects that depression may have on thinking. Several studies on depression support the idea that irrational cognitions are correlated with depression. (For our purposes "irrational" and "illogical" are the same, although some make a distinction here.) However, some disagreement exists about whether unhealthy cognitions cause depression, or whether depression causes unhealthy cognitive styles. Research supports both hypotheses. The conclusion from a longitudinal study on this topic, using a sample of 998 people, is that "people change their expectancies and subscribe to irrational beliefs as a result of being depressed," and not the other way around (Lewinsohn et al., 1981). Other studies (e.g., Miranda and Persons, 1988) also give support to the idea that mood can influence thinking.

The kinds of irrational thinking that often accompany depression include a tendency to see or exaggerate the negative side of a situation and to diminish the positive:

> A depressed patient observed that a faucet was leaking in a bathroom, that the pilot light was out in the stove, and that one of the steps in the staircase was broken. He concluded, "The whole house is deteriorating." The house was in excellent condition (except for these minor problems); he had made a massive overgeneralization. (Beck, 1976, p. 219)

To depressed people the cup is half empty, not half full. Depressed people also tend to minimize their successes and maximize their failures by attributing their successes to external causes and their failures to internal causes. In general, depressives are more critical of themselves than they should be and see the world and their future in a more negative light than nondepressives do. That is why suicide prevention centers must often help suicidal people think of alternatives to their problems. Their ability to see their situations clearly is often impaired by their negative mood. As Schneidman (1985) points out, suicidal people, most of whom are depressed, may see only two alternatives to their dilemma: suicide or some unrealistic solution.

Depression in various degrees is so prevalent that it is often called the common cold of mental illness. Ten percent of college students, for example, exhibit moderate depression (Craighead, 1984). We have a much greater chance of experiencing mild depression some time in our lives, and even mild depression can negatively color our thinking.

Dealing with Depression

Serious depression requires serious psychological or medical intervention by a professional. But if we are suffering from "the blues," we must realize that our thinking about ourselves and about life in general is probably colored somewhat by our negative mood. If possible, we should put off major decisions until our mood lifts or talk to others to help us explore alternative courses of action and achieve better insight into our situation. If we have not already done so, we should exercise, for studies show that exercise can lessen depression (Stein and Motta, 1992). In the meantime, we can try to identify the causes of our depression and take action to correct them or, if necessary, seek advice on handling those causes.

Sometimes the cause of our depression is our own irrational thinking. For example, if we encounter a person who does not like us we may become extremely upset about it and spend much of our waking hours wondering what it is about us that is difficult to like. We may also strive excessively to please that person, and we might even suffer insomnia worrying about it. Through our own reflection or through the help of others we may come to see the irrational assumption underlying our unhealthy reaction: "Everyone should like me because I'm a nice person." If we think carefully about this assumption for a moment we can see there is no truth to this, for plenty of nice people, including Jesus, Ghandi, and Mother Teresa had enemies. No matter how nice we may be, some people will invariably misunderstand us or project on us their own inadequacies. Similarly, students who feel lowered self-worth when they receive a disappointing grade are operating under a different irrational belief: "My worth depends upon my achievements." They need only remind themselves that many psychopaths have done well on college exams to realize the error in this kind of thinking.

Cognitive psychologists help people with dysfunctional thinking to see the irrational nature of their thoughts and then suggest rational replacements. Our friends and colleagues may help us do the same, and we can even learn to do this ourselves. In the paragraph below we can see how one cognitive psychologist challenged the distorted thinking of a student who was fearful of giving a speech (sound familiar?).

PATIENT: I have to give a talk before my class tomorrow and I'm scared stiff.

THERAPIST: What are you afraid of?

PATIENT: I think I'll make a fool of myself.

THERAPIST: Suppose you do . . . make a fool of yourself. Why is that so bad?

PATIENT: I'll never live it down.

THERAPIST: "Never" is a long time. . . . Now look here, suppose they ridicule you. Can you die from it?

PATIENT: Of course not.

THERAPIST: Suppose they decide you're the worst public speaker that ever lived. . . . Will this ruin your future career?

PATIENT: No. . . . But it would be nice if I could be a good speaker.

THERAPIST: Sure it would be nice. But if you flubbed it, would your parents or your wife disown you?

PATIENT: No. . . . They're very sympathetic.

THERAPIST: Well, what would be so awful about it?

PATIENT: I would feel pretty bad.

THERAPIST: For how long?

PATIENT: For about a day or two.

THERAPIST: And then what?

PATIENT: Then I'd be O.K. (Beck, 1976, p. 250)

The resolution of depression is not always easy. Fortunately, most people do not become severely depressed. And most who are mildly to moderately depressed, unless it is a major personality characteristic, will find their depression eventually lifting. In the meantime, we must be careful about the thoughts and decisions we make while depressed and remind ourselves of the cognitive distortions we may be experiencing.

THINKING ACTIVITY 2.5
Five Thinking Errors

The five thinking errors below range in severity and frequency and can be found in all of us from time to time. They are particularly likely to appear in times of emotional strain. As you read them, think about instances in which these thinking errors have distorted your thinking, and how these errors have affected your significant others.

1. *Personalization.* Egocentric thinking, in which the world is seen to revolve unduly around the individual. A person might take responsibility for a disappointing picnic at the lake by saying, "I should have known it would probably rain today; it rains a lot in May. I should have waited until June." Or walking by a woman in a store with an angry look on her face, a person wonders, "Why is she mad at me? What did I do?"

2. *Polarized Thinking.* Also called "black and white thinking" or "dichotomous thinking" (later we examine it as the "either/or fallacy"). For example, in depression, a person may see himself only in a negative light and fail to see the good characteristics he has. Or if a person is not extremely successful, she might consider herself a loser. A man might say, "People either like me, or they hate me," not realizing that people can also have mixed feelings about him. A person with a borderline personality disorder often sees people as either all good or all bad.

3. *Overgeneralization.* Drawing broad conclusions on the basis of a single incident. A student fails one course at college and then believes she is a failure and will not be able to earn her degree. Or after receiving a reprimand duly or unduly deserved, a person thinks, "Everyone hates me." Or after his girlfriend breaks up with him, a man thinks, "I'm never going to find someone who will love me."

4. *Catastrophizing.* A common characteristic of anxious people in which they consider the worst possible outcome of an event. A young man announces to his mother that he is getting married, and she immediately thinks about the likelihood of a deformed baby or even a divorce in his future. A young woman going out on a blind date expects it to be a real disappointment. Or a father, upon hearing that his son intends to major in philosophy, imagines his son permanently unemployed and expects him to be a constant financial burden.

5. *Selective Abstraction.* Focusing on one detail of a situation and ignoring the larger picture. For example, an instructor receives a very favorable evaluation from 90 percent of her students but dwells instead on the unfavorable comments from the few. Or a football player, after an overall excellent performance, curses himself for the one pass that he should have caught. (Beck, 1976)

STRIVING FOR COGNITIVE CONSISTENCY

Cognitive consistency refers to a harmony among our various thoughts, and to a harmony between our thoughts and behaviors. Human beings strive for cognitive consistency, because holding onto thoughts that are inconsistent can create an unpleasant state called *cognitive dissonance* (discord) when the inconsistency cannot be justified. This state of dissonance may lead to psychological tension and uncomfortable feelings. When we find ourselves in a state of cognitive dissonance we will often try to change our thoughts or our behaviors to achieve harmony and thereby reduce the tension.

Festinger and Carlsmith (1959) conducted a now classic study illustrating the effects of cognitive dissonance. They had subjects perform a boring task and then asked them to lie to the next subjects by telling them that the task was actually quite enjoyable. Some of the subjects were paid $1 to lie, whereas others were paid $20. Later the subjects were asked about their feelings toward the task. Results showed that subjects who lied for $1 rated the task more favorable than the ones who lied for $20 (about $75 in today's money). This was exactly what Festinger and Carlsmith's cognitive dissonance theory would have predicted. The group that lied for $20 could more easily justify the inconsistency between their thoughts and their behavior. They might have said to themselves something like this:

> The task was really boring, but I told this other guy that it was a lot of fun. I know I lied, but, hey, wouldn't you for twenty bucks? I mean, it's not like I hurt anyone, you know.

On the other hand, the group that lied for $1 would experience dissonance and pressure to change their belief, because it is not easy to justify the inconsistency for only $1:

> The task was really boring, but I told this other guy that it was a lot of fun. I lied for a lousy buck. Boy do I sell out cheap—a lousy buck. But, hey, when I thought about it, you know, it really wasn't so bad. In fact it was sort of challenging. I mean, turning pegs in a hole a quarter of a turn over and over again for a half-hour. Hey, that's a challenge! Kind of fun. No, I didn't lie to the guy, it was quite challenging and enjoyable actually. Besides, I wouldn't lie for a buck.

Thus we see how our thinking can be influenced by dissonance and the need to reduce tension. Specifically, cognitive dissonance can lead to rationalization, a defense mechanism mentioned above.

The need for cognitive consistency shows up in many areas of life. When buying a car, for example, we might have to decide between two attractive models. If we don't believe in spending a lot of money for a car or paying for a lot of

unnecessary frills but we are somehow talked into doing so, we experience dissonance as our behavior becomes incompatible with our beliefs. We then have two
options to remove the dissonance: (1) we can change our behavior—in this case,
that would mean taking the car back, which is not usually an option—or (2) we
can change our thinking about the car, in other words, rationalize our purchase:

> Compared to the cheaper car I was looking at, this one will last longer, so
> I'll easily get the extra money out of it. Besides, this car is safer than the other
> one. And when it comes to your very life, you can never spend too much.
> As far as the accessories go, well, they'll help to sell the car when that distant
> day arrives. Besides, what's wrong with a little pleasure in life. You only live
> once, you know.

Incongruence among thoughts or between thoughts and behaviors does not
always cause a dissonant state. For example, if a student disliked the school she was
attending but no other school in her area was affordable, there would be no cognitive dissonance. As long as there is sufficient justification for the discrepant situation, cognitive dissonance does not occur. Here's one more example: If a young man
does not believe in premarital sex, but when the moment arrives at which his beliefs
must be put to the test he engages in such sex, then cognitive dissonance would
probably occur—unless he can sufficiently justify the discrepancy somehow, such
as believing he was not free to choose. He might argue to himself that he was drinking that night and didn't know what he was doing. If this argument is convincing,
no dissonance will occur and he will not be motivated to change his thinking about
premarital sex. If, however, he cannot find a source of coercion or justifiable motivation for his behavior, he will probably experience dissonance and be motivated to
either (1) change his thinking about the wrongfulness of premarital sex or (2)
change his behavior. Because he cannot undo the sexual behavior that caused the
dissonance, his only option is to change his attitude, or live with the dissonance.

We can apply the idea of cognitive consistency to relationships in other
ways. Balance theory argues that our likes and dislikes of other people should be
in harmony. For example, if you like Mary and you both are pro-life, then you
have a balanced relationship; there is no disharmony. However, if you like Mary
and she is pro-life but you are pro-choice, you have some incongruence, an imbalance that creates pressure on you to change either your attitude toward abortion or your thinking and feelings toward Mary.

Balance theory predicts that many people would vote for a candidate
because their friend or spouse did. Doing so would create a more balanced situation. When the imbalance grows too strong, some couples won't even talk
about politics or religion, although many couples and friends do openly disagree
with each other and maintain their deep friendship at the same time. Crucial or
cherished ideas create more balance pressure than rather irrelevant ones. Who
cares, for example, what your friend's favorite ice cream is? Relationships do not

change over a disagreement about vanilla or chocolate. However, dissonance would likely occur in a relationship when both persons are quite politically active and share very different political ideas.

Many couples and their mutual friends experience an unbalanced relationship when the couple gets divorced. For example, it is often difficult for an ex-wife to continue her friendship with someone who actually likes her ex-husband. Similarly, it is difficult for the mutual friend to continue her affection for both friends when each criticizes the other in her presence. In order to eliminate her dissonance, she may begin thinking and feeling negatively about one or the other and break off her relationship with that person, or she may find a way to get them together again.

Thus we can see how dissonance and imbalanced situations can change our sexual mores, political views, and attitudes toward our friends, for no other reason than to remove the incongruence and tension we experience. Our need for compatible thoughts and behaviors actually leads to altered thinking.

STRESS

> *It's when I'm weary of considerations,*
> *And life is too much like a pathless wood*
>
> . . . .
>
> *I'd like to get away from earth awhile*
>
> —*ROBERT FROST,* "BIRCHES"

Stress is excessive demand upon the body or mind, producing physical or psychological strain. The sources of stress are numerous: work overload, rapid cultural change, time pressure, conflict, noise pollution, negative life experiences, and daily hassles. These stressors not only contribute to between 50 and 80 percent of all diseases, but they affect our cognition as well. Stress can impair our memory, the basis of much of our thinking, and it can also affect thinking more directly. Stress can lead to preoccupation with an idea, concentration difficulties, deterioration in judgment and logical thinking, and negative self-evaluations. It may also lead to an inability to check our thoughts against reality (Beck et al., 1979) and may seriously interfere with our ability to make decisions (Janis, 1982). Under stress our ability to perceive alternative solutions to a problem diminishes, our capacity to search for information is impaired, and the long-term consequences of our decisions are overlooked. This leads us to make decisions prematurely—an action called "premature closure" (Janis, 1982)—and then creates more stress as we deal with the consequences of our poor decisions:

A professor was asked to speak to a community group. He walked to the wrong room and suddenly realized that the presentation was to be given in another building. Beginning to feel pressure, he trotted out to the parking lot to drive to the other building, which was about a block away. He reached for his car keys and found none. Panic began to build. He could see the building in which he was to speak but could not get into his car to drive over there. It was already five minutes past the time of his talk, so he ran to his office to pick up his keys and then ran back and drove over. Only then did he realize that he could have walked the distance in less time than it took him to go back to his office for his keys.

This is a classic example of how stress interferes with our ability to perceive alternatives.

Because stress affects our thinking in so many ways, it is important that we keep it under control. A number of stress-management strategies can help us with this control. However before we can apply them we must first be aware that we are under stress. This is not always easy for stress can accumulate so insidiously that we underestimate its extent. We may get clues, however, by observing ourselves and noting the signs and symptoms of stress and by listening to what our friends and loved ones say about us, such as, "What's wrong with you lately? You're not yourself."

Signs and Symptoms of Stress

The following signs and symptoms may be indicative of stress. The list is by no means exhaustive. The more of these symptoms you have, the more stress you are likely to be suffering, although no two people respond to stress in exactly the same way. Bear in mind that although stress is a common cause of these ailments, other causes may be responsible.

Cognitive Signs

1. Poor concentration
2. Poor memory
3. Paranoid thinking
4. Low self-esteem, loss of self-confidence
5. Nightmarish dreams
6. Preoccupation with one idea or thought
7. Constant worrying

Emotional Signs

1. Depression
2. Moodiness
3. Irritability
4. Anger
5. Crying spells

(continued)

Signs and Symptoms of Stress *(continued)*

Physical Signs

1. Gastrointestinal problems
2. Inability to feel relaxed
3. Insomnia
4. Fatigue
5. Loss of appetite
6. Ulcers
7. Skin rashes
8. More frequent colds
9. Headaches
10. Worsening of other physical problems
11. Loss of sex drive

Behavioral Signs

1. Withdrawal from others
2. Intolerance of others
3. Displaced aggression toward others
4. Fidgeting behavior (pencil tapping, leg bouncing)
5. Increase in bad habits (fingernail biting, smoking)
6. Increase in facial and other tics
7. Binge eating
8. Increased use of alcohol

Stress Management

Once we know we are under stress, it is important to identify the stressors, or causes of stress, being as specific as possible. Don't settle for generalities like "life stresses me out." That's too vague to suggest a stress-management solution—suicide is not a viable option. By probing further we may find that it is not life itself that is the source of our stress; it's the speech we have to give in two weeks that is causing us strain. Or perhaps it's our children. But what about our children? Are they too noisy? Too demanding? Too disobedient? Do they require too much attention or get us up in the middle of the night? We need to be specific, for each situation requires a different approach to management.

In general, stress-management approaches fall into three categories: (1) removing the outside source of stress, (2) removing the inside source of stress, and (3) managing the body's response to stress. Removing the outside source of stress would be appropriate when dealing with the stress of noisy children, for example. We could set an hour of quiet time every day, remove some noisy toys from the house, establish stricter rules about playing outside, or install more doors and carpet. If the stress comes from the constant attention we must give a child in the middle of the night, the solution may be to ask one's spouse to share in that responsibility by alternating nights. Again, the source of stress should be identified as specifically as possible. Often the appropriate stress-management approach then becomes obvious.

If the outside source of stress cannot be removed, perhaps we can remove the inside source, which involves changing ourselves. Typically this means removing irrational ideas and expectations that give rise to our stress, and changing the meaning we give to the stressor. Often we can change the stressful meaning we give to life events by putting them in proper perspective. If we must give a speech, for example, we could ask ourselves, "What's the worst that can realistically happen? Will I die?" Probably the worst would be to forget our speech and become embarrassed. Life goes on. In one week no one will remember anyway, because people will be too busy with their own problems.

Putting a speech in proper perspective is one way to reduce its stress. Oftentimes this requires addressing and removing irrational ideas that underlie the speech anxiety. For example, we may be overly concerned about our upcoming speech because we believe that we must be perfect in everything we do, that everyone should like us, or that everyone is concerned about how we perform. All of these are irrational thoughts that must be challenged and replaced with more realistic ones.

Sometimes we can extend our perspective still wider to show how small our stressors really are. If we stop to think about how short our lives are and how small we are in this huge universe, certain concerns and worries dissolve away in insignificance. When we remember that we are in a galaxy with billions of stars and that there may be more galaxies than there are grains of sand on all the beaches on this planet, and when we think about how old the universe is (about 15 billion years), and how in comparison our life is shorter than that of a fruit fly, then maybe it doesn't matter any more that we are trapped behind a car going 34 miles an hour in a 35-mph zone, that our spouse rarely gets the garbage out on time, or that our hair won't lie down just right.

> *Life is too short to waste*
> *In critic peep or cynic bark,*
> *Quarrel or reprimand;*
> *'Twill soon be dark;*
> *Up! mind thine own aim, and*
> *God speed the mark!*
>
> —RALPH WALDO EMERSON, "TO J. W."

If we cannot eliminate the source of stress and we cannot change the meaning we give to it, we can always manage our body's response to stress through exercise, meditation, relaxation techniques, adequate rest, and proper nutrition.

This reduces both the subjective feelings of stress and the deleterious effects stress can have on our physical and mental functioning. Exercise, meditation, or relaxation alone can sometimes be enough to remove the feelings of stress. Proper nutrition is important because stress rapidly removes essential vitamins, particularly the B complex, which are vital to healthy physical and mental functioning.

SUMMARY

The extent to which we can think critically is strongly related to who we are. The enculturation process largely determines our prejudices and values, and our self-concept contains specific areas of sensitivity and weaknesses that motivate defensive thinking through the use of ego defenses and self-serving biases. Additionally, our schemata shape, restrict, and stereotype our perceptions and thinking. And depression, anger, passion, and stress can lead to negative, irrational thoughts and poor judgment. Our thinking also seems to be affected by our need for consistency and balance among our thoughts and emotions.

All of these factors lead one to wonder about the extent to which human beings can be rational at all. Certainly, the more we engage in self-reflection and become aware of these biases and limitations, the more we are able to avoid them. Such awareness can help us identify our thinking biases and move our thinking in a healthier, more rational direction. Besides self-reflection, we can take specific actions to remove the causes of bad thinking. But transcending our personal barriers is not easy, and most of us do not completely remove them. Fortunately, better thinking does not require perfection, only one step at a time in the right direction.

BARRIER CHALLENGES

1. List the favorite beer in your town or among your group. Is it your favorite as well? Why?

2. Would you eat cow? Would people in India eat cow? Do you think it's okay to eat dog? Do you know any cultures in which they do eat dog?

3. What does your religion teach you about the right way to think about contemporary issues such as abortion, the existence of God, euthanasia, working hard, and the role of women? In what other ways does your religion shape your values, beliefs, and attitudes?

4. How has your hometown influenced you? To help you find out, write down how you might be different if you had been raised in the following cities: San Francisco, Des Moines, New York, Detroit, Cheyenne.

5. Investigate a major religion that is unfamiliar to you. How might people of that religion view your religious beliefs?

6. How have your friends and school influenced your values?

7. Is there anything unique about the people who live in your state compared with people in other states?

8. Sometimes the people we hate most are those who have the trait we hate most in ourselves. Whom do you hate most? Why? Could that trait characterize you as well? If in doubt, ask others.

9. When was the last time you rationalized? It's easier to look back and see it than to identify it at the time it is happening.

10. When was the last time you failed a test or a task at work? Did you use a self-serving bias to protect your self-esteem?

11. We often see according to our expectations and beliefs. Is your perception of your instructor influenced by what you heard about him or her before? Do significant people in your life complain that you fail to recognize their changed behavior and still perceive them as they used to be?

12. When you are angry, do you typically say things that you don't really mean? Do you tend to overgeneralize or catastrophize?

13. Alexander Hamilton once said, "Why has government been instituted at all? Because the passions of men will not conform to the dictates of reason and justice, without constraint" (*The Federalist*). Do you agree with his statement? What would people's behavior be like without a government? Can you find instances in history to support your answer?

14. When you are depressed, which of Beck's five thinking errors (see page 35) tends to characterize your thinking?

15. Have you ever experienced pressure to abandon a couple who broke up? Did you maintain allegiance to one and not the other? How have you and others you know handled such situations?

16. Did you ever believe one way but act in another? How did you handle the apparent contradiction?

17. What happens to your thinking under stress?

18. Some people define themselves by their possessions, religious beliefs, or abilities. How do you define yourself? These are the topics about which you may have difficulty thinking objectively.

19. What stereotypes do you tend to believe? Do you know people who do not fit these stereotypes? If you can't find exceptions, ask your friends, family members, or college professors. You could also do research on these groups that you stereotype to learn about the diversity within those groups.

20. Recall two or three times when you were angry. Which was worse: the situation that caused your anger or the consequences of venting your anger? Could you have done anything to control your anger?

21. Has passion ever clouded your reason?

3

Sensing

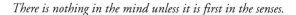

There is nothing in the mind unless it is first in the senses.

—*AQUINAS*

SENSUAL BEGINNINGS

If we were blindfolded, taken to a place, and the blindfold removed for only a second, we would get a flash of visual stimulation. If we were standing where we had never been before, perhaps in a mosque, the one-second glance would reveal a jumble of colors, mosaics, and geometric designs; however, if we were in a city library, we would recognize and understand what we saw. In both cases visual rivers would flow into our eyes, but we would understand the library because we already had the language in our mind. That language would have prestructured our perceptions and would have allowed us to understand and to process the sensual stream of books and desks.

With language already in our mind, it is possible to close our eyes and, disconnected from the outside world, do "pure thinking," but that kind of isolated thinking is rare. Most of our thinking is *sensory interactive;* after all, our brain is enfleshed in our senses. This sensing-thinking connection is so closely interrelated that our thinking often begins in our senses, progresses through additional sensory input, and shapes itself to our sensing habits; conversely, thinking can shape the way we sense.

The statement, "There is nothing in the mind unless it is first in the senses," says, in stark simplicity, that our brain would be empty without our senses. If this view is correct, then sensing would be the main source of raw data for our thinking: if we sense better, we can think better.

Whereas sensing precedes thinking for infants, sensing for adults is concurrent with thinking. As adults we continually return to our senses to refresh the data, to seek new data, to fortify our thinking with tangible examples, and to validate the structures of our thinking. Our sensing and thinking are interwoven: even now as we read this book, as we listen in class, and as we write, we are sensing (with our eyes, ears, hands); conversely, when we bungee-jump, prepare a dinner, or install brakes on a car, we are thinking.

Sharpening our perceptions is crucial for delivering better data to our brains. We need the accurate observations. We need the facts right. We need solid sensory awareness to ground our thinking. We need to perceive beyond appearances and behind false faces.

In this chapter we examine how our senses both enlighten and deceive our mind, we learn how we can sharpen our vital sensing-thinking connection, and especially, we will stress how we can strengthen our two most important senses for thinking: seeing and hearing.

THE POWER OF OUR SENSES

Our senses act as our lenses, amplifiers, particle detectors, and pressure and heat gauges. These sensors are acutely sensitive. Our hearing reacts to a sound vibrating at a frequency as high as 20,000 cycles per second and to a multitude of timbres that allow us to recognize different human voices. Our sight can detect a candle flame on a dark, clear night 20 miles away or discern a single color (mauve or teal) out of millions of hues. Our sense of smell can detect a single molecule of bacon or coffee out of five billion molecules. Our senses feed our brain much as food feeds our body; without their input, our brain would be almost empty.

Is our brain a blank slate at birth, as John Locke says, or is it alive with innate ideas? There are strong thinkers on both sides of this issue. John Locke agrees with Aristotle and calls the mind a *tabula rasa* (blank slate) that our senses and experience write upon. But other philosophers (Plato), psychologists (Jung), and linguists (Chomsky) disagree at least partially with this concept. They say we have innate, or inborn, ideas or structures in our mind. What do you think?

THE DECEPTION OF OUR SENSES

Throughout our life our senses have enriched our brain, and currently our senses link with our brain as we think. Powerful though they are, our senses do not always deliver accurate data to our brain. Our senses do not operate effectively

THINKING ACTIVITY 3.1
Ideas: Innate or Learned?

Where do our ideas come from? List reasons supporting both those who say we are born with ideas and those who say we learn them through our senses.

Ideas Are Inborn	Our Senses Fill the Mind

As you listed reasons, you may have come to a decision in favor of one side or another. If you have not yet decided, weigh those reasons now and check one of the boxes below. As you check the box, be very aware of what is going on in your mind. We will discuss your awareness shortly.

- ☐ We are born with knowledge.
- ☐ We acquire knowledge through our senses.
- ☐ We are born with knowledge; then we acquire more.

How did you arrive at your conclusion? Although the process may be difficult to describe because we are often not aware of our thinking *while* we think, try to describe the thinking processes you went through to arrive at your decision.

_____

_____

_____

_____

_____

_____

Whatever you discovered while you checked the box and wrote about your decision-making process, you sensed and thought together; you interwove sight and touch with your thinking as you read and wrote.

when we are sick, drowsy, or tired; and sometimes, although our senses deliver accurately, the world is not always what it seems on the sensual surface. Our sensual perceptions (using sight as an example) can deceive our brain in three major ways: limited biologically, we see the superficial; corralled by custom, we see the habitual; and blinded by language, we see the general.

Scientists and philosophers have alerted us to the superficiality of our senses. Copernicus stated that the sun did not "set," and Descartes pointed out the "bent" oar in the water. Subsequently, science has shown us the narrow range of our sight from red to violet; all the "colors" from infrared in one direction and ultraviolet in the other through the vast electromagnetic spectrum are invisible to our eyes, as are things very small and very far away. The superficial perception of our senses is weakened further by certain life forms that attempt to deceive, such as the chameleon, the Venus flytrap, and, yes, even humans: "That one could smile and smile and smile and be a villain" (Shakespeare, *Hamlet*).

Likewise custom in the form of habits, interests, and biases, focuses and thus limits our perceptions. A fashion designer, walking into a room, sees that room differently from a carpenter, an antique collector, a gymnast, or a party animal (only the plasterer might seriously study the ceiling). In the following chapter we will study how language also puts reins upon our senses.

THINKING ACTIVITY 3.2
Our Personal Sense Deceptions

Think about how your senses can deceive you. What things appear safe but are dangerous, soft but are hard, fragrant but are poisonous, beautiful but are rotten, true but are false? In the chart list some people or things that can deceive your senses and note what the reality is. Also be aware of your own biases and strong interests that might block, focus, and distort your sense impressions.

Deceptions	Corrections
Vanilla extract smells edible.	Tastes terrible!

SHARPENING OUR SENSES

> *Perhaps my originality boils down to being a hypersensitive receptor.*
>
> —*CLAUDE MONET, IMPRESSIONIST PAINTER*

When we realize that our senses are fallible, then we can begin to adjust to surface appearance and personal distortions. Seeing should not always be believing. The spear-fishing Chippewa Indians of Wisconsin (who don't know Descartes's bent oar) have learned to adjust: they plunge their spear *above* the point where they see the fish. If they didn't, they would go hungry.

We can adjust not just to water but to the entire surface of the earth by turning up the power of our senses. Our eyes now pierce the surface through the electronic microscope, ultrasound, magnetic resonance, and positron emission; our ears amplify apparent silence through the microphone, listen to the shifting earth through seismographs, and hear the echo of the big bang through radar telescopes. Our nostrils smell hidden particles through smoke detectors and Geiger counters; and our sense of touch feels more precisely through the barometer and thermometer. These instruments allow us to perceive beyond the range of our senses to see the molecules and microbes moving. We can then struggle to synthesize the clash between appearance and reality. Our mind can reason, accept the validity of these observations, and know, for example, that invisible species crawl over our skin and that vast spaces exist in the floor upon which we step.

If we try, we can sometimes return to the sensual newness of a child. A five-year-old boy in a mechanic's shop identified his friend Brad's car. His dad glanced at the car and said, "No, that's too rusty." The boy replied, "But it smells like Brad's car." The father asked the mechanic: it was Brad's car. We too can extend our senses. By willing and by trying we can see more and sense more. If we start a program that tries, a few times a day, to absorb more intensely the sensual information around us, we can hone our perceptions to a piercing power of accuracy and newness; by the end of this course we will be perceiving at a higher level. This sharper perception can lead to sharper thinking as we place more specific, concrete, accurate data in our mind; and when our thinking is interacting with our environment, the results will more closely reflect the external reality.

In chapter 1 we made three lists of observations in progressively greater detail. By such methods we can learn to push our senses to see fine details, to notice the rainbow colors of the snowflakes (often we just see white), to hear the wind through the grass (it's different from the wind through the trees), to smell the fragrance unique to each rose, even those coming from the same rosebush (a rose is *not* just a rose just a rose). As we struggle to sense more closely, we might discover the startling fact that no two things are alike: even mass-produced items, like beer cans, pencils, bolts, and coins, have differences easily distinguishable by our sight. We need to break the habit of seeing things in the same general way, largely because we think we know what they look like. One way to break through this habitual pattern is to look at things in extremely small detail and then try to express what we see in new words. Avoid clichés: they are a sign that we are using other people's words and therefore are not describing what *we* are seeing.

THINKING ACTIVITY 3.3
Seeing Anew

1. Pick any two things that you think are identical; if you wish, reach into your pocket or purse and take two coins of the same denomination and begin to notice the differences. Turn and twist them and watch the light reflect off their individual surfaces. Strike them and hear their unique sounds.
2. Focus your senses on those two things as if you were alone in a woods at night and you heard breaking branches on the forest floor.
3. Look so closely, so minutely at tiny sections of the objects that you have no easy words for such small areas of focus. Then try to break the language barrier by describing those differences specifically and concretely.
4. Avoid clichés. Find new ways to describe what you are seeing; use analogies to get your meaning across.

If you practice these steps, your thinking will take root in specific facts and your writing and speaking will glisten with newness.

POWERFUL LISTENING

After seeing, hearing may be our most vital sense. Hearing sends rivers of sound into our ears, from the music of falling waters to the cry of a newborn baby. When we use our hearing to listen to words, listening becomes interactive with our thinking and crucial in communicating.

The Paradox of Powerful Listening

When we were small children our listening was natural and effortless, like the earth receiving rain. That's partly why we were able to learn our language so quickly. Our adult brains can absorb thoughts several times faster than they are spoken: speech runs about 125 words per minute, yet if this rate were doubled (or even tripled through a sped-up audiotape) we could still understand the words. Listening is so simple that, paradoxically, it is hard. Because the rate of speaking is so slow, we can easily allow our mind to roam elsewhere. And now that we've grown older, our listening is drowned by the buzz of our thinking, and is smothered by our poor habits. Because listening is apparently simple, we allow our mind to roam elsewhere while someone is talking. The challenge then becomes, how do we rein in our brain to follow the speaker? How do we not get bored and allow our attention to wander?

How to Listen

In order to listen well, we must want to listen. Here are a few reasons to help motivate us to listen well: (1) we will know more, (2) our decisions will be based on firmer data, (3) we will understand the speaker's values and positions better, (4) our interpersonal skills will be higher, (5) our responses will carry greater effectiveness, (6) we can recall how good we felt when anyone really listened to us, and give that same courtesy to the speaker, (7) the speaker will talk better because we actually partially control the speaker by how well we listen and ask questions, and (8) we will learn more. Can you think of other reasons to listen well?

Even if we think the speaker is boring, if our attitude is receptive we can learn from anyone. Ultimately we are the ones who profit. We are the ones who grow wiser. Consider one final example of the power of listening. A married graduate student reported that he was on a path toward a divorce, so in his busy schedule he set aside twenty minutes a week on Friday nights to listen, really listen, to his wife. The first night, without even knowing why, his wife said, "Gee, hon, we had fun tonight." By continuing to listen, the student said he began to find out things about his kids and his wife that he never knew. He said listening, simply listening, rescued and enriched their relationship.

Once we have set our will to listen, we may need to adjust our environment. MTV, screaming children, trucks winding through their gears, and blasting bands do not provide a good listening environment. If we want to listen, we can move to a place of acceptable noise level and privacy, adjust our chairs so we are close enough, turn our back on windows, televisions, or other distractions, and face the speaker. The environment is ours to control.

Then we need to place our body into a listening posture. First, we square up, sitting or standing directly across from the other person (effective, forthright communication is not assisted by angles—acute, oblique, or otherwise). Second, we relax and open our body to the ideas of the other (folded arms and locked knees are often reflective of our mental locks). Third, we lean slightly toward the speaker (pulling back is a reaction associated with horror, fright, fear, bad breath, or rejection of the other's ideas). Finally and most importantly, we look the other in the eyes without staring, and we appropriately maintain that vital connection while we are listening (eye contact connects us in some ways more strongly than the telephone wire connects our phones). Squared, relaxed, leaning, and looking, our body prepares us for listening.

With our will set, the environment adjusted, and our body posed, we have a better chance of keeping our mind focused. Here are some ways to keep your mind on the speaker. As we present these ideas, think about which ones will work effectively for you:

1. *Listen to the tone of the speaker's words,* to the feelings behind the thoughts. Tone can easily color or contradict the content of the words, but it is rare that content can outweigh tone. For example, if you greet your boyfriend and ask him how he is, and in a small voice he sighs, "Fine," you can believe the tone of his voice and ignore his words. He isn't fine. Something is wrong, and his tone shows it. Because of the connection between tone and truth, voice stress indicators have been developed in an attempt to measure the truthfulness of people's statements.

2. *Read the speaker's body.* Watch the face, the tightness or relaxation around the lips and the eyes; watch the hands. Is any nervous energy playing through the speaker's fingers? A top executive in an advertising firm was a man of forced smiles and memorized names. As he smiled and talked to clients he did not like, his left fist clenched and unclenched. An alert client reading the nonverbal message would know how to deal with him.

Since the work of Edward Sapir in the 1930s, the literature on nonverbal communication has been growing. Body signals, however, can be ambiguous; there is always the possibility that we are "reading" wrongly. With this caution in mind, reading the body can help us stay focused and listen more fully to the speaker.

3. *Use your memory.* Recall earlier meetings and conversations with the speaker and how those ideas fit with the speaker's present words.

4. *Understand the speaker's needs, values, beliefs, and goals.* In the old adage—step into the speaker's shoes and empathize.

5. *Organize what you hear.* Often speakers do not convey their thoughts in perfect prose. Try to group their words into main points.

6. *Paraphrase the speaker's words out loud.* Give feedback by saying something like, "So what you are saying is that you would like to . . . ," and check their response.

7. *Ask questions.* If the speaking situation permits it, asking questions directs the speaker toward topics of interest to you. Also, questions can clarify ambiguities and may spark the speaker alive to new ideas.

8. *Summarize the other's ideas.* This helps both parties focus on the nucleus: on the thoughts to be remembered, on the actions to be taken. Clarity will result.

THINKING ACTIVITY 3.4
Developing an Action Plan

Thinking is intangible, and while you might get some great ideas as you read this book and listen to your teacher and participate in class, unless you *act* on your thinking, your ideas will probably remain intangible. To bring thinking into your life more, you are highly encouraged to develop a *specific, practical* plan of action for each chapter.

To try to listen better, you can make a list of specific steps describing *what* you will do, *when* you will do it, and *how* you will check your progress. A sample action plan might look like this:

WHAT: I want to listen to my friend with more attention. I will try to maintain eye contact and not to interrupt while my friend is talking. I will ask appropriate questions and paraphrase my friend's responses to focus my listening.

WHEN: I will listen for five minutes each day when I return home from school or work.

CHECK: On Fridays I will count the number of days that I was successful, and reflect on the result my listening has had.

Now develop your own action plan in the spaces below. Please pick an idea from class or the book that you would like to try to bring into your life. Remember: be *specific* in describing what you are going to do; when you will do it (days and times and places); and how and when you will check upon your progress.

WHAT:

_____

_____

_____

_____

_____

WHEN:

_____

_____

_____

CHECK:

_____

_____

SUMMARY

We have seen how our powerful senses both nourish and deceive our minds. We have seen that our acute senses can be expanded by the instruments of science, and we have been alerted to the *appearance* of reality of some of our sensations. Furthermore, we have glanced at the deliberate deceptions that occur in nature and human beings. Shakespeare alerts us "that there is no art known to read the mind's construction in the face." We have seen how we can sharpen these vital sensing-thinking connections by looking more closely at the unique world around us. Finally, we have seen how we can focus our powerful mind for effective listening. By keeping our thinking refreshed and sharpened through interaction with our sensing, we will be grounded in a more solid reality as we absorb and seek new data.

SENSING AND THINKING CHALLENGES

1. Do you accept information when it is contrary to common sense? For instance, the earth is closer to the sun in the winter than it is in the summer. Seek the reason for this phenomenon and then think about how your mind struggles with the apparent conflict between your senses and the facts.

2. Galileo convinced the world that Copernicus was right about the orbiting spheres when he pointed a telescope at Jupiter and watched the moons go around it. Is seeing always believing? Can you think of any exceptions?

3. If you are writing a descriptive paper or trying to paint with words, this chapter can help you. Perform Thinking Activity 3.3 several times; that is, try to see on a very small scale, and then search for new words, especially analogies, to describe what you see. Practice this activity on any of the following:
   a. A one-inch square area of the palm of your hand.
   b. A feature (a small part) of someone's face. (In *Canterbury Tales* Chaucer describes a wart on the edge of the miller's nose as having three red sow bristles growing from it. You do not need to choose a grotesque feature, but you should strive for Chaucer's minute level of detail.)
   c. A leaf of some plant.
   d. A petal of a flower.
   e. The shine, color, and reflection in a drop of water.
   f. Any small part of anything you wish.

4. Try focusing one sense, such as smell or hearing, and then shifting to another and focusing sharply. What do you experience?

5. William Wordsworth did not think we were born empty: "We come trailing clouds of glory." What do you think was already in your mind at birth?

6. As a quick test of the effect of your listening, the next time you are in a small group, listen intently and receptively to the speaker: Notice if the speaker begins to look at you longer and more often than others in the group.

7. Do words blind our senses? How might the word *mountain* or *forest* prevent us from seeing the uniqueness of that mountain or that forest, and the uniqueness of the rocks and trees within each.

8. Schedule a few times during the day to *practice* sensing. These times can overlap other things you are doing, such as driving or eating or washing dishes. Focus your mind to become acutely aware of details.

9. Listening is so simple that it is hard. Do you agree with that statement? What do you find particularly easy or difficult about listening?

10. Buddhists engage in a practice of "bare attention" to sharpen their perceiving. This practice is described as "observing things as they are, without laying our projections and expectations onto what is happening; cultivating instead a choiceless and non-interfering awareness" (Goldstein, 1976, p. 20). Whatever you are doing now and throughout the day, give it your bare attention. Try simply to notice things without labeling or evaluating them; remain detached. Afterwards, reflect, write about, or discuss your experience.

11. Have you ever really seen a penny? Which of the following features are on the Lincoln cent? Circle the items that you believe are on the penny, and then inspect a penny. How perceptive were you?
    a. Lincoln facing forward
    b. Lincoln facing to the right
    c. Lincoln facing left
    d. "Give me liberty or give me death"
    e. "In God We Trust"
    f. "One Penny"
    g. "One Cent"
    h. Picture of the White House
    i. "E Pluribus Unum"
    j. "Liberty"
    k. The date of the penny
    l. "United States of America"
    m. Picture of the American Flag

12. Here is a descriptive paper written by a student. What words, figures of speech, and what thought patterns does this writer use to activate our senses?

> Mom and I used to watch the storms that would later resemble life. It was in the springtime of my life when we watched the rain shimmer with moonlight as it fell so delicately to the earth.

(continued)

When I was an adolescent we watched the clouds billow in overlapping layers, covering the entire horizon like a crimson blanket of fog. The lightning danced in a blinding fury to the beat of the rumbling thunder. As we watched, rebelliousness took the stage for my summer years. The wind cried as if it was afraid of the dark. The show gained intensity as the actors prepared for the finale. Then I saw the explosion, and lights like glass shattered everywhere. And the sky cleared and looked again for a new beginning.

I have since matured and mellowed into the autumn of my life. Mom is gone, and now I have taken her place, with my own children. We sit and watch the storms.

4

Brain and Memory

The brain breathes mind like the lungs breathe air.

—HUSTON SMITH, FORGOTTEN TRUTH

THE MYSTERY

Our brain. It lies behind the creativity within the Sistine Chapel and the formulas of Einstein. It has taken humankind to the moon and will someday reach the stars. Perhaps only the universe itself can equal its marvel, yet we know so little of it. How can this physical organ create a private mental world that has no mass and no spatial location? Where are our thoughts? How are they generated by our brain? How has our identity become intricately enmeshed within it? These questions we cannot yet answer, and we leave them to the philosophers and neuroscientists of the future. Here we take a brief, pragmatic look at what we do know about the brain, particularly how it affects our thinking, for though the brain is still a great mystery, we have begun to learn its secrets.

We have also begun to learn the secrets of memory—but only begun. This mystery within a mystery is the bedrock of thinking itself. It, too, has its points of wonder. How is it, for example, that a physical process in the brain can give rise to the memory of your grandfather? If you could take a journey inside your brain, where would he be found? While we can't answer this question, it is worthwhile to think about it, for the activity of thinking enhances thought, just as the activity of memory enhances memory, as we will discuss below.

In what follows we look at the brain, its universe of neurons, the influences on the brain that affect our thinking, and ways to move our brain toward better thinking. We then explore memory, its impermanence, the reasons why we forget, and how we can remember better. With this understanding of our brain and memory, we can lay a stronger foundation for critical and creative thinking.

THINKING AND OUR BRAIN

As you read these words your brain is at work. Relying on earlier learning which associated certain line patterns with letters of the alphabet, your brain checks its own database for familiar combinations of these letter patterns and then recognizes the words or word phrases as individual units. Unfamiliar words, like "phacoemulsification" are flagged and processed with greater attention to each letter or syllable. As all of this is taking place your brain is simultaneously placing these words and word phrases in a context that gives them meaning; the words make sense. Your brain may then continue on to yet another step as you think about the meaning of the sentences themselves. For example, you might wonder about the complexity of this process, the fact that you have little control over it (try not to see the letters as words, for example), or whether there can be any kind of thinking without the brain (as in speculations about an afterlife). As you continue to process these words, you might also judge the value of this information, compare it with other information you already have, or wonder about the point the authors are making. You might even think about whether a machine could ever be developed that can do what you are doing now. All this wondering, valuing, and organizing is done with your brain. Alter the brain or destroy it and the character of this process changes or ceases altogether.

The brain is incredibly complex and has the potential to handle huge thinking demands. It contains more than one trillion cells, about 100 billion of which are neurons. These neurons are the single-cell messengers that carry out the responses that comprise our thinking and movement activities. It would take you about 4,731 years to count them all if you counted one number per second every minute of your waking life! But that's just the beginning, for each of these 100 billion neurons has 1,000 to more than 200,000 contacts with other neurons, each neuron sending and receiving messages up to 1,000 times a second. With this incredible, dynamic interconnectedness, the number of different pathways in the brain is unimaginable!

What we consider to be critical thinking ability is located in the outer part of the brain, that wrinkled cap called the cortex. The cortex is about one-tenth of an inch thick and is convoluted, which explains how its one and two-thirds square feet of surface area can fit within the confines of the human skull. The cortex alone contains more than 10 billion neurons. It is here that all the higher intellectual processes take place. The rest of the brain is responsible for lower functions, such as emotions, hunger, and basic life-sustaining processes, although even these are influenced by input from the cortex.

We are still in our infancy in understanding how our brain's universe of neurons interact to create thinking, but we have made some small progress. We know, for example, that brain neurons do not touch; they communicate by sending molecules of hormones called neurotransmitters across a synapse, the microscopic space between adjoining neurons. Approximately seventy-five different types of neurotransmitters have been identified so far, with perhaps hundreds waiting to be discovered. The balance between these hormones is rather delicate. A glass of wine, a strong cup of coffee, a poor night's sleep, a candy bar, or a common cold pill can affect it. Even falling in love can change the chemistry of the brain. When this chemistry changes, the way we perceive and think about reality changes too. Below we briefly address some of the variables that can impact the brain in a way that affects our critical thinking abilities.

THINKING ACTIVITY 4.1
An Exercise in Mental Discipline

Do you agree with the Eastern analogy of the mind that thoughts jump hither and thither like monkeys jump from tree branch to tree branch? To check out this "monkey mind" analogy, try a simple meditation exercise for ten minutes. Sit in a comfortable chair in a quiet room and try to keep your attention on only one thing, like an inner image of a candle flame, the sound "ah nam" silently repeated to yourself, or a blue vase. When you find yourself thinking about something else, bring your attention back to your object of meditation. After doing this exercise, what do you think about the extent to which you consciously control your thinking?

Food and Drugs

> *O God! that men should put an enemy in their mouths to steal away their brains.*
>
> —*SHAKESPEARE*

Clearly the brain needs food. Like the rest of our body, it requires energy, specifically glucose, which it gets from the body's conversion of starches and sugars.

Like the rest of the body, the brain also needs protein and vitamins for proper functioning. Without adequate nutrients, intellectual impairment results:

> In an intensive study of the children of North American Indians, Dr. Ernesto Pollitt, of the Massachusetts Institute of Technology, demonstrated a 50 percent decrease in behavioral performance in severely malnourished children. Memory, abstract reasoning, thinking, and verbal ability were most affected. (Restak, 1979, pp. 107–108)

But we do not have to be malnourished to notice the effects of nutritional deficiency on our thinking. Simply trying to go through the day with too few calories impairs our ability to concentrate, as any student knows who has tried to concentrate on a lecture on an empty stomach.

Of particular importance to thinking are the B vitamins. Vitamin B deficiency has been linked to problems in memory, concentration, and depression. In acute cases of vitamin B deficiency, particularly thiamine, Korsakoff's syndrome develops. This is a chronic disorder, even after the vitamin deficiency is corrected, which creates gross deficits in short-term and long-term memory. This deficiency is particularly a problem with alcoholics, for alcohol rapidly depletes the body of essential B vitamins.

Besides depleting the body of vitamin B, alcohol also impairs our thinking, particularly judgment and decision making, through its intoxicating effects. Heavy, prolonged drinking changes brain tissue and may permanently retard intellectual abilities.

Besides alcohol, another legal and very popular drug in the United States is nicotine. Nicotine is most commonly absorbed through cigarette smoking. Studies on the effects of smoking on memory and learning are mixed. Some have found that smoking enhances learning and memory, especially short-term recall; others have found it to have a deleterious effect. Reviews of some of these studies (Adler, 1993a; Bower, 1993) suggest that the positive effects of smoking on learning and memory seem to pertain only to simple memory tasks, and these positive effects may benefit only those who are already addicted to nicotine. Regarding more complex memory and learning tasks, however, nicotine has been found to be detrimental, decreasing logical reasoning abilities, impairing performance on complex memory tasks, reducing problem-solving ability, and adversely affecting recall of critical information in essays. Similar effects are experienced during nicotine withdrawal and may linger for one to two months afterwards (Adler, 1993b). While researchers are continuing to explore the possible learning and memory enhancements of nicotine, they seem to agree that cigarette smoking's potential for harm far outweighs any memory and learning enhancement so far discovered.

Marijuana is the most popular illicit drug in the United States. One animal study found that chronic exposure to moderate levels of THC-accelerated brain-cell death in the hippocampus, a very important brain structure for long-term memory formation (Landfield, Cadwallader, and Vinsant, 1988). A later study found that heavy marijuana use reduces attention and learning abilities (Pope and Yurgelun-Todd, 1996). This is consistent with earlier research that has found attention deficits and decreased motivation among regular marijuana users. Even occasional use of marijuana harms thinking. Marijuana intoxication retards learning, inhibiting the transfer of information from short-term to long-term memory. Thus, students who study while smoking marijuana are wasting a lot of their time! And though marijuana smokers believe it enhances their creativity, one study found that in fact it does not (Tinklenberg et al., 1978).

Another drug that can affect thinking is cocaine, a stimulant that, taken daily in large doses, can produce irritability and disturbed concentration. With chronic, heavy use it can lead to paranoid thinking and perceptual disturbances (Grinspoon and Bakalar, 1985).

Other commonly abused drugs, also of the stimulant class, are the amphetamines. These drugs are commonly used to maintain wakefulness and alertness or to increase metabolism and suppress appetite. Although they do have these effects, in heavy use over several days they can cause paranoid delusions, hallucinations, irritability, and insomnia—and distortions in thinking and social functioning that result from these effects. A drug user's "irritability and paranoia may cause fights and unprovoked violence and drive their friends away; their preoccupation with the drug has a disastrous effect on their family relationships and work" (Grinspoon and Bakalar, 1985). When discontinued after prolonged use, they can lead to depression and even suicide.

All of these drugs interact with the brain at the synapse, increasing or decreasing the brain's natural hormone activity. Even though their pharmaceutic effects are different, they all have in common the ability to disrupt our cognitive abilities.

Think About It: *Many people considered to be very brilliant, some to the point of genius, developed ideas and theories that conflicted with those of other very brilliant persons. For every brilliant determinist we can find an equally brilliant proponent of free will; for every empiricist, a rationalist; for every pessimist, an optimist; and for every theist, an atheist. In one sense almost all of them are mostly or entirely wrong, assuming there can be only one correct view. That being the case, what is our basis for considering these people to be extraordinarily brilliant?*

Sleep

We need sleep to think; perhaps that is why we spend one third of our lives sleeping. The important stage of sleep for critical thinking is the REM (rapid eye movement) stage, during which dreaming occurs. When people are more intellectually active during the day they dream more (Smith and Lapp, 1991), and when they are deprived of dream sleep, they have cognitive impairments, such as reduced memory capabilities (Li et al., 1991) and impaired concentration (Horne, 1985). These studies suggest that dreams are crucial for solidifying learning that takes place during the day and that our daily sleep is necessary for optimal cognitive functioning. Although a relationship seems to exist between sleep and a healthy cognitive life, the exact mechanisms involved have yet to be discovered.

THINKING ACTIVITY 4.2
Critical Reading Before We Sleep

To illustrate how mental fatigue can hinder critical thinking and concentration abilities, read the following passage on the unconscious by C. G. Jung and the poem by Emily Dickinson just before you fall asleep, or during some other period when you are mentally fatigued. (Don't do it now!) Then, shortly after you awake, read them again. Granted, you are reading them for the second time and may understand them better because of that, but you should also notice the difference between your ability to concentrate the first time as opposed to the second. How does your first reading compare with your second?

> We cannot overlook the fact that, just as consciousness arises from the unconscious, the ego-centre, too, crystallizes out of a dark depth in which it was somehow contained in potentia. Just as a human mother can only produce a human child, whose deepest nature lay hidden during its potential existence within her, so we are practically compelled to believe that the unconscious cannot be an entirely chaotic accumulation of instincts and images. There must be something to hold it together and give expression to the whole. Its centre cannot possibly be the ego, since the ego was born out of it into consciousness and turns its back on the unconscious, seeking to shut it out as much as possible. Or can it be that the unconscious loses its centre with the birth of the ego? In that case we would expect the ego to be far superior to the unconscious in influence and importance. The unconscious would then follow meekly in the footsteps of the conscious, and that would be just what we wish. (Jung, 1983, p. 218)

(continued)

THINKING ACTIVITY 4.2 (continued)
Critical Reading Before We Sleep

Now read this untitled poem by Emily Dickinson (Selected Poems, 1924, pp. 223–24).

> I heard a fly buzz when I died;
> The stillness round my form
> Was like the stillness in the air
> Between the heaves of storm.
>
> The eyes beside had wrung them dry,
> And breaths were gathering sure
> For that last onset, when the king
> Be witnessed in his power.
>
> I willed my keepsakes, Signed away
> What portion of me I
> Could make assignable,—and then
> There imposed a fly
>
> With blue, uncertain, stumbling buzz,
> Between the light and me;
> And then the windows failed, and then
> I could not see to see.

Our Thinking Potential

If we avoid the substances and practices that can dull our thinking, and work positively on the suggestions in this book to sharpen our thinking, we can begin to fulfill our own unique potential to think. Our brain *can* be moved toward greater thinking.

For our thinking to grow, our brain must grow. Like a muscle, it must be worked to reach its maximum capabilities. Without intellectual work and stimulation, our minds will not develop to their potential. Ideally, this stimulation should begin during the first three years of life. Talking to infants might be the best kind of stimulation they can receive at that young age.

Many studies have shown the effects of environmental stimuli on intellectual development. Some of these studies involved orphaned and other children who were raised in a sterile, impoverished environment. Other studies used rats in an experimental design in which some were raised in a rich, complex environment and others in a sterile one. What these studies find is that a rich, stimulating environment is necessary for the actualization of the brain's intellectual capacity. Raise an organism in an intellectually unchallenging environment and its intelligence becomes stunted.

While it is best to nourish the brain when young, the good news is that even as adults we can improve our brain. One study found that even aged rats who had lived all their lives in a sterile world could benefit from a stimulating environment (Greenough, 1988). Put in a world with mazes, bridges, and spinning wheels, these rats developed an average of 2,000 new synapses *per neuron!* It would be unethical to perform such a study with human beings, of course, but the implication of this research is that it may never be too late for us to start growing toward our potential. And if that isn't enough to motivate us to use our mind, consider this: studies (e.g., Gagnon et al., 1990) have found that the longer we stay intellectually active, the less chance we have of developing dementia, a brain disease that insidiously degrades intellectual functioning. Do you feel like reading a book about now?

If we get our sleep, avoid drugs including alcohol, eat right, and stimulate our brain with intellectual activity, we may expand the potential of our brain. But does the nature of our brain limit our understanding of the world? It probably does, although it is difficult to know the extent to which it does. The situation is something like a blind man trying to know a world of colors and light, which he cannot experience.

If we reflect for a moment on our experience, we can see that we have only five senses that feed our brain the information we use to think. It is possible that there are six, seven, or a hundred ways to experience the world. We have no reason to suppose that we possess all the senses necessary for a complete understanding of the universe. Even the experiences we are given with our senses may not represent the true reality. Is your pen really blue? Or is that blueness just the relationship between your pen and your sense organs, the way your brain processes those sensory data? Does the colorblind man see it wrongly or just differently? Do we have sufficient justification for believing that our brain and sense organs bring the "real" world to us? Could it be that our brain structures reality as much as it discovers it? The philosopher Immanuel Kant believed that causation, space, and time are structures imposed upon the world by our brain. The Oxford mathematician Roger Penrose (1989) takes a similar view:

> The "time" of physical descriptions does not really "flow" at all; we just have a static-looking fixed "space-time" in which the events of our universe are laid out! Yet, according to our perceptions, time *does* flow. My guess is that there is something illusory here too, and the time of our perceptions does not "really" flow in quite the linear forward-moving way that we perceive

it to flow (whatever that might mean!). The temporal ordering that we "appear" to perceive is, I am claiming, something that we impose upon our perceptions in order to make sense of them in relation to the uniform forward time-progression of an external physical reality. (p. 444)

In sum, our brain, as healthily as we might maintain it, probably limits our ability to perceive and think about the world. It is possible that if our neurons fired faster, if they were organized differently, or if our brains were slightly larger, our experience of reality would be quite different than it is today. Thinking is not perfect thinking that yields absolute truths about reality, just the best sound thinking we can do with the brain instrument we are given.

> ***Think About It:*** *We know that drugs can alter our perception of reality and distort our thinking. Yet the brain is also a drug machine in its normal state. Does the normal "drugged" state of the brain limit and distort our thinking too? What state of the brain gives us a "true" picture of reality?*

Brain and Mind

One of the most important philosophical problems concerns the relationship between the brain and the mind, known as the *mind-body problem.* There are two fundamental (and related) questions here: (1) are the brain and mind separate entities? (2) in what way are brain and mind related? The brain is rather simply defined as the physical organ or mass of nervous system tissue enclosed by the skull. Most people know to what we refer when we speak of the brain. There is less agreement, however, about the definition of mind. It is not the physical organ under our skull that we refer to when we speak of our mind. Rather, *mind* is normally defined as the organized structure of our mental processes, including remembering, thinking, perceiving, and experiencing. Sometimes it is seen as synonymous with consciousness, but then what of the unconscious? Is that not part of the mind? One might say that the neuron is of the brain, but our memories of first grade are of our mind, part of our mental world. But what is that mental world? Is it merely a property of the brain? Is it generated by the brain? Or does the brain simply receive mind and interpret mind, much like a radio station receives radio signals? Does the mind drive the brain? Or does the brain drive the mind? Can mind exist at all without the brain? If so, what is its nature without a brain, and how do we account for the apparent connection between the two such that a change in brain tissue seems causally related to a change in mental experience?

(continued)

Brain and Mind *(continued)*

Interestingly, the brain and the mind seem to have different properties. The brain has mass, is public (everyone can see it during an autopsy), and is located in space. Our mental world, however, is private (no one knows what I'm thinking), has no mass, and is not located anywhere in space (so far as it appears). When we refer to our memory of our grandfather, we don't equate it with the sequence of neuron firings that occur during our recollection. So how can a brain, which has properties that our mental life does not, and does not seem to be the same as our mental life, give rise to mind? Or vice versa? Are brain and mind two aspects of something else? Is matter an illusion? (It does seem to disappear as our exploration of it deepens.) Or is mind somehow a form of matter?

Finding the answers to these questions will help to solve other important philosophical problems like determinism versus free will and the possibility of survival after death. There are good arguments on many sides of this mind-body issue, but none has provided a definitive conclusion.

In this chapter we have used statements like "Our brain can be moved toward greater thinking" and "For our thinking to grow, our brains must grow." Obviously these statements could be challenged, depending on one's point of view on mind-brain relationship. It is difficult to satisfy all theoretical points of view on this issue, and we do not mean to support any particular theory of mind.

THINKING AND MEMORY

The past is what you remember, imagine you remember, convince yourself you remember, or pretend to remember.

—HAROLD PINTER, PLAYWRIGHT

Without at least some brief memory, we could not think. For even adding the numbers 6 and 3 requires memory of 6 as we add to it 3. Without memory there could be no thinking based upon experience and there would be no continuity to our world. We would be fully immersed in the present and have no future to imagine, no past to consider. We wouldn't know who we were or where we were going. Being conscious in this perpetual present seems conceivable to some, but thinking in it seems unimaginable.

Thinking and memory are inseparable. What we think depends both on our ability to remember and on the content of that remembering. A poor memory or a distorted memory makes it difficult for us to think successfully. Even a good memory, however, is not perfect. In spite of how certain we may be about prior events, we can be wrong. Therefore, we must listen to the recollections of others and be open to the possibility that their stories offer a more accurate version of what we experienced. We must also back up our memory with hard data and write down events that we know we will be expected to recollect later, and we must work actively to encode information through meaningfulness, practice, and the use of mnemonics. Below we look briefly at how memory can deceive our thinking, why we forget, and how we can improve our memory.

The Changing Nature of Memory

Exactly how memory is laid down in the brain is not yet known. We do know, however, that memories are subject to change. Before reading further about memory, take time to complete the exercise below.

THINKING ACTIVITY 4.3
Memories of Childhood

Take a moment to recollect the first time you learned to ride a bicycle or, if that's too difficult, one of the first times you rode a bicycle. Remember this in as much detail as you can before reading the next paragraph.

If your memory is an exact copy of what you experienced, then you have recalled no more than the front of your bicycle, your arms and hands on the bicycle handlebars, the sidewalk or road ahead, and some houses or trees on the side depending on where your experience occurred. If you remembered more than that and have visualized your head (which you did not see), your grandfather pushing you (whom you did not see), the rear wheel of the bicycle (which you did not see), and so on, you are adding to your actual visual experience. Almost everyone adds information to these experiences. These additions are often consistent with the *meaning* of what happened but are not perfect reproductions of the actual event.

From the above exercise it becomes clear that we actually reconstruct our memories as opposed to retrieving an exact copy of our experience. This reconstruction often, but not always, moves in the direction of the meaning of the experience. That is, although these memories are not necessarily accurate in their details, they may nonetheless be consistent with the meaning that we gave the experience. One of the earliest experiments to demonstrate this (Carmichael, Hagan, and Walter, 1932) found that if we show persons a picture of something that looks like a very thick letter *C* or a very thin quarter-moon and tell them it's the letter *C*, they will tend to remember it later as looking thinner, much more like the letter *C* than a quarter-moon. And when other subjects are shown the same stimulus but are told it is a quarter-moon, they later remember it as much thicker than it was, looking more like a quarter-moon. In other words, people's memories are distorted in the direction of the meaning of the stimulus, in this case the letter *C* or the quarter-moon.

The importance of meaning to our recollections of events cannot be dismissed lightly, because throughout our daily lives we continuously give meaning to the great and small experiences we endure. A dog bite might be experienced at the time as a minor nuisance but remembered as even more trivial than it was. On the other hand, if a dog bite was originally perceived as an awful ordeal, then perhaps with time our recollections of it will make it much worse than it was. The dog becomes larger, the bite more severe, the duration of battle lengthens, and the dog's owner becomes more indifferent, or even sadistic. Indeed, it appears our lives are but true tales embedded in fiction.

> ***Think About It:*** *Have you ever told a story and embellished it to add more excitement to it, and then one day, as you were telling it for the tenth time, you caught yourself starting to believe the embellishments? How often do you suppose you've told such stories, failed to catch yourself slipping over the edge, and ended up believing your own created fiction?*

The memories that are most subject to change are episodic memories, which are memories of biographical events in our lives. Other kinds of memory, such as semantic memory, which includes memory of our own language, what a dog is, and how to add numbers, are less vulnerable to distortion. But what about memories of emotional events that seem to freeze time? Examples of such events are the bombing of Pearl Harbor, J. F. Kennedy's assassination, the explosion of the space shuttle *Challenger*, and the bombing of the Federal Building in Oklahoma City. Many Americans can recall in vivid detail where they were and what they were doing when they heard or saw the news of these events. But as we explore these memories, we find that these, too, vivid as they are, often mislead; in fact, most of our memories are quite subject to change.

Memories are especially vulnerable to distortion under hypnosis. Leading questions by the hypnotist or expectations of the subject under hypnosis can lead to fabricated memories. In spite of what most people think, if people undergo hypnosis to retrieve lost memories, the memories they retrieve are likely to be confabulations (false memories) instead of accurate recollections, and the confabulations revolve around the expectations of the hypnotist or the subject. Such confabulation might describe memories of past lives and has recently been used to explain some false memories of incest abuse (Goldstein, 1992; Wassil-Grimm, 1995).

The following anecdote is a good example, albeit extreme, of the constructive nature and unreliability of memory. The anecdote seems to describe a reconstructed memory that is not consistent with actual events, yet the rememberer considers it to be true.

> The vet had come to this psychologist complaining that he suffered from constant nightmares from his years in Vietnam. He would awaken sweating, heart pounding, surrounded by images of his wounded buddies, visions of blood and gore everywhere. Unable to turn off the state of constant readiness that served him well in the foxhole, he startled at the slightest sound, reflexively reaching for his knife. During sessions the vet would cry about the buddies he'd seen murdered or would scream out in horror at a combat memory. The experienced psychologist treating him would reassure him that the war was over and he was now safe at home.
>
> Nonetheless, the vet could not be saved, and he committed suicide by inhaling carbon monoxide. Following his death, his widow attempted to get his name put on the Vietnam Memorial in Washington, D.C., since she felt he was justifiably a "casualty of the war." An extensive search of the man's military record showed that he had never set foot in Vietnam (Wassil-Grimm, 1995, p. 93).

Forgetting

Not only do memories change and impair our thinking, but we can forget them entirely. Some memories actually seem meant for forgetting, like a telephone number that we will never use again. These *short-term memories* last only about twenty to thirty seconds without rehearsal. Once they fulfill their purpose, they are forgotten and are probably not retrievable.

The memories most important for most of our thinking are our *long-term memories*. These are the memories that we need to perform well on exams, discuss the philosophy of Plato, and think critically about the world around us. Contrary to what most people believe, most of our long-term forgetting occurs shortly after learning; the rate of forgetting tapers off with time. For example, most of what we remember one year after a college course we will remember two years later, but much of what we remember from our reading today will be forgotten in a few weeks.

Recall Versus Recognition

It is much easier to recognize information than to recall it. In one study that dramatically illustrates the power of recognition memory (Haber, 1970), subjects were shown 2,560 photographic slides at the rate of one every ten seconds. One hour after the last picture was shown, each subject was then presented with 280 pairs of pictures. One picture in each pair was from the set of 2,560 pictures; the other was from a similar set. Each subject was asked to identify the picture that was also in the set of 2,560. What do you suppose the accuracy rate was? One might expect an accuracy rate on a recall task of this sort to be no greater than 10 percent. In this recognition experiment, however, accuracy rates were between 85 and 95 percent! This is one good reason why police departments use mug shots to help victims identify criminals. Unfortunately, we often do not have a choice about how we are to recall information. But whenever we do, the recognition option is usually more successful.

Why We Forget

Sometimes we forget because to remember would be painful. This theory of forgetting, called repression, suggests that we forget more of the unpleasant events in our lives than the good. This idea has found some empirical support through numerous case studies. Unfortunately, all of us can remember some bad events; no one knows why some negative experiences are repressed and others are not.

Another reason we forget is because other information, especially *similar* information, interferes with what we are trying to remember. This *interference theory* of forgetting explains the problems and frustrations of cramming. At the beginning of the cram session we may accurately associate names with events and theories, but as the information builds so does interference, and we often find ourselves associating names and events incorrectly. Cramming does increase learning, but because it requires more study time to overcome the interference problems, we would do better to space our study out over time.

Think About It: *The interference theory suggests that we not study two foreign languages simultaneously. What other subjects may pose interference problems if studied concurrently?*

A third reason why we forget is because we can't find the right cues. Cues can be names of categories (tools), the location in which an experience occurred (Washington Park), certain smells (plum trees), and so on. Even our emotional state might serve as a cue. When we are sad we can remember sad things more easily than happy events, and vice versa (Baddeley, 1990). Why we can't retrieve the right cues is unknown, but often it may be that strong, distinct cues were never associated with the information initially. Below we look at ways to lay down better cues, as well as other ways to enhance memory.

How to Improve Memory

The basic strategy for enhancing our memory is to lay the information down well initially because our ability to remember is proportional to the degree to which our memories were originally stored. We must not write our memories with mere chalk; we should engrave them like a chisel on stone. We can accomplish this by making the information more meaningful, by associating information with what we already know well, by using mnemonic techniques, and by repetition and practice.

Make Information Meaningful.　Experiences that are exciting are easy to retrieve because they are particularly meaningful; their memories are laid down effortlessly. Meaningful information is less likely to be forgotten than meaningless information. And though we may not find the world always exciting, we can make it meaningful in other ways. For instance, finding the relevance of the information we are trying to learn and how it can relate to our lives increases its meaning and makes it more memorable. We can also try to understand how the information is organized or, better yet, organize the information ourselves. This provides a meaningful structure that facilitates recollection.

Information can also be made more meaningful by associating the information with what we already know well. The license number KLB100, for example, may be the initials of our name and the age we would like to live to. Noticing this relationship may make retrieval of this number effortless for months or years.

Think About It:　*The fact that we can usually retrieve memories at will suggests that our memories are organized. Estimate how long it would it take you to retrieve the memory of the color of your first bicycle if your memories were not organized and were retrieved at random.*

Use Mnemonic Techniques. Mnemonic techniques are strategies for encoding information so that recall is easier. One strategy uses pictures, rhymes, and associations, another uses a linking technique, and still another uses the familiarity we have with our home environment. Entertainers who impress their audience with their excellent memory usually use these and other mnemonics (see Thinking Activity 4.4).

Repeat. The more we repeat new information and ideas, the easier it is to remember them. College professors who have taught a course numerous times can often teach an entire semester from memory alone. But simply repeating something over and over, without attending to its meaning, does not usually work well to lay down strong memories. For instance, we could read a chapter in a college text repeatedly, but if we did not make it meaningful, organize it, or make associations with it, we would learn and remember very little. There is a place, however, for mere repetition. Poetry, for example, is learned by repetition because we are trying to recall exact words, not just the meaning. But if the poetry is not made meaningful, the words we learn are empty.

Practice. Memory can be likened to a muscle: if it is exercised it grows, if not it weakens. Putting our memory to work increases our ability to remember. As the saying goes, "Use it or lose it."

THINKING ACTIVITY 4.4
Using Mnemonics

Following are some mnemonic techniques. These help to facilitate recall by laying down memories in an organized, meaningful manner.

Rhyme-Association Method

This is a good technique to learn if you want to impress your friends. It allows you to remember lists forwards and backwards and to identify any object associated with any of the numbers. This step first requires memorizing rhymes for each number one through ten such as the following:

One-Bun	Six-Fix
Two-Stew	Seven-Heaven
Three-Bee	Eight-Bait
Four-Floor	Nine-Dine
Five-Dive	Ten-Dog pen

Once you have these rhymes memorized, you associate the idea or thing you are trying to remember with the rhyming word. To enhance recall, these associations should be as ridiculous and lively as you can make them. For example, if you want

(continued)

THINKING ACTIVITY 4.4 (continued)
Using Mnemonics

to remember "alligator," you can imagine biting into a bun, expecting a juicy ham-
burger, and finding a baby alligator instead—who, much to your surprise cries,
"Ouch! What do you think you're doing!" If the eighth word you are trying to remember is "rocking chair," you can imagine fishing with a rocking chair as bait.

For the numbers eleven through twenty, you can develop associations for each
rhyming word in a particular setting, such as on an airplane. For eleven, you might
think of biting into the bun as you hit an air pocket, for example.

Try remembering the following words with the above technique:

dust mask	stapler
computer disk	lamp
sock	quarter
batteries	address book
book	screwdriver

Method of Location
This mnemonic technique is similar to the one above; the main difference is that you
do not have to memorize rhymes first. Instead, you use what you already know, such
as the arrangement of your living room furniture. As you try to remember a list, mentally walk through your living room and associate each word with a living room object.
In the above example, you might imagine an alligator in your houseplant playing love
ballads on his guitar in an attempt to win the affection of the shark lying on your sofa.

Practice using this technique with the ten items above.

The Linking Technique
Sometimes the information we are trying to remember is difficult to picture using
the above techniques. The state of Wisconsin, for example, is hard to imagine lying
on the living room sofa. The linking technique may be better in such cases. In this
technique, all the items to remember are connected to each other. Each item can be
pictured as it is, or something else associated with or sounding like the object can
take its place. For example, if you want to remember the states of Minnesota, California, New York, and Florida, you can imagine a Viking (Minnesota) standing next
to the statue of liberty (New York) wearing a Mickey Mouse hat (Florida) as an earth-
quake (California) rocks the statue and the Viking back and forth.

Practice using this technique with the first thirteen states below. They are given
in the order in which they became part of the United States of America.

1. Delaware	8. South Carolina
2. Pennsylvania	9. New Hampshire
3. New Jersey	10. Virginia
4. Georgia	11. New York
5. Connecticut	12. North Carolina
6. Massachusetts	13. Rhode Island
7. Maryland	

> ***Think About It:***   *Can you think of ways to combine the mnemonic techniques above?*

SUMMARY

The brain is our thinking instrument made up of billions of neurons in a complex connectedness that is unimaginable. For the brain to function properly, for us to reach our potential for thinking, our brain must receive adequate nourishment and sufficient sleep. It must also remain free of drugs, alcohol, marijuana, cocaine, and other substances that can affect the delicate hormone balance in the brain and lead to distorted thinking. But our brain needs more than sound nutrition and freedom from pernicious drugs, it needs stimulation. A rich, challenging environment will build our brain into a stronger thinking organ, and will help to forestall the dementias of old age. Our brain may not solve all the mysteries that concern us—and may actually create as much of the world as it discovers—but it will give us new glimpses and new insights, and most of all, it will move us more completely toward what we can become.

Hidden within our brain is our memory. We have explored some of its nature and mystery and have learned that we must listen to others who disagree with our recollections, for our long-term memory is in constant movement; it may not only revise our past, it may even create it. We've also looked at some reasons why we forget—repression, interference, loss of cues, and failure to lay down memories well in the first place—and we've explored ways to enhance memory through meaning, mnemonics, repetition, and practice.

Through this greater awareness of the nature of memory, we have abandoned our absolute trust in what it presents to us. But we have also learned to improve it and move on to become better thinkers.

BRAIN AND MEMORY CHALLENGES

1. This chapter suggests that we can do a lot to maximize our brain's potential. List some of the ways to improve the working of your brain. Then decide which ones you are going to pursue.
2. We know that the brain is fairly sensitive to coffee, sleep, drugs, and food. What are the implications of this sensitivity for our behavior?

3. We have seen that old people who stay active develop fewer cases of some brain diseases. Do you know any older people who are very mentally alert? What are their mental activities, such as reading, hobbies, talking with people, and so forth?

4. Do you know any young people who do not show much intellectual interest or activity? Do you find any areas in your own life in which you are intellectually lazy? Reading a challenging book is food for the mind. What else could you do to give your mind regular workouts?

5. In the Shakespeare quotation on page 58, what do you think is the "enemy" that can steal away our brains?

6. Using your own experience or the experience of others you know, identify instances in which the drugs mentioned in this chapter clouded thinking and judgment. What were the consequences of the person's reduced ability to think critically?

7. How is it that a physical brain can give rise to a mental world that has properties that the physical world does not? Are there other situations in which physical matter generates something that has non-physical properties?

8. We mentioned that the brain is fed by our five senses. Can you imagine any other sense that could exist? Or is this impossible to imagine?

9. How might your brain be filtering, creating, and structuring reality? Is it possible to know something without the instrument of our knowing (the brain and senses) affecting and distorting what we know? What does it mean to say that we know something as it really is?

10. Do you will the brain to action, or does the brain will you to action? Are you something that exists apart from the brain, or are you something that is manufactured by the brain?

11. Have you ever gone without sleep for several days? How did it affect your thinking and concentration?

12. Your ability to think is related in part to the stimulation in your environment. In light of this, how would you assess your environment?

13. Can you think of other mnemonic techniques besides those mentioned in this chapter?

14. If we can't think without memory, then it is obviously very important to us. In what ways can you enhance your memory?

15. Although memory is vitally important, it is also fallible. Can you recall times when you were certain about some past event and then found out that you recalled wrongly? Can you identify what it was that caused your poor recall?

16. Can you identify areas in which you would not trust your memory? Why? What can you do to strengthen those areas when you need them?

17. Interference can hamper memory. Develop a study schedule that gives you the least amount of interference. Remember, do not overload by cramming, and do not place similar subjects back to back.

18. Firmly laying down a memory is fundamental to recalling it later. What can you do to lay down strong memories so you can recall them when you want them?

5

Language: Our Thinking Medium

The limits of my language are the limits of my life.

—*LUDWIG WITTGENSTEIN*

Language can articulate like an orator or bark like a dog. Language can cut with the ethereal edge of utterance or sweep like a broom in the gutter. It can ring in the courtroom, the boardroom, the classroom, and the bar. It can hold much of our life wrapped in its words.

We think with words. As we read this, we are using language to think. We have defined thinking broadly as the activity of the brain that can potentially be communicated. Although we may think in other ways besides language, such as with images or feelings, language plays a central role in our thinking.

Our main focus in this chapter is to understand language so that we can think better. Instead of linguistic terms such as *semantics, syntax,* and *pragmatics,* we have used common words such as *meaning, word order,* and *context.* In this chapter we examine how language enables, structures, and limits our thinking; we notice the formative influence of society on language; we examine the fundamental, metaphorical nature of language, and we learn how to make metaphors; we point out the limitations of language; then we look more specifically at the rich legacy of English, at its word stock, at its capabilities of definitions, connotations, and word order; we highlight the importance of context and clarity; and finally, we look at some pitfalls to avoid such as vague generalizations, wordiness, illogicalness, redundancies, and clichés.

THINKING ACTIVITY 5.1
Language and Thinking

In his *Tractatus,* Wittgenstein presented a dualistic theory of thought and language: thought is internal and language external. In his *Philosophical Investigations* Wittgenstein closed the gap between thinking and language. He said that thought cannot exist without language, that as one learns language, one learns how to think, that thought and language are one.

1. Do you think that your thinking is internal and that language is merely the external expression of it?
2. Think about the accuracy of Wittgenstein's claim for the importance of language, that thought and language are one. Can you think of ways to support or refute this claim?
3. Can you do any thinking without language?
4. If you believe you can think without language, please do some "languageless" thinking now.
5. Next, if you were able to think without language, try to communicate that "languageless thinking" to someone else, again without using language.
6. What did you discover?

As you were thinking about the role of language, as you were reading these words, and as you were discussing them, you were using language. That use strongly supports a major portion of Wittgenstein's position that language is thinking. Regardless of his or your exact positions, the fundamental connection of language to thinking shows the enormous importance of language.

LANGUAGE AND OUR MIND

The cerebral cortex is like a furrowed field waiting for the seeds of language. With the help of MRI and PET scans, and researchers like Antonio and Hanna Damasio, we are beginning to find out where in the furrows the seeds grow into sounds, verbs, nouns, and sentences. This planting analogy straddles the debate about whether language is innate (Plato, Chomsky) or learned. It is both. Clearly the brain has language capability from birth. Infants spontaneously babble, making many sounds not found in their culture, and then at about ten months they begin to match their sounds to their language environment. In short, the brain is prepared to receive any language, but that language must be learned.

Language is the "software" that allows our brain to think the way it does; without language the cerebral cortex lies largely unused. A brain without language is like that field without seed or a car without gas—all potential and no performance. If you know the story of Helen Keller, you know that when she was young her brain was brilliant but empty of language, and that she acted like an animal. She was deaf and blind; but when the light of language, sensed through the touch of fingers, turned on her mind, she began a learning rush that led to fluency in seven languages. Without language we too might act like animals.

Our thinking is confined within the language that is "running" in our brain. Language is the interpretative medium for the input—the remembering, sorting, creating, judging, and deciding—and language also dramatically shapes those processes. Without language our cerebral cortex, able to conceptualize the universe, would drape uselessly around our lower brain like clothes on a mannequin.

The Universalizing Power of Language

Part of the enormous power of language is its universalizing nature. We have the word *tree* in our head and we, in a general way, know what all trees are like. Although their tips might flaunt buds, blossoms, cones, seeds, nuts, fruit, needles, or leaves, we know that they all have roots, trunk, and branches. In a single word *tree,* we contain all the trees on earth. Often we form this type of universal concept from a single instance. For example, if you saw only one golden tamarin (a fluffy, quick, tiny, eight-inch-long monkey with golden iridescent fur), you would recognize the next one. And even if that next one was a red-mantled tamarin you would easily recognize it; from the single tamarin you would have abstracted universal qualities of "tamarin."

Perhaps some languages have fewer universals. According to Louis Uriarte, a Jesuit missionary who spent several years with an Omagua tribe on the upper reaches of the Amazon River, those natives almost always speak in limiting specifics such as "that panther whose paw print we saw by the river." Omagua parents cannot universalize a warning to their children to "watch out for panthers," but must warn to "watch out for the panther we heard growling by the big rock." We do not know whether the Omaguas have any concepts for *all existence,* but in our language we have the word *universe.* We can figuratively hold the universe in our head! Thus we can ask those fundamentally probing questions of origins and ends.

The Structuring Power of Language

If language is the software of our mind, we can expect it to channel our thinking, but surprisingly language can even channel our perceptions. This means that we see things differently because of our language. This concept of linguistic relativity, often called the Whorf hypothesis after Benjamin Lee Whorf, was popular in the 1950s, was attacked in the 1960s, and returned in a more generalized form in the 1990s. Whorf thought that Inuits (Eskimos) would perceive snow differently because of their many words for snow. Since Eskimos have the same rods, cones, and retinas that we have, do their words for snow enable them to perceive differently? We asked a parallel question of a downhill skier and former captain of a ski team, who uses words like base, fresh, artificial, powder, champagne, corn, granular, slush, Sierra cement, firn, packed powder, hard packed, wind-packed, crust, glare ice, blue ice, bullet proof, and boilerplate. Does having these words in his brain help him to recognize more kinds of snow and to ski better? Yes, and more safely too: "If you are moving fast and pop out of the trees you'd better be able to recognize wind-packed or you could get hurt."

Equally important, when you describe a pain to your doctor, the doctor's perceptions too are structured by language. For instance, if you were having a heart attack and you described the pain as "sharp" you would be less likely to be properly diagnosed than if you had described it as "pressure," "tightness," or "radiating."

Let's look at a few other examples. A first-time car owner who has never worked on cars opens the hood and sees a jungle of wires, metal, and hoses. What do mechanics, with all the words for these parts in their heads, see? An average person listens to a ninety-five piece orchestra and hears a blend of sounds. What does a skilled musician hear? An inner city resident enters the forest for the first time and sees "dark," "big," and "scary." What does the park naturalist see? Much of the differences in perception is the difference in the experiences that are stored in language.

One last example. As a Saturday morning chore, a boy had to dust a maze of ledged baseboards and door frames in his family's old house. In college he learned those ledges were modeled on the seven parts of the Greek column. Today he no longer sees a maze but he can see each of those ledges from the stybolate on the bottom to the cornice on top *because he has a word for each part.*

We see what we see partly because of the language that we learn. Montaigne, the sixteenth-century philosopher, tells us that "the mind cuts [reality] to its own conceptions" (1967, p. 131); therefore, he warns us to be very suspicious of whatever the mind seizes upon or rejects. Bacon calls this distorting process "the idols of the mind." He calls our particular idols "the idol of the cave." Each individual "has a cave or den of his own, which refracts and discolors the light of nature" (p. 336); each of us is unique in mind, body, education, and habit (p. 337); and if we idolize something we usually distort its importance (p. 340). What kind of mind, filled with what kind of language, do you have?

LANGUAGE AND SOCIETY

Language reflects society and is a vehicle for its values. It is only as good as the best minds that have shaped it, and it is only useful to us if we assimilate it. The

THINKING ACTIVITY 5.2
A Brief Mind Sketch

In the chart below list a few areas of interest to you, such as your hobbies. To the right of those areas of interest write a few technical terms that enable you to see particular parts of that hobby. For instance, if you like to work on cars you might write "camshaft," "rocker arms," and so forth. Continue filling in the chart.

Areas I Like	Terms That Structure Perception
Areas I Do Not Like	
Areas I Know Little About	

If we heed Bacon and Montaigne, our lists of likes and dislikes will alert us to some of our stronger perceptual biases. We probably found the last section the hardest to fill in; if we didn't know much about the area, how could we write down the terms? Thus the importance of the last list becomes clear: we need the terms, the language in our mind if we wish to know, to grow, to become successful in school and work (and, we might add, in life). Better language will not make us better people, but it will offer us a better chance to understand more, to think more effectively, and give and get more from life.

English language reflects a rich and varied society and offers us an astonishing array of choices, as we shall see below. It also, at times, shackles our thinking.

In the 1940s George Orwell, in his famous article "Politics and the English Language," declared that the decline of England was reflected in the sloppiness of the English language. Few professionals have sought to corroborate Orwell's connection between language and values. However, if we take a look at the use of words by the U.S. government, the Orwellian observation gains credibility. In the 1970s government reports referred to civilian deaths in Vietnam as "collateral damage." Sounds bloodless, like the "collateral" we might put up to secure a loan. And "pacification," was the term used to make the country "peaceful" by such tactics as laying down a "carpet" of bombs from B-52s. Within such a *peaceful* bombing pattern, who could be offended by a little *collateral* damage? If those twisted terms do not make us flinch, consider the defense of one of those involved in the Watergate cover-up, who said, "Truth comes protected with a cloud of lies." The way we think about these events is no doubt influenced by the language we use to describe them.

In the 1980s information was given to the president in such a deviously crafted manner that the president was able to respond to the questions about the Iran Contra scandal with "plausible deniability." With such a prepared excuse for a president to lie, are we surprised that the "Clean Air Working Group" was a lobby by air-polluting companies to defeat the clean air bill? By comparison, businesses were quite truthful when they said they were "downsizing," instead of firing people, although before long companies did not even like the negative connotation of "down," so they began "rightsizing."

In the 1990s, the Gulf War presented us with the powerful metaphors of "desert shield" and "desert storm." "Desert sword" was one of the original metaphors considered, but it was rejected because it was too harsh and warlike: the bloody sword was softened into the desert storm. In the Yugoslavian war the Serbians killing Croatians called the acts "ethnic cleansing." During a presidential campaign, a candidate was called an "ignoramus and emotionally unstable" until he dropped from the race; then the same people who had called him an "ignoramus" called him "courageous and wise" in order to draw his votes.

Into the second millenium the euphemisms continue. A childless couple becomes "child free." An F (failing) grade is softened into an NP (no pass) or NG (no grade), and those who are failing are called "emerging students." Adults having sex with children, formerly "pedophiles," are referred to as participating in "intergenerational intimacy." A gas station attendant is a "petroleum transfer engineer." "Transsexual surgery" is replaced by "gender reassignment." And finally, frogmen learning how to kill other frogmen are enrolled in a "swimmer nullification program."

Such distortions were not always a part of our American culture. Building on Christian values and Roman law, people thought of the ideal American as forthright and almost rudely honest. We can hear honesty honored in cultural phrases such as "George Washington never told a lie," "he's a man of his word," "you have my word on it," and "I give you my word." Such honesty engenders trust and furthers communication. When language is used to lie, it rips the fabric of trust and becomes a weapon of war.

THE METAPHORICAL POWER OF LANGUAGE

"I myself am hell, where I go hell goes with me," says Milton's Satan. We can feel the power in that thought; it comes from the metaphor that joins the concepts of "myself" and "hell." The metaphor functions at the heart of language. If we can understand metaphors and learn to think with them, we will tap into a richer vein of language and thought. In this section we define *metaphor* in a broad sense. We show how language works metaphorically and how it grew metaphorically, how root metaphors control fields of knowledge, and how, when the metaphor changes, understanding changes.

What Is a Metaphor?

A standard definition of *metaphor* is simply "an implied comparison between two things." Metaphor comes from two Greek words: *meta* means "with," "after," or "beyond," and *phorein* means "to carry." So a metaphor carries another meaning with the original or carries the original meanings beyond into a new meaning. This blending of old meanings produces the new. If the literary critics will forgive us, we are going to use metaphor in the broadest sense of a comparison, which includes similes (explicit comparisons) as well as analogies (extended comparisons). This great reach of the metaphor may be why Aristotle called it the fundamental figure of speech and its use the true mark of genius.

Like the metaphor, language merges two things: sounds (letters or signs) and the reality the sounds signify. In this blending of sounds and reality language itself is metaphorical. Also, in its deep roots, language seems to have grown metaphorically; for instance, the phrase "I am" quite possibly came from an earlier Indo-European form that meant "I breathe." This metaphorical growth expands the meaning of many common words, such as *run* (run up a bill, run the show). When the metaphor of "the information highway" struck at the end of the millenium, within weeks the highway accessories appeared: digital off ramps, information tollbooths, bumper-to-bumper traffic, electronic routes, and even potholes. Because metaphors are centrally connected with the way language works, and because language is connected to the way we think, metaphors are intricately connected to our thinking.

Metaphorical Models Control Thinking

Metaphors are the way we think about ourselves and the world. All fields of knowledge have root metaphors, or models, which began the fields; when those metaphors change, the field changes. For instance, we can watch our understanding of the world change from the Ptolemaic loops around the earth, to the Copernican circles around the sun, to the Keplerian ellipses, to the Newtonian lines of force, to the Einsteinian merger of energy and matter, to Rutherford and

Bohr's solar system of the atom, to the current model of leptons and quarks, "strange," "charmed," and otherwise. As each new metaphor was created, the entire field of knowledge shifted to the new model, and our way of thinking about the universe changed.

To understand the metaphorical nature of those models, let us look at a master metaphor, perhaps the greatest in scientific or literary history, $E = mc^2$. Einstein's insight is basically metaphorical, bringing two things together, but he has gone further and brought them together into an actual identity: mass and energy are the same, are interchangeable.

In genetics, Watson and Crick saw the DNA molecule as a winding staircase (the double helix) with four kinds of repeating steps. Once they achieved this basic metaphorical insight, they set the path for many years in the current genome project to map all the human genes. The double helix model has dominated—almost controlled—all genetic thinking. We understand much about the universe and about our bodies because of the metaphorical models that are in place.

These metaphors also determine the way we think about ourselves. For instance, in *medicine,* an herb (*medica*) is prescribed by an M.D. (*medicus doctor*); influenced by this metaphor, some doctors willingly give us medicine to comfort our "dis-ease" (another metaphor). To understand how this metaphor controls ways of thinking, consider the difference in going to an internist or a surgeon with the same problem. If we go to a doctor of internal medicine for a heart problem, we may be more likely to receive stress- and cholesterol-reducing drugs; if we go to a heart surgeon (the root meaning of *surgeon* is someone who works with the hands), we are more likely to receive a bypass operation. As the metaphor changes, the duties change correspondingly: a "nurse," formerly a breast-feeding "wet-nurse," becomes a "physician's assistant" with more duties and the greater prestige associated with "physician." As the metaphors change, so does our understanding of the universe.

So too we could unfold the metaphorical bases for baseball and business, for philosophy and religion, for working, and for loving. We understand these realms of activity, again, because the metaphors for them have been articulated. However, one key metaphor is missing—the one for the brain. The brain and its operations have been metaphorically referred to as a *tabula rasa,* a black box, a lightbulb, a garden, an enchanted loom, memory groves, memory banks, a machine, a camera, a switchboard, the master organ, a library, a computer, and a hologram. Currently a stunning metaphor has arisen, that of comparing the brain to a metaphor! Since the brain produces metaphors, blends different ideas and images into new forms, one way to understand the brain is to say it works like a metaphor. Although we are partial to this latter metaphor since it illustrates the centrality of the metaphor in thinking, it is probably not yet the master metaphor that will unlock the secret of the brain.

We have seen some enormous claims made for the metaphor, which are pushed even further by literary critic Caroline Spurgeon (1966) who says that the metaphor

---

Language, Lawyers, and Lawmakers

In a national trial the prominent lawyers on both sides used metaphors for truth to persuade the jury: "the embers of truth will glow the more you blow on them," and "it is a house of cards, and the finger of truth comes by and pushes it over." In that context of truth it is fitting that when one of the lawyers was told by the judge to quit dragging out proceedings, the lawyer responded with a metaphorical slip: "We are moving forward, your honor, like a shark through the water." When laughter dotted the courtroom, the attorney quickly changed his metaphor to "like a dolphin, your honor."

A senator from a midwestern state jotted down these miseloquent sayings from his colleagues:

These numbers are not my own; they are from someone who knows what he's talking about.

I'm not confused on that. It's just that I'm too busy to think.

I don't necessarily believe what I think.

My knowledge is no match for his ignorance.

That land in the north has been untouched by nature.

This bill will help sparsely populated large cities.

As long as I'm a senator, there won't be any nuclear suppositories in my state.

I have survived a terminal heart attack.

I know that what I believe is different from what I know are the facts.

People planning on getting in serious accidents should have their seat belts on.

---

holds within itself the very secret of the universe. The bare fact that germinating seeds or falling leaves are actually another expression of the processes we see at work in human life and death, thrills me, as it must others, with a sense of being here in the presence of a great mystery, which, could we only understand it, would explain life and death itself (p. 6).

THE LIMITATIONS OF LANGUAGE

The structuring, universalizing, and metaphorical power of language which enriches our perceptions and understanding can also deaden our perceptions, bend new data into old structures, warp analogies, and distort our memories. To think accurately, we need to be aware of this linguistic twist on thinking. With its universal terms, such as *tree,* language blinds us from seeing the individual characteristics of each tree. Even if language helps us to see more specifically, as in *maple tree,* or still more specifically, as in *silver maple,* the words still blind us within that narrowed definition. With words in our head we think we know what all trees look like (or all silver maple trees), yet each tree and each leaf upon it is unique.

Similarly, as new data enter, we try to fit them into existing patterns, sometimes with dangerous results. For example, most of us are familiar with the road sign that warns trucks of a steep hill ahead. The first time a driver of a car saw a *similar* road sign (of a truck tilted sideways), he perceived it to be the "steep hill" sign that he already knew. Not slowing, he sped into a tire-screeching curve. The sign of a truck tilting over meant "dangerous curve ahead," and he had wrongly interpreted it. Because of the language already in his head, he had failed to notice the subtle difference. Similarly, driving through the eternal wheat fields of Kansas, he saw an unknown checkered pattern in the distance. As he tried to fit it into his urban patterns, it looked to him like an auto junkyard; as he drove closer it turned into a feedlot packed with cattle. Once again his language patterns had distorted his perceptions, this time turning cattle into cars.

Historically, the wrong metaphors have also limited our understanding. As long as people thought that the heart was the center of the affections, they could not understand it. They were imprisoned by the wrong metaphor. Not until Harvey noted blood circulation and Newcomen invented the vacuum pump could they properly describe the action of the heart: it worked like a pump.

Patterns of language may even cause us to remember inaccurately. For example, a boy who grew up around oak trees and could once correctly spell all the states recently confused the state with the tree and misspelled it "Oaklahoma."

So the paradoxical nature of language both sets our mind free and imprisons it. Language "lights up" our cortex with universal concepts, metaphors, and structure. It also partially imprisons our mind within the boundaries of language, blinding us to the subtleties of the world around us.

THE POWER OF ENGLISH

If language imprisons our mind, English is the prison of choice. Our rich multicultural linguistic legacy and the dominant roles England and America have played in history have expanded English across the globe, made it the dominant language of the Internet, and with the *Voyager,* English has gone into deep space. Out of several thousand spoken languages, English has become the most important language on earth, leaving us not so much a prison of the mind but a legacy of more than a million words to think with.

Word Meanings

Although this inheritance is ours, we have to earn it; we are not born with English, we learn it. And considering the importance of language to thinking, to our human interaction, to our understanding of ourselves and the world, and to our ability to reason and make choices that affect our success and happiness, we may wish to learn it better.

> **THINKING ACTIVITY 5.3**
> **The Language in Our Mind**
>
> Below is a series of questions to help you think about the current state of the language in your mind. Since you have seen that your thinking is only as good as your language, this activity may make you aware of a need to strengthen and sharpen your language.
>
> 1. How fluent are you?
> 2. What kind of words are in your mind? How many? You can begin to answer this question by thinking of the types of books you have read and what kind of words you use when you speak and write.
> 3. How clearly can you lay out your thoughts? Can others follow you without many questions or clarifications?
> 4. What is your reading level? What kind of books, if any, do you read? What kind would you like to read more of? Do you need to read more?
> 5. What are the content strengths of your language base? In other words, in what areas are you knowledgeable and can easily think and communicate? What areas do you wish to expand into?
> 6. What is your metaphorical ability? Can you put ideas together into new combinations?
> 7. What is your thinking style? Take a moment to reflect on how words and ideas go through your mind: in random order, in tight sequence, singly, in bunches, in images, with feelings, or in any other mode you can identify.

What does any word mean? The answer lies somewhere between primitive voodoo power in which the word becomes reality, and the anarchy found in Alice's Wonderland: "A word means exactly what I choose to make it mean." Actually, a word means what society chooses to make it mean. For instance, when a young boy who worried about being kidnapped received a puppy, he transferred his personal fears to his linguistic patterns and worried that his little puppy would get "pupnapped." If society accepted that term, if it became common like *carjacking,* then it would enter the language. Both *pupnapped* and *carjacking* sprang into being out of standard English patterns. In order to think more effectively, we will look briefly at the expansive patterns of stems and affixes, at definitions to achieve clarity, and at connotations to achieve subtlety.

Stems and Affixes

Words in the brain are like money in the bank: the more we have the richer we are. We need words to think with, and the wealthier our vocabulary, potentially, the richer our thoughts. The quickest way to verbal wealth is to learn about stems and affixes. For instance, if we know the stem *cog* means "think" (as in Descartes' famous *Cogito ergo sum*), we can begin to guess at the meanings of *cogitate, cogitation,* and *cogitator.* It would be a simple step from there to add a prefix to make *precogitate.* Word awareness, especially of stems and affixes, can quickly increase our word stock which is our thinking reservoir.

The Right Word

An expanded word base should help us in picking the best word; clear thinking depends upon it. Francis Bacon (1625, 1965) tells us "ill and unfit words" can obstruct the understanding and "lead men away into numberless empty controversies" (p. 337). Have you ever heard people energetically arguing about different things when they thought they were arguing about the same thing? Not agreeing on the topic and its definition creates a communication problem similar to the proverbial blind men feeling different parts of the elephant. Definitions can be so powerful that often the person who defines the issue decides the debate. For example, if *pornography* is defined under the banner of free speech, that definition probably wins the debate.

Sometimes users of our language are imprecise. For example, a host of a Chicago talk show said that a "permissive" and a "tolerant" society were the same thing. What do you think about the differences in those words? "Preventive Nutrition" is the title of an article in a medical book. Although we know what it means because some word such as "disease" is implied, normally we do not combine the idea of prevention with a good quality like nutrition. To take a parallel example, how would we respond to the phrase "preventive learning"?

Sometimes the wrong word is used because it sounds close to the word that is sought. Consider a professor in a classroom who said "tubal litigation" instead of "tubal ligation." In one case one is tied up by doctors, in the other by lawyers. Another example of a near miss is from an editorial in a prestigious newspaper that said congress "flaunts" the law. *Flaunts* means to show off; the author meant to say "flouts" the law. Sometimes when we attempt to use a big word, we miss by using another; such malapropisms can be embarrassing.

Sometimes finding the best word is difficult because our language is a sloppy dish to select from: for instance, our tuition might be handled through the billing department, office of financial affairs, bursar's office, treasurer, comptroller, or just plain business office. Or we are cautioned about movies that have nudity, violence, and *language.* Language? Do we wish to return to the silent movies without language? Just because our English language is sometimes sloppy and vague, we do not have to be sloppy in our thinking. If we have a wide selection of tools and some of them are dull, we do not have to use the dull ones. We can select our words and define the issues carefully.

Connotations

Even if we aim our words accurately at their targets, the winds of connotation can blow our meaning off course. Most words are not confined to a single meaning; rather, they have many shades of meaning. One technical college called itself a "terminal" college; a church counseled its members not to "let worry kill you—let the church help"; and a church bulletin noted that "The United Methodist Women have cast off clothing of every kind. They may be seen in the church basement this Friday." Finally, an article appeared in a Chicago paper about raccoons in suburbia. The author compared the raccoons to raiding gangs. People protested. The problem? *Coon* was a term used in the South to apply to southern African-Americans.

These examples show the emotionally laden connotations that some words carry. Words have an enormous power to excite our emotions. Words may not be the things themselves, but they can sometimes slap us in the face with the full force of what they signify.

One helpful way to think about the connotations of words is to judge their positive or negative impact. For instance, concerning overweight people, where would you place the following words on the grid below: *stout, hippo, plump, fatso, tubby, overweight, fat, pig, cow, lump of lard, butter ball, full-figured, hefty,* and *obese?*

```
 -10                           0 neutral                    +10
 ─┬─┬─┬─┬─┬─┬─┬─┬─┬─┬─┬┬┬─┬─┬─┬─┬─┬─┬─┬─┬─┬─┬─
```

THINKING ACTIVITY 5.4
Identifying Our Flame Words

We all have different "flame words." Some examples are *stupid, ugly, liar, cheater, welfare, AIDS,* as well as vulgar terms and racial slurs. List some words that trigger your emotions.

———————   ———————   ———————   ———————

———————   ———————   ———————

Sometimes it may not be the word that inflames us but the tone, which can turn the meaning around 180 degrees.

Change

> *Be not the first by whom the new is tried*
> *Nor yet the last to lay the old aside.*

>   —*ALEXANDER POPE*

Connotations change. To keep our thinking sharp we have to stay abreast of these changes. Clearly we do not wish to refer to our car as a carriage, our word processor as a typewriter, a happy man as gay, or the fragrance of a rose as an odor. Even the Bible changes: in 1990, the revised standard version of the King James Bible changed "What is man that thou art mindful of him?" to "What are human beings that you are mindful of them?" (Psalms 8:4). "*Ir*regardless" of the grammarians, *anxious* (formerly "worried") can now mean "eager"; *aggravate* (formerly "make more severe") can mean "irritate"; and *intrigue* (formerly "connive") can mean "interest."

Think About It: *People used to browse the library, and while some people currently graze the net, most prefer to surf. Think about the changing connotations that are implied in those metaphors. Would you prefer to graze or surf the net? Which activity is fundamentally deeper? Or would you prefer a different metaphor?*

Word Order Creates Meaning

When we think with English, we have to place words carefully because word position contributes to meaning. "Words differently arranged have a different meaning, and meanings differently arranged have different effects," Pascal tells us (Trotter, p. 7). Although this is true of Pascal's French, it is even more true of English: English works on word order. If we move the words, we change the meaning. In the sentences "The dog bit the man" and "The man bit the dog," position alone tells us who got bit. Similarly, we can tell a noun and its adjective from their positions, because the adjective usually comes first: we do not pick the flower yellow, but the yellow flower. We know something about the "sabulous astrachan" without knowing either of the meanings; we know that *sabulous* is an adjective describing the noun *astrachan* (*astrachan* is a type of apple, and *sabulous* means it would not taste very good). Where we place the word makes it what it is. If we carefully place our words and phrases, we avoid confusing structures such as misplaced modifiers and dangling participles. We more closely approach clear thinking.

The Power Parts: Noun and Verb

Our fundamental and most frequent word order is simply: one, two, three; subject, verb, object. These foundational positions in our language and in our thinking are filled by nouns and verbs, the power parts of our language. If we pay attention to the nouns and verbs in our thinking, we usually do not need a list of adjectives to dress up the noun or a string of adverbs to activate the verb. Instead we can select concrete nouns and verbs; for instance, instead of saying, "The huge, hairy, strong, ugly man moved heavily and powerfully across the floor," we can say, "The gorilla thundered across the floor."

Can you feel the powerful difference in that sentence? With less than half the words the "thundering gorilla" strikes the mind with far greater impact. Similarly, if we wish to "move" a woman across the room, we could select from *sashay, stroll, saunter, amble, wiggle, stumble, glide, float, slither, dance, pirouette, undulate,* or *flow.* If we tend to use too many adjectives and adverbs to color our thoughts, we may wish to search harder for the concrete nouns and vivid verbs that form the bull's eyes of our thinking.

Thinking and the Context

Larger than any single utterance is the surround: the speakers, the place, the time, the action, and all that preceded that utterance. *A white sphere on green* makes no sense until the context appears: an outfielder picks it up off the grass; a cue stick strikes the white ball across the green felt toward a fresh rack of balls; a metal club hits the white ball toward a hole in the green. Context is what makes sense of the sphere and the green, and indeed, of almost all the words. Whenever we use words, we want to think about the context. In a nationally televised debate, a vice-presidential candidate said that the cost of his opponent's environmental program would be $100 billion. To make his statement appear true he actually cited the page number in his opponent's book. What the candidate left out was the context that said the environmental program was *international* and that the cost would be borne by many countries such as Germany and Japan. Because the audience was American, they naturally presumed that they would foot the bill. Such distortions approach lying. If the truth is bent, it is no longer the truth.

Context can be so strong that satire or tone of voice can turn a text around. A man at the airport was greeting a friend, hugging and pounding the friend on the back while cursing him profusely. The meaning of the insulting words was reversed by the context. Without context we have no reference points to direct our thinking. Without context we have no ground upon which to build our thinking. Without context we cannot think clearly.

Clarity

Clarity comes from doing everything right. If we are aware that the generalizing power of language can be a weakness, then we are careful to use concrete, exact language. If we are aware of the multiple meanings of words and of the audience's background, we define terms carefully and position our words exactly. Like clear gems, clarity is rare and valuable and greatly to be sought at all points of our thinking.

Clearly Embarrassing

Without clarity and caution some red-faced embarrassment might result. The following quotations are from letters written to a welfare department.

> In accordance with your instructions I have given birth to twins in the enclosed envelope.

> I cannot get sick pay. I have six children. Can you tell me why?

> This is my eighth child. What are you going to do about it?

> Mrs. Jones has not had any clothes for a year and has been visited regularly by the clergy.

> I want my money as quick as I can get it. I've been in bed with the doctor for two weeks and he doesn't do me any good.

> You have changed my little boy to a girl. Will this make a difference?

THE PITFALLS OF ENGLISH

English has the same limitations that all languages have: it structures our perceptions and our memory, and it is subject to inaccurate definitions, conflicting connotations, ambiguous positioning, and distorting euphemisms. In addition, because of the huge and flexible vocabulary of English, if we are not alert we can cloud our thinking with weak generalizations, wordiness, illogicalness, redundancies, and clichés.

Generalizations and Abstractions

Although we need generalizations and abstractions, such as principles, natural laws, formulas, and theories, to help us to understand the relationship between the parts, generalizations and abstractions are greatly overused. To think and communicate clearly, we would do well to flesh out our generalizations with examples. One of those often-used 80-20 rules offers a good norm. Use 80 percent examples, facts, analogies, charts, statistics, concrete words, and specific words to support the 20 percent generalizations and abstractions.

High Specificity

An excellent example of this high ratio of specificity to generalization is the poem "Ode on a Grecian Urn," by John Keats. Keats crafts most of the words in the poem to appeal to the senses as he describes sylvan and pastoral scenes, marble men and maidens, and the melodies and songs of pipes and timbrels before he concludes with this generalization:

> Beauty is truth, truth beauty—that is all
> Ye know on earth, and all ye need to know.

The 80-20 guideline keeps our thinking grounded in facts and ensures that our communication will appeal to the senses.

Wordiness

With more than a million words to think with, it is understandably easy to get trapped in their intricacy and lose sight of straight thinking. Bacon notes that "the first distemper of learning" occurs when we "study words and not matter" (Waihaft, 1965, p. 223). Illustrating this "distemper," the National Bureau of Standards gave this advice to a plumber: "The efficacy of hydrochloric acid is indisputable but the ionic residues are incompatible with metallic permanence." When the plumber could not understand, someone at the bureau wrote: "Don't use hydrochloric acid! It eats hell out of the pipes!" The contrast in these instructions illustrates the challenge to our thinking: keep our statements and explanations simple and brief but also make them accurate and complete. As we will see in chapter 13, "Evaluating," simplicity and brevity are so important that they are sometimes tests of the quality of our thinking.

Redundancies

A certain form of wordiness, called redundancy, is easy to avoid if we become aware of it. Although redundancies do not make our thinking inaccurate, they dilute it, causing it to lose its tight force. For the most part we can avoid expressions such as "in the month of June," but at other times we cannot avoid expressions like "the milky way galaxy," (*galaxy* means milky way, so we are saying "the milky way milky way"). A redundancy is a *needless* repetition, which can be distinguished from an *emphatic* repetition (as in "government of the people, by the people, for the people"), which reinforces our thinking.

Illogicalities

In chapter 9, "Logical Thinking," we will think rigorously and systematically. To do so, we must choose our terms carefully because our language is not always logical. It was not designed by logicians or mathematicians but grew from living speakers. For example, *in*flammable material will burn, but *in*combustible material will not; and *bicentennial,* means every two hundred years, but *biannual* can mean every two years or twice a year. A nineteenth-century mathematician did attempt to give our language the double-negative rule that two negatives make a positive. Literature, however, is full of examples of using multiple negatives to say "no," including King Lear's anguished declaration as he holds his dead daughter: "Never, never, never, never, never!" Sometimes it is helpful to laugh a little at the foibles of language. For instance, why do they have "interstate" highways in Hawaii? And if vegetarians eat vegetables, what do "humanitarians" eat? The more we are aware of the overlapping and illogical nature of language, the better we can choose our words toward clear thinking.

> ***Think About It:*** *The pitfalls inherent in all languages can be compounded by translation. The name of the Chevy model* Nova *means "no go" in Spanish. Would you buy a car so named? The Coca-Cola slogan "Coke adds life" was translated in a Chinese ad as "Coke brings your ancestors back from the dead." Problems occur in translating terms* into *English as well. Two medical remedies were suggested in a book. Would you use them if you knew that* nux vomica *and* rhus toxicodendron *were translated "poison nut" and "poison oak"?*

Clichés

A cliché can be a sign that we are not doing our own thinking. In their original formulation, the thinking behind clichés was brilliant, but time and repetition have worn them into dull emptiness. When we use clichés, we are using someone else's old formulation, and we are probably not aware of our own sensing, feeling, thinking, and communicating; at every level of the thinking process, clichés are embalming. We can avoid clichés by restating them simply, saying "quit" instead of "throw in the towel," for example. Or sometimes we can reforge clichés such as "let sleeping dogs lie" into something like "Don't taunt the tiger."

SUMMARY

Language is the landscape of our mind; it is the mountains and forests as well as the cities and roads. It both carries the content and structures the form. We think with it. Language works intimately with all aspects of our thinking, which we discuss in other chapters: sensing, feeling, remembering, creating, organizing, reasoning, evaluating, deciding, persuading, and acting. As we become more aware of the strengths and weaknesses of language, and as we increase and refine our own language, we will think better.

We have presented language as the software of our minds, without which most of our thinking would not be possible. For the practical purpose of discussing thinking, we have defined thinking as "expressed thought." Language is the vehicle that carries that thought, but more than vehicle, language is both the container and the thought contained.

We have shown that language gives universalizing power to the mind, that language structures our perceptions, and that the metaphor plays a crucial role in the way language works and the way we think. Conversely, we have seen that the universalizing, structuring, metaphorical nature of language can also constrict our minds.

Finally, we have learned that English is a rich language that is still evolving, and that its word order determines meaning. We can more quickly access its huge word bank, thus gaining more words to think with, by paying attention to stems and affixes. To avoid being redundant, wordy, illogical, or clichéd in our thinking, we can define precisely, connote carefully, concretize our nouns, activate our verbs, and seek the power of the metaphor; thus we will energize our thinking.

Although we have concluded a short chapter on a huge topic, we do not leave language behind—we cannot. We think in it.

LANGUAGE CHALLENGES

1. Although we share language with all speakers, we also have our own phrases from our parents, from our local region, and from the unique way we combine all the language we have heard from our birth with our genetic structures and our interests. Try to identify the language structures that are in your mind. This might be difficult because we are often unaware of something so close to us as our language. For example, a good beginning is to analyze something we have written or taped. In the next several months

you might gain greater awareness of your language patterns if you attend to them. Seek the unique state of language in your brain.

2. An excellent way to boost your understanding of English is to read reflectively and listen alertly for patterns and meanings of words. Read one page of any book or article and analyze it. Look closely at the position of each word, the kinds of words used, and the subtle connotations of those words used together in that pattern.

3. One way to increase your language awareness is to listen to a good speaker. Identify different aspects of the speech, such as word order, metaphors, and anything else that demonstrates strong thinking.

4. "If you can't say it, you don't know it." Do you agree?

5. What are some of the underlying metaphors in your major field of studies? Reread the section "Metaphorical Models Control Thinking" for some ideas, if needed.

6. When we don't understand something, we search for a model or metaphor. What are some of the possibilities and limitations of the metaphor as a model for the brain?

7. Can you think of any times when you struggled to explain something and came up with the wrong analogy that was either laughed at or misled your thinking?

8. If George Orwell thought that the decline of England was related to the deterioration of the English language, are the numbers and kinds of euphemisms we use today a sign of the decline of the American culture?

9. What topics or situations prompt you to use euphemisms?

10. Language does not exist as an absolute but is determined by use. Consider the U.S. congressman (who probably did not know he was using an intransitive verb transitively) describing an impending change: "If they don't cut the crap, something's going to happen, and I'm going to happen it." Technically the congressman violated a rule of language yet he communicated effectively. How do you determine when it is effective to break the rules of language to emphasize your point?

11. *Eubonics,* a blend of *eu* meaning "well" and *ebony* meaning "black" caused a stir in the nineties. Some argued that eubonics, based on the language patterns of many African Americans, was breaking the rules of English and others argued that it was a new language. Regardless of that linguistic issue, if people use eubonics are they thinking differently?

12. A sensitivity to patterns influences your ability to think with more accurate words. Language is full of patterns, some of which are not in the grammar books. For instance, what does the *ump* mean in *lump, dump,*

stump, hump, mumps, and *clump?* Can you find any other patterns by looking for rhyming words?

13. Is it true that the metaphor is a bridge that spans our differences and allows us to communicate? If you find any validity in that thought, what does it mean in terms of your future thinking?

14. Word order is so important that it can change parts of speech. For instance Shakespeare changed a noun into a verb when he said, "I'll unhair your head." You might wish to experiment with word order by taking one word and moving it around in a sentence and observing the effects on meaning.

15. In chemistry it makes a great deal of difference whether the water is poured into a container first and then the sulfuric acid, or the other way around; in one sequence there is a solution and in the other an explosion. Likewise, in thinking, placing the right or the wrong word first can lead to communication or disaster. Can you think of examples?

16. In Chicago a man was indicted for molesting children. What do you think of when you hear the word *indicted?* Is the word slowly changing meaning? By definition, the word means "accused." How many people hear the word and presume guilt? Even the indicted man's wife, learning of the indictment, said, "That's why I was so hurt." Does her response suggest that the term implies guilt?

17. How would different metaphors affect the way a child is raised? What if the metaphors were growing a tree, building a house, or making a Stradivarius violin? (Barker, 1998, p. 402).

18. What does Wittgenstein mean when he says that "the limits of my language are the limits of my life"? Do you agree?

6

Feeling

I felt before I thought.

—*ROUSSEAU*

FEELINGS AND THINKING

What does feeling have to do with thinking? Why a chapter on feelings? In some ways thinking and feeling are almost opposites: thinking is cerebral, feeling is visceral; thinking is often clear, feeling is confused; thinking can be readily expressed verbally, feeling often struggles to find words; thinking is strikingly human (*Homo sapiens*) whereas the physiological responses from feelings are shared by many animals. Looking at these contrasts it is tempting to ignore feelings and focus exclusively on our rationality; however, if we do so we will fail to tap an enormous energy source that can animate our thinking and help forge eloquence.

Aristotle calls us "rational animals," but we are more than rational. Proportionally we are far more body than brain. A three-pound brain sits on top of our body, and the thinking part of our brain, the cerebral cortex, is only a covering for the rest of our brain, much of which we share with the animals. If we weigh about 150 pounds, we are about 98 percent body and only 2 percent brain.

But body to brain weight is less important than the connections between them. The rather large body is connected to the brain and directed through a small spinal cord and its neural network. The powerful emotions we feel are triggered by a complex system of glands, hormones, enzymes, and neurons. Our thoughts and feelings fan and fuel each other, blot and cool each other.

In discussing our personal barriers we have seen how feelings can block and bias thought. Here we scan our cultural context, which largely denigrates our feelings, making them hard to understand and use. Then we look at our feelings as a positive force behind our thoughts; we enlarge the context of feelings to include strong beliefs, prejudices, and even values, for, as we will show, there is a strong emotional as well as a cognitive content to those areas of human thinking/feeling. Finally, we will present methods of using feelings to generate powerful thinking in the forms of speaking and writing.

CULTURAL CONTEXT

It is difficult to know our feelings and to use them to think when our society suppresses most public expressions of feelings. This downplaying of feelings is part of our European heritage of rationalism, puritanism, and even stoicism. Our founders such as Thomas Jefferson drew directly from thinkers like Montesquieu and Locke, who thought that the "enlightened" human mind would soon solve all problems, social as well as scientific. This rational foundation combined with the austere religious outlook of puritanism, which fitted the harsh pioneer existence. Out of these forces emerged an early American temperament not unlike that of the Roman stoics. Today some of this temperament is still with us. This same downgrading of feelings and the emphasis upon the mind, emotional restraint, and toughness can be seen in the business world, the church, and the family.

Business

Can you think of any businesses that allow their employees to rant at the boss? How long would their jobs last? On the positive side, can you think of many businesses that allow their employees to emit screams of joy or laughter, let out whoops of exaltation, or show approval with hugs and kisses? Rather, the expected norm is that of the cool, rational, objective, decision processor, the executive who knows the facts, reasons to a profitable conclusion, and then issues the orders. We hear references to "the tough-minded business exec" and the "lean and mean" company. Such phrases imply some limited feelings, but again, mainly along the line of stoicism or strict control.

Church

At times the major religion in our Western society, Christianity, sings hallelujah, but the dominant message from Christian religions has been that feelings can lead us into trouble, called "sin." Sin is often nothing other than feelings out of control. Consider some of the "capital sins" of lust, avarice, gluttony, envy, and vengeance. In all of those sins, feelings have gone to excess. So according to Christianity, it is often feelings that tempt the mind and lead people astray, and, in the worst of scenarios, to hell. Christianity teaches its followers to control and suppress those feelings, for this life is mainly a test of the spirit which will live forever.

Family

Although the American family sometimes allows room to scream and yell, and perhaps even physically fight with siblings, it also carries a clear message to boys—don't be a wimp, control your feelings—and to girls, who have traditionally been allowed more leeway—don't get hysterical or throw tantrums. In short, feelings are frequently looked upon as childish and a sign of weakness.

THE FORCE BEHIND OUR THOUGHTS

Pascal calls the relationship between reason and feeling "an eternal battle." If we view our feelings as Pascal describes them, as battling with our mind, then we have a dangerous adversary; on the other hand, if we join forces with our feelings, we have a powerful ally.

Beneath the Rational Surface

It has been our experience, working with many levels of intelligent, successful persons such as university and college professors, priests, and CEOs, that needs and wants drive thinking. Most of the time people "know" what they want (often this knowing is a feeling), and then they develop reasons to convince themselves or others that their wants are good. Rarely have we met a person who approaches most situations with an objective, data-gathering mind that considers most angles and interests and attempts to make decisions with long-range vision. And paradoxically, sometimes the people who claim to be most objective, who claim to base all their decisions on facts, are least known to themselves. Their feelings are hidden to themselves; consequently, the hidden feelings may function more strongly and perhaps more dangerously.

Closely related to needs and wants are values, beliefs, prejudices, and morals. These *root elements* are usually formed early in life, taught by parents, modeled by peers, and become firmly fixed. Although reasons to justify our root elements are readily available to the mind, the *reasons* are not usually why we hold onto our values, beliefs, prejudices, and morals; the *feelings* are. Thinking and feeling flows both ways. Thoughts can influence our feelings so strongly that cognitive therapy, which changes the way we think about things, is an excellent way to shape our feelings. Fortunately, we are often aware of our thoughts, and thus we have the ability to adjust them and their impact on our emotions; however, we are often less aware of our feelings and therefore we need to identify and deal with them. Our feelings are like the magma beneath the surface which fuels the erupting volcano.

The Importance of Tone

So strong is the force of our feelings that it can override the content of our message. If someone does not like us, behind their attempt to project a friendly voice may be a tone of antipathy. We can hear it. If someone doesn't love us and says they do, we can hear the tone. If our friend is sad and to our greeting of "How are you?" answers "Fine," we can hear the slow droop in the voice. The tone does not easily lie. Voice-stress indicators, already in use in law enforcement agencies, are successful in detecting the tonal stress from someone who is lying. In fact, in almost all instances the tone carries the real meaning; however, rarely can the verbal content override the tone.

THINKING ACTIVITY 6.1
Feelings Beneath Our Thoughts

What are the feelings behind your thinking and acting? What feelings underlie the choices you make? What, deep down, really drives you as you select, choose, and decide? Consider your relationships, school activities, behavior at work, and your cherished beliefs and values. Write down some of these areas below, and then note the feelings that influence your actions and decisions:

_____

_____

_____

_____

_____

Were you able to discover any feelings behind your thoughts. Did you find your feelings to be a bigger part of your thinking than you had expected? If someone you despised approached you, what would you start thinking? Would those thoughts be driven by your feelings toward that person?

Tone is simply the attitude we have toward a subject or an audience. If we detest our topic (maybe centipedes or copperheads), that tone of repulsion will show through. And if we have a superior, haughty, unfriendly, belittling attitude toward those hearing or reading our thoughts, that tone too will show.

Surprisingly, the same truthfulness of tone comes across even in writing. We asked thirteen honor students at the University of Illinois at Chicago to write sincere position papers and another thirteen honor students to write insincere papers. The "insincere" group was instructed to write as if they actually believed their position, using the thoughts and vocabulary of those who held that position; basically, the task of the "insincere" group was to lie as convincingly as possible. Each of the twenty-six papers was read by four other students in the group who did not know the actual position of the authors. The readers had one task, to determine the sincerity or insincerity of the papers. Out of the 104 decisions made ($26 \times 4 = 104$), only two judged incorrectly. Stunningly, more than 98 percent of the time the readers were able to discern the real tone of the papers. Thus even in writing, tone clearly signals its message. So it becomes important to tune in to the tone of others to interpret their expressed thought; likewise, we want to tune into our own tone and match it to our thoughts as we speak and write. If our feeling and thinking are congruent, then our message will carry the force of our personal truth.

GENERATING SPEECH

It is feeling and force of imagination that makes us eloquent.

—QUINTILLIAN, ROMAN RHETORICIAN

How does the pressure of feelings motivate our thinking? Think of a time when you were really happy; perhaps you had just gotten great news, and you rushed to tell a friend. Were your feelings churning out words faster than you usually talk? Or consider a time when you were angry and you told someone just what you felt. Did those words have any trouble coming out hot and heavy and fast? Were you at a loss to find words?

As you can see from reflecting on such situations, feelings can naturally flow into words. We call it fluency. To take two examples, a lawyer who wins most of her cases told us that she researches thoroughly, prepares carefully, takes clients in whom she believes, and then in her final appeal to the jury she "lets it rip." Afterwards, when she listens to the court tapes, she is usually amazed at her own eloquence. Similarly, a college debater who won all of his debates made a similar remark about how he argued his final rebuttal position in one debate. He told us he prepared thoroughly and then got so emotionally involved in the verbal fight that his words poured out on their own. Led by the force of his emotions, his verbal eloquence built and swept over his opponent's arguments like a wave over a sand castle.

> **Think About It:**   *Both of these speakers prepared themselves fully with careful thinking and research. Then they trusted their feelings to strike lightning and thunder.*

GENERATING WRITING

We expect good speakers to animate their thinking with feelings. If they did not, we might become bored, suppress a yawn, or even try to slip out of the audience. A reader can drop a book far easier than someone can leave an audience; therefore, in some ways a writer needs to use feelings even more than a speaker. Because words on a paper are read at the whim of the reader, the words must have a vigorous and appropriately emotional tone. We will look at some ways to use emotions to both generate and enhance one's writings.

The Inspiration Method

Sing to me, oh goddess

—HOMER

Sometimes our thoughts seem to jump into our minds. To the Greek poets, ideas struck so suddenly that they seemed to come from some power seizing the mind. They attributed this force to minor deities, called the Muses, and the Greeks called upon these Muses to inspire their writings. In his *Republic,* Plato called this inspiration "a poetic frenzy that rapts the writer into the seventh heaven." (Because Plato banished poets from his republic, he was probably referring to their drunken Dionysian rites; Plato would certainly not like our using him to support the role of feelings in writing.)

If we wish to use feelings to inspire our writing, the next time we feel a powerful burst of emotions we might pick up a pen and start to write; however, we do not usually have a pen in hand during emotional experiences, as for example, when we are slamming on the brakes to avoid a car collision. So we need to inspire ourselves by artificially arousing our feelings, such as joy or anger, and to work ourselves into a partial "frenzy" before we write. The words will come.

The Recollection Method

Perhaps a more natural use of emotions is to follow Wordsworth's approach to writing poems. Wordsworth says that great writing comes from "emotion recollected in tranquility" (preface to *Lyrical Ballads*). So instead of being immediately involved in the emotional event, we recall it later with pen in hand. We can try this recollection method by first finding a tranquil space. Then we pick an experience that was emotionally moving and begin to write about it without worrying a lot about what comes out, since we can revise it later. If you try this, you may be stunned by the power and fluency of your words.

The Conscious Selection Method

Instead of using feelings to fuel thoughts, the modern poet T. S. Eliot consciously chose words to evoke emotions in the reader. He called his theory the "objective correlative"—a big term that means people hearing a word, such as "mother," have corresponding but different feelings for that word. Eliot employed this principle in many of his poems; for instance, in his poem "The Hollow Men," he showed people alienated and unable to relate by describing their voices as "wind in dried grass" or "rats' feet over broken glass."

We can try this process by first picking an emotion, then by making a list of tangible, seeable words that evoke that emotion, and finally, by consciously constructing phrases from the list. For example, if we want to arouse the feeling of American patriotism, we might list the flag, baseball, George Washington, motherhood, apple pie, the Constitution, "life, liberty, and the pursuit of happiness," the Bill of Rights, the land of the free, and so on. Or if we want to create a serene scene we might use images like a cozy fire, flowers flowing in the wind, a sleeping child, the sun caressing the skin, a soft-throated sax, a sunset water song, an easy chair, or a rainbow over clouds. Perhaps as you read those lists of consciously selected images, you felt the corresponding emotions. If so, Eliot's theory worked.

FEELINGS TOWARD TOPIC AND AUDIENCE

Now that we have seen some of the powerful interactions between feelings and thoughts, we can tap this power. First, we can be aware of how we feel about the topic that we are thinking about, talking about, or writing about. This awareness will help us realize our deep and often buried attitudes, values, beliefs, likes, or dislikes concerning the current topic. This awareness will help us understand and evaluate our thinking and then adjust it toward greater objectivity and accuracy.

THINKING ACTIVITY 6.2
Evoking Emotions

Try Eliot's more conscious manipulation of emotions. Make a list of images that evoke fear, a second list for tenderness, and in the third column below, write images for an emotion of your choice.

Fear	Tenderness	

Now select from your lists those items that best seem to bring out each emotion. Write a paragraph using those items and then discuss with your readers whether your words produce the desired emotion.

Second, we need to check our feelings toward our audience. For instance, if we have negative feelings toward our audience and if we are not aware of the negativity, we will speak or write with a hostile tone. That tone will be picked up by the audience and will harm our communication effort. However, if we are aware of the hostility, we can then choose to be silent, to carefully modulate it, or express it in a number of ways of our choosing, being well aware of the potential impact on our audience. By controlling our feelings and by considering the audience, we can reach the audience more effectively.

Finally, within thoughtful bounds, we can trust our feelings as a positive force. When we feel positive about the topic and the audience, we can let our feelings out and let them work for us. We can use our feelings to bring ourselves alive as thinkers, speakers, and writers. Most great speakers and writers feel strongly about their thoughts. These strong feelings lead to the ringing eloquence of speakers like Patrick Henry, who famously said, "I know not what choice others may take, but as for me, give me liberty or give me death."

SUMMARY

We have seen that feelings are a force behind our thinking; however, our culture, in areas such as business, religion, and family, often denigrates feelings. Nevertheless, these feelings are there and they charge our words with a tone so strong that it cannot be ignored. Our feelings can be the constructive energy to generate our thoughts and deliver them eloquently. More specifically we looked at the inspiration, recollection, and conscious selection methods of using feelings to fuel our thoughts and express them powerfully and positively.

THINKING AND FEELING CHALLENGES

1. Assess Pascal's statement, "Those who are accustomed to judge by feeling do not understand the process of reasoning."
2. Can you remember times when your body was paralyzed by fear? Can you recall times when you have blanked while taking a test or giving a speech or were at a loss for words because of the pressure? If a similar situation occurs, what could you do to manage such emotional forces?
3. How does your language reflect what our culture "thinks" about feelings? For instance, some positive words to describe an emotional male are *sensitive* and *kind;* can you think of other positive or negative words to describe an emotional male? Think of other examples that reflect our culture's attitude toward feelings.
4. How extensive is your vocabulary for describing feelings? To answer this question, begin by listing all the words you can think of to describe love, hate, anger, or fear.
5. To begin to grow more aware of your feelings for certain topics, rate your feelings toward the items on the following list (0 = neutral, 10 = the best, −10 = the worst).

___ snakes	___ sunrises	___ politicians	___ sports heroes
___ flowers	___ earthworms	___ chocolate	___ children
___ teachers	___ ice cream	___ this book	___ parties
___ exams	___ cars	___ houses	___ forests

6. Rousseau said, "I felt before I thought," and e. e. cummings said, "Feeling is first." Are these statements that only romanticists or poets would make? What might they mean?
7. Describe what the American culture thinks about emotions. Give examples to support your description.
8. When you hear the next person talk, listen to the tone, the feelings underneath the thoughts, and describe them. Is the tone congruent with the verbal content?
9. The next time you write something or think about what words you will use to say something to someone, stop and identify your tone. How do you

feel about the subject you are thinking about, and how do you feel about the person who will receive your words?

10. Take any paragraph of this book, and identify the tone that goes with the words. Is the tone strong enough, too weak, inappropriate, or effective?

11. Experiment some more with the inspiration, recollection, or conscious selection method of finding and using your feelings. Begin by taking any topic you feel strongly about and write fast for five minutes. Let your feelings pour and empower the words. When you are finished you might be surprised by both the quantity of the words and a certain raw eloquence. Did your strong feelings help you generate any worthwhile thoughts? Can you keep the words in that form, or do you need to refine them for public communication? If so, refine them, and then discuss your experience and your writings.

7

Creative Thinking

Imagination is more important than knowledge.

—EINSTEIN

"I've got it!" we want to scream. In our sleep, at a ball game, on a bike, in a car, *the* idea springs into our mind, powerfully. So powerful is this burst of insight that when Archimedes discovered how to calculate the volume of gold in the king's crown, he jumped out of the bath and ran naked through the streets yelling, "Eureka! I've found it!"

In this chapter we do not run naked and screaming, but we do yell "Eureka!" Here we see that creative thinking is crucial to critical thinking; we probe our awareness of the elusive moment and process of creativity; and best of all, we find that we too are creative and capable of increasing our creative thinking. More specifically, we define creativity, look at its metaphorical nature, and discuss its limitations and conditions. Then we practice creative thinking through brainstorming, starbursting, and coaxing creativity. Creativity is an early base of our thinking because one of its functions is to produce the thoughts we think with. Creativity operates at the point of acquiring thoughts (in classical rhetoric this process of acquiring thought is called "topics" by the Greeks and "invention" by the Romans). Yet, like all the thinking bases, creativity is used throughout our thinking and can be called upon at any time.

WHAT IS CREATIVITY?

To create, we change the old into the new. We do not create out of nothing. The Wright brothers took four old ideas (a fan blade, a bicycle chain, a gasoline engine, and wings) and "created" the airplane. Edison took three old ideas (a glass container, a vacuum, and electricity through a filament) and created the light bulb.

Creating is taking the old and mixing it, moving it, breaking it, or building it into newness. Sometimes we take a piece of the whole (a tree branch becomes a baseball bat), or two pieces from different wholes (*br* from *breakfast* and *unch* from *lunch* become *brunch*), or one piece and one whole (a typewriter keyboard is added to a computer), or two wholes (music and television become MTV). Sometimes we keep one part and change or add other parts (tea bags become coffee bags, a water ski becomes a jet ski) or we simply move some parts (front-wheel drive). We turn some element around (Dick Fosbury goes over the high jump bar backwards and the "Fosbury flop" becomes the standard). We change an object's use (a glass mug becomes a vase becomes a pencil holder) or omit a part of it (half of a watermelon becomes a fruit dish). We superimpose one concept on another (a carved face transforms a pumpkin into a jack-o-lantern) or impose form on a raw material (a block of marble metamorphoses into Michaelangelo's *David*).

In all of these examples, change takes place and newness results. The mind sees a new relationship or comparison between or among the objects or their parts. This relationship is, broadly speaking, a metaphorical relationship. In short, creating is making metaphors.

METAPHORICAL THINKING

At the heart of creativity, language, understanding, and thinking is the metaphor. We have defined the metaphor as "an implied comparison between two things" (see chapter 5, "Language: Our Thinking Medium"). When we take the old and change it, we are using the metaphorical ability of our mind, the ability to look at one thing and see another. Whether Edison is searching for a new light source or Shakespeare for a new image for life, the process is similar.

Because the metaphor is the way language works (there is no other way), all great communicators forge metaphors. Aristotle calls the metaphor the fundamental figure of speech, the true mark of genius. Homer's warriors are tall trees felled in battle, Confucius speaks of shoots which spring up but bear no fruit, Chuang Tzu's sage tucks the universe under his arm, Christ speaks of seed falling by the wayside, Dante covers the hypocrites in hell with gilded lead coats, and Montaigne calls his book totally his own child because he was both father and mother at once.

Shakespeare was the master of the metaphor. He used metaphors more frequently as his language matured in his great tragedies. Notice how Shakespeare, in this passage from *Macbeth,* takes four common concepts (a candle, a shadow, an actor, and a story) and transforms them into metaphors for the brevity, frailty, and incoherence of life:

> Out, out, brief candle!
> Life's but a walking shadow, a poor player
> That struts and frets his hour upon the stage
> And then is heard no more. It is a tale
> Told by an idiot, full of sound and fury,
> Signifying nothing.

Shakespeare's creativity and communicative power have thundered through the ages. As we learn to know, trust, and tap our own metaphorical mind, we too will think and communicate more effectively.

We know and understand the world through metaphors. If language is the mode in which our mind understands the world, and if metaphors are at the heart of language, then metaphors are at the heart of our understanding of the world. (Not only have we just used a metaphor, but we have also used a syllogism, a form of thinking discussed later.)

THINKING ACTIVITY 7.1
Making Metaphors

To think of other metaphors for the brevity of life, list things that last for a short time.

_____	_____	_____	_____	_____
_____	_____	_____	_____	_____
_____	_____	_____	_____	

You have just used metaphorical thinking. If you take one or two items from your list and give them the proper context, you will probably have metaphors for the shortness of life. Moreover, you have just done one of the more profound tasks that you can perform as a human: you have created! Shortly, you will learn other ways to think creatively.

KINDS OF CREATIVE THINKING

Creativity can take many forms—from cooking to chemistry, from art to archeology, from poetry to physics, from shanty to Chartres, from Mona Lisa to Madonna, from seamstress to surgeon, from baseball to battle, from making laws to making love. Creativity can be seen in the range, kind, and quantity of responses to any given situation. Creativity is barely bound and hardly determined. It swings out with the quasars to the edge of the expanding universe, and it bends inward to the metaphor-making center of our mind. No one has a lock on creativity, and that allows us to think about unlocking our own.

WHO CAN THINK CREATIVELY?

We can all think creatively. In fact, much of our thinking is in some way connected to creativity, constantly there are variations in the processes of our unfolding thoughts. Even when we appear to be thinking in a rut or thinking in circles, if we carefully reflect on the patterns of our thought, we will probably discover that they do not repeat exactly; and even when we are intentionally repeating a pattern, such as memorized lines, the lines do not always march into memory with the regularity of a metronome; often they come haltingly, in pieces, or in tidal waves of changing patterns, even though when we go to speak our thoughts, we might enunciate them smoothly.

People often think of creativity as a talent or a gift held by the few. That's what we as teachers used to think, that creativity was limited to a few students who were creative. Then we performed an icebreaker activity in which each student was asked to come up with an image, or poetic impression, of the other students in class. The results were astounding. Every student created some metaphors, which were often brilliant. We were stunned. Our first guess was that the group of students were extraordinarily bright. We pulled the records and found that the class was carrying a 1.9 average (less than a C)! Our next thought was that perhaps these were all underachieving creative geniuses. We tried the same activity in another class and got the same results: all students produced metaphors, often excellent ones. If you wish to try that same experiment, use Thinking Activity 7.2.

Since that experience and many classes later, we now know that we all are creative. Some people may produce metaphors in greater variety, at greater length, or of better quality than others, but we can all create! The possible variety of our creativity is almost infinite. If we are thinking with an active vocabulary of 6,000 words and if we could think a sentence a second for the rest of our lives, and even if those sentences were shorter than ten words each, we would not exhaust the number of possible sentences. As we stretch our sentences longer

THINKING ACTIVITY 7.2
Poetic Impressions

1. Write the first name of each student in a column down the left side of a piece of paper. Then attempt to get one image each for as many students as you can. A simple example is, "You appear like a mountain, strong and sure of your place in the world." Here is a more complex one: "You appear like a mirror in a foggy room, sometimes the mist clears and I think I see you clear, bright, and smiling, and then at other times you seem to withdraw and I have no idea of how you would react if I approached you."
2. Look at a student and let an image pop into your mind. You can draw upon nature (mountains, lakes, trees, flowers, animals), household scenes (rocking chair, warm fireplace, comforter, kitchen cooking, closed attic), or any other setting, but your image should be a nonhuman one.
3. If an image does not spring to mind, try completing sentences like these: "He/she looks like a _____" (physical image), or "He/she seems rigid and tough like a _____" (personality image).
4. If an image does not come quickly, move on to another student and return later. You might not get images for all students, but the images you do get will demonstrate that *you can be creative.*

than ten words, as we draw deeper from the million-plus words of the English language, and as we abbreviate, adumbrate, cut, and telescope English syntax, the variety increases to a staggering number.

CONDITIONS AND LIMITATIONS OF CREATIVITY

Although creative thinking sometimes seems unlimited, we are absolutely bound by our brain and the language it contains, and we are partially bound by our personal barriers (see chapter 2). The other mind bases that we have examined so far—senses, memory, language, and feelings—operate as conditions of creativity. As those bases grow in firmness, flexibility, and interrelatedness, our creative potential rises.

Courage and calm help us to create. The opposite of courage, fear, can freeze our mind as surely as it can our body. When we worry about how our thoughts will be received, rejected, or ridiculed, we have difficulty thinking of new ideas. In times of fear, the traditional path seems the safe one. But if we can free ourselves of the fear of what others think about us and if we can strike strongly out on our own and let the chips fall where they may, we will increase our creative fluency.

BEGINNING TO CREATE

Brainstorming

Brainstorming allows the mind to flow from thought to thought, each idea stimulating other ideas. All evaluation or censorship of these ideas is suspended, thus helping the normal boundaries of thinking to dissolve, leading to more creative and unconventional thinking.

Research on brainstorming (Mullen, Johnson, and Salas, 1991) finds that it is more effectively done alone than with a group. Apparently, in a group situation people are afraid that their novel ideas will be negatively evaluated by the group, even though instructions prohibit negativity. Also, one person's idea may impede the flow of ideas of the other members. This happens because each member in a group tends to think for a moment about the idea just presented which, not being their idea, tends to stop their own natural flow of ideas. Therefore, the group's efficiency will be greater if the members brainstorm alone and then return to the group with their solutions. The resulting larger number of ideas can then be evaluated by the group. If brainstorming were applied to the topic "Ways to Market This Product," answers such as these might emerge:

Ways to Market This Product

direct mail	take it to the schools
TV ads	identify the trade association
magazine ads	give it to certain leaders
radio ads	go on talk shows
telemarketing	put up billboards
retailing	get the mothers involved
multi-level marketing	create a web site
hire a skywriter	hang posters on cows
door to door	promotional balloons
give-away promotion	get testimonials

Starbursting

> *Many difficulties come when you attempt to answer questions, without first discovering precisely what question it is which you desire to answer.*
>
> —*G. E. MOORE, PHILOSOPHER*

Although brainstorming can generate many effective and creative ideas, it misses some of the larger parameters and assumptions that can come from a different method, which we call starbursting. Starbursting focuses on a topic and radiates outward with *questions*. Here anything goes, any questions are legitimate, and the more the better. Starbursting begins by asking, "What are the questions?" Let's apply starbursting to the same topic of marketing and then compare these results to those of brainstorming:

Marketing: What Are the Questions?

Why market this product instead of another?

Do we want to market this product at all?

Is now the best time?

Why have we waited so long, and will we be faster next time?

Do we want to get more into the marketing business?

Will our company be stronger if we market this product?

Is this the right country for this product?

Why do humans market anyhow?

Do we market to sell or service our customers?

Who does marketing?

What is today's technological marketplace?

Is human conversation disappearing from the marketplace?

Is marketing driven by greed?

Will our customers like this?

How globally appealing is this product?

Would I buy this myself?

From this list we see that starbursting can generate some unexpected questions. Although some of these questions are more philosophical than productive, many of them make sound business sense. Looking at the two lists, which one contains items that need to be considered early in the decision-making process? Which one contains more specific results? Judging from these lists, would it be wise to do starbursting or brainstorming first? These two creative tactics alone can generate enough work, fun, and ideas to free us whenever we feel closed or stifled.

Perhaps you are familiar with the Socratic teaching technique which uses questioning to lead a student toward a conclusion. This method presumes that the teacher knows the goal and that the student has enough knowledge to process the questions. Unlike the Socratic method, starbursting does not use leading questions that probe toward a specific solution. Whereas the Socratic method may produce an answerer, starbursting may produce a questioner.

The difference between starbursting and Socratic questioning, both in method and results, can be seen in two children walking the beach alongside a set of dog tracks. The first was Socratically asked, "What made these tracks?" and the answer was, "A dog or an animal." The second child was asked the wider, starburst question, "What are the questions?" At first there was a puzzled look on the child's face, but after the question was repeated, the child looked around and began asking *questions:* "Why do the waves come in closer here than over there? Why is the water greener over there? What made these (referring to dog tracks)? Why are the tops of the waves white? What is this (referring to kelp)? Why did they put this here (referring to a breakwater)?" Six questions! Instead of being Socratically led down one path, the second child's mind opened like a starburst. If continued through life, starbursting can produce a person who has learned to question, to probe.

COAXING CREATIVITY

Perhaps creativity is slow because our confidence is weak. If creativity doesn't flow, we can give it a nudge. With the process below, we will probably find that we can coax creativity to come, even when we are in the doldrums of the mind.

Step 1: Desire

To become more creative, we must want it. "To change a mind-set may be the most difficult task a human being can undertake." (Hurt, 1998, p. 41) Most of us already would like to become more creative because it translates into more ideas, sometimes more money, and usually more fun out of life.

Step 2: Knowledge and Skills

We have seen that everyone has the capability to create. But to create in a specific field we first need knowledge. If we decided to carve a stone sculpture and knew nothing about working with stone, we would not be successful on our early tries. Fortunately, to create in the field of thinking we mainly use language, and we already have sufficient language skills to create. As we read more books our vocabulary and knowledge base grow and our creative potential expands. More importantly, we are able to create—now.

Step 3: Edisonian Effort

> *Genius is one percent inspiration and ninety-nine percent perspiration.*
>
> *—THOMAS EDISON*

We hear so much about the spontaneous, serendipitous, heuristic, inspirational, and almost accidental aspect of creativity that it sometimes seems out of our control. The good news is that work can cause creativity to happen. At this point enters the effort or "perspiration" of Thomas Edison. Known for his persistence, he asserted that there is no substitute for hard work. He tried over a thousand different filaments before he found one that burned bright enough and long enough to be used in his light bulb. Like Edison, we can apply our skills and begin to push, pull, bend, break, reverse, and spin them into newness. We can take the data and fiddle, fidget, and fool around with them until something new springs out. The activity below can help you to make creativity happen.

THINKING ACTIVITY 7.3
Prepcreation

1. Pick a topic that needs some creative work.
2. Write down three or four headings for important parts of that topic. For instance, if you were going to design an innovative course of study for students, your headings might be:

Students	Job Market	Facilities	Faculty

3. Make lists of anything that occurs to you under those topics. Keep each list in a column on a narrow piece of paper, or cut the columns out neatly so you can slide them up and down next to each other. Begin now by brainstorming a list under "Students," or the first topic you have selected.
4. Place a list of prepositions (such as these below) between any two of your lists, aligning the items in the three lists.

above	about	around
after	because	before
between	beyond	below
beside	down	during
from	for	in front of
inside	in	into
near	next	next to
opposite	outside	out

5. Because prepositions show relationships, you can read possible relationships between the elements you listed from left to right. For instance, taking the first column of prepositions and inserting them between two lists of subtopics, you might have a list like this:

Students	above	Job Market
majors	after	starting job
seniors	between	grad schools
honor	beside	corporation
commuters	from	small business
residents	inside	start a business
failing	near	hot field
bright	opposite	future field

(continued)

THINKING ACTIVITY 7.3 (continued)
Prepcreation
Reading the relationships across we get:

- Take *students above job market* (give them an overview).
- Pick *major after starting a job* (work first, then decide which major to follow).
- Allow *seniors between grad schools* (perhaps allow the seniors to do a joint graduate program at two close universities).
- Take the *honor* students *beside the corporation* (in something like a work-study program, perhaps honor students could work on parallel projects with a corporation).
- And so forth.
  6. Shift one column so all the items slide up or down one notch. For instance, if the preposition column is moved one line up, we get "*students after the job market*" (survey or recruit students after they have been working a while). As you can begin to see, the number of combinations is enormous. Lists can be switched (left to right) and different lists inserted. Also, we can see that not all combinations work, but if only a small percent of the combinations are successful, the process can still yield a huge number of creative ideas.

From this activity we again see that creativity is bringing the old together in new ways. It involves working the data, pushing it into another corner, turning it over, forcing it together into its critical mass, pulling it apart into new forms, and playing with it until it finds its creative form.

Think About It: *Coax or coerce? We have called this section "Coaxing Creativity," yet under "Edisonian Effort" we have talked about making creativity happen. Is this similar to forcing creativity? If so, is force antithetical to creativity?*

Step 4: Fermentation and Insight

When creativity does not strike with lightning-like swiftness and our efforts still do not satisfy our needs, sometimes we have to give the process time or "sleep on it." When we are driving, sipping a soft drink, dreaming, or daydreaming (in another class, of course), our mind seems to sit with the idea and then, suddenly, as Einstein says, while we are eating an apple, the idea appears. After the desire, the effort, and the fermentation comes the payoff: Insight! Solution! Discovery!

Step 5: Evaluation

As great as our idea may be, ultimately it needs to be shared and recognized, if not in our lifetime, then by later generations; otherwise it remains valuable and satisfying only to ourselves. As in the fourth step of the scientific method, our ideas need to be validated; in this case, validation occurs through acceptance, through other ideas building on ours, and through the test of time. We will discuss this process of validation more fully in chapter 13, "Evaluating."

SUMMARY

We have looked at creativity as simply putting the old together in new ways; basically, it is a metaphorical process. Creativity is not confined to the Michelangelos; everyone can create, including ourselves. Hopefully, we have discovered through some of the activities presented that we too can create. We have seen how brainstorming and starbursting can boost creativity, and we have followed a five-step process to coax creativity when the ideas do not readily appear. Sometimes our creativity can generate an astonishing amount of material, and creativity is involved continually in all areas of our thinking. In the next chapter we will learn to organize that information.

Leonardo da Vinci

Although only nineteen paintings survive, da Vinci's notebooks showed an enormously creative and prolific thinker in action. True, his mind spawned more than his hands could build, but he captured these thoughts in writing and in sketches. Not since Archimedes has such a restless, questing mind asked so many questions and sought so many answers.

CREATING THINKING CHALLENGES

1. Describe the most creative persons you know. What are their personality characteristics, living styles, and creating methods?
2. List the subject areas in which you feel comfortable creating. How do you go about creating in these areas? Could you use some of those same processes to create in other areas like painting or writing?
3. We "coerced" creativity by placing lists of words next to each other and joining the words together. Can you find other ways to run ideas together?

4. Be creative and think of a new metaphor for the way the brain works. Some people think of the brain as having storage boxes or pigeonholes; one student described her brain as a bayou where ideas arose like steam. Write a passage beginning with, "My mind works like ... "

5. A "dynamic tranquility" in which we can relax but also remain alert is an ideal state for creativity. As we relax we can begin to disassociate our usual thoughts and let our mind roam freely. We can then assemble the parts of our wandering thoughts into new structures. There are a number of techniques for relaxing, but for the moment, try the way that works best for you and see if you can achieve a creative state. Then try to solve a problem or let your mind brainstorm a topic and notice the results.

6. Try brainstorming for a solution: Mary is divorced, thirty years old, mother of two sons, ages eleven and twelve. She lives in a three-bedroom apartment in a large city. She works full-time at minimum wage and is in a desperate financial situation, unable to pay the rent, credit card bills, auto payments, insurance, and other usual living expenses. Using brainstorming, come up with as many suggestions as you can to ease Mary's financial problems.

7. Try starbursting by asking, "What are the questions?" Pick any idea, issue, or area in which you feel "stuck" and need some fresh ideas. Allow your mind to range freely and ask any kind of question at all. Then look at those questions and pick the ones you want to seek answers for.

8. Shown below is the result of creativity. We have constructed a mnemonic device that covers some major points in this chapter to help us remember how to create. At any time in the thinking process when you find yourself stuck, remember the "ELVES":
   E. Be at *ease.* Relax. Creativity will flow more easily.
   L. Make *lists.* Starburst and brainstorm.
   V. *Vary* those lists between prepositions: prepcreate.
   E. *Eureka!* Recognize and enjoy the insight.
   S. *Select* from your creations; test them on others.
   Take an area in which you wish to generate ideas and try the ELVES steps above.

9. Create your own mnemonic device the next time you have to remember a list of items.

10. Because creativity always occurs in new and different ways, it is difficult to define; it's hard to classify something new with old labels. If you are interested in creativity, you may wish to take on the task of creatively defining it.

11. Was Aristotle correct when he said that "there is nothing new under the sun"? Can you think of new ideas and discoveries since the time of Aristotle, over 2300 years ago? List them.

8

Organizing

And what is organization but the connection of parts in and for a whole.

—*SAMUEL COLERIDGE, LECTURES*

If we have just engaged in a prolific creative process, we may be overflowing with jumbled bits of data. If we could organize these pieces, they might form a stunning mosaic. In this chapter we look at different ways to form that mosaic. If we can find basic orders that are in both the universe and our minds, we can use those strong orders in our thinking. First, we look into the origins of order; then we consider the orders of place, time, similarity, and cause; further, we look at some of the many logical orders that humans have created; last, we apply a method of clustering, analyzing, and prioritizing to some of the more important orders.

ORIGINS OF ORDER

Is the universe orderly? Do we call it cosmos or chaos? Or is order only in our mind? Is our mind born with its own patterns of organization? Or does our mind learn and reproduce patterns of order that it finds around it? Can our mind create its own structures to fit its own needs?

Some powerful thinkers tell us that our mind is not born blank. Plato says we have innate ideas, Kant says space and time are structures of the mind, Hume says that cause and effect are the mind's way of ordering reality, Jung says we have archetypes that we share with other humans, and Chomsky says the mind has the natural ability to learn language and to produce and recognize meaning. Although it would be difficult to verify what these innate structures are, the fact that the brain has general "territories" where certain data are stored and where certain processes take place suggests that there are innate structures. Our brain is prepared to receive and store sensory data, to retrieve that data, and then to process and interpret that data in a higher, symbolical manner of language.

NATURAL/MENTAL ORDERS

Much of the order within our mind seems to be learned from the natural order of the universe. We first look briefly at four natural orders that appear to be both in the universe and in our mind: topical order, analogical order, chronological order, and causal order. Later in this chapter we use these orders to help us organize our thinking.

Topical Order

In the universe most things have their "natural" place, or topical order. Water flows to its lowest level, lead sinks down, and helium balloons go up; planets whirl in orbit as they and the sun pull toward each other in direct proportion to their masses and inversely according to the square of their distances. Even human-made objects are subject to this topical order. Long after the Tower of Pisa leans over too far, the centered pyramids will stand. As we look around we see this topical order, or order of place in the universe.

Analogical Order

All around us we see similarities: between a ball and a planet, a flower and a tree, an apple and a cantaloupe, a mouse and a horse. The power of the mind to recognize such similarities is the same metaphorical power that we discussed in the chapters on creativity and language. This analogical order of insights is found both in the world and in our mind.

Chronological Order

In the universe we observe change and we interpret it. We see day yield to night, planets wheel around the sun, flowers bloom and die, and our bodies grow and age. This change takes place through time; we see things changing in sequence and we call this order of time chronological.

Think About It: *What would our world be like without the chronological order? How safe would it be? Consider the chronological sequence that pilots use before flying: preflight inspection, pre-ignition, ignition, running up the systems, pretakeoff, takeoff, climbing, cruising, descending, prelanding, landing, after landing, securing aircraft. Are we happy that pilots follow a strict chronological order? Are there situations in which we should not follow a strict chronological order?*

Causal Order

Behind these chronological changes we look for reasons. If we hear a loud bang in the next room, we presume someone or some force caused the noise. If a tree falls, we look for cuts, rot, shallow roots, wind, lightning, bulldozer tracks, or the giant pileated woodpecker. Even when we see seemingly chaotic patterns, we look for order. Eighty years ago a hurricane seemed like a disorganized mess of terrible winds and waves. Now with air and satellite reconnaissance we can spot the huge swirling vortex, understand the conditions of heat and cold that spawn and feed it, and somewhat predict its direction and duration.

Our experience (and perhaps matching structures in the brain) has taught us that all changes have reasons; when we find the reasons we call them causes, and the changes they produce, effects. We call this order causal.

THINKING ACTIVITY 8.1
Other Natural Orders?

When you look around you, do you see any other naturally occurring orders in the world that are not human constructs? For instance, is the Darwinian idea of survival of the fittest a natural order? Is the life form with the greater molecular complexity also higher on the food chain? Can you identify any other orders?

THINKING ACTIVITY 8.2
The Order of the Elements

Dmitri Mendeleev placed the elements in rows and columns according to their atomic weights, creating what would come to be called the periodic table. Presuming an orderly universe, Mendeleev predicted that this same pattern would

(continued)

THINKING ACTIVITY 8.2 *(continued)*
The Order of the Elements

continue and the missing elements would be discovered. Shortly thereafter, the three new elements gallium, germanium, and scandium were discovered. These elements fitted Mendeleev's description and behaved exactly as predicted. Does the periodic table help to confirm the order in the universe? Which (one or more) of the four orders (more than one?) do you think Mendeleev used?

MENTAL ORDERS

The above four orders—topical, analogical, chronological, and causal—appear to be both natural and mental; they are found in nature and are reflected in our mind. Other orders that exist are mainly mental because they come largely from human structures. These mental orders can be arbitrary, such as an alphabetical seating arrangement, or they can be logical, as when we decide to store our valuables in different places according to their worth: diamonds go in the safety deposit box, large sums go into the bank, big bucks go under the mattress, daily living money goes in our dresser, spending money goes in our wallet or purse, and change lies loose on the counter. That's a logical order developed by correlating the perceived value of the item with the perceived safety of the location.

Thousands of mental orders have been developed, by carpenters, philosophers, journalists, accountants, plumbers, lawyers, and so forth. These orders are not totally disconnected from the natural physical orders around us. For instance, when a plumber deals with gravity and permeability, the natural order is strongly in effect; but when the plumber applies new methods of connecting and cleaning, the mental orders of cost and reliability come more into play. And when the marketer deals with the four Ps—price, place, product, and promotion—the mental order predominates over the natural.

Some professions have produced logical orders that have excellent applications in other professions. For instance, the journalistic categories (the five Ws— who, what, where, when, and why) have broad applications for lawyers, teachers, writers, detectives, marketers, historians, and so forth. A brilliant professional lecturer who speaks *ex tempore* on many topics keeps his speech organized and complete by following the five Ws in his mind. We too can use this organizational pattern often and effectively to think, write, and read. Journalists are trained to answer these five questions in their first paragraph. Knowing this, if we wish to read fast and get a news summary, we need to read only the lead paragraph of each article.

Another major order, the scientific order, or method, has multiple applications in manufacturing, business, cooking, and indeed in most processes that work with empirical data. The four main steps of the scientific method are so integral to thinking that we have treated each in a separate chapter: *observation* correlates with our chapter on the senses, *hypothesis* with creativity, *experimentation* with action, and *validation* with evaluation.

Logic, with deductive and inductive reasoning as its supporting pillars, is also an order so important that we have set aside an entire chapter on logical thinking. Logical order is used continually in most fields of learning and working. Although the premises change from field to field, we will see that this order of stating a premise, applying a particular, and then drawing a conclusion is basic to much of our thinking.

Planners often use a mental order that defines the objective, develops a plan to achieve that objective, monitors progress, and adjusts the plan.

Some mental orders are mainly arbitrary. Different societies have based their monetary standards upon seashells, copper, gold, or paper currency. Different languages make use of different symbols in their alphabets, such as the Roman or Chinese. For logical reasons we sometimes select an arbitrary order such as the alphabet or a number sequence, or decide the order by a flip of a coin.

Besides the mental orders found in groups, individuals also have their patterns. For example, suppose a pitcher has only three kinds of pitches. When does that pitcher tend to throw which pitch? In what quarter does an NBA All Star usually score most of his points? Judging from the first test, what questions might the teacher ask on the second test?

THINKING ACTIVITY 8.3
Other Mental Orders

What are the orders relied upon by the following?

mechanics _____
teachers _____
manufacturers _____
homeowners _____
real estate agents _____
engineers _____
jewelers _____
computer programmers _____
students _____
nurses _____
journalists _____

(continued)

THINKING ACTIVITY 8.3 (continued)
Other Mental Orders
scientists _____

mathematicians _____

marketers _____

Are any of these orders partially associated with the four natural orders? Are any of these orders purely arbitrary?

Clarity and Memory

Because we have found order in the universe around us and have seen that we create it in society, we naturally expect to find it in our thinking. A structure in our mind makes sense of the universe, our solar system, the atom, our society and even ourselves. What would our lives be like without a structure? Where would we arrive without a map? How would we assemble words without the patterns of language? Organizing the pieces makes sense of the puzzle. Organizing gives clarity to our thoughts. Even as we write this book, we are struggling to give it an organizational format that offers clarity to the reader. Clarity is needed and valued in writing and speaking. It adds to the effectiveness of thinking and delivering our thoughts.

A clear structure also adds to the effectiveness of our memory. We are greatly aided by a clear thesis presented up front in a textbook, speech, or meeting, such as, "In this book we will cover three major topics." Having these major parts clearly distinguished and related prepares our mind to store ideas in a related fashion, and to recall them when needed. Studies have shown that if we memorize nonsense data they quickly disappear without constant repetition, but if the data are organized and we understand what we are reading or thinking about, it is easier to bring them back to memory. The recognition and use of orders adds to our recall, efficiency, and clarity of thinking. Organize.

Think over the orders that were just presented. In your home life, work, and study, when do you use the predominantly natural orders: topical, chronological, analogical, and causal? When might you employ some of the major mental orders such as the scientific method and the five Ws? Can you identify any of your own patterns and orders that you have developed to keep track of things and ideas and to recall them and use them more efficiently?

STEPS IN ORGANIZING

When we need to make sense of information we have generated or received, an effective three-step method is to cluster, analyze, and prioritize.

Clustering

Clustering is simply grouping. For example, let's presume we have done starbursting and brainstorming on the issue of gun control and we are not sure about how to handle the following data that we have generated (below). The first step is to look at the items and see which ones are similar to each other, which items naturally belong together.

guns	police	gangs	death
handguns	protection	freedom	the innocent
rifles	natl. defense	control	outlaw
register	types of gun	permits	place
automatics	statistics	crime	Bill of Rights
drugs	drive-bys	sports	hunting
training	license	survey	criminals
fear	stray bullets	NRA	urban/rural

Place the above items in groups that seem to fit. What kind of clusters become apparent? If you experienced difficulty or spent more time clustering than you would like, here is one way to quickly cluster:

1. Look for similar items.
2. Give a general name to those similar items such as causes, people, results, things.
3. Mark each item with a symbol for that cluster.

Following these three steps, you might label the clusters this way:

I = Instruments
S = Solutions to deal with issue
C = Causes, reasons
R = Results
P = People

I—guns	P—police	R/C/P—gangs	R/P—death
I—handguns	C—protection	C/R—freedom	R/P—the innocent
I—rifles	C—natl. defense	S—control	S—outlaw
S—register	I—types of gun	S—permits	S—place
I—automatics	R—statistics	C/R—crime	C—Bill of Rights
C—drugs	R—drive-bys	C—sports	C—hunting
S—training	S—license	S—survey	C/P/R—criminals
C/R—fear	I—stray bullets	P/C/R—NRA	?—urban/rural

When these items are clustered according to the categories above, they form these groups:

Instruments	Solutions	Results	Causes	People
guns	register	fear	drugs	police
handguns	training	statistics	fear	gangs
bullets	license	drive-byes	hunting	NRA
automatics	control	gangs	natl. defense	death
types of gun	permits	freedom	gangs	innocents
stray bullets	survey	crime	freedom	criminals
rifles	outlaw	NRA	crime	
	place	death	sports	
	criminals	innocents	NRA	
		criminals	Bill of Rights	
			protection	
			criminals	

Analyzing

After clustering, the second step is to analyze both the clusters and the individual items to determine whether we should omit any, add some new clusters, keep them as they are, or change them. These choices are made as we clarify our purpose in using these clusters. For instance, if we favor regulating the guns, we might want to add a new category "History" to show that the authors of the Bill of Rights were speaking of the rural landscape of pioneer days when guns were indeed necessary, but that now the urban landscape does not seem to justify guns. Or, if we do not favor regulation, we might omit the "Solutions" cluster because most of these items deal with some kind of regulation.

Once we have dealt with the larger question of which clusters to use, we can analyze the particular items. Perhaps we wish to remove "automatics" and "rifles" from the list of instruments and focus only on "handguns." Perhaps we

---

THINKING ACTIVITY 8.4
Analyzing the Clusters

Try analyzing the clusters for the issue of gun control according to your purpose. Are you for or against the ownership of guns? Are you against ownership of all types of guns or only handguns and automatic weapons? Do you want all guns or only certain types of guns to be registered. Do you wish to see ownership limited to certain people? Once you have clarified your purpose, think carefully through the clusters and the items and add, subtract, and change them as necessary to support your purpose and give a fair presentation of the other position. Do you need to do any research to add to your knowledge?

want to add more results, such as cities or other countries that have tried gun control legislation, or correlations between various controls and death rates. Often we find that we need to do some research to fill in data that we need to present a full position.

Prioritizing

Finally, we take the analyzed clusters and place them in an order; that is, we prioritize them. This is equivalent to roughing out an outline. For instance, how could we order the clusters above? Here are two possibilities:

    I. People: Who uses guns? Who kills? Who gets killed?
    II. Instruments: What kind of guns are we talking about?
    III. Results: What are the guns used for (the problem)?
    IV. Causes: Why do people fear guns or want guns?
    V. Solutions: What are possible ways to solve the problem?

    I. Causes
        A. Instruments
        B. People
    II. Results
    III. Methods

What are some other possibilities? Can you come up with another organization by changing the orders of the clusters? What determines the order? Can you see a relationship between the parts, a relationship that explains how that particular order coheres? Try to write out a "story" that links the parts together and demonstrates the prioritizing principle involved.

USING THE ORDERS

Now that we have a method to sort, select, and organize our ideas, let's apply this method to some of the natural and mental orders we discussed at the beginning of this chapter. For instance, look at this outline:

    I. Causes
        A. Instruments
        B. People
    II. Results
    III. Solutions

We can see that the outline has a *causal* order. The cause and effect are clear; the people and instruments are the causes and the results are the effects.

We use the *chronological* order when we want to tell what happened. If we want to tell the history of gun ownership or describe some incidents that occurred with or without guns, the chronological order fits fine. It is perhaps the earliest of the orders, for it tells a story. Much of the first recorded literature of ancient cultures (such as Gilgamesh and the Homeric poems) is in epic form, which is often a narrative describing the origin of the world and the human race. If we imagine a scene far earlier than the advent of writing, we can picture our ancestors around a fire telling a story of the hunt, of their injuries and the one that got away.

We use the chronological order often. Journalists, news broadcasters, and news magazine publishers live on it; investigators and prosecuting attorneys link guilt and innocence to it; researchers, archivists, and historians build their reputations on it; writers of business reports, how-to manuals, and economic forecasts make money from it; geologists, paleontologists, and archeologists rigorously search for it; and we—teachers and students—use it constantly. We use it when we answer questions such as, Where did you go? What did you do on your trip? What were the last three jobs you held? What schools did you go to? What are your plans?

Aristotle said everything has a beginning, middle, and end. Those basic, chronological parts fit the megastructure of most writings which have an introduction, body, and conclusion, but we do not always begin with the beginning. Movies frequently make use of flashbacks, and the epic writers as well as modern novelists often start *in medias res,* in the middle of the action. Often in our thinking we see the core of the idea and even the end before the beginning; as Pascal notes, "The last thing one settles in writing a book is what one should put in first" (Trotter, 1958, p. 7). In our writing this principle works well: write it first and then introduce what was written. Often our brilliant introduction comes to mind while we are writing the body of our discourse.

Our organizing method of clustering, analyzing, and prioritizing works quite simply with chronological order: stringing the data along a time line automatically clusters and prioritizes them. Our main thinking task then is to decide what to include and what to omit. We can turn to the chronological order often and with confidence because it is both a natural and a mental order, and it fits easily and naturally into what we already do well.

Analogical order, being both a natural and a mental structure, has a compelling power. We have looked at the force of analogies in the chapters on language and creativity and briefly at the beginning of this chapter. The first step of our organizing method, clustering, fits naturally with analogies. The process of clustering, or grouping similarities, uses the same insight contained in analogies: seeing likenesses. Likewise, the final step, prioritizing, superimposes an analogical structure upon the clusters; to do so, we have to call upon our creativity and mix ideas together until we see the new structure. For instance, Aristotle's beginning, middle, and end as the three parts of a discourse (introduction, body, conclusion) are analogous to a hook, arrow, and anchor. The hook, or the introduction, catches the attention of the audience, then the arrow delivers the message to the target audience, and finally the anchor firmly fixes the conclusion in the mind. A hook, arrow, and anchor is a powerful, analogical, memorable packaging of the chronologically first, second, and third.

Analogical structures have exerted power through the ages. Our youth and old age have been compared to spring and winter, to a sunrise and sunset; and the totality of our life has been compared to a five act play. Here's how two students used forest analogies to animate and structure their writings:

> I ran into the woods to chase her out of my mind. The last shimmering light glowed off the yellow, fall leaves. The landscape was intoxicating like a fine brandy. I sat silently, wandering the dark corridors of inner consciousness, reflecting on our past three years. The memories of her hung heavily on my heart. I sifted through them one last time, returned them to the dark corridors, and walked from the woods free.

*   *   *

> They had surrounded us. Tall silent wooden sentinels, protecting what was left of their world. They pointed their long bony broken fingers at everyone. And the wind cried for them.
>
> Their beautiful uniforms of green, gold, and orange, forever gone. No longer admired for their beauty, they hung their limbs in shame. No mask can hide the reality of their detestation. And the wind cried for them.
>
> The scorched earth pulled away from their feet, adding to their indignity. Their hold on life was gone. We looked, and shook our heads. And the wind cried for us all.

A structure built on an analogy will work for most communication situations. It is often worth our time to find a central analogy that fits the audience and then develop it. We can call such an analogy a "seminal structural analogy." This seedling analogy will grow a clear structure as we write, much like the acorn contains the DNA of the oak. Here is an example of the structuring power of a seminal analogy. Given the title, "My Emotional Mansion," a student wrote:

> You can drive by my emotional mansion but I'm sorry, you can't come in today. My walls are built of sturdy brick that stand too tall to get in or around. I have too much fear so I built these walls for my protection. What's inside that I want to hide? My fears, anger, and trust.
>
> My fears are in the first room as you would walk in, if only I would let you. The room is filled with sadness. Pictures of children with sadness in

their hearts. A lost puppy, curled tightly in a corner of the room. Gloom in the air, no sunlight is allowed in here.

If you were to have walked through the hall you would see a room set off to the right. It's locked most of the time for everyone's protection. That is my anger room. Many times of the day you can feel explosions vibrate through this room. No windows or lights needed. The flames from the burning pit are set in the middle of the room. Pots, pans, glasses, plates, books, all fly through the air from one side of the room to another. We will not go in there right now. You just might get hurt.

There is one more room. It's around the corner, down the hall, and to the left. This room has double glass windows with bars crossing the front. Three locks protect this room. Everything in it is locked and chained down. My furniture, my lights, and even a drinking glass has a chain around it. It's my trust room. As you can see I really trust everyone with all my possessions in this wonderful room of mine. I don't spend much time in here because I don't have to worry when no one else is here.

I did once have a happy room. It's somewhere here in my mansion but I guess I lost it. I remember that at one time I did spend a lot of time in here, but it's so long ago, I forgot where it's at and what it looks like.

So as I said, I'm sorry, you can't come in today.

This piece was written *ex tempore* in class in about ten minutes. It flowed out spontaneously in this form with only a few (corrected) misspellings. The writer produced it easily because the central analogy between the inner self and private house provided an appropiate structure. This house analogy taps the essential power of language and provides structural clarity and originality, and the emotions add an honest personal tone.

The effectiveness of analogical order is clear. It helps us to understand similarities and the differences. It draws on the analogical power existing in nature, which is reflected in our language and perhaps in the function of our mind, and it communicates forcefully.

THINKING ACTIVITY 8.5
Creating a Seminal Structural Analogy

If you want to try your response to the title "My Emotional Mansion" (which is almost guaranteed to produce great papers), begin by writing the opening line "Welcome to my emotional mansion." Then develop a different emotion in each room; for instance, the attic could be your thinking or private room, the basement your anger room, a locked closet your fear room, and so forth. On a blank piece of paper, begin writing rather rapidly without worrying about how the words come out.

Topical order works well with description. It too was probably developed prehistorically. We can again imagine our ancestors returning from a forage and describing some trees with huge globes of fruit that they found in a valley by a stream four hills away. Topical order aids description because objects and places have physical dimension. In describing an object or place we might move from top to bottom, right to left, north to south, little to big, and so forth. Topical orders are used by architects, surveyors, sculptors, astronomers, geologists, farmers, engineers, mechanics, bus drivers, community developers, truck drivers, and many others.

Students also use topical order when they wish to describe. Here is a student's descriptive paper that uses the topical method (along with some brilliant analogies). The topical order can be seen in the first two paragraphs.

Curtain Call

Over the lake the lightning was dancing across the black horizon. Sometimes it was just a quick little jig, other times it was a delicate waltz. It started at the northern end of the sky and jitterbugged its way towards center stage.

The rain stopped, but a heavy curtain of clouds still hung over the inky water. Bolts of electricity still flashed beyond the thunderheads.

Who had choreographed this brilliant display of power? Why had I gotten front row seats? Who else was in the audience, and were they also longing to leap out of their seats for a standing ovation?

A tribute was due, but to whom?

As with the other orders, we can apply the process of clustering, analyzing, and prioritizing to the topical order. If we are attempting to describe, say, a Colorado mountain campsite, we might cluster our list of details into trees, camping equipment, rocks, lakes and streams, mountain peaks, glaciers. We would then analyze what we wished to keep, add, delete, or change. Then we would prioritize our list, perhaps arranging the details of the scene from top to bottom: the mountain peaks, the snow, the rocks, the timber, the lakes and streams, our campsite, and our tent.

Like chronological order, topical order is fundamental; both time and space (place) are basic constructs of the world, of science, and of our thinking. Arranging things, ideas, and words in an orderly fashion allows our thinking to progress solidly and clearly.

SUMMARY

Some people find working with details and exact placement of parts exhilarating. Others find the task of organizing rather boring. For both of these groups this look at organizing our thinking can add satisfaction and excitement. We have searched for and found basic organizational patterns in the universe as well as in our mind. These strong orders are the chronological, analogical, causal, and topical. We have looked at these orders of time, space, analogy, and cause and have stressed choosing one of these orders rather than an arbitrary order whenever possible. We have also seen that there are powerful mental orders such as the scientific method and the five Ws of journalists; additionally, many other orders operate in specific professions. Finally, to deal with the data generated, we can apply our organizing method and cluster, analyze, and prioritize.

ORGANIZING CHALLENGES

1. What orders are found in the following?

   a formal speech
   a dictionary
   a library
   an encyclopedia
   a usual textbook

2. What kind of orders are found in a business that uses these items?

   card files
   data bases
   spreadsheets
   sales reports

3. Do you think your mind is born with organizing structures, or do you discover them, learn them, or create them?

4. How would you organize these items: lion cub, animal, horse, lion, wolf, cow, calf? Why? What were your principles of organization? How did you find those principles? Is another organization possible?

5. Can you develop other seminal structural analogies? Try substituting other words for "mansion" in "My Emotional Mansion." Then substituting words for "emotional." Try to develop one in your major field of study.

6. Why are the journalistic categories—who, what, where, when, and why—so useful? Could you use this pattern to organize a paper you might want to write?

7. Take two or three occupations you are interested in and try to identify some of the logical orders that operate within them.

8. Do any of the logical orders from one professional field also work in any other field? Can you identify the most useful orders or the master models?

9. What is the order of geometry?

10. When historians ask questions about an author's sources, dates, authenticity, and motives, what kind of orders are they using?

11. What is the major organizational principle for marketing?

12. When a real estate agent tries to price a house, what is the order behind the pricing?

13. What books do you know that are well organized? You might want to look at books by Thomas Aquinas and John Henry Newman as two thinkers who present their ideas with optimum structural clarity.

14. How do you use some of the basic orders in your life? Think about how you arrange your house, your work space, or your study area.

15. Are there domestic orders? In our dresser, where is that other sock?

16. We have stated that there is a causal order. The theory of chaos has received a great deal of attention in the sciences (see *Chaos* by James Gleick) and in a different form in the business world (see *Thriving on Chaos* by Tom Peters). Do some formal research in this area, or analyze your own experience. Do you experience chaos in the world around you? Is chaos contradictory to order?

9

Logical Thinking

If we reason it is not because we like to, but because we must.

—*WILL DURANT, THE MANSIONS OF PHILOSOPHY*

Thinking logically and identifying reasoning fallacies in one's own and in others' thinking is the heart of critical thinking. In this chapter we examine the basic rudiments of both deductive and inductive logic. We explore deductive logic primarily through its basic form, the syllogism, and look at various ways in which people err in deductive thinking. Deductive logic is then distinguished from inductive reasoning, which is presented with its own set of inductive thinking errors. Finally, we look at some other common reasoning fallacies. Because this chapter treats material that is at the very heart of thinking itself, we spend more time addressing this information. You will find this chapter to be longer and perhaps more difficult than the others. But patient effort will pay off handsomely in your ability to become a more careful and independent thinker.

DEDUCTIVE THINKING: THE SYLLOGISM

Deductive thinking is the kind of reasoning that begins with two or more premises and derives a conclusion that must follow from those premises. The basic form of deductive thinking is the syllogism. An example of a syllogism follows:

All massive bodies that circle a star are planets.
The earth is a massive body that circles a star.
Therefore, the earth is a planet.

Usually our thinking is not as formal as this but takes on a shorter form: "Because the earth is massive and circles the sun, it is a planet." To understand the logic behind our shortened thought, we need to understand the structure that supports it: the syllogism. A syllogism is a three-step form of reasoning which has two premises and a conclusion. (Premises are statements that serve as the basis or ground of a conclusion.) Not all syllogisms are alike. We will look at three types: the categorical, the hypothetical, and the disjunctive.

CATEGORICAL SYLLOGISMS

The classic example of a categorical syllogism comes from the philosopher Socrates. Updated for gender, it goes as follows:

MAJOR—All human beings are mortal.
MINOR—Ann is a human being.
CONCL—Therefore, Ann is mortal.

We can see that categorical syllogisms categorize. In the example above "human beings" are put in the "mortal" category. "Ann" is in the "human being" category. And in the last statement "Ann" is in the "mortal" category. If the first line of the syllogism above read, "Some human beings are mortal," then only some human beings would be in the "mortal" category.

A categorical syllogism is a form of argument that contains statements (called categorical propositions) that either affirm or deny that a subject is a member of a certain class (category) or has a certain property. For example, "Toby is a cat" is a categorical statement because it *affirms* that Toby (the subject) is a member of a *class* of animals called "cats." "Toby is brown" affirms that Toby has a *property* of brownness. Similarly, "Toby is not a cat" and "Toby is not brown" are categorical statements because they *deny* that Toby has the property of brownness and that Toby belongs to a class of animals called "cats." *All valid syllogisms must have at least one affirmative premise.*

In the standard form of a categorical syllogism, the major premise always appears first. It contains the "major" term (in this case "mortal"), which is the term that appears as the predicate in the conclusion:

MAJOR—All human beings are **mortal.**
MINOR—Ann is a human being.
CONCL—Therefore, Ann is **mortal.**

What is a predicate? It is simply the property or class being assigned to the subject in the last line. In our example above, the subject in the last line is Ann, and the property of Ann is that she is "mortal." If a syllogism concluded with the words "Robert is intelligent," then "intelligent" would be the predicate because in this sentence it is the property of the subject, "Robert." "Intelligent" is also the major term and would appear in the first (or major) premise:

MAJOR—Our students are **intelligent.**
MINOR—Robert is one of our students.
CONCL—Therefore, Robert is **intelligent.**

Let's look at the other parts of the syllogism and see how they combine to form a valid argument. The minor premise introduces the minor term (in our examples, "Ann" and "Robert").

MAJOR—All human beings are mortal.
MINOR—Ann is a human being.
CONCL—Therefore, Ann is mortal.

MAJOR—Our students are intelligent.
MINOR—Robert is one of our students.
CONCL—Therefore, Robert is intelligent.

The minor premise makes a connection between the minor term and the major term. It makes this connection through the "middle term," which then disappears in the conclusion:

MAJOR—All **human beings** are mortal.
MINOR—Ann is a **human being.**
CONCL—Therefore, Ann is mortal.

MAJOR—Our **students** are intelligent.
MINOR—Robert is one of our **students.**
CONCL—Therefore, Robert is intelligent.

The minor term then becomes the subject of the concluding premise:

MAJOR—All human beings are mortal.
MINOR—**Ann** is a human being.
CONCL—Therefore, **Ann** is mortal.

MAJOR—All of our students are intelligent.
MINOR—**Robert** is one of our students.
CONCL—Therefore, **Robert** is intelligent.

The diagram below summarizes the parts of the syllogism discussed in this section.

(middle term)
does not appear in conclusion
↓

major premise → All **human beings** are **mortal.**
↑
(major term)
appears as predicate in conclusion

(minor term)
is subject in conclusion
↓

minor premise → **Ann** is a **human being.**
↑
(middle term)
does not appear in conclusion

conclusion → Therefore, **Ann** is **mortal.**
↑   ↑
(subject) (predicate)

Three Kinds of Propositions

You may have noticed by now that some of the premises refer to all members of a class, as in "All humans are mortal." These kinds of propositions are called *universal propositions.* They may also take the obverse form, "*No* humans are *im-mortal*" or simply "Humans are mortal," when the statement implies "all humans." *All syllogisms must have at least one universal premise.* The syllogisms above have only one universal premise, but two universals are also allowed:

> **All** students are human beings.
> **All** people who attend classes are students.
> Therefore, all people who attend classes are human beings.

It is important to note that in modern logic, universal propositions do not imply that the subject actually exists—only that *if* the subject exists, it would have the characteristics of the predicate. Thus, "All dibberdillies are red" does not imply that dibberdillies exist, but only that if they do, they would be red. Of course, in our everyday use of logic, we usually know that at least one member of the subject exists, as in "All students are human beings."

The other two kinds of propositions are particular and singular. *Particular propositions* refer to *some* members of a class, as in "Some humans are female." In logic, *some* means "at least one." "Some humans are female" means that at least one human is female. In logic, *some* also leaves open the possibility that *all* members share the predicated characteristic. In other words, "Some dinosaurs were cold-blooded" leaves open the possibility that we might later find out that all dinosaurs were cold-blooded.

Singular propositions refer to only one member of a class. The statement "Robert is one of our students" is a singular proposition.

Four Figures

In the diagram on page 137, the middle term appears as the subject of the first premise and as the predicate of the second premise. This is one of four possible variations, or figures, of the categorical syllogism called figure one. In the other variations the placements of the major, minor, and middle terms are different. Therefore, we cannot, for example, identify the major term simply as the predicate of the first premise and the minor term as the subject of the second premise; this is not always the case, although the major term appears in the first premise as a general rule in writing syllogisms. The four figures of the syllogism are presented below. S stands for the subject of the conclusion (which is the minor term), P stands for the predicate of the conclusion (which is the major term), and M stands for the middle term (which never appears in the conclusion).

Figure 1:	M	P	All NBA players are people making a good salary.
	S	M	Jones is an NBA player.
	S	P	Therefore, Jones is a person making a good salary.
Figure 2:	P	M	All Christians are believers in God.
	S	M	No atheists are believers in God.
	S	P	Therefore, no atheists are Christians.
Figure 3:	M	P	Some teachers are wise.
	M	S	All teachers are educated people.
	S	P	Therefore, some educated people are wise.
Figure 4:	P	M	No basketball is a football.
	M	S	All footballs are things to be kicked.
	S	P	Therefore, some things to be kicked are not basketballs.

THINKING ACTIVITY 9.1
Drawing the Conclusion

In the following syllogisms only the premises are provided. Test your natural deductive thinking ability by attempting to draw the conclusion for each syllogism. You may not agree with the premises or with the conclusions, but given these

(continued)

THINKING ACTIVITY 9.1 (continued)
Drawing the Conclusion
premises, what conclusions follow? For some of these syllogisms there is no conclusion that can be derived from the premises. Later, you learn ways to analyze a syllogism to make a task like this one easier. For now, consider it a fun activity.

1. All theories that are not good are theories that will be abandoned.
   Some ethical theories are theories that are not good.
   Therefore,   .

2. No nonhuman animals are moral creatures.
   All furry creatures are nonhuman animals.
   Therefore,   .

3. Some sports enthusiasts are people who love football.
   All sports enthusiasts are conscious creatures.
   Therefore,   .

4. All dillies are bobbers.
   No thingamajigs are bobbers.
   Therefore,   .

5. No human being is a person who is perfect.
   All highly creative beings are human beings.
   Therefore,   .

6. All galaxies have stars.
   Some stars have planets.
   Therefore,   .

7. All nature's creatures are creatures that have a right to live.
   All fetuses are nature's creatures.
   Therefore,   .

8. No creatures without a brain are creatures that can experience pain.
   Only creatures that experience pain are creatures that have a right to life.
   Therefore,   .

9. Some books are things that are full of information.
   Some things that are full of information are worth reading.
   Therefore,   .

10. All mean people are creatures that are not pleasant.
    Only creatures that are not pleasant are creatures that will be disliked.
    Therefore,   .

THINKING ACTIVITY 9.2
Finding Terms and Figures

Identify the major, minor, and middle terms for each syllogism below. Then go back and identify the figure for each syllogism.

(continued)

THINKING ACTIVITY 9.2 (continued)
Finding Terms and Figures

   1. No cute creatures are creatures that have scary faces.
      Some rodents are cute creatures.
      Therefore, some rodents are not creatures that have scary faces.

      Major term: _____
      Minor term: _____
      Middle term: _____
      Figure no: _____

   2. Some Americans are patriotic citizens.
      All Americans are people who love apple pie.
      Therefore, some people who love apple pie are patriotic citizens.

      Major term: _____
      Minor term: _____
      Middle term: _____
      Figure no: _____

   3. No cloudy days are cherished days.
      All rainy days are cloudy days.
      Therefore, no rainy days are cherished days.

      Major term: _____
      Minor term: _____
      Middle term: _____
      Figure no: _____

   4. All people are mortal.
      No angels are mortal.
      Therefore, no angels are people.

      Major term: _____
      Minor term: _____
      Middle term: _____
      Figure no: _____

   5. All human beings are self-conscious creatures.
      All self-conscious creatures are creatures that fear dying.
      Therefore, some creatures that fear dying are human beings.

      Major term: _____
      Minor term: _____
      Middle term: _____
      Figure no: _____

Validity of Categorical Syllogisms

All of the syllogisms above are valid (except for some of those in Activity 9.1). By *valid* we mean that the argument, which is the reasoning from premises to a conclusion, is accurate. Arguments can be valid or invalid, but not true or false (only premises and conclusions are true or false). An argument can be valid even if it contains false premises and a false conclusion. Conversely, it is possible to have an invalid argument with true premises and a true conclusion. Let's examine these possibilities in the following syllogisms.

> All men are intelligent.
> Andy is a man.
> Therefore, Andy is intelligent.

In the above syllogism the major premise is false because not all men are intelligent. Nonetheless, the syllogism is valid because the reasoning is correct: *if* the premises were true, then the conclusion would have to be true. In this way a valid syllogism can yield a false conclusion.

It is important to note that the conclusion of a valid syllogism with false premises could still be true, but coincidentally, and not because of the premises:

> All redheads are aggressive.
> Mary is a redhead.
> Therefore, Mary is aggressive.

The above syllogism is valid, but the first premise is obviously false. And if Mary happens to be an aggressive blonde, instead of a redhead, then both of the premises are false and yet the conclusion would coincidentally be true.

Let's now look at a syllogism that is invalid but has true premises and even a true conclusion:

> Some animals are brown.
> All dogs are animals.
> Therefore, some dogs are brown.

In this syllogism each premise is true and the conclusion is true, yet the syllogism is invalid; the argument is not constructed so that the conclusion can be derived from the premises.

The goal of a good thinker is to develop syllogisms that have both true premises and validity. When we have a valid syllogism with true premises we have what is called a *sound argument*. In sound arguments the conclusion *must* be true—and therein lies the beauty and usefulness of the syllogism.

THINKING ACTIVITY 9.3
Identifying Valid Categorical Syllogisms

There are many valid forms of categorical syllogisms. They are often expressed using the letters X, Y, and Z. These letters are substitutions for syllogistic expressions about subjects, properties, and classes. For example, "No X are Y" would be the expression for "No rich ladies are drivers of Ford Pintos." Carefully examine the four forms of categorical syllogisms below. Which ones do you think are valid?

1. Some X are not Z.
   All X are Y.
   Therefore, some Y are not Z.

2. Some X are Z.
   All X are Y.
   Therefore, some Y are Z.

3. No X are Y.
   All Z are X.
   Therefore, no Z are Y.

4. Some Z are X.
   No X are Y.
   Therefore, some Y are not Z.

THINKING ACTIVITY 9.4
Using Venn Diagrams

One way to test the validity of a syllogism is to diagram the two premises. If the syllogism is valid, then the conclusion is found in the diagram of the premises. If the conclusion is not evident in the diagram, the syllogism's conclusion cannot be supported by the premises and the syllogism is deemed invalid. A good way to diagram a syllogism is to use the system developed by John Venn. A Venn diagram uses three intersecting circles, one for the subject (S) of the conclusion (the minor term), one for the predicate (P) of the conclusion (the major term), and one for the middle term (M), which does not appear in the conclusion. To practice this technique, we will use the following simple syllogism:

No cats (M) are dogs (P).
Some animals (S) are cats (M).
Therefore, some animals (S) are not dogs (P).

(continued)

THINKING ACTIVITY 9.4 (continued)
Using Venn Diagrams
Begin by drawing the three circles in the following manner:

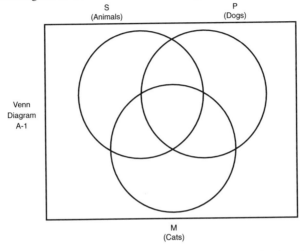

Shading an area of a circle means that there are *no* entities in that shaded area or classification. Therefore, we would illustrate the first premise, "No cats are dogs," by shading out the space shared by the cat and dog circles, as in diagram A-2. This indicates that there are no cats that are also dogs.

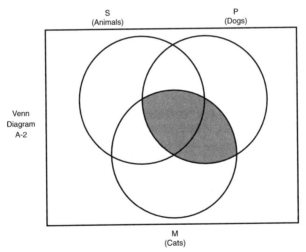

Placing an X in an area means that there is at least one entity in that class; the X is used to represent particular statements. The X cannot be placed in a shaded area because it would lead to a contradiction. Thus, we would diagram the second premise, "Some animals are cats," as in diagram A-3.

(continued)

THINKING ACTIVITY 9.4 (continued)
Using Venn Diagrams

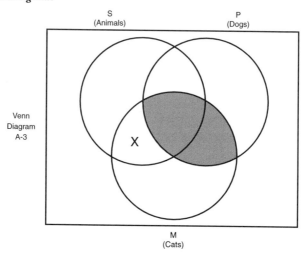

Venn
Diagram
A-3

Now we look to see if the conclusion, "Some animals are not dogs," is represented in our diagram. In this case we find an X in the animal circle and outside the dog circle, indicating that there are some animals (which are cats) that are not dogs. Because the conclusion is represented in our diagram of the first two premises, our syllogism is valid.

Sometimes when we diagram particular statements, the X could go in either of two areas. In that case we put the X on the line dividing the two areas, which means that in at least one of those areas there is an entity, but we don't yet know in which one. Diagramming the following syllogism illustrates this process.

Some fortunate people are wealthy.
All fortunate people are earthlings.
Therefore, some earthlings are wealthy.

The first premise, "Some fortunate people are wealthy," is diagrammed by putting an X in the space shared by the two circles representing "fortunate" and "wealthy." But since that space is divided into two sections, and since we do not yet have enough information to tell us in which section(s) the X should go, we place it on the line, as indicated in diagram A-4, indicating that there is an entity in at least one of the adjacent areas.

(continued)

THINKING ACTIVITY 9.4 (continued)
Using Venn Diagrams

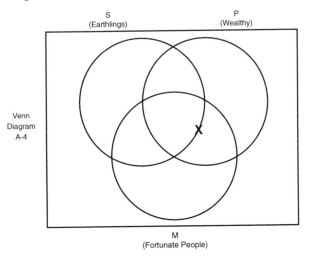

Venn
Diagram
A-4

S
(Earthlings)

P
(Wealthy)

M
(Fortunate People)

The second premise, "All fortunate people are earthlings," leads us to shade in one of those areas. We are then forced to put the X in the only alternative space left, as shown in diagram A-5.

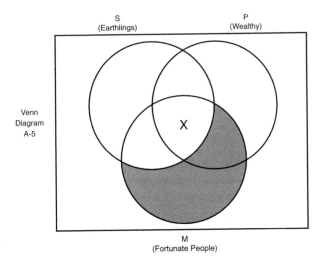

Venn
Diagram
A-5

S
(Earthlings)

P
(Wealthy)

M
(Fortunate People)

Checking the conclusion, "Some earthlings are wealthy," we find it expressed in our diagram. Thus the syllogism is valid. But remember, a Venn diagram only illustrates the validity of a syllogism; it does not test the truthfulness of its premises.

(continued)

THINKING ACTIVITY 9.4 (continued)
Using Venn Diagrams

Let's look at one more example, this time using an invalid syllogism:

All college students are brilliant people.
Some elderly people are college students.
Therefore, all elderly people are brilliant people.

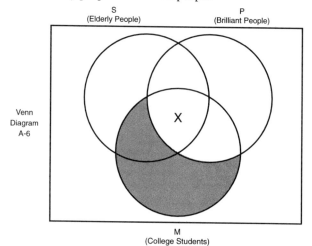

S
(Elderly People)

P
(Brilliant People)

Venn
Diagram
A-6

X

M
(College Students)

In Venn diagram A-6 we diagram the first premise, "All college students are brilliant people," by shading out portions of the college student circle so that all college students must fall in the brilliant category. (Remember, an area that has been shaded has no entities.) The second premise, "Some elderly people are college students," is indicated by placing an X in the only area that allows for elderly people to also be college students. We can now see that our syllogism is *not* valid. The conclusion of the syllogism, "All elderly people are brilliant people," is not apparent in the diagram. If it were, the largest area of the elderly people circle, the area that allows for elderly people to be outside the brilliant people circle, would be shaded. Since it is not, it leaves open the possibility that some elderly people exist outside the brilliant people circle.

We must be careful when diagramming syllogisms that have a conclusion that is particular but premises that are universal. Some of these syllogisms are valid, but X, which usually indicates particular statements, will not appear in the diagram. However, a careful look at these diagrams will show that if we assume that the subject of each universal premise exists, then the conclusion will be found in the diagram if the syllogism is valid. Try diagramming syllogism 5 in Thinking Activity 9.2, which is an example of this kind of syllogism.

Now diagram syllogisms 1–4 in Thinking Activity 9.3 to check your assessment of which are valid and which are not.

ENTHYMEMES AND SYLLOGISMS IN EVERYDAY LIFE

We use categorical syllogisms all the time, but often they are in a shortened form called an *enthymeme*. An enthymeme is a syllogism with an implied premise or conclusion, one that is not explicitly stated. Consider the following: "I'm a minority, so I'll never get this job." We have one premise (I'm a minority) and one conclusion (I'll never get this job). The missing premise is "No minority will get this job." The implied syllogism looks like this:

> No minority will be a person who will get this job.
> I am a minority.
> Therefore, I am not a person who will get this job.

Let's look at some more examples of the complete syllogism that is implied in the shorter enthymeme:

> "He's the president, so he deserves respect!"
>> All presidents are people who deserve respect.
>> He is a president.
>> Therefore, he is a person who deserves respect.

> "We trust you; you're a teacher."
>> All teachers are people who can be trusted.
>> You are a teacher.
>> Therefore, you are a person who can be trusted.

> "He's a dentist. I'll bet he's got a lot of money!"
>> All dentists are people who have a lot of money.
>> He is a dentist.
>> Therefore, he is a person who has a lot of money.

When enthymemes and their missing premise are laid out in a formal syllogism, we can more clearly see any thinking errors that may be occurring. For example, in the syllogisms above, we can see that the premises containing the word "all" are not true.

Using enthymemes is common. And if they are stated in the order of premise and then conclusion, the implied syllogism is not difficult to see. But in colloquial speech our premises are often hidden, and we sometimes state conclusions first, and then we state our premise or premises. This can make the underlying syllogism more difficult to find. Let's consider some examples of syllogisms hidden in common language:

ANDREW: That new manager at Wal-Mart is hard to work for. Maybe I ought to think about quitting my job there and moving on.

MARK: I thought you said yesterday that you looked forward to working with someone new. Besides, I didn't think you had met the new manager yet.

ANDREW: I didn't. But someone said it's a woman who has been hired for the position, and you know how women are.

This argument takes the following syllogistic form:

All female managers are hard to work with.
   (All X's are Y's.)
The new manager is a female.
   (Z is an X.)
Therefore, the new manager is hard to work with.
   (Therefore, Z is a Y.)

We should note that although the above syllogism is valid, because the conclusion is derived from the premises, the conclusion cannot be considered to be conclusively true because at least one of the premises is not true. In this example, the major premise that states that all female managers are hard to work with is based on an erroneous stereotype.

Sometimes our deductive thinking involves more than two premises and one conclusion. In these cases we can generally form additional syllogisms, with the conclusion of one syllogism serving as a premise for the next one. To illustrate how common arguments have more than one premise and form two or more syllogisms, consider the following argument:

ISAAC: I'd be worried about living next to those new neighbors of yours.

ROBERT: Why is that?

ISAAC: They're the kind that make noise, rough stuff, you know? I mean, you could even get shot!

ROBERT: Isaac, what are you talking about?

ISAAC: Didn't you see them? Their car! Their clothes! The car has got to be twenty years old. And their clothes look like they came from the seventies. Are you blind? They're obviously on welfare. Yea, I'd move if I were you. Can't trust that bunch!

The first syllogism in the above argument goes as follows:

All people who drive old cars and wear old clothes are on welfare (premise 1).
Robert's neighbors drive an old car and wear old clothes (premise 2).
Therefore, Robert's neighbors are on welfare.

We have made one categorical syllogism out of the above argument. But the argument continues to assert that these people are dangerous. The way the argument proceeds is by making the conclusion of the first syllogism the minor premise of the next syllogism:

> All people on welfare make noise, engage in rough behavior, and shoot people (premise 3).
> Robert's neighbors are on welfare (premise 4 and conclusion above).
> Therefore, Robert's neighbors will make noise, engage in rough behavior, and shoot people.

The above argument has four premises and forms two syllogisms with two premises and one conclusion each. For the final conclusion to be conclusively true, all premises in both syllogisms must be true. In this example premise 1 is false, which forbids the conclusion of the first syllogism from being conclusively true. Because this conclusion has questionable truth value and is also the fourth premise, the fourth premise could easily be false. Of course, the third premise is certainly false, expressing nothing more than an inaccurate stereotype. Only one premise would have to be false for the final conclusion of this argument to be false. In this case there are actually two or three false premises.

Let's look at one more example of hidden, multiple syllogisms in common parlance:

JOB INTERVIEWER 1:	Tony's our next candidate.
JOB INTERVIEWER 2:	You can interview this guy. It's a waste of my time.
JOB INTERVIEWER 1:	Why do you say that? Do you know something I don't? His resume looks okay.
JOB INTERVIEWER 2:	Look at his school record.
JOB INTERVIEWER 1:	Came from a good school. Straight A's.
JOB INTERVIEWER 2:	Yea, straight A's—a regular geek.
JOB INTERVIEWER 1:	What's that got to do with anything?
JOB INTERVIEWER 2:	Geeks don't work out here. We've tried 'em before.

The first syllogism in the above conversation attempts to argue that Tony is a geek. It does so through an enthymeme. The missing premise is "Everyone who got straight A's is a geek." The first syllogism takes this form:

> Everyone who got straight A's is a geek.
> Tony is a person who got straight A's.
> Therefore, Tony is a geek.

The last sentence in the conversation is not a conclusion, but a premise in the second syllogism: "Geeks don't work out here," meaning "Geeks don't work out in this company." When we add the conclusion of the first premise, "Tony is a Geek," we get the second syllogism with the final conclusion.

Geeks don't work out in this company.

Tony is a geek.

Therefore, Tony won't work out in this company.

Again, even though the two syllogisms are valid, the final conclusion *may* be false if we can find an erroneous premise in either syllogism. If "geek" means a strange and eccentric person, then the first premise in the first syllogism can certainly be challenged.

THINKING ACTIVITY 9.5
Finding Multiple Syllogisms and False Premises

In the following discussion there are three categorical syllogisms leading to the conclusion that Ellen deserves what she gets. Can you find them? Are there any false premises in these syllogisms?

SANDY: Say, I heard that your neighbor Ellen lost all her money to some con artist. Is that true?

CAROLYN: Yes, poor girl. Fifty years of savings down the tube like that!

SANDY: Did they catch the person?

CAROLYN: No, I guess they haven't got a clue. She'll never see her money again.

SANDY: Oh well, I wouldn't feel too sorry for her. She's so naive, you know; she deserves it!

CAROLYN: I don't know why you say that. Just because someone gets taken in by a con artist doesn't mean that they are necessarily naive.

SANDY: I agree, but she does belong to that cult located outside of town, doesn't she?

CAROLYN: Yes.

SANDY: Well, . . . like I said, naive! And if you ask me, naive people deserve what they get.

CAROLYN: How do you figure that?

SANDY: Look, Carolyn, the way I figure it, people become naive by their own choices. They choose not to work hard in school, not to read the papers, not to catch the news. These are choices they make and, quite simply, people should be held responsible for their choices. They deserve what they get—that's all.

CAROLYN: Mmmm. I see. But I still feel sorry for Ellen.

SANDY: Have it your way, but I still think she deserves what she gets!

SOFT DEDUCTIONS

We have seen above that one requirement for a valid syllogism is at least one universal premise which explicitly states or implies the word "all" as in "All humans are mortal." In a lot of our deductive thinking, however, we do not use a universal premise, but use terms like "generally" or "most" instead of "all," as in "Most physicians are wealthy." Such premises do not form classic syllogisms, and they do not provide conclusions that are absolutely true. Intead, they form *soft deductions,* but we can use them in deductive thinking as long as we are aware of their limitations. Let's examine one example:

> Most physicians are wealthy.
> Wanda is a physician.
> Therefore, Wanda is probably wealthy.

As in a classic syllogism the conclusion cannot be considered absolutely true if either of the premises is false. So one can first analyze this kind of thinking by considering the truthfulness of the premises. If the premises are determined to be true, then one will get a conclusion of *probability* only. Moreover, this conclusion must be put in proper context; it must be measured against any other information we have about the terms in our deduction. For example, if we know that *young* physicians are not wealthy and we know that Wanda is a young physician, then the conclusion, "Wanda is probably wealthy" must be discounted, even though both premises are true.

Whenever possible we can strengthen our deductive argument by adding critical adjectives and qualifiers, such as "older," "married," "in love," and so on. Watch the progression in the strength of the following deductions as we move from general to more specific premises.

> Most people are happy.
> Reggie is a person.
> Therefore, Reggie is probably happy.

> Most married people are happy.
> Reggie is a married person.
> Therefore, Reggie is probably happy.

> Most married people who are in love are happy.
> Reggie is a married person who is in love.
> Therefore, Reggie is probably happy.

We can still discount the conclusion in the last argument if we have other critical information. If, for example, unemployed people are typically not happy and we know that Reggie is unemployed, then the conclusion that Reggie is probably happy would be weakened. The advantage to making premises with qualifiers is that it leaves open fewer possibilities for weakening the conclusion. In the first argument above, we could weaken the conclusion by pointing out that Reggie was unmarried, and in the second argument the conclusion could have been challenged by someone who knew that Reggie was not in love with his wife.

Even if the conclusion cannot be discounted or weakened because of other critical information we may have, the conclusion must be interpreted in the correct way. Consider the argument concluding that Wanda is probably wealthy because she is a physician. In fact, Wanda is either wealthy or she isn't. There is no such thing as anyone being probably wealthy. A conclusion of probability simply means that for those of us who do not know the true state of affairs, we would more likely be correct if we make an assumption in the direction of the conclusion than not, assuming other known information we have does not weaken the conclusion. In other words, we are more likely to be correct in assuming Wanda is wealthy than in assuming she is not.

In interpreting the conclusion, we must be careful not to interpret "probably" to mean "highly probable" or "most likely." Let's take an obvious example:

> Most dogs are mongrels.
> Ladybird is a dog.
> Therefore, Ladybird is probably a mongrel.

How much money would you bet on Ladybird being a mongrel? Probably not much. The conclusion does not mean that there is a high probability that Ladybird is a mongrel, especially if there are only a few more mongrels than purebreds. The chances of Ladybird being a purebred might be almost as good as Ladybird's chances of being a mongrel.

We can get conclusions that have high probability if our premise states "almost all" instead of "most." "Most" means more than half, but "almost all" means just that.

> Almost all Christians will celebrate Christmas.
> Sandy is a Christian.
> Therefore, Sandy will probably celebrate Christmas.

In this example "probably" means "very likely," but it still does not mean "certainly." And in truth Sandy will either celebrate Christmas or she will not. If we know that Sandy is bedridden and living alone, with no living relatives and no friends nearby, then the conclusion is substantially weakened.

Besides the word "most," many people use the term "generally," which is subject to the same interpretations and cautions as "most." In the premise "Generally, men will open a door for a woman," "generally" seems to mean "most of the time" and might mean "almost always." Without knowing how to interpret the term we are left with only the equivalent of "most men" and without a conclusion of high probability.

We can test the validity of soft deductions by eliminating "generally" and "most" and replacing them with "all." If the syllogism is not valid with "all," then the softer deduction is not valid either. Consider:

> All ambassadors are political friends of the president.
> Andy is a political friend of the president.
> Therefore, Andy is an ambassador.

If we diagram this syllogism we will find it to be invalid. Therefore, the argument would also be invalid if the term "all ambassadors" was replaced with "most ambassadors." But this general replacement rule only applies to arguments that have only one premise that is weakened with such words as "most" and "generally."

When two premises are stated with such qualifiers the argument will not be valid. To illustrate, consider the following argument with two weakened premises:

> Most dogs are mongrels.
> Most mongrels live long.
> Therefore, most dogs live long.

Imagine that there are only fifty dogs in the world; thirty of them could be mongrels and the first premise would be true. Of the thirty mongrels eighteen could live long and the second premise would be true. But that would mean that only 18 dogs out of 50 live long, which is contrary to the conclusion. In this way we can see that such arguments are not valid.

Remember, in a true syllogism there must be one universal premise. Even though we can make softer and valid deductive arguments using "most," "generally," and "almost all," these are not technically syllogisms and should not be seen as exceptions to the rule requiring a universal premise in a syllogism.

THINKING ACTIVITY 9.6
Challenging Soft Deductions

For each of the following arguments, try to think of some critical information that could weaken or discount the conclusion. How could the argument be expressed to eliminate the weakness?

1. Generally, women prefer men of high status.
   Celestina is a woman.
   Therefore, Celestina probably prefers men of high status.

2. Generally, Toyotas are very reliable cars.
   Tony drives a Toyota.
   Therefore, Tony probably drives a reliable car.

3. Almost all people want to live.
   Carlos is a person.
   Therefore, Carlos probably wants to live.

4. Almost all Americans speak English well.
   Chavela is an American.
   Therefore, Chavela probably speaks English well.

5. Most Americans believe in God.
   Siddhartha is an American.
   Therefore, Siddhartha probably believes in God.

6. Almost every person will eat a chocolate chip cookie if offered one at lunchtime.
   Penelope is a person.
   Therefore, Penelope will probably eat a chocolate chip cookie if offered one at lunch time.

REASONING ERRORS IN CATEGORICAL SYLLOGISMS

Now that we have seen the basic logic of syllogisms that underlies our common arguments, let's look at some errors in thinking that violate this logic and render the conclusions worthless.

Undistributed Middle

In a categorical syllogism the middle term (the one not mentioned in the conclusion) must be distributed at least once:

All B are C.
All A are B.
Therefore, all A are C.

To distribute a term means to comment on all of the members of the term. In the first premise above, "All B are C," the term B is distributed. If we say, "Some B are C," the term B is not distributed because we are not talking about all the members of B, only some of them. If the middle term of a syllogism is not distributed, the argument commits the fallacy of the undistributed middle:

All C are B.
All A are B.
Therefore, all A are C.

At a quick glance this syllogism might seem to make logical sense. But if we add real terms, the fallacy becomes apparent:

All public buildings are air-conditioned.
All schoolhouses are air-conditioned.
Therefore, all schoolhouses are public buildings.

Here the middle term B, or "air-conditioned," is undistributed. If the second premise read, "All air-conditioned buildings are public buildings," then the term "air-conditioned" would be distributed and the argument would be valid. We should note that in the above syllogism the term "air-conditioned" is the predicate, not the subject, of both premises. In positive universal statements, which both of these premises are, the predicate is considered undistributed. When we say, "All schoolhouses are air-conditioned," we know for sure only that *some* air-conditioned buildings are schoolhouses. There is no statement about *all* air-conditioned buildings; thus "air-conditioned" is undistributed.

In a negative universal statement, such as "No public buildings are air-conditioned," both predicate and subject are distributed. Essentially we are making a statement about all public buildings, that none of them is air-conditioned, and about all air-conditioned buildings, that none of them is a public building.

It is obvious that subjects of particular statements, such as "Some A are B," are not distributed, but what about their predicates? In *positive* particular propositions the predicate is not distributed. Thus, "Some birds are flying creatures" does not distribute "flying creatures" because it does not say anything about *all* flying creatures; we can gather from this statement only that *some* flying creatures are birds, though this statement allows for the possibility that all of them are. With *negative* particular propositions, however, the predicate is distributed because these propositions refer to the entire predicate class. For example, "Some birds are not flying creatures" means that the *entire* class of flying creatures is excluded from *some* birds.

A singular proposition, such as "Socrates is a man," distributes its subject because the subject is the entirety of its class; there is no such thing as "some Socrates."

Here are two more examples of the undistributed middle:

Some women are lawyers.
All people seeking abortion are women.
Therefore some people seeking abortion are lawyers.

Some people under a lot of stress are not intelligent.
All married people are under a lot of stress.
Therefore, some married people are not intelligent.

Think About It: *Is any term distributed in the proposition, "Only human beings are creative thinkers"? If you have difficulty with this question, read "Valid Conversions" beginning on page 168 for a hint.*

Illicit Process

Illicit process occurs when a term is distributed in the conclusion but not in a premise. The fallacy of illicit process has two variants: illicit major and illicit minor. The error of *illicit major* occurs when the major term is distributed in the conclusion but not in the premise:

Illicit Major

All X are Y. (Notice that Y is not distributed.)
No Z are X.
Therefore, no Z are Y. (Notice that Y is distributed.)

The above syllogism may appear logical, but actually no conclusion can be made from the two premises; Z may or may not be Y. If we substitute common expressions for the terms, we can see the mistake:

All dogs are four-legged creatures.
No cats are dogs.
Therefore, no cats are four-legged creatures.

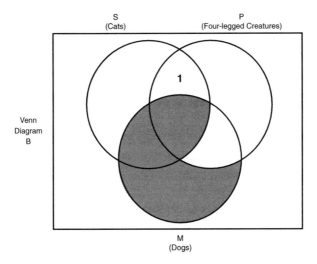

Area 1 of the diagram shows that there is a possibility that some
cats are four-legged creatures. This possibility contradicts
the conclusion of the above syllogism.

Unfortunately, many people succumb to this logical error. Five examples
are given below:

All Christians are people who believe in God.

No Moslems are Christians.

Therefore, no Moslems are people who believe in God.

> (In fact, they do. *Problem:* "People who believe in God" is distributed in the con-
> clusion, but not in the premise.)

All Catholics are baptized people.

No Lutherans are Catholics.

Therefore, no Lutherans are baptized people.

> (In fact, they are. *Problem:* "Baptized people" is distributed in the conclusion
> but not in the premise.)

All full-time university professors are college graduates.

No full-time carpenters are full-time university professors.

Therefore, no full-time carpenter is a college graduate.

> (In fact, many are. *Problem:* "College graduate" is distributed in the conclusion
> but not in the premise.)

All diets rich in meat fat are unhealthy diets.

No vegetarian diet is rich in meat fat.

Therefore, no vegetarian diet is an unhealthy diet.

> (In fact, some may be deficient in protein or other essential nutrients. *Problem:*
> "Unhealthy diet" is distributed in the conclusion but not in the premise.)

All divorced women are previously married people.
Sally is not a divorced woman.
Therefore, Sally is not a previously married person.
  (Sally could be a widow. *Problem:* "Previously married people" is distributed in
  the conclusion, but not in the premise.)

The other form of illicit process, *illicit minor,* occurs when the subject of the conclusion (the minor term) is distributed in the conclusion but not in the minor premise:

Illicit Minor

All X are Y.
Some Z are X. (Notice that Z is *not* distributed.)
Therefore, all Z are Y. (Notice that Z is distributed.)

All alcoholics are unhealthy.
Some women are alcoholics.
Therefore, all women are unhealthy.

Of course, the conclusion should read, "Therefore, *some* women are unhealthy." The mistake is that the term "women" is distributed in the conclusion but not in one of the premises. The argument would be valid if the second premise above read, "All women are alcoholics." In that case the term "women" would have been distributed in one of the premises as well as in the conclusion.

In this example it is easy to see the logical error; in fact, in most cases the logical error is quite obvious when the argument is stated in the formal syllogistic form. But in casual conversation, these logical errors often go unchallenged. Consider the following conversation:

BETSY: Say, Sally, I just had to call you. I just read this article about people who beat their spouse. God, it's awful. There's this one lady who used to be a model until her husband disfigured her. Now she's on AFDC and can't get a job. She says she's so depressed she just wants to die. Sally, how could someone do that?

SALLY: I know what you mean, Betsy. They're just scum. Nothing but scum— anyone who would do that to their spouse, to anyone for that matter. Pure scum, I say.

BETSY: That happened to Sharon, you know. Her husband did her in good— real good. I mean, she couldn't work for a week. Said she had a cold. Yea, right. Everyone saw the bruises when she finally came back. I didn't say anything though. Not like some.

SALLY: Men are scum, Betsy. Pure and simple.

BETSY: You got *that* right.

Although Sally and Betsy might feel angry toward those two husbands, they have generalized from two cases to all cases. While we might not know any men who are "white knights," we probably know a few gray ones, and certainly many men who are not scum.

The argument above takes the following form:

All people who beat their spouse are scum.
Some men are people who beat their spouse.
Therefore, all men are scum.

THINKING ACTIVITY 9.7
Finding Undistributed Terms

Circle the undistributed terms below that should be distributed. Then, to the left of each syllogism identify whether it is an example of undistributed middle (UM), illicit minor (IMI), or illicit major (IMA).

_____ 1. Some men are more intelligent than most women.
            Andrew is a man.
            Therefore, Andrew is more intelligent than most women.

_____ 2. Some thingamajigs are watchamacallits.
            All dillybobbers are thingamajigs.
            Therefore, some dillybobbers are watchamacallits.

_____ 3. All muscular men are narcissists.
            No wimp is a muscular man.
            Therefore, no wimp is a narcissist.

_____ 4. Some brilliant people are not wise.
            Some Democrats are brilliant.
            Therefore, some Democrats are not wise.

_____ 5. All people who believe in God will be saved.
            Martha does not believe in God.
            Therefore, Martha will not be saved.

_____ 6. All saved people will experience eternal joy.
            Only people who believe in God will be saved.
            Therefore, all people who believe in God will experience eternal joy.

_____ 7. Some U.S. citizens have the capacity to be president.
            All students in this class are U.S. citizens.
            Therefore, some students in this class have the capacity to be president.

The Four-Terms Fallacy

A valid syllogism has only three terms. The major and minor terms connect through the middle term. Because the middle term has linked both major and minor terms, the conclusion can connect the major and minor together. If four terms are introduced, the conclusion is invalid. An example of an invalid four-terms syllogism is as follows:

> All alcoholics are ill.
> Bill is someone who drinks alcohol.
> Therefore, Bill is ill.

There are actually four terms in the above argument. The major term is "ill," the minor term is "Bill," and then there are two middle terms "alcoholics" and "someone who drinks alcohol." Because one can drink alcohol without being an alcoholic, these two terms are separate. Thus we have four terms and an invalid argument. Let's look at one more example:

> All academics are egotists.
> Susan is someone who works in a university.
> Therefore, Susan is an egotist.

The four terms in the above argument are "academics," "egotists," "Susan," and "someone who works in a university." Someone suggesting the above argument would be equating "academic" with anyone who "works in a university." But this is a false identity because many people who work in universities, such as cooks, custodians, and security guards, are not academics. Thus there are four terms, not three, and the syllogism is invalid.

Equivocation

Sometimes the four-terms fallacy occurs when we give two meanings to the same word, fail to recognize the distinction, and treat the word as one term. When this occurs, the fallacy of equivocation has been committed (as well as the four-terms fallacy). In such an argument, the conclusion cannot be derived from the premises:

> Everything that is good is right.
> Using drugs feels good.
> Therefore, using drugs is right.

In this example the term "good" has two meanings; it is equivocal. It is first used to denote a moral quality, and second to denote a sense of pleasure. Thus, there are actually four terms in the syllogism, rendering it invalid.

Notice the equivocal term "love" in the following discussion:

> SALLY: Mark says that he loves to go to work more than anything.
> JOHN: My God, does his wife know that?
> SALLY: She's the one who told me.

> JOHN: It must be awful to know that Mark doesn't love her as much as his work. What did she say?
>
> SALLY: She doesn't seem bothered by it at all. Pretty dense, I'd say.
>
> JOHN: Definitely.

Mark's wife may not be dense. She probably understands that love has different meanings and that the term "love" used by Mark to describe his feelings about his job is different from when he uses it to describe his feelings about another person. Sally and John make the mistake of perceiving "love" to have one meaning.

In disjunctive syllogistic form (to be discussed later) Sally's and John's argument could be described as follows:

> Either Mark loves work more than anything else or he loves his wife more than anything else.
>
> Mark said he loves work more than anything else.
>
> Therefore, he doesn't love his wife more than anything else.

This makes no more sense than stating:

> Mark loves apple pie more than anything else or he loves his wife more than anything else.
>
> Mark said he loves pie more than anything else.
>
> Therefore, he doesn't love his wife more than anything else.

When the term "love" has two meanings, as in this argument, it makes the disjunctive either/or statement false, for it implies that one can have only one or the other alternative and not both, yet both are of course possible. One can love apple pie more than anything else and also love one's spouse more than anything else. The statements *seem* exclusive, but what they mean is that one can love pie more than any other food and love one's spouse more than any other person.

The Importance of Agreed Meaning

When the terms of a syllogism are not clearly defined or when people disagree about the meaning of the terms, the conclusion of the syllogism may be rejected or rendered ineffective. In Tolstoy's *The Death of Ivan Ilych,* for example, Ivan denies that the conclusion of a syllogism, that men are mortal, applies to him. Motivated by his fear of death, he attempts to do this by questioning the meaning of "man" as used in the first premise:

> Ivan Ilych saw that he was dying, and he was in continuous despair.
>
> In the depth of his heart he knew he was dying, but not only was he not accustomed to the thought, he simply did not and could not grasp it.

(continued)

The Importance of Agreed Meaning *(continued)*

> The syllogism he had learned from Kiezewetter's Logic: "Caius is a man, men are mortal, therefore Caius is mortal," had always seemed to him correct as applied to Caius, but certainly not as applied to himself. That Caius—man in the abstract—was mortal, was perfectly correct, but he was not Caius, not an abstract man, but a creature quite, quite separate from all others.

Clearly an argument, even as solid as a valid syllogism with true premises, is worthless if people do not agree on the meaning of the terms.

Because terms can be used to signify different meanings, it is important that they be properly defined to avoid confusion. If two people believe that all men are created equal, they may still be believing in two different things. What does it mean to say that all men are equal? Similarly, if two people believe in God, they could be believing in two different ideas. Therefore, it is almost imperative when someone asks the question "Do you believe in God?" to respond with "What do you mean by 'God'?" For until you know the meaning that person gives to the term, you cannot respond properly to the question.

RULES FOR THE CATEGORICAL SYLLOGISM

The following summarizes the basic rules for the valid categorical syllogism.

Structural Requirements

1. At least one affirmative premise ("All humans *are* mortal")
2. At least one universal premise (*"All* humans are mortal" or "*No* humans are immortal")
3. Exactly three terms

Logical Rules

1. If one of the premises is negative, the conclusion must be negative.
2. If both premises are positive, the conclusion must be positive.
3. If one of the premises is particular, the conclusion must be particular.
4. If one of the premises is singular, the conclusion must be singular.
5. The middle term must be distributed at least once.
6. A term distributed in the conclusion must be distributed in a premise.

Remember, even if a syllogism meets all these rules, if the premises are false, we cannot rely upon the conclusion.

THINKING ACTIVITY 9.8
Identifying Invalid Syllogisms

Identify the rule(s) which these syllogisms violate.

1. All communists are mortal; no Baptist is a communist; therefore, no Baptists are mortal.
2. Some people are Republicans; some gentle creatures are people; therefore, all gentle creatures are Republicans.
3. No schoolhouses are made of wood; no people live near schoolhouses; therefore, some people are living near brick homes.
4. All good people attend church regularly; all Catholics attend church regularly; therefore, all Catholics are good people.
5. All people are liars; all liars are guilty; therefore, all people are sinners.
6. All Democrats care about the poor; all people who care about the poor are Democrats; therefore, no Democrat cares about the wealthy.
7. Some vegetarians live longer than average; Alan eats vegetables; therefore, Alan will live longer than average.

HYPOTHETICAL SYLLOGISMS

If you prick us, do we not bleed? if you tickle us do we not laugh? if you poison us, do we not die? and if you wrong us, shall we not revenge?

—SHAKESPEARE, MERCHANT OF VENICE

Much of our thinking in everyday life is hypothetical. This kind of thinking takes the "if-then" form. The angry employee states, "If I have to work one more night, then I will quit!" The student faced with an exam might think, "If I fail this test, then I will fail this class. And if I fail this class, then I will not graduate this semester." And the frustrated parent reprimands a child in hypothetical language: "If you come home late one more time, then you will be grounded for the month!"

These hypothetical statements can be put in syllogistic form. A *pure hypothetical syllogism* is one in which the two premises and the conclusion are hypothetical, or *conditional;* that is, they take the form of if-then statements. The "if" statement is called the *antecedent,* and the "then" statement is called the *consequent:*

If P, then Q.
If Q, then R.
Therefore, if P, then R.

If my neighbor waters his lawn, then my basement will leak.

If my basement leaks, then my boxes will get wet.

Therefore, if my neighbor waters his lawn, then my boxes will get wet.

If I don't cut this credit card into pieces, then I'll have to file bankruptcy.

If I have to file bankruptcy, then I won't be able to buy a house for many years.

Therefore, if I don't cut this credit card into pieces, then I won't be able to buy a house for many years.

Not all hypothetical syllogisms are pure, having three hypothetical statements. Some of them are mixed. In a *mixed hypothetical syllogism* only the major premise takes the if-then form; the other premise and the conclusion are categorical. There are positive (*modus poems*) and negative (*modus tollens*) mixed hypothetical syllogisms. A positive mixed hypothetical syllogism takes this form:

Positive

If P, then Q.

P.

Therefore, Q.

If God is dead, then there's no hope for anyone.

God is dead.

Therefore, there is no hope.

If I get a raise, then we can take a vacation.

I got a raise!

Therefore, we can take a vacation.

If the stock market falls, then it will be a thin Christmas.

The stock market fell.

Therefore, it will be a thin Christmas.

Notice that the minor premise affirms the antecedent P, in the major premise, and thus *affirms* its consequent, Q.

A negative mixed syllogism *denies* the consequent:

Negative

If P, then Q.

Not Q.

Therefore, not P.

If it rains, then the streets will be wet.

The streets are not wet.

Therefore, it did not rain.

If I am poor, then I am not happy.

I am happy.

Therefore, I am not poor.

Because the proposition "If P, then Q" means that whenever there is P there will be Q, we can deny P by denying Q. However, this last example may be confusing because the second premise appears not to be a denial; that is, "I am happy" seems to affirm, rather than deny, something. On closer inspection, however, we can see that it is in fact a denial of the consequent, "I am not happy."

Reasoning Errors in Hypothetical Syllogisms

Denying the Antecedent

A common error in thinking is to deny the antecedent in a mixed hypothetical syllogism. We have already seen the valid form of the mixed hypothetical syllogism (*modus tollens*), which denies the consequent:

> If P, then Q.
> Not Q.
> Therefore, not P.
>
> If the sun dies, the earth will become barren.
> The earth is not barren.
> Therefore, the sun did not die.

Now watch what happens when we deny the antecedent:

> If P, then Q.
> Not P.
> Therefore, not Q.
>
> If the sun dies, the earth will become barren.
> The sun did not die.
> Therefore, the earth is not barren.

Again, the difference is that the valid syllogism denies the consequent of the first premise (Q), whereas the invalid argument denies the antecedent (P).

We can validly deny the antecedent in a hypothetical syllogism *if there is a qualification:* "If P, then Q" must be understood as "*if and only if* P, then Q." It is true that if the sun dies the earth will become barren. But it may also become barren through nuclear war or some other disaster. Therefore, the conclusion that the earth will not become barren if the sun does not die is invalid unless the major premise is qualified or understood as "If and only if the sun dies will the earth become barren." Here are some other examples of denying the antecedent:

> If it rains tonight, then the grass will be wet tomorrow.
> It did not rain.
> Therefore, the grass will not be wet.
>   (Dew could make the grass wet if it doesn't rain.)

If I lead a decadent life, then I will have a tumultuous life.
I did not lead a decadent life.
Therefore, I did not have a tumultuous life.

> (Even good people are victims of circumstance and are forced into a tumultuous existence.)

If he hits me, then he does not love me.
He doesn't hit me.
Therefore, he loves me.

> (Obviously, one may not hit and not love at the same time.)

If I do not study hard, then I will not pass.
I studied hard.
Therefore, I passed.

> (Studying hard does not always lead to a passing grade.)

Affirming the Consequent

Another logical error related to the syllogism occurs when we affirm the consequent of the first premise instead of its antecedent. A valid positive hypothetical syllogism affirms the antecedent:

If P, then Q.
P.
Therefore, Q.

But sometimes people argue in the following invalid manner by affirming the consequent:

If P, then Q.
Q.
Therefore, P.

If I walk to the store, then I will be tired this evening.
I am tired this evening.
Therefore, I walked to the store.

In the above example, it is possible that one could be tired in the evening even if one did not walk to the store. Therefore, being tired does not mean that one necessarily walked to the store. The conclusion cannot be assumed to be correct. However, if the statement read, "If and only if P, then Q," it would be valid to argue in this manner.

The two logical errors above concern only hypothetical (if-then) syllogisms, and they serve to remind us that we can only affirm an antecedent and deny a consequent—not the other way around.

DISJUNCTIVE SYLLOGISMS

A third kind of syllogism is the disjunctive syllogism, which uses "either/or" statements such as "Either the plane is in the air or on the ground." This kind of syllogism has two forms. The first disjunctive form (*modus tollendo poems*) denies one term in the minor premise and then affirms the other term in the conclusion. It looks like this:

Denial-Affirmation

Either P or Q.
Not P.
Therefore, Q.

Either the plane is in the air or on the ground.
The plane is not in the air.
Therefore, the plane is on the ground.

(Although this denial-affirmation pattern is valid in the disjunctive syllogism, we saw earlier that it is not valid in the hypothetical syllogism without qualification.)

A variant of this type of syllogism is to deny Q:

Either P or Q.
Not Q.
Therefore, P.

Either the plane is in the air or on the ground.
The plane is not on the ground.
Therefore, the plane is in the air.

The second form of the disjunctive syllogism (*modus poems tollens*) affirms one term in the minor premise and then denies the other term in the conclusion:

Affirmation-Denial

Either P or Q.
P.
Therefore, not Q.

The preacher will read either from Matthew or from Mark.
The preacher read from Matthew.
Therefore, the preacher did not read from Mark.

In this form we can also affirm Q and deny P:

The preacher will read either from Matthew or from Mark.
The preacher read from Mark.
Therefore, the preacher did not read from Matthew.

This affirmation-denial form, or *mood,* of the syllogism is valid only if P and Q are seen as exclusive of each other, that is, where P and Q cannot both occur. As we will see below, sometimes people make the mistake of creating an either-or proposition in which they use "or" in the exclusive sense when in fact it is nonexclusive.

Think About It: *Is the disjunctive statement "Either P or Q" equivalent to "Either Q or P"?*

Reasoning Error in the Disjunctive Syllogism

Affirming a Nonexclusive Disjunct

Sometimes the disjunctive syllogism uses "or" in a *nonexclusive* manner. Consider the following examples:

> Either Karen went to the store or she went to the bank.
> Karen went to the store.
> Therefore, Karen did not go to the bank.

> Either Bob starts showing up to work on time or he will be fired.
> Bob started showing up to work on time.
> Therefore, Bob will not be fired.

It is possible that Karen went to the store *and* went to the bank. And it is possible that Bob started showing up to work on time but was fired for another reason. In these cases, some might argue that the either-or propositions were false disjuncts. Nonetheless, people use "or" in this manner frequently and then by affirming one, they attempt to deny the other. To affirm one of the disjuncts in the first premise and therefore deny the other is to commit the fallacy of *affirming a nonexclusive disjunct,* unless the two disjuncts cannot both occur. (For further clarification of the truth value of premises using "and," "or," and if-then statements, see the appendix on propositional logic.)

VALID CONVERSIONS

You may have noticed by now that many of the premises of a syllogism can reverse their predicate and subject with no loss of meaning. This process is called *conversion.* For example, the statement "No X is Y" ("No Republican is a Democrat") can be converted to "No Y is X" ("No Democrat is a Republican") without loss of meaning. Similarly, "Some X is Y" ("Some computers are malfunctioning machines") can be converted to "Some Y are X" ("Some malfunctioning machines are computers").

Two other propositions that are convertible, with proper changes, are "All X is Y" and "Some X are not Y." We must be careful about these last two, for their conversions are not simple reversals. If we say, for example, "All X are Y" ("All model T's are black cars"), we cannot say "All Y are X" ("All black cars are model T's"). Nor, to further illustrate, can we convert "All very intelligent creatures are human" to "All humans are very intelligent creatures." Obviously this is false. What we can do with "All X are Y" is convert it to "*Some* Y are X," or "*Some* humans are very intelligent creatures." Another legitimate conversion of this proposition is "*Only* Y are X" ("*Only* humans are very intelligent creatures"). However, unlike the conversions above, the conversion of "All X are Y" to "Some Y are X" does not lead to an equivalent proposition. We have gone from a universal statement to a particular statement (from "all" to "some") and have lost some of the import of the original statement. Moreover, because a universal statement does not mean that a member of the subject class actually exists, and because "some" means that at least one member of the subject *does* exist, this conversion is possible only when we know that there are members of the subject class, in this case, when we know that at least one X exists. The Venn diagram below illustrates the logic of the two conversions of "All X are Y."

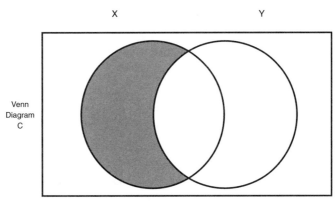

From "All X are Y"
it is true that "Only Y are X"
and (if X exists) "Some Y are X."

One must also take precaution with the example "Some X are not Y," for it is not valid to convert "Some X are not Y" to "Some Y are not X." The "not" must go with the Y. To say, "Some lawyers (X) are not rich people (Y)" is not the same as saying, "Some rich people are not lawyers." Even though in this case the conversion is a true statement, it does not follow logically from its conversion and for this reason it is invalid.

Let's apply the same logic to another example to illustrate more clearly the invalidity of this conversion. Consider the true statement "Some human beings (X) are not great thinkers (Y)." This cannot be converted to "Some great thinkers (Y) are not human beings (X)." This conversion leads to a false statement because only human beings can be great thinkers. Thus, converting "Some X are not Y" to "Some Y are not X" is not a valid maneuver, even though sometimes the conversion results in a true statement. The truth of such statements is not derived logically from the conversion but is known by experience. The statement "Some humans are not fast runners" converts (invalidly) to "Some fast runners are not humans." We know through our experience with animals that this conversion happens to be true, but we do not know it from logic. For example, it is possible to imagine a time on earth when the fast nonhuman animals have become extinct. If that would happen, then the conversion of "Some humans are not fast runners" to "Some fast runners are not humans" would result in a false statement. Thus it cannot be logically derived.

The valid conversions of categorical statements are listed below:

1. No X is Y → No Y is X
   (No girl is a boy → boy is a girl)

2. Some X are Y → Some Y are X
   (Some cats are black creatures → Some black creatures are cats)

3. All X is Y (assuming X exists) → Some Y is X
   (All model T's are black things → Some black things are model T's)
   All X is Y → Only Y are X (All model T's are black things → Only black things are model T's)

4. Some X are not Y → Some not-Y are X
   (Some animals are not humans → Some not-humans are animals.)

There are many invalid conversions, and it would only be confusing to list them all. However, one popular invalid conversion deserves special mention: the conversion of a hypothetical (conditional) statement. It is not valid to convert "If P, then Q" to "If Q, then P." Consider the statement "If Jack wins the lottery, then Jack will be very happy." Its conversion is "If Jack will be very happy, then Jack will win the lottery." Unfortunately for Jack, this conversion is not logical. If all of this sounds familiar, it's because the conversion is nothing more than a variation of affirming the consequent, an invalid maneuver described above. The invalid syllogism that expresses this example is:

If Jack wins the lottery, then Jack will be very happy.
Jack is very happy.
Therefore, Jack won the lottery.

THINKING ACTIVITY 9.9
Writing Valid Conversions

Write a valid conversion for the following propositions.

1. Only in politics can people make a significant contribution to their country.
2. All mathematicians are introverts.
3. No human being is a saintly person.
4. Some wealthy people are not stingy.
5. Some fathers are gentle creatures.
6. Some celestial bodies are not planets.
7. Only creatures with a brain can have a mind.
8. Some atheists are not evil.
9. All homosexual people support gay rights.
10. All people who own guns oppose gun control.

INFORMAL DEDUCTIVE FALLACIES

We have examined the different reasoning errors associated with each kind of syllogism. Other reasoning errors are not directly related to syllogisms but are still errors in deductive logic. We explore three of them below: the fallacy of division, circular reasoning, and the either/or fallacy.

The Fallacy of Division

People who have never visited the United States might erroneously assume that all citizens of the United States are rich. Their reasoning commits the *fallacy of division,* which is the attempt to argue that what is true of the whole (the United States) is true of its parts (its citizens). There are, of course, many instances in which the parts do share characteristics with the whole, but this is not because of logical necessity. There is no logical rule that allows us to make such deductions. To say that a minority group in the United States is oppressed does not allow us to conclude that each and every member of that minority group is oppressed.

We must be careful not to confuse this issue with universal propositions. From the statement "All animals are sentient creatures" we can assume that each and every animal is a sentient creature. But this is because "All animals are sentient creatures" means the same thing as "Each and every animal is a sentient creature." But "All cars are heavy objects" does not mean the same thing as "All parts of cars are heavy objects." Because the car as a whole is different from the parts that make it up, we cannot conclude for logical reasons that any of its parts are heavy. Consider the nature of the human being: a human is a totality that is far more complex than any of our human parts. The sodium and potassium ions of our nervous system, for example, do not seek God, love, knowledge, and apple pie. (See "Fallacy of Composition," page 185, for the opposite of this fallacy.)

Circular Reasoning

> *In his book,* What Social Classes Owe to Each Other *(1883), sociologist William Graham Sumner . . . argued that the upper classes deserve their privilege because the mere fact of having it demonstrated their greater fitness. The main problem with this argument is that it is circular and thereby true by definition: If we accept the idea that wealth is a valid measure of fitness, then by definition the wealthy must be more fit than everyone else.*
>
> —A. JOHNSON, HUMAN ARRANGEMENTS: AN INTRODUCTION TO SOCIOLOGY

Circular reasoning, also called "begging the question," is an error in deductive logic in which a person's conclusion is already assumed to be true in one of the premises or, more simply, when a person's conclusion is simply a reformulation of the premise. If we say, "The Bible is the word of God because it says so right in the Bible," we have engaged in circular reasoning. That the Bible says that it is the word of God is important only if it is already assumed to be the word of God, yet that is what one needs to prove.

The longer the circular statement, the easier it is to forget about where we began. When circular statements or arguments are short, it is not very difficult to spot them. We are most vulnerable to accepting circular reasoning, either our own or others', when the argument is more lengthy and the propositions are more numerous.

The Either/Or Fallacy

The either/or fallacy has also been called the all-or-nothing fallacy, black-and-white fallacy, and false dilemma. In the disjunctive syllogism we saw a deductive argument that had as its first premise an either/or statement. We showed that if the two alternatives are exclusive of each other, we can affirm one and deny the other, or vice versa. This is valid. However, if the first premise is not an accurate representation of the situation, then the syllogism, although valid, may yield a false conclusion. It is important that the first premise be a true statement. In other words, when setting up the either/or condition, all possibilities must be accounted for in the statement or the conclusion may be false.

Specifically, the *either/or fallacy* is the portrayal of a complex situation in simplistic either-or terms, not acknowledging that (1) both alternatives could be true, (2) gray areas exist between the two alternatives, or (3) other possibilities exist. It is one thing to state that John either failed or passed the test, and another to state that the

United States Congress is either good or bad. The former statement is a true disjunctive statement, as one cannot both pass and fail at the same time. But, in the latter example, we have an either-or fallacy, for parts of the United States Congress might be good for the country, whereas other dimensions of it might be bad. It might, for example, be good for our country's relationships with other countries but bad for our country's domestic economy. Or it could be good for many people, but bad for many other people, and so on. In this example, a complex state of events is reduced to simplistic alternatives. In reality, the United States Congress is probably both good and bad, yet the disjunctive statement implies that it is either good or bad but not both.

The either/or fallacy is also committed when there are gray areas between the alternatives. Consider the statement "Tom is either a heterosexual or a homosexual." This statement fails to recognize the continuum that exists between the two alternatives. It is possible that Tom is bisexual; that is, he is heterosexual most of the time, but engages in homosexual behavior from time to time.

Oftentimes people present us with either/or options when other options are available. This ploy is often used by salespersons. To motivate a customer to buy a product, a salesperson might say, "The sale ends tonight, so either you buy it this evening, or you'll end up paying full retail price for it. I'd hate to see that happen." What the salesperson leaves out are the many other options: you could wait until the next sale at this store, you could choose not to buy the product altogether, you could go to another store, you might find it in a wholesale catalog, you might be able to bargain with the store manager later, you could possibly get a deal later by asking the salesperson to give up some of the commission, you could buy a cheaper alternative that's not on sale, and so forth.

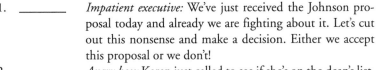

THINKING ACTIVITY 9.10
Identifying the Either/Or Fallacy

The either/or fallacy is committed when someone sets up a disjunctive proposition that does not allow for all of the options. Of the statements below, identify the ones that commit the either/or fallacy. Write "yes" in front of those that do and "no" in front of those that do not commit the fallacy.

1. _____ *Impatient executive:* We've just received the Johnson proposal today and already we are fighting about it. Let's cut out this nonsense and make a decision. Either we accept this proposal or we don't!

2. _____ *Angry boss:* Karen just called to see if she's on the dean's list. Will you get back to her quickly, please. Either she is or she isn't. It's that simple.

(continued)

THINKING ACTIVITY 9.10 (continued)
Identifying the Either/Or Fallacy

3. _____ *Same angry boss:* Say, is that colleague of yours a pretty bright guy? In other words, would he be good for the company if I offered him a job? *Answer:* Well, yes and no. *Reply:* "Yes and no!" What kind of answer is that? Either he is or he isn't!

4. _____ *Mad scientist:* Is there life on Mars? Or are we alone in the universe?

5. _____ *Parent to daughter:* Does your boyfriend believe in God? Or is he an atheist?

6. _____ *Chauvinist:* Are we going to have a good time fishing this weekend? Or are you bringing your wife along again?

7. _____ *New parent:* Is it a boy or a girl?

8. _____ *Philosopher:* Either each of us lives on eternally after death or we each give up our lives forever. To affirm one is to deny the other.

Reductio ad Absurdum

A deductive argument can be attacked by pointing out that the conclusion or premise of the argument leads to an absurdity or contradiction. This approach to disproving an argument is called *reductio ad absurdum*. For example, consider a speaker arguing the following:

> Mind is nothing but the cause-and-effect process of our physical brains. Freedom, my friends, is an illusion. All your thoughts, behaviors, and feelings are nothing but the effect of complicated cause and effect interactions.

A *reductio ad absurdum* argument attacking this position might go as follows:

> Mr. Speaker, you say that all thoughts are nothing but cause-and-effect interactions and therefore we are not truly free. If that is so, then even your thoughts about thoughts are not free and your statements about our lack of freedom are only cause and effect productions. Yet, you come here today to share with us this information which has taken years of study and reflection as though you have come to it freely, as though it reflects truth, as though you have something objective and absolute to offer us. Perhaps you should have prefaced your speech today with a notation that you could not help but come here, that we could not help but attend, that you could not help but discover what you discovered, and that you believe what you're saying to be true because you can't help but believe it to be true. And then you should say that your helplessness in believing is a mere product of cause and effect—and so is this insight, and so on.
>
> And then, Mr. Speaker, at the end of all your qualifying statements, which you cannot help but qualify, we will have listened to nothing but the

(continued)

Reductio ad Absurdum *(continued)*

conclusions of your physical brain, the simple effect of untold causes. And, because we cannot help it, we will treat it with amusement, and nothing more, not unlike the story of Alice in Wonderland or Pooh and the Honey Bear. And if you take offense at us for this disrespect, at least do not blame us, for we'll have had no choice, as you say, to have done otherwise.

This *reductio ad absurdum* argument challenges the proposition that thoughts are nothing but the effect of myriad causes by reducing the proposition to absurdity, or at least to a position that the speaker would not, or could not, accept. It forces the speaker, in this case, to either reject his proposition or to refine it so it cannot be reduced to absurd consequences.

INDUCTIVE THINKING

In the previous section, on deductive thinking, we learned that valid deductive thinking begins with at least one universal premise and leads to a conclusion that is believed to be contained in the argument's premises. Indeed, if the premises are true and the argument form is valid, the conclusion must be true. The universal statement in a syllogism allows us to move from a proposition about an entire class to a statement about some or all members of a class. In this section we look at arguments that move from a particular premise to a universal conclusion. Such arguments are examples of *inductive thinking*.

Inductive reasoning begins with a set of evidence or observations about *some* members of a class. From this evidence or observation we draw a conclusion about *all* members of a class. Because of this move from the particular to the general, the conclusions of good inductive reasoning *likely* or *probably* follow from the observation; they do not absolutely follow. By moving from the particular to the general, the conclusions of inductive reasoning are not logically contained in the premises. We can see this in the following inductive argument:

> Every day I notice that the sun rises in the east and sets in the west. Though I'll be dead in one hundred years, I know that my grandchildren will also see the sun rise in the east and set in the west.

In all likelihood the grandchildren will make the observations predicted. However, it is not necessarily the case. It could be, although it is unlikely, that the earth will encounter some cosmic matter or force that unsettles its rotation such that the sun rises in the north and sets in the south. The only way we will know for sure is to wait until the grandchildren observe the sun.

In inductive reasoning the premises of the argument consist of the evidence or observations from which we derive our conclusion. As in deductive arguments, these premises can be challenged. For example, if we see three black crows and conclude that all crows are black, someone could say, "Well, you saw them far away, didn't you? Don't you know that colors disappear with distance, and even if they were red they would have looked black to you?" Thus the observation is challenged. Science, which relies heavily on the inductive method, often faces challenges this way, as when someone points out that the results of a particular experiment are flawed because of poor experimental design (see chapter 10, "Scientific Thinking").

Often deductive arguments contain premises that are inductively derived. Consider the following:

> If the stock market crashes, then the suicide rate will rise.
> The stock market crashed.
> Therefore, the suicide rate will rise.

In this hypothetical syllogism, the first premise is really a conclusion of inductive reasoning: "Whenever the stock market crashed in the past, the suicide rate went up. Therefore, if the stock market crashes again, the suicide rate will go up." Many of the syllogisms we looked at earlier contain premises that are based on inductive reasoning. And as we learned, these inductive premises can often be challenged, thereby weakening the deductive argument.

Inductive reasoning can also be challenged by finding evidence contrary to the conclusion. Let's go back to the evidence in our example with the black birds: "I saw three crows today and all of them were black." The conclusion is that therefore all crows are black. The conclusion of this argument would be refuted instantly if someone found a red or blue crow. Thus, the conclusions of inductive arguments, *even with true premises,* are always open to the possibility, however unlikely, that they are false, for they are statements of probability, not certainty. In contrast, the conclusion of a deductive argument cannot be false, given true premises and valid syllogistic form.

Consider the following inductive argument: "Because no other planet in the solar system has any signs of even the lowest form of life, we must conclude that we are the only intelligent creatures in the universe." Here the argument went from the particular "no life on any other planets in *our* solar system" to the general "no life on any other planets in *any* solar system." This conclusion can be disputed in several ways: we can attack the methods that have been used so far to search for life, that is, attack the observation; we can argue that the number of planets that we have observed is too small to justify a generalization to all planets; or we can actually discover life on another planet, a possibility that is not foreclosed by the inductive conclusion.

Discovering life on another planet would definitely refute the conclusion above. However, one commonly attacks the inductive argument with another inductive argument, that is, with evidence or observation that suggests a contrary conclusion. For example, astronomers have discovered planets revolving around nearby stars and can argue from this evidence that our planetary system is not unusual, that many or most stars have planets. Therefore, considering the billions of stars in each galaxy and the billions of galaxies in the universe, it is highly unlikely that life exists only on earth. This evidence of other planetary systems in our galaxy does not refute the previous conclusion that there is no life in the universe except on earth, but it certainly weakens it.

Given induction's apparent uncertainty, is there any such thing as a sound inductive argument? We have seen that sound deductive arguments are valid arguments with true premises and therefore conclusively true conclusions. Some philosophers, such as the skeptic David Hume, argue that there are no absolutely sound inductive arguments—that all inductive arguments fall short of yielding conclusions as certain as those in sound deductive arguments—but there are good practical inductive arguments. If the argument is based on repeated, accurate observations, and as we will see, if the analogies used are based on strong significant similarities rather than on weak ones, then the induction may be, practically speaking, rather solid. Such strong inductive arguments can be referred to as *sound* as long as we understand that their conclusions are not absolute, as they are in sound deductive arguments.

We use sound inductions every day; indeed, it would be difficult to live without them. Here are some examples:

1. Driving to work after a fresh snow we notice several cars in the ditch. Just after this observation we see a car ahead of us spin out of control. We conclude from these observations that the roads in our area are slippery because of the new-fallen snow. We slow down and drive very carefully the rest of the way to work.
2. We let our cat out of our house and notice that it runs behind a neighbor's garage. We let our cat out the next day and it runs there again. And on the third day our cat again runs behind our neighbor's garage. We conclude from these observations that our cat will run behind the garage upon being let out. We decide to talk to our neighbors to see if they mind if our cat roams on their property.
3. We are dropped off from work and wave our friend on before we open the door. We have the keys to the house and we know that we will be able to get in. We know this because our keys have worked in our lock hundreds of times before.

Conclusions of good inductive reasoning are highly probable, but never certain. In the above examples, the conclusions could have been wrong. Consider these possibilities:

1. The roads were only slippery along this stretch of road because a water main broke and the water froze under the snow. All other roads were just fine.
2. The cat went behind the neighbor's garage because the neighbor had some garbage from Thanksgiving Day back there, and the cat had a fancy for turkey. After the garbage was collected the cat was no longer interested.

3. We waved our friends on knowing that we had our keys and could get in. Unfortunately, the keys didn't work this time because the lock was broken.

THINKING ACTIVITY 9.11
Distinguishing Between Inductive and Deductive Arguments

Analyze the seven statements below for the kind of reasoning used. Place an "I" in front of the inductive arguments and "D" in front of deductive ones. Be careful that you do not confuse premises derived through induction with the inductive form of argument.

1. _____ Anything that questions the fact of its own existence must exist. I question the fact of my own existence. Therefore, I must exist.

2. _____ Every person who questions the fact of their own existence is depressed. Mary has recently been questioning the fact of her own existence. Therefore, Mary must be depressed.

3. _____ If a woman gets married, she will regret it. Sharon is getting married soon. Therefore, Sharon will eventually regret it.

4. _____ My friend is a very intelligent person but also quite neurotic. So, I think intelligent people in general, perhaps because they are so overdeveloped in their intelligence, must be underdeveloped elsewhere, leaving them with somewhat disturbed personalities.

5. _____ I have never won a thing in my life, and I never will. It's not in my karma.

6. _____ No human being lies all the time. Therefore, Mary does not, as you suggest, lie all the time—maybe a lot, but not all the time.

7. _____ No species on this planet has survived for more than 100 million years. The human race will be no exception.

THINKING ACTIVITY 9.12
Considering Past Errors

List examples of erroneous inductive reasoning that you have used in the past. Consider reasoning that you do at work, at home, and in your relationships. For each example, identify why your conclusions were wrong. Were they based on too few observations, or were the errors due to some very unusual circumstances?

(continued)

THINKING ACTIVITY 9.12 (continued)
Considering Past Errors

1. Example:_____

_____

    Reason for Error:_____

2. Example:_____

_____

    Reason for Error:_____

3. Example:_____

_____

    Reason for Error:_____

Think About It: *Are the conclusions of deductive arguments any more conclusive than inductive arguments if one or more premises of the deductive argument are the result of inductive reasoning?*

ANALOGICAL ARGUMENT

Analogical argument is a form of inductive reasoning that rests on the similarities between two things. In this kind of argument we reason that if A and B are similar in some features, then another feature of A will also be found in B, when it is unknown or uncertain if B has that feature. For example, one could give reasons why child neglect will inhibit a child's development, or one could say, "As a rose with too little water will fail to bloom, a child who receives too little love will fail to grow." The strength of this argument rests on the degree to which a child and a rose are similar. They are both living things requiring nourishment; they are both "born"; they both grow, flourish, and die; and they both depend on their environment for life and proper development.

The above analogy has a metaphorical element, the likening of a child to a rose. A more straightforward analogy is found in the following, which likens one tyrant to another:

We should remove this tyrant from his throne! Merely punishing him will be ineffective. Hussein was punished for his tyranny and all too quickly returned to terrorize and slaughter his enemies again.

The more similar A and B are to each other, the stronger the analogical argument will be. But even with few similarities, if the similarities are strong and compelling, the analogical argument can have force. The two examples above are reasonably good analogical arguments.

We have no foolproof test to determine which analogies are strong and which are not. However, the degree to which the similarities match and strike most people as appropriate and effective, as opposed to the degree to which the dissimilarities of the analogy strike most people as dissonant, is one way to gauge the analogy's effectiveness. No analogy can be used to "prove" something because no two things are identical in every respect. But one can consider the similarities and differences between the two elements being compared and accept those analogies in which the similarities are striking. It is reasonable to assume that if two things are known to have a lot in common, they may share other similarities as well.

Chuang Tzu's Analogies

Analogical argument has been in use for thousands of years. The Taoist philosopher Chuang Tzu, who lived in the fifth century B.C.E., used them copiously. In one of Chuang Tzu's stories Hsu Yu was offered the opportunity to rule the Chinese empire. Hsu Yu declined:

> When the Tailor Bird builds her nest in the deep wood, she uses no more than one branch. When the mole drinks at the river he takes no more than a bellyful. Go home and forget the matter, my Lord. I have no use for the rulership of the world! (Watson, 1968, pp. 32–33)

This analogy recognizes the similarity of the human being to other natural creatures. We find in nature that creatures take only what they need. If human beings are to live as nature intended, we too should take only what we need. Does this analogy work? Is it a good one? There are many differences between a human being and a Tailor Bird, but are those differences outweighed by the similarity that we share as creatures of nature?

Chuang Tzu uses another analogy, this time between the senses and understanding. Lien Shu chastises Chien Wu for his refusal to believe some remarkable tales about a sage:

> We can't expect a blind man to appreciate beautiful patterns or a deaf man to listen to bells and drums. And blindness and deafness are not confined to the body alone—the understanding has them too, as your words just now have shown (p. 33).

(continued)

Chuang Tzu's Analogies *(continued)*

Is the understanding sufficiently similar to the senses of sight and hearing that we can be convinced that it, too, can become "blind" and "deaf?" Would you consider one of these analogies to be better than the other?

THINKING ACTIVITY 9.13
Using Analogies

Using one or more analogies, try to make a brief argument for or against some of the most debated moral issues of our times, such as abortion, gun control, euthanasia, or capital punishment.

CAUSATION

One common use of inductive thinking in our everyday life is the search for causes. Discovering causes uses inductive thinking because it is based upon observations of particular events from which we then generalize to all similar events. For example, we conclude that lowering water temperature causes it to freeze because on prior occasions it has done so. Philosophers remind us that our conclusion about what causes a particular event is not based on logical necessity, as in a deductive argument, but upon experience. Therefore, our conclusion about a cause-and-effect relation does not necessarily follow from our observation; it only *probably* follows. In other words, experience cannot tell us what must be, but only what has been; it is possible to imagine otherwise.

Although in a strict, philosophical sense we may never be absolutely sure about what event causes another, it seems essential to living that we act in the world with confidence about our ideas concerning cause-and-effect relations. This confidence can be strengthened by understanding the different kinds of causes that exist for the different events we experience.

According to one typology, there are four main classes of causes: necessary cause, sufficient cause, necessary and sufficient cause, and contributory cause. A *necessary cause* is one that must be present for an event to occur, but its presence alone does not lead to the event. For example, for uncontrolled drinking to occur it is necessary that there be ready access to alcohol. But ready access to alcohol does not by itself cause uncontrolled drinking. A *sufficient cause* is one that by itself can bring about an event, such that whenever the cause is present the event occurs. A sufficient cause of an automobile's failure to start, for example, is an empty gas tank. However, this is not a sufficient and necessary cause of automobile failure because it is not necessary for an automobile to have an empty gas tank in order to fail. There are other causes of automobile failure. A *sufficient and necessary cause* is one that must be present to cause an event and is sufficient itself to cause the event. HIV is a necessary and sufficient cause of AIDS because one can get AIDS only through HIV, and HIV by itself leads to AIDS; no other factor also needs to be present.

The last category of causes is contributory cause. A *contributory cause* is not necessary for an event to occur and is not sufficient for an event to occur, but it helps to bring about the event, such that an event becomes more likely because it occurs. For example, the assassination of a president in a country already ridden with strife might contribute to a civil war. Such an event itself is not a necessary cause of the war nor a sufficient cause, but it adds more tension and hostility to a situation already aggravated and leaning toward conflict. Thus, one might want to say that the assassination led to the war, because the war followed soon after. In fact, however, the assassination may have been only a contributory cause, not the necessary cause of war and not a sufficient cause either.

THINKING ACTIVITY 9.14
Thinking About Causation

Cases abound in which one spouse's behavior toward the other motivates the other to abuse alcohol in an attempt to escape from an oppressive, physically abusive, or otherwise stressful situation. What kind of cause is this? Is the marriage a necessary cause, sufficient cause, necessary and sufficient cause, or contributory cause? Explore the kinds of causal relationships a marriage could have to a spouse's drinking problem. To what kind of cause are people referring when they say, "Her marriage led her to drinking"?

INFORMAL INDUCTIVE FALLACIES

When done well, inductive thinking gives us reasonable, although not absolute, conclusions that we live by. Unfortunately, considerable unsound inductive thinking also occurs. Below we look at some of the major kinds of inductive reasoning fallacies. If we can learn to avoid them, we will think more competently.

Hasty Generalization

A *generalization* is a statement about a class of objects or situations based on observation of *some* members of that class. All inductive thinking uses generalization as it moves from the particular to the general.

There are reasonable generalizations and there are hasty ones. A *reasonable generalization* is one that has a large enough sample to warrant an inference. For instance, if we randomly surveyed forty percent of the women in a small college about their attitudes toward men, we could reasonably assume that the results of our sample reflect the attitudes of women in general in that college. On the other hand, had we asked only a few women about their attitudes and concluded that all women at that college feel the same way, we would be making an error, specifically, a hasty generalization.

A *hasty generalization* occurs when a conclusion is drawn from a sample that is too small or in some way atypical. For example, a man who has one bad experience with a woman might conclude that all women are nothing but "users and losers." Or a student who has taken her first college course and encountered an egotistic teacher might conclude that all college teachers are egotists. It is easy to see how these hasty generalizations can fuel stereotypes. One bad experience with a person of another race, creed, or economic status might leave one concluding, "All those people are like that."

Hasty generalizations often occur in arguments between couples. In the heat of anger, a woman might accuse her partner of being a very selfish person because during the past year he acted selfishly a few times. Or a man might accuse his spouse, who occasionally forgets to do the dishes, of never helping in household chores. The accuser can easily remember the many times in which the dishes were not done but forgets or fails to notice the more numerous times that they were done. One might call this selective attention, noticing the bad and not the good. Nonetheless, the sample of cases on which the accusation is based is too small to warrant the conclusion.

There is no hard and fast rule that one can use to determine whether a generalization is reasonable or not; each case requires a different set of facts. It is even possible that one datum would be enough to form a generalization. If a woman suffers an attempted rape by her neighbor, for example, she shouldn't have to wait for a dozen or so experiences before she can conclude that the man is dangerous. Similarly, if a man wins a race far ahead of the other outstanding competitors, one wouldn't have to suspend judgment very long to conclude that the man is fast.

Post Hoc Ergo Propter Hoc

One of the more persuasive and powerful fallacies is *post hoc ergo propter hoc* ("after this, therefore, because of this"). Because a cause always precedes an effect, it is an easy fallacy to assume that if an event comes after X, it is therefore caused by X. Obviously this could be the case, but it certainly is not necessarily so; to assume such is to generalize well beyond what the data allow. It is true that if A causes B, then B follows A, but just because B follows A does not mean that A causes B.

Some associations are merely coincidental; the two things associated have nothing whatever to do with each other. The death of a parent, for example, might be followed by a son's divorce. It is illegitimate to argue, however, that the parent's death led to the son's marital dissolution simply because the dissolution followed the death. Many tragic events happen every day soon after sunrise, but we would not want to conclude that the rising sun caused the tragic events. Similarly, we could not legitimately conclude that a woman's marriage caused her drinking problem just because it started soon after she got married. There could be other causes of the drinking—a change in jobs, the death of a parent, conflict with colleagues at work, excessive school demands, and so forth—that just happened to coincide with her marriage.

Think About It: Post hoc ergo propter hoc *reasoning can be the source of much superstitious thinking. If one sees a black cat on the road and then soon after has a flat tire, one might conclude that seeing a black cat leads to some misfortune on the road. Do you have any superstitious behaviors or beliefs that were started because of this fallacy?*

Extravagant Hypothesis

We have just seen how people sometimes jump to conclusions about the causes of things just because one thing follows another. People jump to conclusions in yet another manner when they commit the *extravagant hypothesis* fallacy, which is the formulation of a complex or unlikely explanation for an event when a simpler explanation would do. A principle called "Ockham's razor" states that the simplest explanation for an event is to be preferred over a more complex one, so long as the simpler one is adequate. The principle of Ockham's razor has shown itself to be a good thinking principle over the centuries. As an example, compare Ptolemy's earth-centered system of the universe with Copernicus's sun-centered model. The former model is rather complex, whereas the latter is simpler. Scientific evidence has supported the simpler model.

As an example of an extravagant hypothesis, consider the following, somewhat common, experience:

> I went to bed last night at my usual time. My husband was already sleeping. I found I had no trouble going to sleep but something awakened me shortly thereafter. I know I was awake, but I was unable to move. I was paralyzed

and very frightened. I tried to call out to my husband but I couldn't. He was sound asleep, unaware of the trauma I was experiencing. As I was lying there paralyzed with fear I sensed a presence in the room. I can't tell you what they looked like, but it seemed like there were several creatures standing at the end of my bed. I felt helpless, and tortured with fear. After many minutes had passed, I was able to move again. I sat up in bed with acute anxiety, as I expected to see some small creatures, but they were gone.

Some people might believe that this experience is a visitation by UFO aliens who have arrived to abduct the paralyzed victim for a scientific examination—quite an extravagant hypothesis. Others see this as a simple case of "sleep paralysis," a common but often frightening nuisance that is often accompanied by hallucinations.

Commonly people imagine brain tumors instead of tension headaches or interpret an unfamiliar phone number on a piece of paper as evidence of infidelity instead of guessing it is the phone number of the dentist or some other innocuous person. People with hypochondriacal and paranoid disorders are especially vulnerable to creating wild hypotheses, but it is in no way restricted to them. Students who haven't been called on by their professor might assume that their professor dislikes them, whereas those who are called on more often might imagine a romantic interest. To the chagrin of some, the world is often simpler and duller than we imagine it to be.

False Analogy

A *false analogy* is one in which the similarities between the two things being compared are not enough to assume that other characteristics of the one apply to the other. Someone might argue, "Just as an apple tree under some stress bears more fruit than another tree that lacks for nothing, so too a woman under stress bears more children than one who suffers nothing at all." Obviously this analogy is false. The similarities between a woman and an apple tree regarding fertility are weak and superficial; the differences far outweigh any similarity.

The Fallacy of Composition

Similar to hasty generalization, the *composition fallacy* assumes that what is true of the whole's parts is true of the whole. Although it may often be true that characteristics of the parts are also characteristics of the whole, it does not logically follow that this is the case. For example, if we know that Allison is pleasant to be around and her husband Jeremiah is pleasant to be around, we cannot conclude that they are a nice couple to be around, for when they are together they might engage in competition with one another and become argumentative. As we can see from this example, the parts of a whole do not exist in isolation from each other; instead, they interact with one another. This interaction can create synergistic effects in the whole that are not shared by the individual parts. Twenty outstanding musicians may or may not create an outstanding orchestra, nor do a hundred great individuals necessarily make a great United States Senate. If you doubt this fallacy, add two soft ingredients, water and plaster of Paris, and see if you get a soft product.

Slippery Slope

Water slides are becoming increasingly popular in theme parks; they also exist with some popularity in our "thinking parks," although they have no place there. The *slippery slope* argument is fallacious reasoning which argues that, as on a water slide, once a person initiates an action, there is no stopping it until it hits bottom. This argument has been used, for example, by opponents of gun control laws. These laws generally aim at removing handguns and have no intention of eliminating hunting rifles, knives, and so forth. Nonetheless, it is not uncommon to hear a rebuttal to handgun control that sounds like the following:

> Sure, they want to take away our handguns. That's what they want now. But what are they going to want to take away next? Soon it will be our hunting rifles, next it will be our hunting knives. Soon we will have a police state in which only the oppressive government will own arms. Give them an inch today and they'll soon take a mile. In short, giving away our handguns is nothing less than giving away our freedom!

The erroneous assumption behind this argument is that each step between the removal of handguns and ultimate oppression is very small and thus there will be no stop to the action until all steps have been taken. In other words, the assumption is that one must inevitably slide from handgun control to severe oppression; there is no stopping in the middle. This argument often sounds quite convincing, but no logical necessity supports it. On innumerable occasions people do stop along the slippery slope and travel no further. Some people do stop at two drinks, and some do eat only a few potato chips.

Human relationships provide many occasions for slippery slope arguments. Sometimes a man and woman become uncompromising because of the fear that one compromise will lead to another until one person is eventually dominated entirely by the other, sometimes sliding down the slippery slope to a divorce.

The slippery slope argument holds human appeal, but logically it is fallacious. If it weren't, smokers would never quit, every drinker would become a drunkard, every sexual fantasy would lead to adultery, and every violent man would eventually rape and murder.

OTHER REASONING FALLACIES

The following reasoning fallacies are difficult to classify exclusively as errors in either deductive or inductive thinking. Nonetheless, they are common and egregious errors.

Appeal to Authority

> *The book that you are holding purports to give a description of the physical world.* Why do you believe what I tell you? *Because I am a professor of physical chemistry and have canvassed your vote?*
>
> —BRIAN SILVER, THE ASCENT OF SCIENCE

People sometimes justify their values and ideas by appealing to an authoritative source. This is not necessarily fallacious. In the complex world in which we live, no one can master all subjects. We consult our doctor about matters of health, our auto mechanic about our car, the child psychologist about child-raising practices, and so on. However, these people are not always correct in their judgments. Therefore, a belief that something is true because an expert said so is usually a good bet, but it is not necessarily true. Nonetheless, relying on experts is still prudent given our general lack of knowledge about most of what goes on around us.

Although appeal to authority is often reasonable for obtaining knowledge about the world around us, there are many instances in which it is abused. One such instance is the appeal to false authority, such as movie stars, athletic heroes, and prominent musicians when they are presented to us as authorities in areas well outside their fields.

Even appeal to legitimate authority is not without its problems. Consider the number of authorities in the fields of philosophy, physics, psychology, and so forth who disagree with each other on important matters within their field. Carl Jung and Sigmund Freud disagreed about the role of sexual motivation in human behavior. Both of them were authorities, both of them had brilliant minds, but at least one of them was very wrong!

Likewise, books, including this one, are not an absolute source of authority. Students in classrooms often appeal to a text to argue against their professor. The assumption is that if it's in the text, it is therefore more accurate than the professor's knowledge. Individuals write books, and these individuals are fallible.

Another kind of book to which people often appeal is the Bible. Some people consult their Bible for matters that are outside the authority of the Bible, such as matters of astronomy, health, and anthropology. These subjects are better left to astronomers, physicians, and anthropologists because the Bible has been shown to be unreliable in these matters when it is compared with scientific studies.

In sum, any time we appeal to an authority that is not a source of accurate information on a topic, we are engaging in an invalid appeal. And given the dissension among even legitimate authorities, we must be cautious in these appeals. Whenever practical, we must rely on the validity of the authority's arguments and the strength of the evidence presented, rather than on that person's word alone.

> ***Think About It:***   *Aristotle believed the heavens to be crystalline spheres, physicians used to engage in bloodletting, chemists used to practice alchemy, and church officials believed in witches who made pacts with devils. Can you think of other authorities who have been wrong?*

Appeal to Tradition

Tradition has a strong appeal. Traditions are rooted in family and corporate structures and in religious and political rituals. If those traditions are sound and healthy, and have proven successful in raising people or producing corporate products, they can be referred to as "tried and true" and should be kept ("if it ain't broke, don't fix it"). But because something has always been the case does not mean that it is right or appropriate now, or that it was ever right or appropriate. Appeal to tradition is an attempt to justify a practice or policy because it has "always" been that way. This is fallacious reasoning because innumerable instances can be cited of things having been traditionally done wrong. Moreover, given the changes in knowledge that science has brought us and the rapid cultural change that has taken place throughout the world in the last several decades, a position or idea that was once appropriate may be wholly inadequate now. For example, consider this argument: "A woman's place is in the home. That's the way it's always been, and that's the way it ought to be." Such an appeal to tradition will not sway the millions of women who would not return to a world that oppressed and subjugated women for hundreds of years.

One gentleman tried to return merchandise to a store for a cash refund. The store clerk refused, saying, "That's been our policy for thirty years." One could certainly argue that that's been a poor or unfair policy for thirty years. (It certainly resulted in the loss of at least one customer.) As another example, a man was having some remodeling work done on his home. The owner questioned some unorthodox practices of the builder, only to be told that "that's the way I've been building these things for fifteen years." After the project was completed, a more competent builder looked at the project and identified a dozen examples of poor construction. For fifteen years this person had been building incompetently.

In short, one cannot get an "ought" from an "is." It is the case that people sing in church, but that does not mean that people ought to sing in church. Likewise, it is not the case that people ought to smoke because people do smoke or ought to steal because people steal. Simply because something has been tradition does not mean it should remain so.

Bandwagon Appeal

Similar to appeal to tradition is the bandwagon appeal, which is an appeal to popularity. It is the attempt to justify a position on the basis that "everybody is doing it." Most people have heard of the "bandwagon effect" with respect to political elections. It is well known that a good segment of our society does not want to be associated with losers. Thus, when they learn that a particular candidate is falling out of favor or is capturing the attention of large audiences, they adopt the stance that the majority is taking, in effect, siding with the winner. To take a contrary opinion requires significant self-esteem and courage. Thus we find politicians eagerly sharing any poll they can find that puts them in the lead; the bandwagon effect only enhances their lead that much more.

Of course, just because most people are doing something does not justify it, for it is possible that they are wrong. History is replete with examples in which the majority of a population adhered to erroneous ideas, made poor choices, or acted unjustly. The wide support of Hitler is but one example.

To help us resist the bandwagon appeal, we should remember that all great ideas, such as our model of the solar system, the theory of evolution, Einstein's theory of relativity, and the double helix model of DNA, were once novel ideas. Most great ideas were not accepted instantly; they had to compete with less accurate but more popular notions. Even the automobile was scorned by many. Fortunately, novel ideas can overcome the obstacle of contrary popular opinion, for without novel ideas, there could be no growth; without people with the courage to be different, there would be only stagnation.

Appeal to Ignorance

If people can't find an authority, tradition, or majority to appeal to, sometimes they resort to an appeal to ignorance. This is not an appeal to one's stupidity, as the name suggests. Instead it is supporting a position by either appealing to the fact that no one can prove it wrong, or to the fact that no one can prove it right. When a presidential candidate accused the incumbent president of deliberately spreading false and negative propaganda about him, one of the president's representatives responded by saying that he didn't believe there was any evidence to prove that. In other words, because the allegation cannot be proven correct, it is therefore false. Whether true or not, the response to the accusation was an appeal to ignorance.

On the other hand, we can imagine a hundred mythical monsters, but we cannot legitimately argue that they all exist simply because there is no proof that they don't. In sum, having no evidence against a position does not amount to having evidence for it; and having no evidence for a position does not compose evidence against it.

SUMMARY

Along with creative thought, inductive and deductive logic comprise the bedrock and substance of all our thinking. We explored deductive thinking through the three major types of syllogisms: categorical, hypothetical (if-then), and disjunctive (either/or). We explored some formal fallacies, such as denying the antecedent and affirming the consequent, and we emphasized the importance of clear definitions for our terms. Valid and invalid conversions were also addressed; we learned that we cannot always simply reverse the elements of a statement without changing its meaning.

We also explored soft deductive arguments which use terms such as "most," "almost all," and "generally" instead of "all." We learned that conclusions of these arguments can only be statements of probability, and that these statements of probability do not always mean "very probable." We also learned that these softer arguments must be put in the context of other information we have about the terms before we can embrace their conclusions.

At the end of the section on deduction we explored some informal deductive fallacies. Here we learned that we should not assume that the parts of wholes share their characteristics. Nor should we engage in circular reasoning by assuming what we are trying to prove or fall prey to the either/or fallacy by reducing complex issues into simplistic alternatives. In this section we also learned to refute arguments by exposing these and other reasoning errors or by reducing a proposition or conclusion to its absurdity.

Finally, inductive thinking, reasoning from the particular to the general, was explored and contrasted with deductive thinking, reasoning from the general to the particular. We explored the analogical argument as a valid form of inductive reasoning, even though a precise test for a strong analogy cannot be found. We then identified common errors in inductive reasoning such as false analogy, hasty generalization, fallacy of composition, extravagant hypotheses, and slippery slope thinking. We also explored errors in causal thinking through discussion of *post hoc ergo propter hoc* and the different types of causation: necessary, necessary and sufficient, sufficient, and contributory. Finally we looked at the fallacies of appeal: the bandwagon appeal and the appeals to authority, tradition, and ignorance.

LOGIC CHALLENGES

1. Because causal laws of nature are descriptions of past events, on what basis should we assume that past events must be the same in the future?

2. How do the emotions of anger and depression affect your ability to think logically?

3. If someone could take one of your cherished beliefs and show that it is based on faulty reasoning, would you readily abandon it?

4. How logical do you think most human beings are?

5. Identify beliefs and attitudes of those around you that you believe are founded on poor logic. Can you find illogical thinking embedded in our cultural beliefs?

6. Should people who are uninformed and reason illogically be allowed to vote for issues and candidates that determine the course of the country? Why?

7. Identify examples in which we reason logically but do not act accordingly. What are some reasons for this inconsistency?

8. To what extent can we discover truths about the world through reasoning alone, without science? Are there truths that we will never discover through reason?

9. What would you think about someone who was so logical that he or she always acted rationally, never allowing feelings to get in the way? Is this the ideal person? Or would this be a flawed person? Why?

10. How often do you use "or" in a nonexclusive manner? When you use it this way, do others know how you are using it?

11. The next time you get into a serious debate or argument, write down a summary of the points made on both sides. Can you identify any reasoning errors?

12. Can you think of deductive arguments using "most," "generally," and "almost all" for which it would be difficult to find critical information to challenge the conclusion? One example might be the following: "Almost all girls like cookies; Sharon is a girl; therefore, Sharon probably likes cookies." Aside from knowing that Sharon doesn't like cookies, is there any category that Sharon could fall under that would lead us to believe that she probably would not like cookies?

13. What kind of thinking errors do you think are most commonly made, inductive or deductive? What kind of thinking errors do you most commonly make?

14. What kind of thinking errors lie behind stereotypes?

15. How have you responded in the past to the question "Do you believe in God?" Did you ask for the meaning of God before you responded? How many different meanings of "God" can you think of? Can you think of other questions that should be qualified before answering?

16. What issues do you tend to look at in black-and-white (either/or) terms?

17. Think of the complex network of causes that have led to your existence. What are the odds of your creation?

18. When was the last time you made a *post hoc ergo propter hoc* error? Describe it.

19. Can you think of any popular hypotheses for events that would be considered extravagant? Are all extravagant hypotheses in error? How would you respond to someone maintaining an extravagant hypothesis who says to you, "Prove I'm wrong"?

20. Some analogies are weak and some are strong. Can anything be proven even with a strong analogy?

21. What hasty generalizations have you made recently?

22. Identify some popular slippery slope arguments for contemporary issues today.

23. In some families incest and child abuse are traditional, being passed from generation to generation. Can you think of other traditional practices that ought to be abandoned?

24. What illegitimate authorities have you appealed to in the past?

25. To what extent should we rely on any authority for information? Is this approach ever a reasonable way of knowing? What would it be like to live in a world in which we believed only in what we experienced and never in what we heard from others?

10

Scientific Thinking

There are ten astrologers for every one astronomer.

—*CARL SAGAN*

Science. It is almost a second language as well as a method of inquiry. Rarely a day goes by when we don't hear about some new discovery in fields such as medicine, psychology, and physics. To think more critically about such discoveries, such as a cure for cancer, new treatments for depression, evidence for life on other planets, or an advertisement for a new "wonder drug," we need to know the language and methods of science.

In this chapter we explore the nature of science, beginning with the basic steps of the scientific method. We identify some of the assumptions and requirements of this method and contrast it with other ways of knowing. We look at the empirical nature of science and its limitations, and we briefly consider the problem of proof. We also explore the different research designs, their drawbacks, and the experimenter biases of the scientists themselves. Our goal is not to become scientists but to learn about the basis of research in order to become intelligent consumers of scientific information.

THE SCIENTIFIC METHOD

The worldwide technical and scientific literature was over 60 million pages a year by 1970 (Toffler, 1970). If scientific information comes close to doubling every

193

twelve years as some suggest (Marien, 1998), it may now easily exceed 250 million pages. This explosion in knowledge began with an increased reliance on the scientific method as the tool for understanding our material and psychosocial universe. This method, which has so radically transformed our world, is a type of inductive thinking which moves through four major steps:

1. Observation
2. Hypothesis formulation
3. Experimentation or data collection
4. Verification

These same four steps were used by Galileo when he studied the effects of gravity on falling objects. Galileo observed bodies appearing to fall faster the longer they fell. He then formed a hypothesis that falling bodies increase their speed at a steady rate. He experimented by rolling balls down an inclined plane and measuring their speed at different points. He then attempted to verify his hypothesis by analyzing the experimental results, which showed that the balls increased their speed at a constant velocity of 32 feet/second every second, in agreement with his hypothesis. To further verify his results, Galileo and others ran his experiment again.

Observation

The scientific method relies primarily on systematic observation of the world. It uses formal procedures for testing ideas about cause-and-effect relationships between variables. It can be used in many fields of study, including the social sciences, biology, chemistry, and physics. We might observe, for example, that many human beings are stricken with cancer. This observation might then lead us to wonder about the cause of cancer or about possible treatments. This kind of wondering about cause-and-effect relationships can be called scientific thinking. Scientific thinking can begin with observation, prior experience, previous knowledge, or common sense, and it can lead us to the second step of the experimental method, the hypothesis.

Hypothesis

A *hypothesis* is a tentative statement about the relationship between two variables, usually in the form of a prediction: "If A, then B." For example, if (1) we had observed that people dying of cancer are usually heavy cola drinkers, (2) we were aware that cancer rates were lower before cola was invented, and (3) there was considerable scientific debate about the safety of cola additives, then our thinking and observation might lead us to suspect that the cause of cancer is excessive cola drinking. We could express the hypothesis in an if-then statement, such as "If people drink large amounts of cola, then they are more likely to develop cancer." This if-then hypothesis could be simplified into a single statement: "The cause of cancer is drinking too much cola." No matter how the hypothesis is formulated, it must be tested for its truthfulness because the casual observations alone are not enough to support it.

Experimentation

The testing of the hypothesis is done through research and experimentation, and is the third step of the scientific method. There are many ways to conduct these studies, each with its own advantages and disadvantages, as we discuss later. For instance, in our cola example, we could feed large quantities of cola to chimpanzees and after a while compare their cancer rates with those of a group of chimpanzees that did not receive cola. Or we could find human beings with a history of excessive cola consumption and compare their cancer incidence with that of humans who avoid such consumption. Once the experiment or a data collection is complete, we move on to the last step of the scientific method, verification.

Verification

Verification is the analysis of our data to see if the data support or deny the hypothesis. In our example, we would analyze the results of our experiment to see if the excessive cola drinkers did indeed have a higher incidence of cancer. If they did, then our hypothesis was supported (but not proven). If there was no difference between the groups, then we must go back to our first step to look for new observations or begin thinking about other cause-and-effect relationships that might explain our observations. This last step of the scientific method can be fortified through replication, which means running the study again to ensure that the results are reliable. It is especially helpful if other researchers replicate the results. Verification can also be fortified through prediction, which is the ability to use our study's conclusions to reliably predict other outcomes.

These are the basics of the scientific method, a model of inquiry that is sometimes supplemented with hunches, intuitions, good luck, and creative play:

"To our knowledge, no one has ever been able to grow neurons from the brain, probably from any animal, much less a human," said Dr. Solomon

Snyder.... "We didn't expect it to work. We can't tell you why it did work.... We did it by diddling around, by being at the right place at the right time." (Bor, 1990)

> **Think About It:** *While creating technological marvels and producing vast amounts of worthwhile information, the products of the scientific method have also created an ecological nightmare, extended humankind's ability to kill a thousand-fold, and raised ethical issues that seem to transcend our capacity to answer them.*

Science and Other Ways of Knowing

The scientific method can be further understood by distinguishing it from other ways of knowing, such as philosophy and appeal to authority. Like science, philosophy has systems for investigating the world, and the questions philosophers address may be inspired by a set of observations. However, philosophy differs from science in its greater emphasis on reason for solving problems as opposed to observation. The two also differ in the objects of their investigations. The domain of science is the world of observation, also known as the empirical world. Philosophy, on the other hand, often makes its inquiry outside the empirical world, investigating values, meaning, existence, and so on.

The scientific method can also be distinguished from appeal to authority. Many people seek knowledge by appealing to an authority figure. This figure may be a well-respected doctor, teacher, or religious book. The scientific method, however, is at great odds with this way of knowing. When we appeal to authority, we believe something is true because an authoritative figure said so, and we do not require a set of systematic observations to support it. During the Middle Ages, for example, the Catholic Church taught that all the heavenly bodies revolved around the earth. Most people accepted this teaching because it came from the church's interpretation of an authoritative source, the Bible, and *casual* observation supported it: the heavenly bodies did appear to go around the earth. But from the scientific point of view, this observation led only to a hypothesis, which was not tested scientifically. There were, as we know now, other explanations that would just as well have supported the observation that planets and stars appear to go around the earth. These explanations were not tested scientifically because the hypothesis was assumed to be true since it came from an authoritative source. When the church's teachings were eventually challenged by Copernicus and Galileo, they were deemed heretical, not because they were at odds with observation, but because they were at odds with authority!

Think About It: *Is science at the end of its useful life? Will it ever find another physical law? Will it ever discover the roots of consciousness? Will it ever find out what happened before the big bang? Will it ever answer the big questions? Or will it just give us technical trivia about esoteric matters that will have no real impact on our lives?*

Copernicus and Galileo

In the sixteenth century, Copernicus argued that the earth moved around the sun. His idea was contrary to the teachings of the Catholic Church, which believed that the celestial bodies revolved around the earth. Needless to say, Copernicus's teachings inflamed many Christians, including Martin Luther who considered him a fool who wanted "to turn the whole of astronomy upside down" (Crowther, 1969, p. 48). In 1616, sixty years after Copernicus's death, the Catholic Church, fearing a great scandal and dissent if Copernicus's views were taken seriously, put his text outlining a heliocentric (sun-centered) theory of the solar system on the *Index of Prohibited Books.*

Although Copernicus is credited with introducing the heliocentric solar system, it was Galileo who was prosecuted for supporting such a view. Relying on scientific observation of the sun, planets, and stars, instead of on religious doctrine, Galileo found strong empirical support for Copernicus's theory and was unafraid to go public with his views. Even though forbidden by the church, Galileo published a book in 1632 supporting Copernicus's ideas and was consequently forced to stand trial for heresy. Found guilty, he was ordered to recant his views and was sentenced to house arrest, which remained in effect until he died eight years later. Such was the price of science. Only in 1992 did the Pope finally recant and admit that Galileo was right.

This story shows that appealing to authority is not always going to yield a valid picture of reality, and it shows the power of our worldviews to inhibit our consideration of opposing beliefs, no matter what the evidence. In this case, Christians had a worldview that placed earth and human beings at the center of the universe. This view prevented them from thinking objectively about alternate views, even when the scientific evidence was substantial. This story also shows us the necessity for courage in our critical thinking, courage to abandon beliefs that make us feel safe and secure, and to stand up for an unorthodox view that may make us vulnerable to criticism from others. Without such courage, thinking cannot take the creative leaps often necessary for a breakthrough in knowledge.

THE EMPIRICAL NATURE OF SCIENCE

The world of science is the empirical world, the world of observation. In order to apply the scientific method scientists must be able to make observations and measurements. Therefore, all variables under study in science must be defined in observable, measurable terms. By giving *operational definitions* to variables in this way, we make it clear to others what those variables are and what observations or measurements will indicate their presence. Physicists must decide what physical traces from an atom collision will indicate or define certain atomic particles. Astronomers must define a black hole in a way that they can recognize it when it is present in their observations of deep space. And psychologists must define variables such as love, frustration, and stress in such a way that they can be observed and measured.

An example of a *nonoperational definition* is Webster's definition of *love* as "strong attachment" and "warm affection" toward another. Although this definition conveys to others the meaning of the term love, it does not indicate to others what observations or measurements are necessary to indicate the presence of love. With only Webster's definition in mind, with no observational measures to indicate its presence, imagine trying to ascertain the percentage of passersby who are in love. But if we define love as walking hand in hand with someone for at least sixty seconds, then we are defining love operationally and we would be able to observe and count the number of people passing by who are in love. But have we, in this case, defined love accurately?

Erroneous Operational Definitions

When variables are defined operationally, they are sometimes defined incorrectly. When this happens, the conclusions of the research may be in error. In medical research, for example, an operational definition of low-fat eaters has been based on a person's response to a questionnaire designed to determine how much fat a respondent eats now—not in the past, not in the future. That information is then used in studies twenty years later to see if low-fat eaters had, for example, more or less cancer than the high-fat eaters over the twenty-year period. Since people's eating habits do change, one can certainly question whether twenty years of low-fat eating can be adequately defined by only one questionnaire twenty years ago.

As another example, consider a 1991 survey by the National Centers for Disease Control ("Good News," 1991). According to the survey, 45 to 75 percent of Americans have "sedentary lifestyles," *sedentary* being defined as "fewer than three 20–minute sessions of exercise each week." One can imagine the reactions of millions of parents whose days are completely filled by employment, childcare, and housekeeping responsibilities that include miles of walking, hundreds of flights of stairs, and lifting babies and heavy bags of groceries, with no time left over for a regular exercise program. We could hardly call these people sedentary! We can see that, despite the good intentions of scientists, sometimes the concept under study is one thing, whereas the operational definition of that concept is another.

Think About It: *In the above operational definition of* love, *the meaning of love may have been lost by defining it as handholding for sixty seconds. When we count handholding, are we really counting love? Are we missing anyone? A better definition might be to define love as a "yes" response to the question "Are you in love?" Can you think of a better operational definition?*

Operational Debates

Operational definitions that are acceptable to everyone are sometimes very difficult to achieve. Such difficulty often leads to debate. One area of debate in psychology, for instance, is whether or not the hypnotized state is an alternate state of consciousness. First, researchers have to define in nonoperational terms what they mean by an alternate state of consciousness, and then they have to define this state in observable, measurable terms. Those who believe that hypnosis does not lead to an alternate state typically define *alternate state* operationally as a pattern of brain waves different from those of the waking state. They then point out that such brain wave change does not occur during hypnosis, and therefore hypnosis is not an alternate state of consciousness. Supporters of the alternate state theory might respond by challenging this operational definition. They might argue that it is possible for a person to be experiencing an alternate state of consciousness even though their brain waves indicate nothing more than normal waking consciousness. Given that possibility, critics of the alternate state theory of hypnosis could be relying on an invalid operational definition!

The Limits of Science

Without an operational definition, the scientific method cannot be employed. Science cannot, for example, tell us whether or not a biblical heaven or hell exists. Such metaphysical concepts are generally not reducible to operational terms. They lie outside the realm of observation and are best left to the areas of religion and philosophy.

Besides metaphysical questions, questions of values and ethics also lie outside the domain of science. Consider the issue of abortion. Is abortion right or is it wrong? The answer cannot be found through observation. Scientists cannot find an answer to this question by looking through microscopes, observing biological changes in laboratory dishes, or observing how human beings respond to the abortion issue. The question of abortion is one of values, and although science can give us information that can be useful in answering such a question— for example, ascertaining when the heart starts beating in a fetus—it cannot by itself evaluate ethical statements. Value questions lie within the realm of religion and philosophy and outside the realm of science.

Consider the value statement "It is wrong to kill human beings for any reason but self-defense." Can you imagine any scientific way to support or refute such a statement? Where would we look for the answer? Perhaps, you might say, in our emotions, for most human beings find killing emotionally repulsive. But how do you determine that human emotion should be the criterion for determining values? Is that a scientific fact or a philosophical statement? No kind of scientific observation could possibly tell us that human emotion is the criterion

---

THINKING ACTIVITY 10.1
Creating Operational Definitions

If you were proposing to study the following variables, which ones could you operationally define? Which ones could not be so defined? The key to determining your success is to ask, "What could I observe that would indicate the presence of the variable?" and "Could my definition be defining another variable instead?" Try your definitions out on others to see if there is agreement that your definition indeed defines the term without losing its meaning.

1. Frustration	16. God
2. Obesity	17. Immoral behavior
3. Aggression	18. Prejudice
4. Soul	19. Meditation
5. Scientist	20. Hypnotized subject
6. Depression	21. Psychological stress
7. Thumb sucking	22. Altruistic behavior
8. Migraine headache	23. Happiness
9. Multiple personality	24. Life
10. Nothing	25. Consciousness
11. Black hole	26. Thinking
12. Gravity	27. Death
13. Telepathy	28. Beginning of human life
14. Evolution	29. Intelligence
15. Pain	30. Heaven

for determining values. Once again we are back to the realm of philosophy and have left the domain of science.

THINKING ACTIVITY 10.2
The Domain of Science

For which of the following questions would science be the appropriate method of investigation?

1. Do human beings have free will?
2. How can we reduce pollution in the environment?
3. Is there life on other planets?
4. Is a person the same person from birth through old age? If so, what is it that makes her so?
5. Does God exist?
6. At what point in fetal development do brain waves occur?
7. When does human life start?
8. What is life?
9. What principles should guide a person's behavior toward others?
10. What is the origin of the human race?
11. How can we increase our longevity?
12. What was Shakespeare's purpose in writing *Romeo and Juliet*?
13. What is the human mind?
14. Should human beings be punished for evil deeds?
15. Are human beings basically good, or are they basically evil?
16. What is beauty?
17. Does stress cause most cases of depression?
18. Does wearing a seat belt decrease the incidence of highway fatalities?
19. Does drinking milk before bedtime aid sleeping?
20. Is there life after death?
21. What is intelligence?

SCIENCE AND THE UNDERSTANDING OF HUMAN NATURE

A scientific conception of human behavior dictates one practice, a philosophy of personal freedom another.

—B. F. SKINNER, SCIENCE AND HUMAN BEHAVIOR

Because of the remarkable success of science in understanding the material universe, psychologists and sociologists have applied scientific thinking to the understanding of the psychological and sociological dimensions of human beings. From a philosophical viewpoint, this scientific thinking rests upon a foundation of determinism, which leads to some interesting problems when applied to the study of human beings. Below we explore the validity of this application of science through a discussion of determinism.

Determinism as Foundation

Scientists seek not only to discover phenomena but to discover the order underlying various phenomena, that is, the cause-and-effect relationships between things. The psychologists' lengthy surveys, the biologists' dish cultures, and the physicists' atomic accelerators are all designed to discover the components of nature and the laws that govern the actions of these components, whether those components are human beings, tsetse flies, or atomic matter. Scientists assume that the world is orderly, predictable, and operating through complex mechanisms of cause and effect. In other words, they assume a *deterministic* universe. If the world were not determined, but completely chaotic, scientific investigation could not lead to the discovery of natural laws.

There is considerable debate among philosophers and scientists about the extent of determinism, but most agree that for the macrocosmic physical universe determinism is a valid description of events. The debate centers on the role of determinism in the microcosmic world of particle physics and in the behavior of human beings. We will concern ourselves with the latter.

Human Beings and Determinism

Social scientists are concerned with the understanding and control of human behavior in order to promote optimal social and psychological functioning. The assumption, in whole or in part, behind this concern is determinism: social scientists assume that genetic, psychological, and social forces in each person's history govern the character and behavior of each individual. Although not all psychologists adhere to a deterministic view of human nature, their dominant tendency to look for explanations of human behavior by examining past events seems to assume such a view, especially when the general goal is to determine laws or principles that may govern human behavior. Here is an example:

STUDENT: Why did Mark become a psychopath?

PROFESSOR: Well, our answer lies in the genetic, social, and psychological forces that shaped Mark through his early development. Interestingly, Mark's father was also a psychopath and might have passed on some "psychopathic genes" to him. Moreover, being a psychopath, Mark's father did not teach him a healthy value system and actually served as a negative role model for Mark. Mark's mother, of course, had to work ten hours a day, six days a week, because Mark's father was often unemployed and was not a reliable source of income. Consequently, Mark's mother was not around to help shape Mark's values either and never really formed a strong bond with him. She often neglected Mark and physically abused him when she was under stress, which was more often than not. Sadly, there was never any sign of affection expressed toward him at all. And that's why Mark became a psychopath!

If Mark's behavior was shaped by his genetic constitution and his psychological and social environment, can he be held responsible for anything that he does? Hard determinists must answer "no," for they believe that every element of Mark's behavior, including the choices, judgments, and assessments underlying that behavior, are nothing but the result of a complicated chain of cause-and-effect relationships. Hard determinists argue that if all the variables about Mark were known, they would be able to predict his behavior with perfect precision. The reason they cannot ever predict perfectly what someone will do is not because people are free, but because they never know all of the variables bearing on that behavior. Thus, they talk about probabilities. They say that, given a certain kind of parenting style and a certain social environment, the chances are good that someone will become a psychopath. But rarely, if ever, can they be certain.

Opposed to determinism are the *indeterminists,* who believe that much of our life is shaped by genetic and psychosocial forces but that there is still an element of free will behind our behavior. We are free in the sense that we could have done otherwise, but we chose not to, and thus we are accountable for our actions.

If the indeterminists are right about our freedom, can scientists ever understand and predict our behavior? Some philosophers argue that prediction and freedom are not incompatible. For example, you may know your friend well enough to know how he would *choose* to behave in a given situation. Thus, even though he is acting freely, you can predict his behavior. Then again, maybe you can't:

> I have observed instances of a person deliberately upsetting the predictions simply to reaffirm his unpredictability and therefore autonomy and self-governance. For instance, a ten-year-old girl, known for being always a good citizen, law-abiding and dutiful, unexpectedly disrupted classroom discipline by passing out French fried potatoes instead of notebooks simply because, as she later said, everyone just took her good behavior for granted. A young man who heard his fiancée say of him that he was so methodical that she always knew what to expect of him, deliberately did what was not expected of him. Somehow he felt her statement to be insulting. (Maslow, 1966, p. 42)

Would any scientist have been able to predict that the ten-year-old girl would hand out french fries? The determinist, of course, would argue that an inability to predict the girl's behavior only reflects the complexity and enormity of the variables behind that behavior and in no way undermines determinism. Nonetheless, most of us would agree that a strong sense of freedom is evident in the example above. So strong is that sense of freedom in our lives that it may be more the burden of the determinists to show that we are not free than it is of the indeterminists to show that we are.

The point is that social scientists generally act under the assumption of determinism when they look for the causes of human behaviors and thoughts, even though their subjects feel free and are held responsible for their acts by others. For example, when Mark the psychopath murders, we react with outrage, not against a social-psychological system that made Mark what he is, but against Mark himself as though he is responsible for what he did, as though he could have chosen otherwise. Thus we have a contradiction between the deterministic assumption of social scientists which absolves Mark from responsibility and the reaction of the world in general which presupposes Mark's responsibility and freedom. One determinist explained the contradiction this way:

> All of this suggests that we are in transition. We have not wholly abandoned the traditional philosophy of human nature [that we are free]; at the same time we are far from adopting a scientific point of view that our behavior is determined without reservation. We have accepted the assumption of determinism in part; yet we allow our sympathies, our first allegiances, and our personal aspirations to rise to the defense of the traditional view [of human freedom]. (Skinner, 1953, p. 9)

Think About It: In his statement above, B. F. Skinner explains the contradiction between the deterministic assumption of social science and our general assumption of free will as due to an inability to fully embrace determinism because of our loyalty and attraction to the idea of free will. Do you agree? Is our "love" of free will and its implications getting in the way of straight thinking about it? Or are there solid reasons for defending free will?

Although we have not determined the extent of human free will, we can say with some confidence that the precision of social science may be limited by the extent of it; the greater our freedom, the less the rule of cause and effect applies and the more difficult human behavior is to predict and control. And if human freedom exists at all, then perhaps the goal of social scientists ought to be to encourage it. As Maslow (1966) wrote, "If humanistic science may be said to have any goals beyond sheer fascination with the human mystery and enjoyment of it, these would be to release the person from external controls and to make him *less* predictable to the observer" (p. 40).

Determinism and Probability

Although determinism underlies the scientific work of the physical and social scientists, many scientists work more with the concept of probability than with the concept of determinism. Probability is concerned with the *likelihood* of a particular event occurring in a particular situation. In quantum mechanics, for example, physicists work with Werner Heisenberg's uncertainty principle. This principle states that, because atomic particles are so small, the methods we use to observe and measure those particles change them. Therefore, physicists can observe and measure the exact momentum of a particle, but they cannot simultaneously determine its exact velocity because that would have been changed by the act of observing momentum, and vice versa. If physicists want to know both momentum and velocity, they can only make statements about the probability that a particle will fall within a particular range of values; for a given probability, the smaller the range for one value, the larger the range for the other.

Social scientists also deal with probability. Much of their research is done with groups of people as they compare the average value of one group with that of another. If, for example, they find that a group of people exposed to noisy working conditions have poorer marital relations than a similar group that is exposed to quiet working conditions, they might conclude that exposure to a noisy work environment leads to poor marital relations. However, not everyone in the noisy conditions is necessarily going to be affected that way. There are usually exceptions in every group. Thus, for a given individual who is exposed, we can talk about probable effects on marital relations, not certain effects.

Do these probability theories undermine determinism? Not necessarily. Einstein, for example, thought that the uncertainty principle reflected the limitation of our ability to measure atomic particles, not an inherent indeterminism of atomic elements. Similarly, the work of social scientists with probability may only reflect their limitation in assessing all of the important characteristics of each individual; for although a group may have similar people, they do not have identical people. Those unmeasured differences foil our ability to predict behavior with certainty.

PROVING A THEORY

We cannot pretend to offer proofs. Proof is an idol before whom the pure mathematician tortures himself. In physics, we are generally content to sacrifice before the lesser shrine of plausibility.

—*A. EDDINGTON, "DEFENSE OF MYSTICISM"*

Imagine being a traveling nurse who cares for leukemia patients in a large city. After several months and hundreds of patient visits, you notice that many of your patients live very close to high-voltage power lines. You at once suspect that the magnetic fields from those power lines may be the cause of leukemia in your patients. At this point you have formed a hypothesis, a tentative statement of the relationship between events generally based on casual observation. Now you proceed scientifically. You look up the addresses of all your patients and find that 85 percent of them live within 1000 feet of high voltage wires or an electrical transformer, both of which generate a strong magnetic field. You then go to the city health department and collect addresses of all leukemia victims in the last ten years and find that most of them lived in urban areas, which is where high-voltage lines are more common. Furthermore, you find that as distance from high-voltage lines decreases, leukemia rates drop. You then write an article and state your theory that strong magnetic fields cause cancer in children at rates directly related to the strength of the magnetic field.

Have you proven your case? No! There are other possible explanations for the results. For example, it could be that all the high voltage lines run through the more industrial parts of the city, and the industrial pollutants could be responsible for the leukemia. The fact that most of the cases come from urban areas may be nothing more than a reflection of the distribution of the population in the United States: most cancers are in urban areas because that is where most people live!

> ***Think About It:***   *Can you think of other explanations for the leukemia results that are not connected to high-voltage lines?*

Suppose your research is so good that we just cannot think of any other explanation for your results (except the theory that you have formulated). Have you then proven your theory? You may have a strong case, but you would not want to say that you have proven your theory. Scientists generally do not like to use the words *proven* and *proof* (despite how often you hear them in commercials), for even though no other explanation for one's results is available, there might still be one. Moreover, the amount of data necessary to convince one person of the validity of a theory may be insufficient to convince another. Who determines how much data and what kind of data are necessary to prove a theory? And how do we determine the amount of data necessary to prove a theory? Certainly if someone proposed a theory that challenged our worldview, we would want more data than if that person proposed a theory that did not usurp conventional beliefs. As we saw in chapter 2, people are very resistant to changing their worldviews; a great deal of data would be required to do so.

One scientist who challenged our worldview was Albert Einstein. His theory of the universe confronted basic beliefs about space and time. His idea, for example, that time is relative, that two individuals traveling at different speeds through the universe age at different rates, or that a person at the base of a mountain ages at a different rate from a person living at the top, seriously disturbs the commonsense view of time held by most people even today. Nonetheless, his theory has been supported by numerous experiments throughout the last several decades. Has his theory been proven? It certainly has to many physicists and mathematicians; however, because proof is subjective, with each individual requiring more or less data or different kinds of data, some people probably won't accept relativity as proven until they actually travel through the universe at different speeds.

In the rest of this chapter we explore the many ways that science can make progress toward "proof," and we illustrate in more detail why it is important for researchers and consumers to be cautious about jumping to hasty conclusions.

> ***Think About It:***   *Relatively few people fully understand Einstein's theories of relativity. How can a layperson become convinced of the validity of his theories?*

CONTROLLED EXPERIMENTS

A *controlled experiment* is any research design that allows the experimenter to control the variables so that the results of the experiment can be attributed to certain conditions, thus better establishing a cause-and-effect relationship. A controlled experiment generally requires an experimental group and a control group. The experimental group is the group that receives the treatment; the control group is the comparison group. Theoretically, the two groups are identical except for the treatment. If a chemist wants to find out if a new chemical added to ordinary detergent will improve its cleaning efficiency, one group of clothes will be washed with the new chemical, while the other will not. Both groups must be washed in water of the same temperature, with the same amount of water, and so on. Except for the added chemical, the washing conditions must be identical. If this identity has been achieved, we have a well-controlled experiment

To illustrate the importance of having control over as many variables as possible, consider a fictitious study that is not well controlled: Dr. Smith wants to find out if hot weather causes human beings to be irritable. He administers an irritability test to people waiting in line to buy tickets outside a movie theater on a hot day. He then administers the same irritability test to theater patrons leaving the theater after two hours of sitting in an air-conditioned environment. He finds that the people standing in the heat of the day scored higher on the irritability test than the air-conditioned patrons. Thus he concludes that heat makes human beings irritable. But Doctor Smith erred, because he did not control enough variables to make the two groups identical except for temperature, and therefore he cannot conclude with any degree of certainty that heat causes irritability. For example, maybe the people outside the theater were frustrated from waiting in line so long, and it was the frustration and not the heat that caused the increased irritability. Or perhaps the people waiting in line were hungrier, not having had an opportunity to eat popcorn like their counterparts in the theater. Dr. Smith should have controlled for these variables of frustration and hunger, which could explain the differences in irritability.

These variables and others need to be controlled so that only one variable distinguishes the two groups, thus giving us only one explanation for the results of the experiment. For example, in the above experiment, it would have been better to have both groups see the same movie at the same time of day with the only difference being that one group watched the movie in high heat while the other did not. If the groups are the same with respect to every variable (frustration, time of day, hunger, and so forth) except one, then that single variable would be the cause of any difference between the two groups. How do researchers know which variables are important to control and which are not? (For example, should both groups see the movie in the same theater? On the same day of the week?) They use common sense based on other information they already have about the research topic.

Much to the embarrassment of researchers, someone often comes along with another explanation for their results. The experiment must then be run again, this time controlling for the variable that slipped by last time. So next time you hear a commercial claim that says something like "Rinsing with our product before bedtime kills twice as many odor-causing germs as brushing alone," think! What other variables could explain the results? The researchers compared their product to brushing without rinsing, but did they compare their product to rinsing with *water* before bedtime? Perhaps it is rinsing with a fluid that's important in the removal of germs and not the expensive product's "special ingredients."

CORRELATIONAL DESIGNS

Instead of a controlled experiment, researchers will sometimes use a correlational design. Correlational designs differ from controlled experiments in the way the comparison and experimental groups are selected. In a simple controlled experiment researchers *create* the difference between groups by dividing a homogeneous group into two equal groups and then introducing the variable under study to only one group, the experimental group. Theoretically the groups are equal except for the variable under study, so it becomes easy to say that that variable is the explanation for any outcome differences between the groups.

In the *correlational design,* however, researchers *find* the groups that have differences. For example, in order to discover the effects of meditation, we find meditators and nonmeditators, instead of dividing a homogeneous group into a control and an experimental group, and then teaching the experimental group meditation. After finding the two groups we measure them on some outcome variable, such as emotional stability. If the meditation group is psychologically more stable than the nonmeditation group, we might conclude that meditation increases emotional stability. The problem with the correlational method, however, is that groups that are found generally have other differences between them besides the variable being studied, and those differences may be the real explanation for any outcome differences. In the example above, meditation may not be the only difference between the two groups. If it's not, how are we to know if it is meditation that causes emotional stability or if it's one of the other differences?

What other differences might there be? Perhaps people who meditate are more educated than people who do not. Or maybe people who meditate also tend to be vegetarians. Or maybe people who choose to meditate have more leisure time and less stress. Or maybe they were spiritually inclined, which led them to take up meditation. Who knows? The point is, any one of these other variables, called *hidden variables,* could explain the outcome differences between the two groups. In other words, education, vegetarianism, leisure time, or spiritual inclination could have been responsible for the increased stability of the meditation group and not the meditation itself.

Whenever we find differences between groups instead of creating differences, we run into the problem of hidden variables (also called the "third-variable problem"). Scientists attempt to control for the variables that may obviously explain the differences by, for instance, making sure that the meditators and nonmeditators both eat meat, have the same level of education, and so forth. But what about intelligence, drug abuse history, or early family experiences? All of the variables cannot be controlled, and these hidden variables might be the real reason for the differences. Suppose you hear about a correlational study that compared vegetarians with nonvegetarians and found that vegetarians live longer. Most people uninformed about correlational designs would quickly conclude that adopting a vegetarian diet will increase longevity. But the cause-and-effect relationship is not that obvious in correlational designs. For example, it could be that vegetarians happen to be the kind of people who care about their health more than the typical nonvegetarian, and not only do they avoid meat, but they also avoid alcohol and tobacco more than nonvegetarians and tend to see their doctor more frequently for regular check-ups. So is it vegetarianism that leads to longevity or the other good health habits that tend to accompany vegetarianism?

Another problem with correlational designs is determining the direction of cause and effect. Suppose you hear about a study that finds a positive relationship between marital satisfaction and work motivation. Does this mean that marital satisfaction somehow leads to more positive work attitudes, or is it that industrious people tend to put more energy into their marriages, consequently creating more marital satisfaction? The correlational research method can determine if a relationship exists between one variable and another, but it cannot always determine the direction of cause and effect in those relationships, although common sense and advanced statistical methods can often help to clarify the directional problem.

Given all these problems of correlational designs, why do we have these kinds of studies at all? One reason is that correlational designs yield statistics about the degree to which two variables are related, that is, the degree to which they correlate. The higher the degree of correlation, the more precisely we can predict one of the variables if we know the other. Life insurance companies, for instance, use correlations when they assess the gender and health habits of new subscribers to determine death potential and insurance risk.

The other reasons for using correlational designs concern matters of practicality and ethics. Some research questions simply are not practical to perform under more controlled conditions, and others are absolutely unethical. Imagine assessing the effects of child abuse on later personality development. The more controlled procedure of the experimental method would require that we separate a homogeneous group of children into two groups, a control group and an experimental group, then abuse the children in the experimental group, and compare them on personality variables. Obviously this would be unethical.

> ***Think About It:*** *How would you conduct an ethical study on child abuse and personality development?*

Arguably ethical problems might be avoided by using animal subjects instead of humans. A controlled experimental design looking for the possible cancer-causing effects of a particular drug would be conducted with animal subjects. However, there is the problem of generalization when using animal subjects instead of human ones. Generalization is the assumption that what is true of the sample is true of the larger population under study. To assume that a drug that causes cancer in laboratory mice also causes cancer in humans is to make a statement of generalization. Given the differences between human beings and animals, there is room for skepticism about such generalizations. In sum, although correlational designs are beset with problems of hidden variables and ambiguity about the direction of cause and effect, they are often the preferred research design because, along with giving us predictive ability, they more easily avoid the ethical and generalization problems of the controlled experiment alternative.

> ***Think About It:*** *The problem of generalization aside, can you think of any topics for social science research in which we could not use animals?*

SIGNIFICANCE

Sometimes the differences between groups on the outcome variable occur through chance. This statement does not imply that the world is chaotic or that some miracle occurred to cause our results. *Chance,* as we use the term here, means that in spite of all the precautions taken to select our study sample wisely, there is a possibility (chance) that faulty sampling occurred, and our results are due to the sampling error, and not to one of the variables being studied. For example, it is possible that the two groups of subjects we selected for the study may have differed from each other at the outset on an important variable that is responsible for the outcome. In the mouthwash example above, for instance, it is possible that the group using the mouth rinse was different from the comparison group such that they would have had 200 percent fewer germs anyway even if they had not rinsed at all! No matter how much one tries to control the variables so that the two groups in a study (the mouth rinsers and the nonrinsers) are equal in every respect but one (mouth rinsing), there is a chance that they are not. In other words, a possibility exists that rinsing had nothing whatsoever to do with the difference observed between the two groups.

Let's illustrate this issue with another example. If we want to find out if people in Wisconsin are more overweight than people in California, we are not going to assess the weight of every Wisconsin citizen and every Californian. Instead, we get a sample of people from Wisconsin and compare them to a sample of Californians. Suppose we get a hundred people from each state, compare their weights, and find that the people in our California sample are, on the average, ten pounds heavier than those in the Wisconsin sample. We want to conclude, on the basis of our sample results, that Californians are heavier than Wisconsin citizens. But isn't there a chance that such is not the case at all? Isn't there a chance that we just happened to get too many extra-thin people in our Wisconsin sample and/or an unrepresentative number of overweight people in our California sample? Even if we obtained a random sample of both California and Wisconsin citizens, making sure that we select people from all income, educational, and geographical brackets, there would still be the possibility that our samples do not reflect the real weight averages in those states.

Obviously the larger our random samples, the less likely our samples will be unrepresentative of their state's population. But even with 500,000 people in each sample, the possibility still exists, however remote, that the samples do not reflect the true state of affairs. What is the chance of that happening? That chance, called the *significance level,* is statistically calculated based on the size of the samples, the amount of variability within those samples, and the size of the difference in outcome between the two groups, in this case ten pounds. There is always a chance of error, no matter how small, unless we take the entire population!

Obviously, when the odds of our results occurring by chance are one out of a million, we have great confidence that our results reflect a real difference between our groups. But what if the odds were one out of a thousand, or one out of fifty, or one out of ten? At what point do we lose confidence in our results? In the social sciences, for example, there are two acceptable standards: significance levels of .01 and .05. If research results are significant at the .01 level, the chance of the results occurring because of some sampling error is only one in one hundred, or 1 percent; thus we can be quite confident—but not certain—that our study is not that one time out of a hundred in which the results could have occurred by chance. A significance level of .05 is less stringent, indicating a 5 percent chance that the results are due to sampling error, but it is still acceptable to most scientists as indicating the likelihood of a real difference, that is, one not due to chance but to the variable being studied, such as heat in the frustration experiment or mouthwash in the germ-killing study.

How are we ever to know if it is chance or one of the variables under study that causes our results? We can become more certain if we repeat the study and find the same result. This is the importance of replication in the last step of the scientific method. Unfortunately, many studies are not repeated because researchers rely on the confidence levels of .01 or .05 or fail to be interested enough in a project to engage in a replication. But even results significant at the .01 level could still be due to chance. If someone else repeats the research design and gets the same results, however, then chance is probably not the explanation. Year after year we hear of possible cancer cures, only to be disappointed when others repeating the experimental design fail to get the same results. In 1989 the American public had a major disappointment when a supposedly successful cold fusion experiment failed replication tests. These replication failures suggest that something else other than, or in addition to, the variable being studied was responsible for the initial positive results in these experiments.

In sum, when we hear about the results of a study, we must think about the role of chance and exercise appropriate caution in our interpretation. We should ask ourselves if the results are consistent with other findings; if not, it might be prudent to wait for replication studies.

Think About It: *How much confidence do you need to take action? What level of confidence do you need to run a red light, engage in unprotected sex, sky-dive, bungee-jump, or bet $1,000 on the lottery?*

Sizeable Effects

A *sizeable effect* is a large effect. Just because a study's results are significant at, say, .01, does not mean that there's much to be concerned about. It's one thing to say the results of a study are not likely the result of sampling error; it's another to say the study demonstrates a sizeable effect. If a study finds that people who eat liver are less likely to get cancer, and the study has significance at .001, we can be quite confident that the results are not due to sampling error, especially if the results are replicated. But we can still ask, "How much does eating liver reduce the risk of cancer?" "Just a tad," the researcher might reply. In that case, we need not change our diet to include the insufferable liver. On the other hand, if eating liver cuts our risk in half, then it's time to change our palate! Unfortunately, the popular media often presents study results without mentioning the size of the effect.

EXPERIMENTER BIAS

No intellectual activity, science included, is ever free from the shaping force of one particular ideology or another.

—W. BEVAN, CONTEMPORARY PSYCHOLOGY

Sometimes experimental failures are not due to sampling error or poor research design but to the experimenters themselves. This kind of error is known as *experimenter bias*. Experimenter bias is the tendency on the part of researchers to make errors in perception or judgment because of their expectations or desire for a particular result. It is part of a general tendency among all of us to see what we would like to see or what we expect to see. Sigmund Freud, Carl Jung, William James, and others argued that objective, rational inquiry may be more a fiction than a reality, a mere rationalization dictated by unconscious motives, seething emotions, and cherished beliefs. Our liking or disliking of a person, event, or idea can alter our perceptions, even if the foundation of our liking is based on nothing more than hearsay or unhealthy personal needs. Such bias affects teachers grading student exams, jurors judging a defendant, and scientists conducting research.

Many psychological studies have demonstrated this effect. In one classic experiment (Rosenhan, 1973), normal graduate students lied to gain admission to a mental health hospital, were given a psychiatric diagnosis, generally "schizophrenia," and then behaved normally thereafter. Their normal behavior, however, was often seen by the hospital staff to be pathological. The label "schizophrenia" biased the staff's perception and judgment of normal behavior.

In another early experiment (Rosenthal, 1966), two groups of graduate students were given mice to run in a maze. One group was told that their mice were "maze bright," that is, bred particularly for adeptness at maze running. The other group was led to believe that their mice were "maze dull." In fact, however, the students were working with the same population of mice. But graduate students who were told that their mice were maze bright recorded significantly fewer maze-running errors than the other group and perceived their rats to be brighter, more pleasant, and more likeable. Other studies support these findings.

When interpretation of experimental variables is open to subjectivity, special care should be taken to guard against experimenter bias. Because such biased interpretation is not a conscious process, it is not enough to rely on a scientist's good judgment and care. What is needed are more objective means of defining the variables, or special procedures in the research protocol itself.

A common procedure is to make sure that the researcher is unaware of some critical conditions of the experiment that would otherwise allow for experimenter bias. For example, if Dr. Z invented an antidepressant drug and runs an experiment to find out if the drug really can alleviate symptoms of depression, then Dr. Z, having a great deal of reputation and money at stake, might unknowingly bias his interpretation of the results. It would be more than just a little unwise to let Dr. Z assess the patients' recovery when at the same time he knows which patients had his drug and which did not. It would be better to keep him ignorant about who took the real drug or have someone else who is unaware of these facts do the assessment of the patients' recovery.

The motivation of the researcher or research organization is obviously something that everyone should be wary of. There is a big difference in credibility between the research of Burt's Chemical Corporation on the carcinogenic properties of their own weed-control product and the research of an independent group that has nothing at stake in the outcome. It is certainly not impossible for good research to be conducted by organizations that have a vested interest in the research outcome, but the potential for experimenter bias effects and outright fraud is significant. Therefore, the special interests of the researcher or research organization must be taken into consideration when assessing experimental results, and those results must be weighed against any independent sources doing research on the same subject. If the television industry cites studies supported financially by the television networks that show television violence to have no impact on the viewer and if those studies conflict with well-conducted research from independent sources—well, you be the judge.

A similar problem arises in the political arena in which, for example, a politician is expected to carefully weigh arguments for and against gun control while at the same time receiving generous amounts of campaign money from the National Rifle Association. As suggested in chapter 2, the politician's ability to think objectively would very likely be impaired by motivational considerations. In science, one's ability to judge, perceive, and assess are also subject to these motivational factors. Unfortunately, safeguards against these factors are not always implemented, either for practical reasons, out of disregard for the bias tendency, or out of a deliberate attempt to defraud the public. In the mid 1990s the American public became painfully aware of the potential for scientific fraud and bias when the tobacco industries were found to have suppressed research that suggested nicotine was addictive. As it turned out, tobacco science was nothing more than "politicized science," as one politician correctly put it.

The Placebo Effect

A researcher's beliefs and expectations must be controlled for in any research in which it could be a problem. But subject belief must also be controlled for, because subject belief can often confuse study results. If subjects are given a drug that they believe will cure them, the belief itself may cause the cure and not the drug. This is called the *placebo effect*. To control for this, only the study's experimental group is given the real drug while the control group is given a placebo, a pill containing no medicine, but led to believe that it's the real drug. If belief is responsible for the cure, both groups will be cured. If it's really the drug and not belief, then only the experimental group will be cured. The extent to which belief can cure is suggested by the Sapirstein and Kirsch study (1996). They analyzed thirty-nine studies involving a total of 3,252 depressed people and found that 50 percent of the response to antidepressant medication was due to the placebo effect. Clearly this study underscores the need to control for it in research.

Cases of Fraud

The following are examples of misconduct cases resolved by the Public Health Service between 1989 and 1991 (Wheeler, 1991, p. A7).

[Oregon Regional Primate Center] R. P. S., assistant scientist in the division of neurosciences. A center investigation found he had used the same photographs of cells to represent different sets of data in published papers.
[Tufts University Medical School] R. S., research associate in neuro-science. A university investigation determined that R. S. had altered and fabricated data.
[University of California at San Francisco] P. P. D., adjunct assistant professor of neurology. A university investigation found P. P. D. had fabricated data in two published papers, an unpublished paper, and an unpublished book chapter.
[University of Iowa Medical School] H. S., advanced research fellow in internal medicine. A university investigation found H. S., who was visiting the laboratory from Japan for an academic year, had altered data.
[Harvard University Medical School] M. B., research fellow in surgery. A university investigation found M. B. had fabricated data for a draft manuscript and published abstracts.
[Northwestern University] D. O. N., associate professor of physiology. A university investigation found that D. O. N. had fabricated data for two published abstracts and had submitted a document with the forged signature of a graduate student to the investigating committee.
[Stanford University] P. A. B. and S. M. S., professors of psychiatry. A National Institute of Mental health investigation found that Dr. B. had misrepresented the status of research subjects in nine papers. Dr. S. was the lead author on two papers the investigation found to be "seriously misleading." Both men were also found guilty of plagiarism in writing a book chapter.

In most of the above cases, the offenders resigned from their university positions and were barred from receiving federal grants for several years. Journals that had published the falsified data were notified.

Cases of fraud occur at all levels and in all disciplines. As you can see, some of the country's most prestigious universities were associated with the cases above.

THE SURVEY

One of the most convenient and relatively inexpensive way to gather data for research is through a survey. A survey is simply an instrument with questions designed to assess our attitudes and opinions about various issues. This instrument can be given to a subject through an oral or written medium. We have probably all experienced the oral method when we were approached in a shopping mall by someone who wanted to ask us a few questions about a new product, or when we answered a phone call from an independent research firm with questions about our leanings in an upcoming election.

Without the survey method it would be difficult or impossible to acquire information about people's beliefs, attitudes, and opinions. We might be able to infer some attitudes and beliefs by observing someone's behavior, but much of a person's subjective life cannot be reliably measured in this way. However, with the survey method a person's political affiliation could be operationally defined as a "yes" response to the question: "Are you a Republican?" The survey technique transfers a political view, which we cannot see and measure, into an oral or written response, which we can observe and measure. Some information would otherwise be nearly impossible to accurately define operationally, such as people's secret fantasies, their conception of God, their attitude toward gun control, their sexual behavior, or their worst regrets.

Surveys are a very popular method for accumulating data on large numbers of people, principally because of their relatively low costs, ease of administration, and ability to assess personal information and private experiences. However, surveys must meet four conditions for them to be efficient research tools: (1) they must be administered to people in a way that encourages honesty, (2) the questions must be clearly stated and written or asked objectively, that is, without bias in one direction or another, (3) they must reach a representative sample of the population being studied, and (4) they must be returned in an unbiased manner. If any of these conditions is not met, the survey results become invalid.

The best way to encourage honesty in survey responses is to assure the person that his or her answers will remain anonymous. This is especially important when dealing with sensitive topics like sexual behavior, childhood sexual abuse, and problems of addiction. A face-to-face interview by a stranger about sexual habits does not provide the anonymity required for honest answers. However, an uncoded survey given to a class of two hundred students with instructions to answer the questions in the privacy of their home and to place them in a closed box upon returning to class does meet the anonymity requirement.

Anonymity alone, however, does not ensure valid results if the questions are asked in a biased manner, that is, by pressuring, intimidating, or otherwise indicating how they are to be answered. One "State of the Nation" survey violated the rules of anonymity and unbiased questioning when it instructed respondents to return the survey with their name on it and prefaced the survey with a four-page letter on how to vote. Part of the letter appears below:

> May God strengthen you as you continue to speak out against abortion, homosexuality, communism, pornography, anti-Christian TV programming and secularism in government. . . . There are more well-funded liberal activists than ever at work on Capitol Hill. They smell victory in the making because it appears on the surface that the Christian agenda has been

defeated. . . . You and I must show them they are wrong. . . . Radical feminist groups, the American Civil Liberties Union, and People for the American Way would like nothing more than to see ministries like Coral Ridge silenced.

A few years later the Democratic National Committee mailed a seven-page survey with sensitive political questions as part of its Democratic Party membership acceptance form. At the top of each page of the survey was printed the respondent's name.

One would think that academic institutions would be one place where good surveys would be found, since this is where survey design is taught. But even in these institutions bad surveys are generated. It is not uncommon for college administrators to send surveys to faculty with questions about the repondent's age, sex, race, department, and highest degree. Obviously, in small departments such information is devastating to anonymity.

Survey bias can also be found in academic arenas. One college survey on the topic of student retention asked respondents to rate the potential of various programs to improve retention from "low potential" to "high potential." Following each variable name, such as "advising" or "admissions selectivity," a paragraph explained the value of such a program. For example:

> *Academic Advising.* The importance of academic advising as a retention strategy is well documented in the literature. Advising provides the most significant mechanism by which students can clarify their educational/career goals and relate these goals to academic offerings.

The above paragraph certainly steers respondents away from "low potential" and "moderate potential" ratings. Oftentimes administrators, managers, church leaders, and others have good intentions, but are not well prepared in survey design.

Even if a survey guarantees anonymity and objectivity, it is not necessarily going to generate useful data if no one returns it or if only a certain kind of person returns it. Probably the most difficult challenge in using the survey technique is selecting a representative sample and ensuring an unbiased return. An unbiased return occurs when everyone in the sample returns the survey or when the surveys are returned by a representative sample of people from the sample itself. But even an unbiased return is not going to yield valid results if the sample receiving the survey is not representative of the larger population being studied. For example, if we want to find out what men's attitudes are about the feminist movement, we need to solicit the views of men who are rich as well as poor, Protestants as well as Catholics, young as well as old, educated as well as uneducated, and so on.

A popular survey among the American public in the 1980s was the Ann Landers survey that asked women if they would "be content to be held close and treated tenderly" and forget about the sex act (Landers, 1984, Nov. 4, and 1985, Jan. 14 and 15). This question generated the second-largest response in the history of her column and, to the amazement of many, men in particular, the results came back overwhelmingly in support of being held instead of having sex. But the manner in which the survey was conducted gives us little confidence in the validity of the results. One might argue that an Ann Landers survey does not reach a cross section, or representative sample, of American women. It might be that only certain types of women read Ann Landers or that women who read Ann Landers are disproportionately a certain type of woman compared with women in general in the United States. If this is true, then the results need to be qualified: *among women who read Ann Landers,* a certain percentage of them would rather be held than have sex.

But even this conclusion may not be justified. There might also have been a problem of return bias in the Ann Landers survey. Because there was no motivation to fill out the survey other than the desire to do so, we might wonder why some women desired to fill it out and send it in, whereas others did not. Clearly not every woman who read the survey sent it in. Is there something special about the women who did respond?

Psychologists have shown that people who have strong negative feelings about an issue are more likely to express themselves on that issue than people who have strong positive feelings. With this knowledge in mind, we might suspect that women who were dissatisfied with their sex lives and were emotionally unfulfilled might be more inclined to send in the survey. If this is true, then Ann Landers received a biased return; that is, she did not get responses from a representative sample of her readers, but instead she received a disproportionate number of survey returns from readers in emotionally unfulfilling relationships. All that we can conclude from her survey is that some women prefer to be held rather than have sex. We can conclude nothing about American women in general, nor can we even make general statements about Ann Landers readers.

Unscientific surveys, such as the Ann Landers survey, magazine surveys, and so forth, are abundant in American media. Even evening news programs are using them when they solicit their viewers' opinions by asking them to dial a telephone number to express their view on a certain issue or when they request a response to an internet questionnaire. These unscientific surveys may elicit responses from only certain kinds of people, who may not be typical of the larger population. Internet questionnaires, for example, are only going to be available to those who have a computer with an internet connection. And though most people have a telephone, when a news program asks its viewers to dial a telephone number to record a vote on a political issue, it is likely that those who have the strongest feelings and greater wealth (because there is a charge for these calls) will be more inclined to respond. People on tight budgets with moderate feelings about the issue are less likely to be reached by such a survey, yet they may constitute the majority of the public. One is reminded of the telephone survey conducted during the Dewey versus Truman presidential campaign. A phone survey was conducted to find out which candidate was likely to win the election. The phone survey showed such a lead for the Republican candidate Dewey that the Chicago Daily Tribune did not wait for election results and announced his win in the morning paper the day after the election. It turned out that Truman won. The mistake? The phone interviews reached only the wealthy, for at that time only wealthier people could afford the luxury of a phone. And wealthy people tend to vote Republican. So the survey amounted to nothing more than asking Republicans who they were going to vote for!

CASE STUDIES

We have seen that in order to generalize from a sample of people to a larger population we need to have a representative sample, which requires an adequate and unbiased return. Without representativeness we cannot make meaningful statements about a larger population of people. This problem of generalization is especially acute in case-study methods of investigation. The case-study method involves studying one person thoroughly as opposed to studying a large sample of people. It was the principal research method used by such famous psychologists as Sigmund Freud and Carl Jung. But because only one person is being studied, statements of generalization cannot be made from a case study. Yet people make them all the time:

PROFESSOR SMITH: According to a well-conducted study, the principle of reciprocity, contrary to the strategy of "playing hard to get," suggests that we are more likely to succeed in attracting others by expressing a positive interest in those people whom we find attractive.

STUDENT: I don't think that's right at all.

PROFESSOR: And why is that?

STUDENT: Well, I got my husband by playing hard to get, so I think playing hard to get works just fine. It sure worked for me.

In the above example, the student is using herself as a case study and then generalizing to others. Such reasoning is not valid. No one should question the student's honesty about her experience; what ought to be questioned, however, is the generalizability of the student's experience to everyone else's experience, particularly when the student's experience contradicts the results of a well-conducted study.

Technically speaking, case studies can be conducted within the physical sciences as well. But in the physical sciences it is legitimate to discover certain principles about a single physical event or object and then assume that those principles apply to all other events or objects identical with the one studied. If one discovered, for example, that adding two atoms of hydrogen to one atom of oxygen produced water, we could assume that that would be the case for all hydrogen and oxygen atoms. Studying human beings, however, is a different matter entirely, because no two human beings are identical in their histories or constitutions. Finding out that Joan developed a multiple-personality disorder because she was severely abused as a child does not mean that we can assume that anyone severely abused as a child will develop a multiple-personality disorder, or anyone with a multiple personality disorder was abused as a child (though, in fact, most of them were). Maybe Joan's manner of developing a multiple personality was atypical, which is not unusual given each person's unique genetics, family history, peer relations, and interpretation of life events.

If we cannot generalize from case studies in the social sciences, of what value are they? Case studies are valuable for clinical work with patients, and they can give us hints about what might be transpiring in *similar* cases. (When comparing human beings there are never identical cases.) These hints can then be tested using a larger sample of people.

Pseudoscience

True scientific inquiry uses the steps of the scientific method in a careful, well-controlled, and objective manner in an attempt to reach some truths about the world. At the same time it is open to the possibility of error in its conclusions, considers alternative explanations, and weighs the evidence for and against various theories. Further, true science develops hypotheses and theories that are testable and falsifiable. Subjects of inquiry that pretend to be scientific but lack these characteristics are called pseudosciences. Their fault is not that their beliefs are false, but that the beliefs are deemed true without careful scientific testing or in spite of it. One might say that *pseudoscience* is the unquestioned belief in extravagant hypotheses without scientifically testing more conventional theories. Some commonly labeled pseudosciences are astrology, UFOs, parapsychology, and creationism. Some of this pejorative labeling is undeserved, however, for sound, scientific studies have been conducted in these areas. The label "pseudoscience" seems to be applied because of a preponderance of bad scientific thinking, which parallels the genuine scientific investigations into these topics, or a continued belief in those areas in which good evidence strongly suggests otherwise.

One common characteristic of the pseudosciences is the tendency to give a *post hoc* (after-the-fact) explanation for an unfulfilled prediction without testing the explanation or to give it in a manner that is untestable. Many religious and cultic groups have prophesied that the world was going to end; when it did not, they

(continued)

Pseudoscience *(continued)*

explained their apparent error as, for example, an intervention by God to reward them for their efforts to save souls and warn others. Such an explanation is untestable and appears only to save face. Similarly, so-called psychics have offered face-saving reasons to explain their failure to perform psychic readings and feats, as when a failed seance or reading is attributed to "bad timing," an "uncooperative spirit," or "negative energy."

Creationism, astrology, parapsychology, and UFOs involve themes of power, religion, spirit, savior, and mystery—themes that human beings grasp onto quickly and tenaciously. Such themes may make it difficult for some believers in these phenomena to open their systems up to scientific scrutiny.

Think About It: *Is the distinction between genuine science and pseudoscience black-and-white? To what extent if any do the more acceptable sciences have some of the characteristics of the pseudosciences?*

SUMMARY

Because we live in an era in which science permeates our culture, it is important to understand its basic methodology, assumptions, and limitations in order to think more critically about the world around us. The methodology of science consists of four basic steps: observation, hypothesis formation, experimentation, and verification. It differs from other forms of inquiry primarily in its emphasis on systematic observation. This is also its limitation, for science can study only the empirical world, the world of observation and measurement. Answering metaphysical questions and determining values, for example, are outside the reach of science.

Although many scientists work with the concept of probability, science generally assumes a deterministic and orderly universe, including the universe of human behavior. Considerable debate occurs about the extent of this determinism when it is applied to human beings. Ironically, we tend to judge people as though they are free, but we study them as though they are not.

The methods of researchers are many and include case studies, surveys, controlled experiments, and correlational designs. Because the correlational method must find the difference between groups instead of creating the difference, as is done in a controlled study, it has more problems with hidden variables as alternative explanations for the results. Moreover, cause-and-effect relationships cannot as easily be inferred from correlational designs. In spite of these limitations, correlational methods are useful in making predictions and are used when controlled studies are impractical or unethical. Sometimes the use of animal subjects avoids ethical problems and allows scientists to use a controlled study. However, the question about the validity of generalization arises when using animals to learn about human beings. Generalization is a problem in all studies if the sample is not representative of the larger population. And it is invalid to generalize from a single case study.

Even when there are no problems in the studies themselves, there is always the question of the results occurring by chance. Results are generally accepted if their significance level is .05 or better, meaning that the results could have occurred by some sampling error five times out of a hundred or less. Replication of research can help to strengthen confidence in study results. Such increased confidence, however, does not prove a theory, because everyone's standard for proof varies.

Researchers are human beings with cherished beliefs, pet theories, and great hopes like everyone else. These biases can consciously or unconsciously influence their judgment of the research variables. Such influence is called experimenter bias. It is important for researchers to insulate their research from this bias as much as possible. One technique, used particularly in drug experiments, is to make the experimenter and subjects ignorant about crucial conditions in the experiment.

The techniques of controlled, objective observation make science a valuable tool for unraveling the mysteries of the world. A failure to use science where it belongs or a haphazard use of it is considered pseudoscience. Here the themes of power and mystery may overwhelm our critical, scientific sense and lead us to false beliefs about the world.

As our awareness of the strengths and shortcomings of scientific procedures increases, we can make better judgments on the claims we see and hear, and we can apply the solid principles of science in our own thinking and research designs.

SCIENTIFIC THINKING CHALLENGES

1. Is it possible to have a cause-and-effect order in the universe without determinism? Explain.
2. What kind of research method would you use to test the effects of depression on thinking?

3. Imagine you heard the following: "Doctors found a relationship between being underweight and having cancer." What third, hidden variable can you think of that might explain this relationship?

4. Were you ever in an argument in which you tried to *prove* a point and were unsuccessful? Why?

5. Short of actually discovering intelligent life elsewhere in the universe, what would it take to prove to you that such life probably exists?

6. Outline different ways in which you could determine if broccoli or some other food prevents cancer? What are the strengths and weaknesses of each method?

7. List the ten most important things that you would like to know. For how many of them is science the appropriate tool for finding an answer to your question?

8. When you hear the claim "Doctors recommend Goody's Pills," what questions should you ask?

9. How satisfied are you with significance levels of .05 and .01 for determining confidence in experimental results? Can you think of situations in which you would want stricter criteria?

10. Are you free enough to be held responsible for what you do? How much does your social and psychological environment determine your behavior? How much is it determined by your genetics?

11. Is experimenter bias a factor in the classroom?

12. Given that the speed of light is constant, if you shine a flashlight ahead of you as you travel forward at half the speed of light, how fast would the light from your flashlight travel? If you find this intriguing, read a book for the layperson on Einstein's theory of relativity.

13. What do you think about one writer's definition of pseudoscience as "scientific work undertaken by anyone of whom one disapproves" (Sutherland, 1989, p. 351)?

14. Conduct your own survey about a topic of interest using the four criteria for good surveys. How did you do? Can you generalize from your sample to a larger population?

15. Ask people the same question but in different ways. Do you tend to get different responses depending on how the question is asked?

16. Surveys are often conducted in shopping malls. What is a drawback to this technique?

17. Have you ever made the mistake of using your personal experience and then generalizing to a larger population?

18. If you noticed poverty and crime in mainly inner-city areas, what would be some of your hypotheses?

19. If you conducted a survey on the internet in such a fashion that you picked up a representative sample of internet users, what do you think would be the makeup of your respondents?

20. The views of astrologers have not been supported by scientific studies. Why then do so many people continue to believe in astrology?

11

Persuasive Thinking

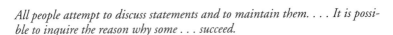

All people attempt to discuss statements and to maintain them. . . . It is possible to inquire the reason why some . . . succeed.

—*ARISTOTLE*

WHAT IS PERSUASION?

Simple to define, difficult to do, persuasion means influencing someone to accept our message. To persuade well is a demanding and delicate art. We must understand human nature, control our emotions, and think carefully; and we must be aware of the time, the place, our involvement, the message, the receivers, and their values. We must also articulate meticulously; one slip of a feeling or one wrong word and the architecture of persuasion collapses.

In this chapter we attempt that adventure. To craft a strong persuasive structure we use all of our thinking bases and abilities: we discuss the ethics of persuasion, think about what persuades us, and learn to analyze audiences to find how they differ from us. We then follow a persuasive process that leads our audience to a new position, but one that continues to meet their basic needs and concerns. We also look at some maneuvers that others typically use in their attempts to persuade us, so that we can better defend ourselves against manipulation.

THE ETHICS OF PERSUASION

If we try to persuade people to do something solely for our advantage, we are using them. That is manipulation. If we try to get them to do something that we believe is for their, our, and society's good, is that manipulation or persuasion? We should realize that the distinction between persuasion and manipulation is complex; few, if any, definitions, decisions, or discussions are black or white. Consider, for example, the chairperson of a college department who told us that she knew what her faculty members needed better than they knew themselves. The chairperson never openly told them what she thought they needed, but she acted, issued directions, and spoke to them in a manner to achieve her goals for them. Was the chairperson manipulating, persuading, or both?

> ***Think About It:*** *Do we ever have a right to get people to do things without their knowing why?*

On the surface, all persuasion is presumptuous because it presumes that we know what is best. What right do we have to persuade people to change their thoughts, beliefs, feelings, or actions? On the other hand, although we do not know for certain what is best, we still cannot avoid persuading. At home, at work, and at school, we are constantly choosing and interacting with others; as Aristotle said, "All men attempt to discuss statements and to maintain them" (1954, p. 19). Our choices affect others whether we intend them to or not. Even if we try to march only to the drum we beat, our marching influences others. Unless we march right out of society, and that exiting march would also influence, we cannot stop persuading; to live is to persuade and be persuaded.

THINKING ABOUT WHAT MOVES US

Because persuading is part of life, we need to understand it and learn how to become powerful persuaders. Understanding begins with ourselves, for some of the same forces that move us move others. We are more likely to be persuaded by someone who is knowledgeable, objective, rational, honest, attractive, convinced, similar to us, and by someone who appeals to our values, our needs, and our wants.

Confucius, Christ, and Kant

Ethical thinking can be a complex task. For the moment, if you find yourself in a difficult situation, you might rely on a simple rule used by many people that was first stated by Confucius, restated by Christ, and reformulated by Kant. Confucius stated it passively: "What you do not want done to you, do not do to others" (*Analects* 15:23). Christ stated it actively: "Do unto others as you would have others do unto you" (Matthew 7:12). And Kant formulates it: "Act only on that maxim whereby thou canst at the same time will that it should become a universal law" (*Fundamental Principles of the Metaphysic of Ethics,* 1955, p. 46). This Golden Rule which has transcended cultures and time can be helpful when we are faced with tangled ethical choices.

Knowledge

> *To know that you do not know is the best. To pretend to know when you do not know is a disease.*
>
> —*LAO TZU*

If you were awed by the beauty of butterflies, would you rather listen to an engineer or a lepidopterologist with a vast and stunning collection? If they both told you why the cloud-covering migrations of the monarch were thinning, whom would you believe? No contest. We like to listen to people who know what they are talking about. Likewise, if we are to persuade anyone, we had better ground our persuasion in knowledge. Wise persons know what they know *and* what they don't know.

Objectivity and Honesty

If the lepidopterologist were selling butterfly specimens, would we begin to suspect what he had to say? If we were offered free trips to Brazil to see the various butterflies, would we feel uneasy? ("I fear the Greeks bearing gifts," Virgil wrote.) Suppose the persuader made an up-front statement such as this: "If you appreciate the beauty and purpose of the butterfly, I'll show you ways you can help preserve the monarch through personal action and donations." Now it is easier to believe the persuader. We tend to believe people who are unbiased and honest and who have nothing to gain by lying. Aristotle calls this persuading through personal character. We believe *the person.*

Biases

Biases show. They warp our arguments and repel our audience. We tend to use arguments that support our biases, and we reject opposite arguments. The audience will notice our biases and begin to close their minds, because our biases will surface in our connotations and become apparent in our tone.

The first step in dealing with biases is to recognize them. "Know thyself," said Socrates. We can suspect a bias whenever we feel strongly about one side or another, and we can recall some of our particular biases that we may have identified as psychological barriers in chapter 2. Once those biases have been identified, we have to keep them caged like a tiger; a slight snarl or a gleaming fang and our audience will recoil. Even better, of course, is to let go of our biases and approach the issues objectively by looking at all points of view. If our audience believes that we are not aware of other viewpoints or that we are afraid to address them, then our credibility suffers. Audiences with at least a high school education seem to be persuaded more easily when we also address the other side. If we control our biases and attempt to address the issue objectively, we will strengthen our position and increase the audience's receptivity.

Likability

If a persuader was knowledgeable and objective but was also condescending, haughty, belligerent, and wore smelly sweat clothes, would we listen eagerly? If the person did not show that she respected us, would we find it easy to listen to her? Sometimes what you are speaks so loudly that no one can hear what you're saying. We listen to people we like, and we are more open to receive their ideas. So when we persuade we must take care about our appearance and maintain a positive and respectful attitude toward our listeners. If we like them, we should let them know it, for the operative principle behind interpersonal attraction is reciprocity; we tend to like those who like us.

Motivation and Purpose

To understand our motivation we need to answer the question "*Why* do I wish to persuade these people on this topic?" If we can answer this question clearly, we can proceed to persuade with congruency and candor, without a hidden emotional agenda that might derail our appeal. If our biases are part of our motivation, we may wish to rethink whether we are the right person to attempt to persuade this group at this time.

Motivation is related to purpose. To find our purpose, we must answer the question "*What* do we wish our audience to think, feel, or do?" A purpose helps us select and direct all of our ideas and appeals toward the target. A purpose, like a beacon in a fog, helps us sail our persuasion home.

The Rational Appeal

"Proof or apparent proof" can persuade, Aristotle said (1954, p. 25). When we have proof in the form of facts, evidence, undoctored photos, or reliable witnesses, we can convince all but members of the Flat Earth Society. But often our proof is not overwhelming, and we need to turn to logic to construct solid arguments (see chapter 9, "Logical Thinking"). We respect people who, by persuading rationally, rise to the top of their fields. Most CEOs can process data logically according to the impact on "the bottom line"; they can use examples with inductive reasoning and theories applied in syllogisms; and they can use statistics, analogies, and cause-and-effect relationships to convince the board of the accuracy of their interpretations and projections. We need to appear rational to others, for rationality is one of our cultural norms. We live in a world of *apparent* rationality; politicians and business leaders, criminals and baseball players all give reasons for their actions. Sometimes the reasons are far from logical—they may be ludicrous, laughable, pitiable, self-serving, or lies—but people still give reasons. Reasons that appear illogical or contradictory or lead to absurd consequences, however, can hardly have persuasive force. We do not respect someone who, like an uncontrollable child, simply says, "I want it," or someone who relies on power alone, saying, "I'm the boss, that's why." Although they may force temporary compliance, they have not achieved permanent persuasion.

The Emotional Appeal: The Root Elements

Logic can convince thoughtful people, but logic is just the surface of the mountain. Much of the persuasive pressure that drives the mountain upward lies deep in the mantle, deep in our root elements: values, needs, biases, and beliefs. These forces are established early in life, and they drive the emotional tone beneath our convictions; thus we refer to these forces as the root elements. They drive the emotional meaning of our rational or rationalizing words.

We might not always recognize or wish to recognize these deeper forces, for they do not always flatter our idea of ourselves as "rational creatures," a concept called into question by philosophers such as Schopenhauer, Freud, Jung, and William James. Because of our desire to appear rational, we tend to cloak our emotions with reasons. Aristotle's "rational animals" often use logic to cover their animality. Freud called this cover-up "rationalization." Evidently "apparent proof" (Aristotle, p. 25) is enough to appear rational.

Recognizing this human emotionality, Aristotle tells us to "stir the emotions of our hearers" (p. 25). Our emotions are closely connected to our beliefs and prejudices, most of which were instilled in us as children; for instance, if we follow a religion it is likely the one passed on to us by our parents. Although some adults change their religion, it is often for an emotional reason such as loving and marrying someone of a different faith. Logic blows over the heads of Moslems bowing in Mecca, of Jews chanting in Jerusalem, and of Catholics kneeling in Rome; few adults, such as John Henry Newman (*The Grammar of Assent*), choose their religion through an intellectual process. In chapter 2 we examined this process of enculturation.

All of us use emotional appeals in our arguments. The following is an example of how one student effectively played upon our emotions:

> My world is small, hard and mostly barren. The bleak landscape is broken by a couple of pleasant objects, my color TV, stereo system, and of course my books. Though a hard place it offers many amenities: 24 hour security, three hot meals delivered daily, laundry service, all personal toiletries, art supplies, and of course the bookmobile comes to my door twice weekly. The health and dental plans are excellent, no deductible, co-payments or premiums. And let me not forget the gymnasium. All this for only $24,000 per year.
>
> Why do I live here? That's easy—I killed three people. Not my fault really, they were in my way and had to go. I was sent here to this place called "Death Row," supposedly to join the three people I killed. There's a possibility that I will die here, in say, oh, thirty or forty years, of old age or natural causes. But I'm thankful that I live in America where the humane moral majority will not let them kill me. I thank you. When I first came here I was slightly concerned about my old lady and three kids, but welfare gives them almost $10,000 a year, so they get by and she sends my smokes.
>
> I keep up with the news while in here and am hoping that the recession will end soon so all you citizens can return to work. After all we shouldn't tolerate people being delinquent on their taxes in this fine country. Taxes, like voting, are responsibilities held by all citizens. So this fall when the death penalty is on the ballot I beseech you to vote NO. Isn't my life worth that simple vote, and it only costs $24,000 per year. Well, back to my school.

Is this emotional appeal effective? How do you think it would affect someone who was very much against capital punishment because of religious beliefs?

THINKING ABOUT WHAT MOVES OUR AUDIENCE

Persuasion assumes "that we have studied well the human heart" (Pascal, 1958, p. 6). Our understanding of the human heart begins with ourselves. When the audience is similar to us, our self-knowledge works well: it's not difficult for a Parisian to praise the Parisians in Paris. But when our audience differs from us, our words and our approach must also differ.

If we wish to persuade, we must understand how other people are different from us. Perhaps the greatest error in persuading, and the hardest to overcome, is to presume that people are exactly like us and do things for the same reasons we do. They don't. For instance, we know a person who has actually found and returned a bag of money, then later stole a piece of chocolate. This tendency to think that what moves us will move others may cause us to miss our audience.

Although we might think our arguments are steel-tipped arrows, they may fall upon our audience like gentle snow. We need to analyze our audience objectively.

Demographics

It certainly helps to know what our audience already knows about our topic. If we presume that they have information which they do not, or if we present information that is too simple, we run the risk of losing the audience through their ignorance or boredom. Demographics, or the study of subgroups in our population, can help us estimate the information level of an audience.

Demographic data are objective data describing people according to categories, such as age, education level, and occupation. Demographic information is often used by marketers to target products. Some of the standard questions that marketers ask are those that would be discriminatory to ask on a job interview; they concern age, gender, race, religion, marital status, and political party. Other questions might relate to income level, occupation, education, hobbies, and affiliation with groups such as the National Rifle Association, the National Organization of Women, the Nature Conservancy, the American Civil Liberties Union, and so forth. For instance, if you were giving a speech on abortion or gun control, how would that speech change if your audience was young, female, Afro-American, college graduates, and members of the National Organization of Women? How would your speech on gun control or abortion change if your audience was old, male, white, republican, baptist, and members of the National Rifle Association? Making some generalizations based on demographic information can paint for us a pretty clear picture of our audience.

THINKING ACTIVITY 11.1
A Demographic Analysis

What are the demographics of the students in this class? Using the lists of demographic features above, make some educated guesses about their age, gender, race, religion, and so forth. How did you arrive at some of your descriptions? How would you check your accuracy?

Values and Needs

Values and needs, those deep-seated forces, are more difficult to determine than demographics because often they are not even known to the people holding them. We can begin to identify those values by using the chart in Thinking Activity 11.2.

THINKING ACTIVITY 11.2
Identifying Values and Needs

As you read through this chart, rate the importance of each characteristic from 1 to 10, 10 meaning that the value is of the highest importance, and 1 the lowest. In the columns to the right, Y stands for you, O for a significant other such as a spouse, lover, friend, or boss, and C for an estimate of the average person in this class.

	Need	Description	Y	O	C
H	To help	Enjoys helping others; does work in community			
U	Understand	Likes reading; broad interests			
M	Material things	Likes to own, save, collect things			
A	Autonomy	Likes to make decisions, run things			
N	Newness	Likes change, adventure, creativity			
S	Safety	Needs security at work, at home			
A	Appearance	Looks: clothes, house, car			
N	Natural functions	Health concerns: eating (three meals), exercise, sleep (eight hours)			
D	Dollars	Needs to save; preoccupied with money			
N	Number one!	Likes to win, beat the competition			
E	Excel	Sets high standards			
E	Esteem	Wants recognition, admiration			
D	Details	Likes order, everything in its place			
S	Socialization	Likes people around, joins groups			

The values and needs chart can help us identify some of the root elements that are behind the positions people hold. For example, the need for safety may supply the motivation for gun control. People who wish to control guns may be afraid that guns might kill them or their loved ones. They may not like holding or even seeing a gun. Surprisingly, the same need drives many of those who wish to have access to guns. They want guns to protect themselves. A gun in their hand gives them the confidence that they are a match for most criminals. Some gun owners do not know or admit that they want a gun for their safety; they often give other reasons such as sports, hunting, or collecting (in some cases these are the main motivations).

Once we've identified safety as a root element behind gun control, we then have to be sensitive to this value in our audience. We would acknowledge their reasons or supposed reasons for supporting gun control and build a rational case to show that they would actually be safer with another program. This approach will not remove their need for safety but will simply replace one program with another.

Using the same chart above, ask your significant other to rank your values and his or her own values. How close do your assessments match each other? Our ability to persuade depends upon a fairly accurate assessment of the needs and values of our audience; you may have just discovered how difficult this can be.

Adjusting Our Goals

After analyzing and understanding our audience, we need to adjust our goals. How far can we go in changing our audience's thinking, feeling, or acting? That depends on how deeply they are entrenched in their present position and on the power of our appeal. If we are arguing against a root element such as racial prejudice or religious belief or if we are confronting a volatile topic such as abortion, we will be forcing the audience to run up a steep mountain in a single sprint. We must recognize where they are on the mountain and how far we can lead them in the time available. When we know they have deep convictions opposed to our message, our goal might be to get the audience just to begin to question their present position, we cannot expect an instant conversion. On the other hand, if the audience is near the top of the mountain, if they have already intellectually assented to a new position (for example, many smokers know the disadvantages of smoking and some would like to quit), our goal might be to move them to action, to take the last steps to reach the top of the mountain.

ORGANIZING FOR PERSUASION

Once we have analyzed the audience, identified root elements, and gathered ideas for persuasion, how do we structure this information? This question is pivotal, for the careful placement of our thoughts, like weights on a balance, will tip the

THINKING ACTIVITY 11.3
Motivation Mountain

The "motivation mountain" diagrammed below can help us picture the relative positions of our audience. For instance, "granite" groups might include certain political, religious, and ethnic groups and associations such as the NRA and the ACLU, which are known to be unbending. Where might other groups fall?

    Once the position of the audience has been established, then the task is to take them gently up to the next level. We cannot ask them to instantly leap to the top of the mountain.

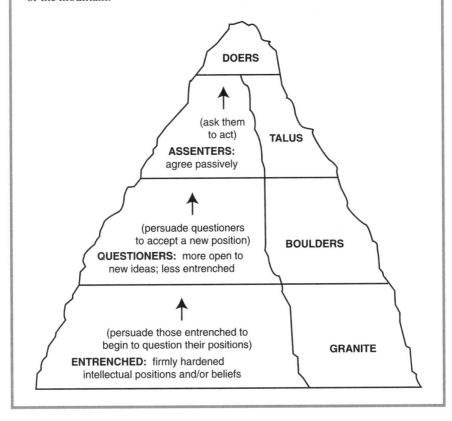

scale favorably to our side. Depending on the audience, the speaker, and the time available, our approach will differ, yet most approaches can be adapted to most audiences. One of the strongest persuasive structures we can create moves through five steps: (1) we establish our credibility, (2) we acknowledge the audience's position, (3) we develop our own position, (4) we show them how this new position offers them a more satisfactory way to meet their needs, and (5) we ask for a change in thinking, feeling, or acting.

Step 1: Establishing Credibility

First impressions, although often shallow and wrong, are nevertheless vital. Whether in a speech or in a paper, our audience can close their minds or drop the page—and quickly. First impressions become increasingly important when the audience is hostile. Facing an antagonistic audience, we cannot be militant or cowards or liars: "To thine own self be true. . . ." We have to reach deep into our character and show ourselves to be knowledgeable, believable, likable, rational, unbiased, and convinced.

Not having a lifetime to establish these qualities, we can do so quickly by objectively acknowledging both sides of a disputed topic. For instance, on the topic of gun control, an objective opening for either side might state, "Gun control is a hotly debated issue in our nation. Thoughtful citizens offer reasons on both sides. . . ." Here is an objective opening written by a student on the inflammatory topic of abortion:

> The debate over abortion is complex. It involves theological, moral, medical, and social issues. It touches the mysteries of human sexuality and the process of reproduction. Consequently, it is a highly emotional subject.

Step 2: Acknowledging the Audience's Position

This step can be encapsulated in a quote from Pascal: "Notice from what side they view the matter, for on that side it is usually true, and admit that truth to them" (1958, p. 4). With remarkable insight, Pascal asks us to do three things. First, we need to see the issue from the other side. While this advice is expressed in many common sayings, such as "Walk a mile in their shoes," it is seldom followed.

Second, and perhaps harder to accept, Pascal says that the way others see the issue "is usually true." Usually true? How can that be if it is the opposite of what we believe? A partial answer is that the opposite side starts from a different point, from different values and different presuppositions; naturally they reach different conclusions.

Third, Pascal asks us to "admit that truth to them." This does not mean that we have to be hypocritical or dishonest. We do not have to agree with their position; we merely state that we understand that people holding that position are reasonable, intelligent people and we understand why they came to their conclusions. By this single stroke of acknowledging their position and admitting the truth of it, we have shown ourselves to be knowledgeable, objective, and empathetic. We have prepared the ground for planting our idea because we have first listened to the audience. The chances are now greater that they will listen to us and allow the seed of our idea to grow.

THINKING ACTIVITY 11.4
Recognizing the Other Side

In the space below try to apply Pascal's first two steps to a contemporary issue such as abortion or gun control. First, review your own position on the issue. Then write down the *other* side:

Issue:_____

The Opposite Side:

_____

_____

_____

_____

_____

_____

_____

Now try to see the truth of the opposite position. Pascal said that if we see the issue from the other side, it is usually true. Here you are challenged to see the truth of a position with which you do not agree. To do this you must make an effort to almost adopt this position, make yourself vulnerable to the appeal of this position, to empathize with them.

The Truth of the Opposite Side:

_____

_____

_____

_____

_____

_____

Notice how difficult it can be to actually see the world from the opponents' point of view. You may want to test how well you did by sharing your response with people who actually hold that view. How well do they think you have captured the truth of their side?

At this point our argument, like a new sprout, is fragile, so we must place our steps with precision. Our audience is tentatively with us because until now we have been on their side. But we will lose them if they sense any hostile rhetoric. After restraining ourselves and admitting the truth of their position, it is natural to want to unleash the full force and feelings of our position. But we cannot wildly charge forward. We need to rein in our emotions, which might easily trample our delicate, budding argument. From this point onward we must guard our tongue or our pen and not let slip a single inflammatory word that might slam shut the door of the audience's opening mind.

Step 3: Constructing Our Rationale

Now we can construct our rationale in a positive way using facts, statistics, authorities, and our strongest reasoning from logic, analogies, precedents, examples, and cause and effect. Our goal is not to prove our audience wrong but rather to offer them something better. Whereas Aquinas might refute his opponents or a trial lawyer rip away at the opposition, we are not in a medieval-style debate to intellectually vanquish our opponents, nor are we in a court of law to prove them guilty. We do not want to leave them humbled before our brilliance but, rather, excited by a better way of thinking or acting.

Step 4: Transplanting the Root Elements

If we have crafted our persuasive message sensitively and strongly, if we have approached our audience's root elements carefully and respectfully, if we have offered our audience a more solid rationale that satisfies their needs better than the one they currently hold, then change is likely. We are not so much painfully extracting their root elements as we are transplanting them into a package that is stronger and which feels better to the audience. For instance, they now believe they will be safer with (or without) gun control or capital punishment. They have now accepted a different supporting logic, they have changed, they are persuaded.

Step 5: Asking for the Response

So now we have convinced them to vote for us, but will they go to the voting booth? If the first four persuasive steps were sound, this final step is achieved by merely asking for it. It is similar to the salesperson who has convinced the buyer and "asks for the order." At this concluding point, we need to get an agreement from the audience that they will do it, that they now hold a new line of thinking, and that they formally accept the new position they have adopted. Without this formal "sign on the line," it is easier for the newly persuaded to slip back into their habitual patterns of behaving and thinking. We have worked hard arranging our thoughts and controlling our feelings, so we want to remember to add the capstone to our persuasion by asking for the response.

DEFENDING OURSELVES AGAINST DECEITFUL PERSUASION

Forewarned is forearmed.

—*CERVANTES*

Persuasion is most powerful and enduring when it is both honest and built upon a solid foundation. And it is in our best interest when it involves accurate facts, clean logic, and persuaders who have integrity. However, some persuaders are deliberately inaccurate, illogical, or dishonest; they bend and distort their messages to satisfy their own needs for power or possessions. Against this onslaught of deceitful persuasion, we need to be aware and armed. Below we look at twelve common persuasive techniques that others are likely to use on us. We've organized them in three categories: manipulative tactics, invalid attacks, and abuse of language. By learning about them, we can more easily protect ourselves from their influence, separate the wheat from the chaff, and emerge rather unscathed.

Manipulative Tactics

Seven psychological tactics are used intentionally by others to persuade us. These tactics have great potential to be manipulative. These seven tactics are the foot-in-the-door technique, door-in-the-face technique, lowballing, spending time, and the three appeals: appeal to pity, appeal to fear, and appeal to pride.

Foot-in-the-Door Technique

The basic strategy of the *foot-in-the-door technique* is to get a person to comply with a small request and then ask them to comply with a larger request later. Getting the person to comply with the larger request is the real objective. In one study of this technique (Freedman and Fraser, 1966), two groups of women were asked to put a large sign in their yards that read "Drive Carefully." Only one of the groups was previously asked to comply with a smaller request to put a small sign in their front window; most of that group agreed. Amazingly, 76 percent of those who complied with the smaller request later complied with the larger one, but only 17 percent of the other group did.

Why does the foot-in-the-door technique work? Perhaps complying with the small request changes a person's self-definition. By putting a small sign in the window we may begin thinking of ourselves as people who care, as people who get involved in this issue. Then, when someone approaches us later for a larger request, they are approaching a person who cares, a person who gets involved, and are more likely to gain compliance from us than from those who haven't yet defined themselves in this way. Thus, beware of letting the vacuum cleaner salesperson into your house, for once we let the person in, we have complied with a small request; we have defined ourselves as someone who must be somewhat interested in vacuums, for why else would we let the salesperson in? Now the salesperson is selling to "someone who is interested" and thereby increases his or her chances of success.

Door-in-the-Face Technique

Mix the spirit of cooperation with a pinch of guilt and you have the ingredients of the *door-in-the-face technique*. It is just the opposite of the foot-in-the-door technique. This time the first request is so large that one expects it to be rejected, that is, to have the door slammed in one's face. Then, shortly thereafter, one follows with the real request, which now appears much smaller than it otherwise would have. Denying this smaller request might be difficult because of a feeling of guilt about not compromising. Many teenagers have learned to use this technique on their parents:

TEENAGER:	Mom, may I have the car this weekend—I mean *all* weekend? My friends and I want to do something different for a change. You know, hit the streets in the city for a while. May I?
MOM:	Absolutely not! You know that's the only car we have. How am I supposed to function without a car all weekend? Besides, hitting the streets in the city does not sound like a healthy idea to me.
TEENAGER:	I knew you would say that. You just don't want me to have any fun. (Teenager walks away.)
TEENAGER RETURNS:	Um. Mom. I know you don't want me to go this weekend and take the car and all. And I'm willing to accept that. But could I at least have the car for a few hours Friday night to take Terry out? I mean, you never let me use the car for anything, you know.
MOM:	I suppose.

Unlike the foot-in-the-door technique, this strategy works only when the same person makes both requests. Our sense of cooperation and fair play easily extends to the individual who appears to be compromising.

Lowballing

While watching an exciting football game on TV, a young man was interrupted by his neighbor who asked for help to move the refrigerator in his basement. Since it was halftime, the young man complied, believing it would take only about fifteen minutes. After moving the refrigerator up from the basement, the young man was expected to help move it onto his neighbor's pickup. Once that task was accomplished, his neighbor said, "All we have to do now is take it to my grandma's house." The young man reluctantly got in the truck and proceeded to drive to grandma's house, located on the other side of the city. When he arrived, he helped to unload the refrigerator, set it up in grandma's kitchen, and finally returned home two hours later. "Had I known," he said, "that I would miss the rest of the game and be gone for two hours, I never would have complied in the first place."

The technique of *lowballing* asks someone to comply with a request without giving them the whole story; specifically, negative aspects of a task are withheld in order to ensure compliance. Lowballing helps to ensure compliance to a large request, not by getting someone to comply first to a small request in order to change their self-definition, but by making a large request appear small and then relying on the other's commitment. This technique seems to work because (1) we tend to feel obligated to follow through with our commitment to a person, although we may blame ourselves for making it hastily without getting all the details; (2) we are often inched along, as when gas prices jump a penny or two per month, each step being too small for us to raise a serious objection; and (3) we might lack the necessary assertive skills to say "no" when we realize that we are being manipulated. This last aspect is quite serious, for it makes us more vulnerable not only to lowballing but to all forms of manipulation. Assertiveness is a quality and skill of character that allows us to act on our thinking and reject manipulation. Fortunately, assertiveness can be learned if we need it.

Think About It: *Monday you agree to help Bill supervise some Cub Scouts while they do "a little fishing" this Saturday. Bob calls you in the middle of the week to tell you that it would also involve participating in recreational sports and you wouldn't be getting home until 11:00 p.m. that evening. Would Bill's lowballing technique work to sustain your commitment?*

Investing Time

A former car salesman shared with us a technique he learned in a training program to motivate customers to buy a car. This technique involved nothing more than *spending time* with the customer. "When you spend a lot of time with them," he said, "they feel guilty walking away with no commitment, with no purchase. Here I am working perhaps two to three hours showing the car and trying to get a good deal for them. That's almost half my day. Many people feel guilty taking up half a person's day and then leaving them with nothing."

One woman succumbed to the foot-in-the-door technique used by a vacuum cleaner salesman. Once he was inside the house, she had a difficult time getting rid of him. "He was there for hours," she said. Although she did not make a purchase, she felt great pressure to do so. Moreover, she felt so guilty using his time up that day without a sale that she invited him for supper!

Appeal to Pity

People can evoke our sympathy and empathy by an *appeal to pity*. A school board might be led to retain a school principal who was convicted of ballot fixing at the high school prom, or a college instructor might pass a failing student. Such is the influence of pity.

Sometimes an appeal to pity is appropriate in motivating people to take benevolent actions, as in a plea to provide food and shelter for hurricane victims or to help the needy in impoverished countries. We must be wary, however, of pleas based on pity that stand alone and have little to do with the argument or situation. For example, a young woman who had received a D grade in a college course approached her professor with a plea for a C; in the middle of her plea she began crying uncontrollably, explaining that her father would reject her if she received a failing grade. And an employee defended his high salary because of his retirement needs and the number of mouths he had to feed at home.

In sum, if pity is not the basis on which we ought to make certain decisions, then it is usually invalid to appeal to pity to modify those decisions. Some of us are less vulnerable than others to this form of appeal; while retaining empathy and compassion, we can resist false appeals to pity.

Appeal to Fear

And the Lord God commanded the man thus, "From the tree of the knowledge of good and evil you must not eat; for the day you eat of it, you must die."

—*GENESIS 2:16*

Another appeal that is often used in persuasion is the *appeal to fear*. Cigarette smokers are warned about the cancer-causing potential of smoking, automobile drivers are encouraged to buckle up or risk death in an accident, and children are told to brush their teeth to avoid painful cavities. These uses of fear are legitimate because the fearful consequences may really happen if we do not heed the message. Sometimes, however, the degree of danger and the probability of it happening are exaggerated in an attempt to manipulate our behavior or attitudes. Politicians warn us that if we vote for their opponent the economy will collapse and our jobs will be lost. Automobile insurance companies may recommend increasing our coverage lest we lose everything in a lawsuit. And makers of water and air purifiers might warn us about an increased risk of disease if we do not use their products. These claims may contain some truth, but they are usually greatly exaggerated.

Do such fear messages work? Research has found mixed conclusions. Generally fear is more effective in persuasion than no fear at all, but whether strong or moderate fear works better is still in question. A strong fear message without specific instructions on how to avoid the danger may lead to denial, as when cigarette smokers are told that they are killing themselves and are not told at the same time how to break the habit. If we can't stop smoking, we're likely to block out the fear message to alleviate anxiety. Surprisingly, in such situations of total denial, moderate fear may work better, such as a warning about smoker's breath or the financial drain on the household budget.

THINKING ACTIVITY 11.5
Your Vulnerability to Fear Appeals

To help you find out where you are especially vulnerable to fear appeals, organize the following list of fears from most fearful to least fearful. Add others if you feel some important fears are missing.

1. _____ fear of change
2. _____ fear of failure
3. _____ fear of injury
4. _____ fear of death
5. _____ fear of controversy
6. _____ fear of financial loss
7. _____ fear of embarrassment
8. _____ fear of abandonment
9. _____ fear of rejection
10. _____ fear of _____
11. _____ fear of _____

Try to find examples of fear messages that appeal to each of these fears. You may find most of them in advertisements or news items in various media, but also attend carefully to your conversations with friends; they too try to persuade us through fear.

In sum, appealing to fear does work. There are legitimate fear messages with real and likely dangers, but some fear messages are designed to manipulate us by exaggerating the danger of a situation.

Think About It: *The appeal to fear was effectively used against the front-runner in a presidential election. The other candidate pointed out that as governor, the frontrunner had pardoned a convict who, upon being released, killed again. This issue evoked fear in the voters and was heavily credited for the candidate's defeat.*

Appeal to Pride

> *Of all the causes which conspire to blind*
> *Man's erring judgment, and misguide the mind,*
> *What the weak head with strongest bias rules*
> *Is pride, the never-failing vice of fools.*
>
> —*ALEXANDER POPE*

At times persuaders appeal to our pride, "great intelligence" or "uncommon wisdom." An *appeal to pride* may work in two ways: it may increase our liking for the other and thereby increase that person's persuasive power, or it may inhibit us from consulting with others or listening to their sound advice.

As an example of appeal to pride, consider the salesperson who pays us a compliment about our superior intelligence and good taste compared with her other customers. She tells us that *we* wouldn't be duped into buying an inferior line of products, that for us only the best will do (the best is more expensive, of course). Feeling flattered, we may be more willing to buy her items. When we point out that the other retailers in the area have suggested that we not invest in the better product line, she asks us why we would even consider their views on the matter. Certainly, she tells us, we are not the kind of person who is told what to do. We are to lead, she says, not to follow. Whereupon we nod smugly in agreement and sign her purchase contract.

Erroneous Attacks

The Ad Hominem Argument
Reason, if it is against you, is a powerful enemy. Those who confront the power of reason without a rational defense often resort to the *ad hominem argu-*

ment, that is, an argument against the person (literally, "to the man"). This is an attempt to discredit a person's argument or position by attacking the person's character. *Ad hominem* arguments are commonly used by politicians in an election year; they're called "mud slinging" or "negative campaigning." Such arguments can sink presidential candidates, especially when they involve sexual impropriety, unpopular affiliations, illicit drug use, or questionable military service.

Ad hominem arguments are erroneous because the character of the person has nothing to do with the merit of one's position or argument. Someone who experimented with marijuana in his twenties *can,* later in life, advance reasonable arguments for controlling drug use; a man who is unfaithful to his wife may yet be a successful politician; and a draft dodger in the sixties can, thirty years later, have valid reasons for the arming or disarming of America. Yet in spite of its invalidity, the *ad hominem* argument does influence Americans' attitudes against the attacked person. That is why it is so commonly used in politics.

MS. A: . . . And that's why I am running for election against my opponent.

OPPONENT: Well, we have all heard Ms. A's eloquent speech, and the numerous faults she finds with my political record. Funny how she can find faults with others so easily but not with herself. A woman who has married two draft dodgers can hardly expect to have the respect of patriotic American people, no matter how eloquently she speaks. Of course she doesn't talk about that, does she? Nor does she mention her experimentation with marijuana in college. Is this the kind of woman we want in office? She talks about being committed to the American people, yet she herself can't even stay committed to her husbands. Two divorces and rumors of infidelity won't sell commitment to the American people. How can anyone take this woman seriously as a contender for office?

Ad hominem arguments are even less legitimate when they attack the person's former character. Such an attack assumes that people always remain the same. If that were so, each of us would be fully mature by our twenty-first birthday and experience would be no teacher at all. The view that no change occurs in a person's character or wisdom during a lifetime of experience flies in the face of social science theory and research, not to mention common sense.

> *Think About It:*   *Are attacks on character ever justified?*

The Straw Man Argument

It's not hard to attack a scarecrow. A *straw man attack* distorts the opponent's position or assumptions in a manner that makes his position easily refutable. By arguing against a fabricated weak position, one can easily gain the upper hand. The "straw man" is usually a simplistic or extreme restatement of the opponent's real position. For example, one might argue against abortion by claiming that no one should have the right to kill babies. But this claim is an oversimplification of a very complex issue involving questions such as what human life is, when human life begins, how we know when human life begins, how we determine the value of human life, when human life becomes more valuable than the human life supporting it, and so on. To reduce the moral and scientific complexity of the issue to "killing babies" is to attack a straw man.

Abuse of Language

Withholding Quantification

Sometimes people try to persuade us by withholding information. Qualifiers such as "all," "some," "only," "usually," and "always" are left out of statements in the hope that the listener will fill in the desirable quantifier but one which is contrary to fact. This type of language abuse is called *withholding quantification.*

Withholding quantification might be used in a mild *ad hominem* argument as follows:

> Soldiers did drugs in Vietnam. Everybody knows that. And here is Dean standing before you bragging about his military service. We know, too, that soldiers suffer from post-traumatic stress disorder. Do we really want Dean serving in our government as state senator? Granted, he is not to blame for his status; we applaud him for fighting for us. Nonetheless, we must face the facts: drug abuse and PTSD are no laughing matters.

In the above argument the speaker suppresses quantification by not specifically mentioning whether all, many, some, or just a few soldiers did drugs in Vietnam. Clearly he would like his audience to fill the quantity "all" or at least "most." In his statement about post-traumatic stress, the speaker again withholds the quantification. What percentage of soldiers actually suffer PTSD? And for how long? The speaker doesn't say, so we must fill in the blanks. The speaker's argument works only if we assume that all or most soldiers did drugs and all or most of them develop PTSD.

Suggestion

Withholding quantification is a form of suggestion. *Suggestion* occurs when we hint at something without really stating it. In the example above, the speaker doesn't say that *all* soldiers used illegal drugs, but he suggests it by concealing the quantification. Another way to suggest an idea without actually stating it is to couch it with words such as "hope," "might," and "maybe." The statement "The board might want to question this person's integrity" suggests that it ought to. But a person making such a statement can appeal to the literal interpretation and claim that he did not say that the person's integrity was questionable. Similarly, the statement "I hope your party can handle this tough job" could suggest doubt about the party's ability to do so. However, it could also be quickly reinterpreted as a goodwill gesture by changing the meaning of "hope."

People may try to persuade us by suggesting we will receive favors or advantages if we comply with their requests, only to back down later by appealing to the literal interpretation of their promises: "I said *maybe* I'd speak to the boss on your behalf if you cooperated with me on this project. I didn't say I *would*."

In sum, we must be careful about assuming what is only suggested in a statement. Reading and listening carefully for "*mights*" and "*maybes*" and being cautious about filling in missing quantifiers will help us think more critically about the claims we hear and will decrease the likelihood of being persuaded by misleading statements.

Ignoring the Question

Listen carefully. Sometimes it's not so much what we hear as what we do not hear. A person trying to persuade another with an argument may face a threatening challenge or question. One common way of responding to such a challenge is to ignore the question altogether. This tactic is quite common in politics: the candidates avoid answering questions that might cost them votes.

> **Think About It:** *In the first century* B. C. E., *Publius Syrus, author of the maxim "A rolling stone gathers no moss," also said, "It is not every question that deserves an answer." What questions can you think of that do not deserve an answer? How should we respond to such questions?*

SUMMARY

It could be said that persuasion, of all the types of communication we engage in, demands the most thinking. Besides having a command of the subject matter, we must think carefully about how we present ourselves, think thoroughly and empathetically about the audience, hold a tight reign on our emotions, and present our rationale in a positive, sensitive way that supports the audience's needs and moves them to accept our position. Then we can ask for their response, a commitment to take action based on that position.

We have presented an ethical thinking process that can lead to honest, solid persuasion; but there are other routes, deceitful and often effective, that we need to recognize and reject, including lowballing, which doesn't give us a fair picture of our options; the foot-in-the-door technique, which moves us toward a redefinition of ourselves and a new level of commitment; the door-in-the-face technique, which takes advantage of our sense of fair play; spending time, which uses our sense of guilt to pressure us into an action; attacking a straw man, which dethrones a simplistic version of our argument; hitting our human weaknesses with *ad hominem* attacks; appealing to fear, pity, and pride; and abusing language through suggestion, withheld quantification, and ignoring the question.

In short, by thinking carefully, by deflecting cunning persuasive tactics, and by crafting sensitive, logical persuasive techniques, we can most effectively persuade.

PERSUASION CHALLENGES

1. This chapter presents a strategy of persuasion that respects those with other views and is sensitive to their values. Although we addressed changing views rather than values, are there any situations in which you might want to change the values of others? When would this be justified? Do you think the suggestions in this chapter would be useful in such an endeavor?

2. *Ad hominem* arguments, particularly in politics, often attack people as they *were*. Are such attacks ever justified? In what sense, if any, are we the same person from one decade to another? What stays the same?

3. In this chapter we left out a step of Pascal's persuasive process which is to "reveal to him the side on which [his view] is false" (1958, p. 4). Our reason for excluding this tactic was that we are trying to persuade, not win a debate. Do you think this fourth element has a proper place in persuasion?

4. Can you identify the root elements of people on both sides of these issues: capital punishment, abortion, gun control, AIDS testing, drug legalization, flag burning, and euthanasia?

5. During the next week, from magazines, conversations, news, commercials, and TV programs, observe and record any manipulative tactics that you see.

6. Some of the manipulative tactics we've discussed are similar and work quite well together. To help your understanding of them and how they might be applied, try to create scenarios in which more than one tactic is used. Is it possible to use all seven?

7. Under what conditions, if any, is it ethical to use the manipulative tactics of door-in-the-face, foot-in-the-door, and lowballing?

8. Do you believe that there is a distinction between manipulation and persuasion? Or is all persuasion manipulation?

9. Our rationale for presenting deceitful forms of persuasion is that awareness of them and how they work can reduce their effectiveness. Do you agree? Are there situations in which awareness alone will not lead to a solid defense against these techniques?

10. If you believe that someone is using one of the deceitful techniques on you, what would be an appropriate response?

11. To what extent are you encouraged at your place of employment to use deceitful persuasions for your own or your employer's gain? Do you rationalize away the questionable ethics of using such techniques?

12. We have listed only some techniques for persuasion that could be construed as manipulative. Can you think of other manipulative strategies? For example, what tactics are used in grocery stores?

13. Identify a recent appeal to pity that was justified and one that was not. Is the distinction an easy one to make?

14. There are many kinds of fear but some may be used more than others in persuasive appeals. For the next week be especially watchful for appeals to fear and identify the fears that are targeted. Are some kinds of fear targeted more than others?

15. Most people engage in some kind of pernicious behavior, such as smoking, drinking, and so on. Identify any pernicious behaviors you have and the fear messages that are commonly used to try to influence that behavior. Is denial a mechanism that you use to fight such persuasion? Do you deny denying?

16. *Ad hominem* attacks are popular in politics. What other occasions invite frequent use of such attacks?

17. Do some people have so little pride in themselves that an appeal to pride doesn't work? Does the appeal to pride work better the more pride we have? Explain.

18. Identify popular debatable issues and fabricate a straw man for each side. Are you guilty of using such attacks? To answer this question, think of positions that you hold with conviction and emotion. Now list the opposing position and your common arguments against it. Are your arguments against a simplistic version of the other side?

19. Create an argument that intentionally misleads by withholding quantification. Read it to some friends and see if they accept it uncritically.

20. Intentionally ignore a question that is asked of you and notice the effect on the speaker. How easy was it to evade the question?

21. Develop a persuasive essay or speech following these steps:
   a. Name your topic.
   b. Describe the audience.
   c. What is your purpose? What do you want the audience to do, feel, or think?
   d. What are your motivations, biases?
   e. Empathetically, in *their* words, describe the position that the audience holds now.
   f. Gently, objectively, introduce your position. Be careful to avoid any inflammatory words.
   g. Show how this position actually better meets the needs of the audience based on their root elements.
   h. Now ask them to move to this new position.
   i. It is often prudent to test your approach on people who are similar to the audience you want to persuade. If you lose them at any point, ask them to identify where you went astray and then improve that section. Some students in class probably hold the opposite position and can act as a test group.

12

Problem Solving

At least some *of the problems of life are novel and must therefore have novel solutions.*

—ABRAHAM MASLOW, MOTIVATION AND PERSONALITY

Impasse. The road is blocked. The job isn't working. The relationship is drifting apart. We have a problem that needs solving. *Problem solving* is applying critical thinking to achieve the goals and personal harmony that are important in our personal and professional lives. From day to day we face personal problems involving bad habits; psychological problems of adjustment; material problems like trying to figure out why our car won't start; interpersonal problems, as when our loved ones complain that we don't love them or that we don't spend enough time with them; and problems with values and beliefs, like wondering if God really exists, if prostitution is really wrong, or if there is life after death.

Some of these problems can be solved primarily through thinking and some through thinking ending in action. In this chapter we focus on common problems that can be solved through action, such as meeting our goal to graduate in four years, paying the bills on time, taking care of children while in college, getting a commitment to marry from our beloved, meeting financial goals in business, keeping morale high in the workplace, or meeting the needs of both employees and managers who have different interests and objectives.

In this chapter we attack problems in five steps: We define the problem; we remove barriers; we generate possible solutions through the strategies of information gathering, brainstorming, and creative thinking; we select a solution through preliminary evaluation, trial and error, evaluating pros and cons, working backwards, and through practical problem-solving tips; and finally, we evaluate and monitor the solution.

Hopefully we will emerge with a greater ability to solve some of the problems in our lives that would otherwise decrease our joy in living or hinder our occupational success. As we wrestle with these problems, we may find comfort in Carl Jung's words: "The meaning and purpose of a problem seem to lie not in its solution but in our working at it incessantly" (Jung, 1969, p. 394).

DEFINING THE PROBLEM

We cannot solve a problem unless we know what it is. If our car doesn't start, we wouldn't want to define the problem as "Life is one frustration after another." Even something like "My car doesn't work right," although more precise, is still an ill-defined problem. Defining the problem carefully means being as precise and as specific as possible. We could state, "My car doesn't start," or better, "My car doesn't start in the morning," or better yet, "My car doesn't start on wet mornings." This more specific definition enables us to identify the possible causes of the malfunctioning, and it shortens our path to the solution of the problem.

Consider a person who is suffering a lot of stress, which is making her life quite miserable. Her vague statement of the problem might be "Life stresses me out." If life itself stresses her out, then the solutions are limited and suicide might seem to be a reasonable option. On the other hand, a closer examination might show that on weekends life is pretty good. That might mean her problem lies at work or at school. Because she finds that work gives her a sense of accomplishment and camaraderie, she might narrow the problem to school. She reflects for a moment and realizes that she does enjoy some of her classes, such as psychology and American literature, but that her speech class fills her with an anxiety that lasts most of the week. The problem is now coming into focus: her enormous fear of giving speeches every week! Now this fairly well-defined problem can be addressed in a variety of ways. In sum, defining the problem as specifically as possible helps us focus on appropriate solutions.

Problems concerning human relations are often intricate and difficult to define. Suppose two people in different departments are not getting along very well. Management might define the problem as "Those departments can't stand each other." However, it may be that the employees are frustrated because the goals of one department are interfering with the goals of the other. One department, for example, may focus on production and the other on quality. In this case, a better formulation of the problem would state that one department's goal of quantity is interfering with the other's goal of quality. Without this precise definition, the manager might get the two departments together on the same company baseball team to improve camaraderie or change the office design so that members of the different departments are integrated. With these solutions, the problem would likely remain. In short, formulating the problem precisely and carefully is worth the time it takes; it is rewarded by a more rapid solution to the problem and might even yield an obvious solution.

Discovering Causes

Part of defining and understanding the problem is to look for the cause of the problem. A writer, for instance, could be experiencing frustration. She may find that her frustration comes from an inability to concentrate, and her lack of concentration stems from problems in a personal relationship. This discovery of the root cause allows her to try to work out her relationship problem and thereby regain her ability to focus on her writing.

   We can discover the causes of our problems by noticing the relationships among details. For example, if we notice that our concentration is impaired only when our children are playing in the house, we can be fairly confident that our children distract us. By noticing that whenever we feel time pressure we make mistakes, we can identify time pressure as the cause of our poor job performance. By noticing that our car starts well except on rainy days, we identify dampness to be a partial cause of the problem. And when we notice that low staff morale corresponds to an office restructuring, we might suspect restructuring to be the cause of the problem. In short, when variables continually coincide with each other, we can gain confidence that a cause-and-effect relationship is at work. (See chapter 10 for more discussion on deriving cause and effect from correlation, and chapter 9 for the different kinds of causation.)

   However, just as it is easier to spot a deer on the run than one standing still, it is usually easier to identify a cause-and-effect relationship when the causes of our problems come and go than when they are fixed. Our relationship problems, for example, may stem from a *persistent* negative attitude about people in general, or a basement water seepage problem may be caused by a *permanent* clay soil condition.

   Sometimes looking for correlating variables is a tedious task that can take years of observation before a cause-and-effect relationship is discovered. Fortunately, many of life's problems are not nearly as difficult to decipher as are cold fusion and quantum mechanics.

Problems Without a Cause

Some problems calling for answers do not have a cause. For instance, members of a product-marketing committee gridlocked over a marketing strategy for a new product do not look for causes but for creative ideas to sell their product. Another example of a causeless problem is the classic nine-dot problem. The challenge is to connect all nine dots with only four straight lines without the pencil leaving the paper. A search for causes will not help you.

$$\begin{matrix} \bullet & \bullet & \bullet \\ \bullet & \bullet & \bullet \\ \bullet & \bullet & \bullet \end{matrix}$$

For these and other problems for which solutions are not obvious when the causes are discovered, we need to generate ideas to find the solution that we desire.

REMOVING BARRIERS

Perhaps the first step in finding solutions is to examine two thinking barriers that inhibit our full problem-solving potential.

The Myth of Perfection

One barrier that clearly stands in the way of problem solving is the irrational wish for a perfect solution and the related belief that one best solution exists. In our world, perfection is generally a myth. There are ideas of perfect machines, but none exist, and there are ideas of perfect humans, although no one has yet become one. For many problems, many solutions will work, each with their own advantages and disadvantages, but rarely will one of them be perfect. If we search for the perfect solution, we waste time and energy and we may miss *good* solutions.

Often our striving for perfection is rooted in our fear of being unloved or unaccepted by others. We believe that if our solutions are less than perfect, then *we* are less than perfect. We believe that we might suffer ridicule, humiliation, and loss of self-esteem. It may be admirable to do the best we can with the situation and talents we are given, but it's irrational to continually insist on perfection.

> **Think About It:** *In what areas do you try to be perfect? Is your goal of perfection realistic? If not, practice accepting the less than perfect results.*

The Myth of Genius

Everyone has problem-solving ability. Problem solving requires creativity, which correlates only modestly with intelligence (Barron and Harrington, 1981). Thus, one does not have to be Immanuel Kant or Albert Einstein to be a good problem solver. That does not mean that we are all qualified to solve advanced problems in philosophy and science, however, for problem solving also requires knowledge; without knowledge of a discipline we cannot solve problems in that area. Fortunately, most of our problems involve knowledge that is readily obtainable and understandable by most persons. In short, what is generally lacking is not the intellectual ability to solve but the self-confidence to solve.

GENERATING SOLUTIONS

Once we let go of our barriers, we can begin to generate solutions by gathering information, thinking creatively, and brainstorming.

Gathering Information

Trying to solve a problem without information is like trying to drive a car without a steering wheel. Consider a college student faced with a scheduling problem and in a dilemma about what courses to take this semester. If she chooses her courses without adequate information about the college's policies and course scheduling, she may never see graduation. However, if she acquires information that answers the following questions, she will likely find a way to graduate on time: (1) what courses are required for the major? (2) do those courses require a prerequisite? (3) which of those courses are offered only once a year or every other year? (4) how many upper-level courses are required? (5) how many credits are allowed to transfer from other institutions? (6) what courses are offered during the summer session? (7) is independent study an option to meet a degree requirement when a scheduling conflict occurs? (8) are there any conditions under which course substitutions are allowed? (9) what general requirements must still be completed? And so on. Without gathering this information, she may not be able to solve her scheduling problem adequately.

With inadequate information, the solutions are weak. Consider the problem of controlling criminal behavior in the United States, which has one of the highest rates of violent crime in the world. Some common proposals to combat violent crime in America are to increase the size of the police force, develop stiffer prison sentences for offenders, increase the use of capital punishment for murderers, and increase the role of religion in our lives. Most of these solutions are not supported by social science research. For example, compared with other countries, the sentencing policies of the United States are actually stricter than many countries whose crime rate is a fraction of what it is in the United States. Capital punishment does not seem to make an appreciable difference on crime (Bailey, 1990; Newbold, 1990). And as far as religion goes, the percentage of people in the United States who attend church and believe in God is one of the highest in the world!

The research suggests instead that we might be better off addressing the variables that do correlate with increased violent behavior, such as great economic inequality among the different social classes, high unemployment, lack of attachment to significant others, parental abuse, and television violence. As we pointed out in chapter 10, "Scientific Thinking," a correlation does not necessarily mean a causal relationship exists between the variables, but it is certainly a good place to start.

> ***Think About It:*** *Is there a problem that you, your company, or the United States government is trying to solve without adequate information? What information seems to be missing?*

Identifying the Components

The more information we can collect, the better we are able to solve the problem. We can gain comprehensive information by identifying each known component of the problem and then obtaining information about each one. The components of any problem are the persons and objects involved in the problem, as well as the problem goal itself. If Green College, for example, has a declining enrollment, the components are the faculty, the administration, the community, the students, and the goal of increased enrollment. How knowledgeable, enthusiastic, and caring are the faculty? How competent, effective, and supportive is the administration? What is the college's image in the community? Who are Green College students? Why do students choose to attend or not attend Green College? How old are they? Where do they live? What social class are they from? Finally, Green College must look at the goal itself. Is increasing enrollment a realistic goal given the demographics?

> ***Think About It:*** *Sometimes we create our own problems. Our standards of performance are unrealistic, the time line we arbitrarily set is too short, the activities we engage in are too many. Which of these could you change to reduce your life's problems?*

THINKING ACTIVITY 12.1
Identifying Problem Components

Identify the components in each of the following problems. What questions would you ask about each component?

1. The president of the alumni association at the local university is having difficulty getting enough financial support from its alumni to meet the university's contribution goals this year.

2. The local community needs a highway bypass to decrease traffic through its city, but the proposed bypass route takes it through a residential area of a suburb. The threat of increased congestion, pollution, and noise has the suburbanites in an uproar.

3. NASA is frustrated because its radio signal is not firing the satellite's rocket booster in time to put it into orbit around the planet it is approaching.

4. A college student's goal of graduating in May is being thwarted by class-scheduling problems. Her last two required courses are offered at the same time!

5. Mark and his wife Elizabeth are unable to meet the demands of work and domestic life. Their job demands do not leave enough time for cleaning and maintaining their home.

6. A secretary cannot get her new computer to send her document to her printer. The document must be printed for an important business meeting beginning in fifteen minutes!

Sources of Information

When the problem concerns human relations, information can be requested of the other person or persons involved. What is their understanding and perception of the problem? What do they need and want? How do they think it should be solved? Simply talking with those involved often helps us to understand better. However, many married couples, parents and children, managers and employees are often uncomfortable with direct communication. For them counseling is an option. Counselors spend their lives primarily aiding people in the communication of their feelings, needs, and desires in order to solve their problems.

Experts are a prime source of information. We might communicate with a psychologist about discipline problems with children, an accountant about a financial crisis, an auto mechanic about our car problems, or a lawyer about our legal problems. One word of caution: the experts must be objective. A stockbroker may push high-commission stocks and bonds instead of low-commission ones. One particularly valuable expert (and not particularly biased) is the local reference librarian, who can lead us to data such as the changing demographics in a small town, the pros and cons of various investment strategies, neighborhood crime statistics, changing property values, effective child-raising techniques, and manuals for repairing and building almost anything.

The last important source of information is ourselves. We all have a wealth of experience to bring to bear on many problem areas in our lives. Perhaps we live with the person involved in our problem and know that person better than anyone else, perhaps we can find similarities between our current and our past problems, perhaps we can use our ability to empathize with others to more fully understand even a novel interpersonal problem, or perhaps we can use knowledge acquired through years of education to understand more completely the problem and its components.

Creating a Healthy Communication Climate

Most problems involving people require some kind of communication with others. Such communication can help define the problem, identify causes of the problem, or help generate solutions. But communication will not be effective if we do not provide the right communication climate. Below are some tips that will improve the chances of productive communication with others.

1. *Avoid loaded words.* Some words inhibit people's true expression of their feelings by stirring up emotions and defensiveness or by setting a person up for rejection. Words like "stupid," "childish," "idiot," and so on should be avoided whenever possible. Instead of saying, "What do you think of that *stupid* slogan the marketing department came up with?" try, "What do you think of the marketing department's new slogan?" If someone actually likes the new slogan, the adjective "stupid" will make them feel that he will be rejected or laughed at if he expresses his true opinion. In this way loaded words inhibit the expression of true feelings and do not further communication.

2. *Avoid status barriers.* People are easily intimidated by signs of status and have a more difficult time expressing their true opinions when they feel less than equal to the person they are talking to. If we are sitting in a large chair at a large desk in a large room, with numerous diplomas decorating the walls, the person we are talking to might feel intimidated. It is better to come out from behind the desk and offer the person a seat in a chair that is equal in height to our own. It is also important to avoid a judgmental or superior attitude that sometimes accompanies a high-status position.

3. *Avoid defensiveness and anger; be a safe person.* No one is correct all the time, including ourselves. We need to remind ourselves that we are still worthwhile

(continued)

> ### Creating a Healthy Communication Climate *(continued)*
>
> persons when we make mistakes. If we can accept this, we can listen to the criticism of others without turning the communication into a hostile win-or-lose situation. If we can drop our defensive posture, we will also listen better, hearing what is being said instead of rehearsing our defense. Moreover, if we are known to turn every attempt at constructive criticism into an angry situation, others will stop talking to us about important matters.
>
> 4. *Be open-minded.* If we convey an attitude of intolerance for others' ideas before we even hear them, there is a good chance we never will hear them. We must be willing to let go of our tenacious grasp on our own ideas, for no matter how certain we are that we have the right insight or the correct solution to a problem, we may be wholly wrong. A rigid attitude only discourages honest communication.
>
> 5. *Rephrase communication.* In order to make sure that we understand what others are saying to us, it is important to restate their position back to them in our own words. This reassures them that we are listening and gives them an opportunity to correct us if we have misunderstood them.

Think About It: *Can you think of any communication that you have experienced recently in which one or more of these suggestions were ignored? What was the effect on the communication?*

CREATIVE THINKING

After we have gathered information and identified components, if a solution is not apparent, we can use methods of creative thinking to help us find solutions. In thinking creatively we must strive to transcend our usual ways of seeing. We should not limit ourselves to seeing what we are supposed to see or thinking about things as we were taught to think about them. We must learn to see and think without assumptions, stereotypes, or expectations, much as a painter does when looking at a penny lying on the floor, seeing it as oval instead of round or as brown with a white sheen instead of copper.

To think creatively we must transcend the world of dos and don'ts and enter the world of the impossible, the frivolous, the vulgar, and the absurd. We must see things not for what they are or for what they were meant to be, but for what we can imagine them to be. This world of the creative is in each of us. We need only watch a young child play to realize the creativity that was once present in all of us.

THINKING ACTIVITY 12.2
Functional Fixedness

Seeing things only for what they were meant to be used for and not seeing things for what they can be used for is called *functional fixedness*. A book is meant for reading, a waste basket for waste, and a hair dryer for drying hair. But a book can be used for a weight or a booster seat, a wastebasket for a flowerpot, and a hair-dryer for drying paint.

Try to transcend functional fixedness to solve the two problems below:

> *Problem 1:* Two strings about four feet long are suspended from an eight foot ceiling at opposite points in a room. Each string is about three feet from the nearest wall. Your task is to tie them together. Although the strings are long enough to meet in the middle, holding on to one of them prevents you from grasping the other, which is just two feet out of your reach. Nearby, and within reach as you hang onto one string, is a desk with some tools on it: a hammer, a pair of pliers, a screwdriver, and a penknife. What do you do? (adapted from Maier, 1931)

> *Problem 2:* On a table is a full box of kitchen matches, a candle, and some tacks. Your task is to attach the candle to the wall in a way that wax will not drip on the floor. What do you do? (Duncker, 1945)

SELECTING SOLUTIONS

When all ideas have been generated, we can best select solutions by *preliminary evaluation,* in which we use our imagination to assess the value of a solution before it is even implemented. We can also select solutions by assessing pros and cons, by using the trial-and-error method, by working backwards, and by following a few other tactics and tips.

Preliminary Evaluation

> *[Newton's] peculiar gift was the power of holding continuously in his mind a purely mental problem until he had seen through it.*
>
> —*JOHN MAYNARD KEYNES*

Sometimes we imagine the solution to a problem so automatically that we may not realize we have solved a problem. For example, how would we remove three pennies from the bottom of a tall glass if we were only given the choice of using a clothespin, coat hanger, or long, thin tongs? Which would we choose? Undoubtedly we would pick the long tongs and reject the other items; in essence, we "evaluated" imperceptibly.

> ***Think About It:*** *There are ways to get the pennies out of the glass with the other items. Do you know how?*

Just as we browse through the shopping malls and imagine how we would look in certain clothes, in preliminary evaluation we picture the problem, but with this difference: we attempt to consider many more components and possible responses to the proposed solution. Most men and women probably do not imagine how a piece of clothing would fit when they raise their arms, nor are they likely to imagine how it would look on them as they run to the bus stop; some may imagine how it would look sitting down or bending over, but many do not. In preliminary evaluation we must imagine implementing the solution, while considering the solution's effects on as many variables as possible.

Problems in Anticipation

> *I remember the rage I used to feel when a prediction went awry. I could have shouted at the subjects of my experiments. "Behave, damn you, behave as you ought!" Eventually I realized that the subjects were always right. It was I who was wrong. I had made a bad prediction.*
>
> —B. F. SKINNER, WALDEN TWO

Anticipating becomes more difficult when there are many components and possible interactions. For instance, in order to predict our weather perfectly, we would have to know all of the variables precisely. If one small weather variable were miscalculated, it could eventually affect the entire forecast for a given area in the future. Failure to accurately measure the ocean's temperature in one rather small area, for example, could lead to warmer or colder air than predicted and make or break the formation of a storm. The immense difficulty in this type of forecasting has generated the mathematical and scientific theory of chaos.

Anticipation is also confounded by "*wildcard" variables.* These are variables that arise unexpectedly, such as the sudden separation and divorce of the company's president and its effects on the president's competence and risk-taking behavior, volcanic eruptions and their effects on the weather, a sudden coup in a foreign country and its effects on the stock market, and an ex-spouse's sudden refusal to pay child support and its effects on the other spouse's plans to earn a college degree.

Perhaps the most unpredictable variable is the human variable. Behind people's actions are their goals, their life meanings, their personal histories, as well as whether or not they ate breakfast that morning or suffered insomnia the night before. Any predictive solution involving the human component is only a fragile prediction.

In sum, because numerous problem variables (especially human ones) and their numerous interaction effects are difficult to predict, our preliminary evaluation cannot be totally accurate, but it can be careful, intelligent, and well-intentioned; in other words, our evaluation can be good but it will never be perfect.

Chaotic Systems

Much of science has been dominated by the great laws of nature, concerning motion, thermodynamics, nuclear periodicity, and relativity. These laws work well when applied to simple movements such as those of a planet, an airplane, or a baseball, producing such accurate predictions that the universe appears to be determined. However, other areas of nature seem to be impossible to determine. These areas are called *chaotic systems*. According to chaos theory, chaotic systems are extremely sensitive to "initial conditions," meaning that any uncertainty or error in the measurement of the system's variables at a given time will eventually lead to conditions that were not foreseeable. Changing weather, liquid turbulence, and the branching of trees, blood vessels, and neurons in the brain are examples of chaotic systems. Even economics and human behavior can be seen as chaotic systems.

In chaotic systems, if we cannot measure the crucial variables with infinite precision, then our prediction will go awry at some time, the more errors, the sooner it will go awry. And because infinite measurement is impossible, these systems are only roughly predictable at short intervals and theoretically unpredictable at long intervals. As time goes by, small errors in measurement mount to make the difference between, say, a hurricane and ideal golfing weather, and they can make the difference between our solution's failure or success. In short, there are many uncertainties in problem solving, particularly in searching for long-term solutions; the further out in time we project our solution, the more likely chaos will intervene.

Pros and Cons

Problem solutions are imperfect; a solution may often have strengths on one side and weaknesses on another. We must then determine whether the strengths outweigh the weaknesses enough to justify implementing the solution. Assessing the strengths and weaknesses of situations is sometimes called *cost-benefit analysis*. This analysis looks at both quantity and quality. For instance, a solution may have two drawbacks and one advantage; the drawbacks seem to win from the quantity point of view. But if the single advantage were very important, it would outweigh the numerically superior drawbacks.

The strengths and weaknesses of a solution depend on the value we assign to different outcomes. For instance, if a solution looks profitable it may be adopted despite serious drawbacks to human psychological and physical health. This can be seen in U.S. policies on air quality. On more than one occasion, deadlines for meeting air-quality standards have been extended because industries have complained of the expense. In the meantime, millions of human beings suffer the consequences of air pollution, including death. Yet, if one gives high value to the dollar and low value to health hazards, the solution may be seen as a good one. Values are intricately linked to our assessment of a solution's worth.

Other variables to consider when weighing pros and cons are timeliness, effectiveness, reliability, reversibility, and the risk of making a bad decision. A great solution that cannot be implemented for some years may in fact be no solution at all because it is not timely. Effectiveness is the extent to which the solution actually resolves the problem. Reliability is how consistently the solution will work. And reversibility is the ease with which the solution can be retracted without serious consequences. Supreme Court decisions, for example, are not easily reversible.

The risks of making a bad decision can be gauged by asking, "What's the worst that can happen?" Would someone die? Would we remain unhappy for the rest of our days? Would we be fired? Would someone be injured? Obviously, if the costs of implementing a wrong solution were high, we would hesitate and look for a better alternative or do a more careful preliminary evaluation before implementing it.

Other important questions remain to be asked in a cost-benefit analysis of the solution. Is it ethical? How will it effect our family and other relationships? Are the human resources available for implementation? And so on. All the variables described above call for active thinking to determine the best possible solution.

Rejections on Minor Grounds

It is not usually reasonable to reject a proposal because there is one drawback to it. Often very good ideas may have one or two disadvantages. Unfortunately, it is quite common to have such solutions rejected because of minor drawbacks, even though the advantages far outweigh the disadvantages. The failure of those who reject the proposal might lie in one of two areas: they assume that a perfect proposal exists, or they fail to recognize the advantages of the solution over the disadvantages. Many good solutions have been rather quickly dismissed because of one salient drawback. The real issue, however, may be a need to protect some personal interest or simply a fear or reluctance to change. Awareness of these irrational rejections will help us objectively weigh the advantages and disadvantages of a given solution.

THINKING ACTIVITY 12.3
Weighing Pros and Cons

Identify the pros and cons of the following solutions to curb the handgun homicide rate in the United States.

1. Make it illegal to own a handgun and create severe, mandatory sentencing for violation of this law.
2. Require that people convicted of theft or violent crime after the age of twelve be forbidden forever to own a handgun.
3. Require that the punishment for any crime committed with a handgun be double what it would have been without a handgun.
4. Require every middle school and high school in the United States to set up metal-screening devices in school entrances and conduct thorough locker checks at random throughout the school year.
5. Require that all citizens carry a handgun in their cars, places of business, and homes for their own defense.
6. Forbid the television industry to broadcast programs with scenes of gun murder.
7. Require parents to lock up all handguns and ammunition they own and remove children from the home of any parent who fails to abide by this law.
8. Tax the wealthy more in order to reduce the income inequality that leads to greater poverty and frustration among the lowest economic class.
9. Initiate an education program starting in elementary school that instills self-esteem, teaches self-restraint, and explores alternatives to violence for solving personal problems.
10. Enlist the services of the United States Army in the control of illegal substances in the United States.

Subgoal Analysis

Sometimes a problem can be broken down into smaller problems, each having its own solution. The apparently insurmountable goal of writing a term paper, for example, can be broken down into many subgoals: write the pros, write the cons, write the conclusion, and write the introduction. Instead of one goal involving ten pages, we have four goals involving two or three pages each. Even subgoals can often be further broken down. In this way overwhelming tasks become manageable problems. As another example, consider the goal of building a substantial savings. The first goal might be to get a good-paying job, the second goal to pay off all debts, and the third goal to invest in appropriate mutual funds or stocks. Each of these subgoals is a problem in itself, but as smaller problems they are less threatening and easier to manage, and solutions are easier to come by.

Moreover, as we find ways to achieve each subgoal, we gain reinforcement, self-confidence, and the motivation necessary to achieve our ultimate goals.

Trial and Error

The trial-and-error method of problem solving, involving little preliminary evaluation, is the process of trying solution after solution until we happen upon the correct one. Such trials may be guided by nothing more than a hunch or simple experimental inquisitiveness, or they may be slight modifications of earlier trials that almost reached the mark.

Often we use this hit-or-miss approach because we do not understand the problem very well, critical information is lacking, or the problem components and possible interactions among them are too numerous for us to be able to anticipate a solution. The trial-and-error method may sound rather primitive and inferior to a more methodical approach, but as a last resort it can be an exciting way to solve problems. Before beginning trial and error, however, we must be careful about serious negative consequences that might result. If the cost of a mistake is high, such as serious injury or losing one's life savings, then the trial-and-error method is inappropriate.

> **Think About It:** *Should the trial-and-error method be used in medicine? If so, under what circumstances?*

Working Backwards

> *In solving a problem of this sort, the grand thing is to be able to reason backward.*
>
> —*ARTHUR CONAN DOYLE, A STUDY IN SCARLET*

Another problem-solving technique that involves little or no preliminary evaluation is to start with the goal, imagine the step just before the goal, the step before that step, and so on, until we arrive at the first step. That first step is then implemented, as are the others, in forward order. Suppose, for example, that we want to move our library books into what is now the bedroom, so that the old library room can become the new baby's room. Thinking backwards about this problem might go something like this:

> I can't move the library into the bedroom because the bedroom is occupied with furniture. So I'll first move the furniture into the spare room that will be the new bedroom. But the spare room is full of boxes with all my precious

memorabilia. Of course that can go in the basement. But the basement leaks water, which means I'll have to stack the boxes on shelves. Shelves! I don't have any shelves. So I'll first have to get some shelves. But I can't load heavy shelves into my car. Maybe my brother can help me. I'll give him a call. But I don't have his number; he just moved. Mom has it; I'll give her a call.

In this way we've discovered that the first step in moving our library is to call mom. As simple as this working backwards procedure is, many people fail to use it and find themselves stuck in the middle of a mess.

Problem-Solving Tips

When we encounter what appears to be an unsolvable problem, sometimes a solution is waiting to be discovered. Here are a few tips that can help to break the impasse.

Tip 1: Change deadlines.   When we are overwhelmed with a number of activities or cannot find the human or other resources in time to accomplish the task, we can remember that deadlines are often not firmly fixed (epitaphs are written in stone, but even the IRS grants extensions). Sometimes we set a deadline for ourselves and never consider extending it, even though an extension would cause only minor inconvenience. At other times, of course, we are at the mercy of deadlines set by others. It is often worth approaching others for an extension, because many deadlines are set rather arbitrarily in the first place.

Tip 2: Compromise.   Sometimes our problem component is a person who appears unyielding on an issue, such as the hours he will work or the kind of work he will do. We need to remember that people are not always as rigid as they seem to be and that some people are influenced by good reasons to change. Look for a compromise to solve the problem.

Tip 3: Check the facts.   Things are not always what they seem. In the world of human relationships, we often get a problem picture that is a gross misrepresentation of the real situation. We might hear, for example, that employees in department B are angry at management and are threatening to quit en masse if certain demands are not met. This would be a serious problem, except that it may be entirely fiction, a mere rumor grown to enormous proportions. Therefore, it is always worth checking to see if the problem as we understand it is the problem as it really is.

Tip 4: Use empathy.   Empathy is seeing and feeling the world from the other's point of view. In working on problems involving people, it is essential that we learn to empathize with the situation of others, for only then can we truly understand the problem.

Tip 5: Take time to reflect. When we are faced with a complicated and challenging problem, it takes time to acquire the information and understanding necessary for a good solution. It also takes time to do an adequate preliminary evaluation. A hurried approach may give us a brief sense of accomplishment and temporary relief from pressure, but only until the solution fails. Even worse, a quick and haphazard approach may exacerbate the problem. For example, a quickly and poorly thought-out decision to engage the enemy in war instead of in diplomatic dialogue could grow into global warfare. On a lesser scale, imagine the consequences of making a hasty decision about our major in college, whom to marry, or how to deal with a serious relationship issue. Some problem solutions can be revoked with little or no effect; others, however, may leave irretrievable marks.

Tip 6: Anticipate potential problems. It is better to have potential problems worked out ahead of time. Anticipating problems can often lead us to take a course of action that avoids them altogether. And if a potential problem emerges, we will have alternatives ready.

Tip 7: See problems as fun! Most problems can be viewed as challenges or oppportunities, and solving them can even be fun! This perspective reduces stress and makes problem solving enjoyable. Of course, this attitude is difficult to achieve if deadlines are pressing and unyielding or the consequences of a wrong decision are enormously serious.

EVALUATING SOLUTIONS

After the choice is implemented, the solution should be monitored to measure its effectiveness. If the problem remains, the solution may be rejected in favor of an alternative one. However, we should hesitate before rejecting the solution outright; often some slight modification will allow the original solution to work properly. If the modification required is major, the modification may then be treated as another problem to solve.

SUMMARY

We have focused on everyday problems that can be solved through action. The first step in problem solving is to define the problem as precisely as possible. If we define our problems precisely we can often identify the causes, sometimes leading us immediately to a resolution. Not all problems, however, are approached correctly by searching for causes.

In working toward a resolution, we must remove barriers such as irrational ideas about perfection, fear of failure, and fixed ways of thinking. We can then begin generating solutions by gathering full information from experts, personal experience, librarians, and the people involved in the problem itself.

Sometimes finding a solution requires thinking creatively about the world. We can then select a solution through preliminary evaluation, assessment of pros and cons, identification of subgoals, or working backwards. If key information is lacking, or the problem is too complex to anticipate a solution, the trial and error method can be tried as long as the consequences of a wrong decision are not critical. Finally, we can recall some problem-solving tips: (1) change deadlines, (2) compromise, (3) check the facts, (4) empathize, (5) take time to think, (6) anticipate problems, and (7) see the problem as a challenge. We then implement and monitor the solution.

PROBLEM-SOLVING CHALLENGES

1. Have you ever solved the wrong problem by buying or fixing the wrong part? How could this have been prevented?

2. In what way is the search for a clear definition to a problem similar to searching for the cause of the problem?

3. Solving a mechanical problem is simple compared with a human problem. How might you solve the problem of a relationship that is going sour?

4. Select a personal problem and apply the problem-solving strategies in this chapter. Do any of the problem-solving tips apply here?

5. Select a huge social or economic problem (such as teenage pregnancy, rampant crime, drug abuse, the high divorce rate) and write a paper on how you would go about solving this problem using the approaches in this chapter.

6. If we can name the problem we are half way to solving it. Do you think this statement is accurate? Why or why not?

7. What are your barriers to solving problems?

8. Why are more managers in manufacturing plants now listening to their line workers?

9. In this chapter we ask you to think forwards (anticipate how the solution will work) and to think backwards (to get a starting point). Think forward and imagine where you want to be in five years. From that point, think backwards to find the next significant step you must take to get there.

10. Having a list of pros and cons can give you greater objectivity. Take a major personal concern of yours right now (or a social concern, such

as whether all Americans should be tested for AIDS) and list the pros and cons.

11. What constitutes a good solution? How do we know when a problem is solved? Although this question sounds simple, it may take more thinking than we expect.

12. Trial and error may seem scary or risky. When would you use it? When would you not use it?

13

Evaluating

The test is: will the concept work? Does it give an unforced unity to the experience of man? Does the concept make life orderly, not by edict, but in fact?

—*JACOB BRONOWSKI, SCIENCE AND HUMAN VALUES*

What a great idea! Sometimes we are struck by our own brilliance: the idea *is* great. It might be applauded by others and we feel duly appreciated, but sometimes it is rejected or outrightly scorned. What then? Does the rejection and scorn make our idea bad? When we rethink our idea we may understand why it was rejected, we may see the flaw in our thinking, or the poor factual foundation, but at other times we may still be convinced of the greatness of our idea. Who's right? How then do we validate our thinking?

When we evaluate our thinking, we are judging it. We are calling upon that function of our mind that psychologist Benjamin Bloom considered one of the highest acts of the human intellect. We are sitting in judgment with Solomon and the great Supreme Court justice John Marshall, exuding wisdom—or so we hope. In this chapter we use our judging intellect to understand how we need to test our thinking through dialogue; we consider the tests of reproductivity, simplicity, predictability, perspective, balance, completeness, and longevity; and we revisit our thinking bases—our senses, feelings, language, memory, logic, creativity, and organization—as major checkpoints to evaluate our thinking. Although our approach here is systematic and thorough, in our individual acts of evaluating we do not usually move systematically through each checkpoint;

rather, we tend to sweep across the bases and examine those areas that seem to contain weak thinking.

THE NECESSITY TO TEST THINKING

Testing, or validation, is the final step of the scientific method, and whenever possible we need to apply it to our own thinking. Without testing, the scientific method can fail miserably. The Hubble telescope was not tested before it was sent into orbit; it was aimed at a distant formation and gave blurred results; then it was discovered that the mirror was inaccurately ground and did not focus light precisely. Astronomers and taxpayers were angry, frustrated, and rather incredulous that such a simple step had been overlooked. NASA sent a multi-million dollar piece of equipment into space before seeing whether or not it worked.

Testing is a step we need to apply to our thinking whenever possible. How many times have we had a great idea and, when we tried it, were embarrassed because we had overlooked an obvious obstacle. In the abstract, our thinking can seem fine. For instance, a group of students were trying to get everyone over a wall as part of a character-building program. At first thought it seemed natural that the bigger students would boost the smaller ones to the top of the wall, so that is what they did. At the end, the last and largest student was stuck on the ground. By trying out their idea, the group found that they had to reverse their thinking plan and get the bigger students to the top of the wall first because it took many smaller students to lift them. The bigger students could then reach down and pull up the lighter students. Sometimes our thinking seems fine until we try it out, but without testing it first, our thinking could fail like the Hubble telescope.

It is not always simple to test our thinking and rarely can we achieve conclusive results. Although we might like to have a scientific "certainty" in all realms of thinking, often the best corroboration we can get is strong agreement from others.

The Crucible of Critical Dialogue

Critical dialogue is to thinking what testing is to science. We test our ideas in the crucible of active interchange, refutation, modification, and acceptance of ideas. In a community of thinkers, what is written can be critiqued and what is said can be debated and discussed. Unless our thinking is to remain valuable to us alone, we must express it and test it, or it will die with us.

If marketers want to know whether a new product will sell, they form focus groups of typical customers, give them the product, and listen to their criticisms. If an author wishes to test her book, she sends it to readers and asks for their reactions. Similarly, all areas of human living such as cooking, poetry, work, art, architecture, fashion, entertainment, and sports are critiqued by others.

Ultimately others became our jury. Writers turn to readers, politicians turn to voters, marketers turn to buyers, and ministers turn to parishioners. Sometimes we can select our jury before the actual trial. We can take our thoughts and papers to those whose thinking is respected by the community, to those who are knowledgeable, to those who are not biased toward us or our ideas. Even as you now read this book, you are part of the jury for the authors' thinking. You can evaluate the work. Did it help you understand the nature of thinking? Did it spark further ideas? Did it provide answers? Did it lead to further questions?

THINKING ACTIVITY 13.1
Using Dialogue

List three or four ideas you have had or actions you have taken that would have been better if they had been tested by dialogue. List a few times when you did talk with someone about your ideas and were glad you did. List two or three decisions you might be making in the future that would be aided by critical dialogue. Who are the people you want to talk to?

Critical Monologue

When we do not have competent critics at hand, we have to go it alone to test our own thinking; we have to hold a dialogue as it were, with ourself. In that case, as we noted in chapter 1, writing is one of the best tools to objectify, or mirror, our thinking. After we have written out our thoughts, we should set them aside. The longer we wait before we read them, the better chance we have to read them critically, as if they were not our own, as if the words on the paper were the only clues to the meaning of our topic.

One way to gain this objectivity is to imagine our harshest critics reading our writing while we are watching and getting their reactions. Under such scrutiny we will write nothing that we cannot support. Through this critical monologue, our thinking will tighten.

The Elegance of Simplicity

> *Genius is the ability to reduce the complicated to the simple.*
>
> —*C. W. CERNAN*

Since many great insights are simple, simplicity can sometimes be part of the evaluation process. Consider a few simple but great ideas: if we roll a ball, it keeps going until something stops it; when a bullet explodes from the barrel, it recoils back on the rifle; the sun and the earth, or any two objects, attract each other, and the bigger and closer they are, the more they attract. These three examples are the three great laws of motion stated by Newton, and they are elegantly simple. So too is the simple pattern of the DNA molecule, which varies only four steps up a winding staircase (adenine, thymine, cytosine, and guanine); and Mendeleev's periodic table, which embraces all matter, simply counts protons from 1 to 92: 1 proton = hydrogen, 2 protons = helium, and so forth.

$E = mc^2$ is beautifully simple.

Simplicity is valued in most fields; complexity is often a failure to communicate simply. In philosophy we have referred to the elegant simplicity of Ockham's razor. In language we saw the clarity and force of brevity. Some of the most-quoted passages in literature are profoundly simple. What would you think of a six-word passage in which five of the words had only two letters and the sixth word had only three letters? "To be, or not to be, that is the question." Most of us have been frustrated by the compounded intricacies of legal documents. (We know one author who spent longer negotiating a publishing contract than she spent writing the book.) Against this legal verbiage Montaigne affirms simplicity: "The most desirable laws are those that are fewest, simplest, and most general" (1967, p. 345). Suspect complexity. Think simple.

The Flattery of Imitation and Development

Fertile ideas reproduce. If our testing has upheld our thinking, we may be rewarded with the imitation and expansion of our ideas, both of which are additional tests of the worth of our thoughts. Imitation is a high form of flattery and a partial validation of an idea because good ideas are often repeated. Without imitation of some kind, a loudly proclaimed idea can collapse like the "discovery" of cold fusion.

An even higher form of flattery occurs when the ideas are so good that they are used as the basis for other ideas. This expandability is also a partial test of the worth of an idea. Plato and Aristotle's foundational ideas were expanded into the towering structure of Western philosophy. Shakespeare's rhythms and metaphors form the center of the last 400 years of literature. Freud opened the door to the unconscious mind through which countless psychologists still walk. Watson and Crick began unraveling the spiral DNA, and the massive unfolding of the genome continues.

The Power of Predictability

Like expandability, predictability also tests the worth of ideas. Mendeleev's simple table predicted all the elements long before they were found. Einstein's relativity theory predicted that mass would bend light—an occurrence that eventually was measured during an eclipse as starlight bent around the sun. The contemporary quark/lepton theory predicted that six quarks would be found, and described the nature of each: the discovery of the last quark, "Top," was announced late in 1992. So we should ask ourselves, does our thinking help to predict how other ideas or pieces of the puzzle might fit around this one?

Perspective, Balance, and Completeness

Mount Everest used to be called "Peak 15." That's because it didn't look big to the British survey team that first named it, they were too far away. Without the proper perspective the highest mountain in the world was just another large peak. The perspective we have changes our view. If we are lying in the grass, we have a limited view; if we stand up we see more. If we climb a tree, board a plane, or look down at the earth from a satellite camera, our perspective changes. Which is better—in the grass or up in a satellite? It depends. Are we studying an ant or the earth's weather patterns? We need the correct perspective for the thinking task at hand. Pascal cautions us:

> If we are too young or too old we do not judge well. If we think too much or not enough about a topic we can get infatuated or obstinate about it. If we enter something too soon or put it off too long, if we are too close or too far away we cannot see accurately. (1958, p. 103)

Keeping perspective takes balance. As Pascal notes, extreme distance, age, effort, and time can all cause distortions in judgment. We need balance, the balance of Aristotle's golden mean. This is not a lukewarm mediocrity but the balance on a high wire, the tension in a pre-war debate in congress, the judge upholding the law and being merciful to one who stole out of hunger. *Virtus stat in medio.* ("Virtue stands in the middle"). And we might add *veritas.* Truth in thinking threads the needle.

Part of keeping *balance* is completeness. Do all three legs of the tripod touch ground? Are all of the necessary facts involved in the thinking (remember the blind men feeling different parts of the elephant)? A newspaper described the first-place and third-place awards in a sand-sculpting contest. Readers were disturbed that second place was not announced, even though they did not know the participants. Completeness of thought is part of evaluating thought; as Shakespeare says, "Ripeness is all."

The Test of Time

Chronology is a quick test. Does our information line up in the order it happened? Chronology is also a long test: will our thinking stand the test of time? Aristotle's old idea that there is nothing new under the sun has been assailed by newness yet has stood the test of many sunsets. Of course we cannot wait centuries to test our thinking, but if our ideas are sound and profound they will likely grow and endure; if they are fragile and faddish, they will likely flash and fade. Although time is an old test, however, it is good to remember that not all old ideas are true, for as Montaigne tells us, "Truth is none the wiser for being old" (1958, p. 364).

THINKING ACTIVITY 13.2
Does Time Always Test True?

If it lasts it's good; if it doesn't, it's bad. How accurate is the test of time? Can you think of any historical people, events, or inventions that were misjudged by "time"? Can you recall any idea that has stood the test of time, even for centuries, but has now been "proved" wrong? If time was wrong in that interim, how do we know it is right now? How many ways can time be wrong? Make some guesses about which current ideas or authors will become classics, that is, will still be valued hundreds of years from now.

TESTING AGAINST OUR THINKING BASES

Let's quickly return to our thinking bases to evaluate the effectiveness of our thinking.

Personal Barriers

When we do not have the counterpoint of vigorous dialogue, we especially need to be wary of our personal barriers. If the topic we are thinking about elicits strong emotions from us, we need to think carefully and objectively to avoid any distortion in our thinking. We need to be careful that we are not thinking in a stereotypical and encultured manner and that our personal wishes and personal pride are not overwhelming our good sense. We must also be aware of our level of stress, the condition of our body, and the effects these may have on our ideas.

Perceptions and Memory

A quick check: do we have the data right? Are we sure of our sensual perceptions? Do the appearances reflect the reality? Have we listened acutely and sensitively, and can we trust the speaker or writer? Are our facts correct? Are we confident that our memory is accurate? If any of our sensual sources or recollections is suspect, we can express our thinking conditionally and then research our doubts.

Language

Remember, our language does not just carry our thoughts, it is inextricably inter-twined with our thinking. If we have time to write out our thoughts, we can analyze the language of our thinking. We want to use clear definitions, appro-priate connotations, fitting analogies, correct word order, contextual awareness, concrete nouns and active verbs, and we want to keep our thinking as tight and precise as possible.

"Brevity is the soul of wit," says Shakespeare's verbose Polonius in self-reflecting mockery. And we can be sure that Polonius would have railed pompously against bureaucracy if he had heard Chicago officials announce three days after the Chicago River surged into the tunnel system and shut the city down, "Chicago is speeding up its paper work in order to get the Federal Govern-ment to declare it a disaster area." Amazingly, the third largest city in the United States closed while waiting for paper work. Can our thinking be like the gov-ernment? Can we afford a bureaucracy of words?

Brevity adds to clarity, and although brevity is the sister of simplicity, it is not simple to be brief. It is hard to trim our thinking, which is, says Montaigne, our child. However, if we take the attitude that trimming our thinking makes our child smarter, stronger, and more beautiful, it is easier to place the good (but inappropriate) thoughts into other files.

> ***Think About It:***   *Voltaire said, "I would have written a shorter let-ter if I had more time."*

Feelings

Are our feelings there? Can we reach down and identify them? Thinking with-out feeling is often cold and sterile. We need these feelings as the force behind our thoughts. How do we feel toward the topic? Toward the audience? We need to harness the powerful, positive force of these feelings as the heart behind the eloquence of our mind.

Creativity Check

Do our ideas glisten? Or is our mind a desert and our thinking dry? If so, we can be sure that the sand dunes will mount in our receiver's mind. We need water-spring metaphors for our thoughts to bloom. Remember the metaphor—the heart of language, of thinking, of newness, of great thinkers. If our thoughts are clichéd, our thinking will be repetitious, unoriginal, and boring, as desiccated as the desert. We want to remember to starburst, brainstorm, and in other ways coax our creativity to find that key analogy that will connect our thinking to the world and to other people.

Organization

Does our thinking have a clear structure: chronological, topical, analogical, causal, or other natural or mental structure? Can we state our goal clearly? Can we name the three or four most important supporting ideas? Do all the ideas link together? Does our thinking have the perspective, balance, and completeness to stand the test of time?

Logic Check

Is our thinking well-grounded and tightly constructed? How sound are our premises and our assumptions? Will they be accepted by our audience? Do we reason solidly down from these premises, following the laws of logic, to a valid conclusion? Is our inductive thinking based on solid and repeated observations? Is our cause-and-effect analysis sound? Have we avoided reasoning fallacies, especially those that are deceptively appealing to us?

THINKING ACTIVITY 13.3
Our Tone Toward Our Thinking

In a reflective move, turn your analysis inward and try to discover what your own feeling, or tone, is toward your own thinking. How do you feel about how you think? In reading this book, have you become more aware of your own thinking processes? How did you formerly feel about your thinking? What is your feeling about it now: wonder? confusion? pride? fear? excitement? Try to reflect on the positive aspects of your thinking and feel optimistic about your ability to think, and to think better.

SUMMARY

We have considered the tests of dialogue, simplicity, expandability, predictability, perspective, balance, and longevity; and we have touched back on former thinking bases to evaluate our thinking. We have found that we need accurate data provided by our senses and memory: clear, concise, contextually accurate language; controlled and effective feelings; clear structure; and solid logic. When we have evaluated our ideas as good and our thinking as solid, it's time to act. The next chapter will show us how to put thought into action.

VALIDATING CHALLENGES

1. How do you know when to accept the thinking of others as valid? How do you know when your own thinking is accurate?

2. What do you do to gain perspective? Are there some things or people (such as parents or good friends) who are too close to you to judge objectively? List those persons.

3. Are there some topics you are too far away from to have a reasoned opinion about? Give some examples.

4. Who are some of the people with whom you might engage in critical dialogue about specific issues? Would different people be better depending on whether the thinking area is professional, educational, or personal?

5. How long does an idea have to last to be good?

6. What types of thoughts are foundational, the kind on which others can build?

7. Take a piece of your writing and trim it down with Ockham's razor, cut out all unnecessary words.

8. Alexander Pope tells us, "Be not the first by whom the new is tried, nor yet the last to lay the old aside." Is this advice cowardly or wise, or does it depend on the situation?

9. How do you achieve balance in your own thinking? At what points or on what topics are you likely to stumble, or lose your perspective?

10. Much is made of the golden mean as the test of human excellence. What keeps this golden mean from turning into lukewarm mediocrity?

11. How do our courts of law evaluate guilt? Does this legal evaluation involve any of the methods for evaluating thinking discussed in this chapter? You may wish to read Bertolt Brecht's *The Caucasian Chalk Circle* and compare the unorthodox validation methods of a wise judge in the play with those of our legal system.

12. When you hear, "Mr. X was indicted for murder," what do you think about Mr. X? What does the term *indicted* actually mean? If Mr. X is found innocent, how will the media handle the news? How do you evaluate your thinking about the word *indicted*?

13. A critical monologue is one way to evaluate our thinking. Horace tells us that when we have written something, we should put it away for nine years, evaluate it, edit it, and then publish it only if we still find it worthy. Nine years seems excessive, but how much intervening time do we need before we can evaluate our own thinking?

14. Part of the evaluation process is taking care of the final details. In writing, we revise and proofread our thoughts to avoid costly or ridiculous errors;

for example, one book in the draft stage accidentally carried the word *feces* instead of *faces*. A small letter but a great difference. What methods do you use to give a final polishing to your thinking?

15. Like science, we want results; but unlike science, the results of our thinking do not approach certainty. Consequently, much of our judgment lies in the area of probability. How do you know when you have enough probability to judge your thinking to be worthy of action?

16. Write a personal assessment of your evaluation methods, considering both strengths and weakness. Review the chapter and decide what you do well and what you need to work on to judge your thinking more accurately.

14

Decision
and Action

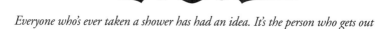

Everyone who's ever taken a shower has had an idea. It's the person who gets out of the shower, dries off, and does something about it who makes a difference.

—*N. BUSHNELL, FOUNDER OF ATARI*

WHY ACT?

Once we have thought something out carefully and our thinking meets all our tests, we need to act. Our thoughts must give birth to action or remain sterile. Thinking without acting is like chewing food without swallowing. The complete thinker is the doer. "Suit the action to the word," says Shakespeare. If our knowledge goes into action, if we act on our best thoughts, we have our best chance to feel good about ourselves. And if we make good decisions frequently, we may some day be called wise. Further more, following our thoughts with action may even improve our thinking, as the old proverb says:

> I hear and I forget.
> I see and I remember.
> I do and I understand.

Montaigne describes an ideal decision: he wants nothing to take "place that has not the consent of every part of [himself], without divisions and without inner rebellion" (1967, p. 13). Yet decision-making is rarely that harmonious. Sometimes life or death is at issue when we choose, support, or vote for euthanasia, abortion, suicide, war, or capital punishment. Sometimes the result of our decision is simply to go to a movie or stay home. Whatever the case, we do need to decide. To live is to decide, and to live fully is to decide well.

In this chapter we explore how to decide. We look at a process of deciding; we present some difficulties that block our deciding such as fear, lack of knowledge, confusion, and conflict of values; we learn ways to deal with these difficulties by facing fears, firming our facts, drawing on character, using our feelings, role-playing, and imaging; we look at the timing of decisions, the actual moment of decision, at the action, and the evaluation after the action; we draw up an action plan to solidify these steps; and we practice turning thinking into action.

DECISION

An American Indian said he had two dogs fighting inside himself, one mean and the other good. When asked which one wins, he replied, "Whichever one I feed the most."

I will. I won't. I'll go. I'll stay. I should. I shouldn't. Yes. No. Yes. Maybe. At times we teeter on the cliff of decision. We feel stressed by indecision as we vacillate through "decisions and revisions which a minute will reverse" (T. S. Eliot). Our thinking bases have already laid the groundwork for deciding. If our thinking has been solid, usually the decision will follow. When it doesn't, we can assist it through a three-step process by considering the goals, alternatives, and probable outcomes of each alternative. The goals are what we would ideally like to result from our decision and action. The alternatives are the ways we get those results. The probable outcomes are what we think will happen after we have chosen the alternatives. Let's look at an example:

Step 1: State the goal.

To get rich; more specifically, to acquire $1 million by age 55, retire, and then live off my investments.

Step 2: List the alternatives.

1. Starting at age twenty-five, save $5,000 a year, earning 10 percent compounded in a tax-deferred plan.
2. Set up a specific investment plan in stocks and bonds.
3. Set up a progressive real estate purchase plan.

Step 3: Describe the probable outcomes.
1. Plan will work if I can earn, save, and get the 10 percent.
2. Plan might work with a good brokerage firm and some luck.
3. Plan might work with a knowledgeable agent in an area of the country that is appreciating in value.

Difficulties in Deciding

Although the three-step process may appear simple, our mind does not work like a machine, nor do human institutions such as the stock market and real estate market follow a linear projection. Frequently we struggle to formulate goals, to assess the data, and to project possible outcomes. We also struggle with our own values. Let's look at some of the difficulties we can run into.

The Fear of Deciding

What if I'm wrong? Probably the greatest block to deciding is fear, which we have also seen hampers our creative thinking and our problem-solving abilities. William Harris suggests that one's anxieties, fears, and doubts may be critically involved in leadership decision making (1998, p. 29). Fear chokes our thinking. When we worry about how our thoughts will be received, rejected, scorned, or ridiculed, we have difficulty deciding. It is safer to tread the traditional path and avoid decisions that cause change and threaten our self-esteem. When we feel we always need to be right, then often we will fear to decide. Or when we fear the conclusions we are reaching, we might abort the decision-making process. What if our lover doesn't love us? What if the boss of our company is crooked? What if our friends have betrayed us? In these instances we might not want to embrace the truth because it is harsh. We do not want to lose our lover, our friends, our job, so we avoid following our thoughts to a decision.

The Grip of Habit

Lack of knowledge is another reason (and usually a good one) to hesitate before deciding. However, even when we have the knowledge we do not always act. For example, modern studies show that physical punishment is no more effective than other forms of discipline and has serious drawbacks; consequently, the American Academy of Pediatrics has urged that it be outlawed in schools and avoided at home. Echoing this position, the surgeon general in 1985 said corporal punishment should be forbidden in schools and discouraged at home; yet in a survey published in the *Journal of the American Medical Association* (June 17, 1992), 59 percent of pediatricians and 70 percent of family physicians still supported spanking, though their positions have recently changed. Why do these experts seem to act contrary to expert conclusions? Have they learned to doubt their colleagues? Or is it that old habits run deep?

Too Much Thinking

Sometimes we have too much information. It may be confusing, conflicting, or we may think too much about it. Thinking too much can stall action. Perhaps we know people like this or have met them in literature. The *Underground Man* by Dostoevski is a prisoner of his own thinking. *Hamlet* is a study in thought, in thinking too long and acting too late. Hamlet reflects on his own inaction:

> And thus, the native hue of resolution
> Is sicklied o'er with the pale cast of thought
> And enterprises . . . lose the name of action.

We have Hamlets in the classroom. One English major thought, double-thought, triple-thought about everything before he spoke or acted; finally he became so enmeshed in his terrible mind-lock that he found it difficult to speak at all. Not just in literature but especially in philosophy, some students begin to think so intricately and involutedly that they actually question whether they are real or not. One philosophy major said, "I don't know if I am alive, if I'm dreaming. I don't know anything for sure."

Clashing Motives

Conflicting needs, drives, and values can stop our decisions. St. Augustine fought the battle of two wills: his body wanted sex yet his mind wanted chastity. Sometimes we act one way even when we think another way is better. One chocolate ice cream addict placed a half-gallon of it deep in the basement freezer away from temptation. That same day he descended the stairs with a spoon in his hand and refused to listen to any guilt-producing thoughts. If we want something badly enough, we will try to suppress or ignore our thinking.

Below a student captures some of the feelings, tensions, insights, and results of a decision:

> My mind screamed NO! My thoughts argued with each other repeatedly. The fear had my speech and body paralyzed. Only my mind was functioning, tossing the negative messages like liquid mercury separating when put on a hard surface. I closed my eyes when I heard the Justice of the Peace say, "I now pronounce you man and wife." I started to cry! My new husband mistook those tears as joyful tears. Only I knew of the estranged feelings that existed, knowing instantly that I had done myself a violent injustice. The

vivid echoing memory of those vows creates a haunting mirage distressing all functions of my well being.

I was a young know-it-all of seventeen. A typical sample of a teenager. I had my mind made up to disband my family. I was spiteful. I wanted to prove my parents wrong! This dishonoring ill attitude that existed is still unexplainable to this day. I know I longed for some acceptance.

Fifteen years too late, the reflection is clear why I accepted those vows. I fell in love with my husband's family. His mom and dad loved me back. I had a new family that loved me just the way I was. Yeah, I really felt important being a wife and daughter-in-law. These roles turned stale real fast. This was the beginning of my devastating trials in the adult world.

I've often thought of what my life would be like if I had made a different choice. This choice resulted in a brutal, costly divorce. It left me financially and emotionally distraught. An important part of my life was wasted and a long recovery was ahead of me. I can't replace the precious time lost, but I've learned to balance and weigh all my choices.

Each choice is a drop of water. That drop of water forms a puddle in time, this then becomes a stream to go on flowing as the river of life.

How to Decide

Facing Fear

If fear is the greatest obstacle to deciding, then courage and calm help us to decide. If we can free ourselves from obeisance to others, if we can strike strongly out on our own and let the chips and opinions fall where they may, we increase our decision-making power. An example of high praise given to a citizen activist was "He put his body where his words were." Courage is not bottled and sold, but it can be bought with hard work. We can change our thinking with mantras such as "I think it's right; I'll do it; others can do what they want." Easier said than done, but courage can build with practice.

Firming Our Foundation

When the decision is important and we have the time, the more thorough we are in our thinking preparation, the easier our decision will be. If we have covered our thinking bases, we have gone a long way toward deciding. We can make our thoughts objective and visible by writing them down.

A good way to capture our thoughts and facilitate decision-making is to make a list of pros and cons. (See chapter 12, "Problem Solving.") Pick any topic you wish (changing jobs, asking someone out on a date, breaking up with someone, taking a certain course, and so forth). Write it down on the following chart, then write all the thoughts for and against that decision.

Decision Issue:			
PROS	wt	CONS	wt
			✓
Total =		Total =	

Sometimes these lists surprise us. Perhaps one list is much longer than we would have guessed, but does the longest list win? What if one of the cons is that we will die? That single con would outweigh a long list of pros. To make our list more accurate, we can weigh the items for importance by writing a 1 to 10 in the box alongside each item, using 10 if it is extremely important and 1 if it is of negligible importance. Now simply total the boxes and watch the scales of decision begin to tip in one direction.

Each decision we make has its own set of relevant criteria. For example, before buying a house we might want to consider criteria such as location (neighborhood, urban or rural setting, proximity to schools, churches, and stores), price, size, materials, condition, and market comparisons. Before applying for a job we might consider the job description, our qualifications, the hours, salary, and benefits. Before bidding on the construction of a house we look at the blueprints and specs. Before marketing a product we do consumer surveys and profiles. The more complete our information, potentially, the better our decision.

Calling on Character

Sometimes, no matter what we know, the decision is hard because the results may be hurtful to us or to those we care about, or because the decision pits our greed against our good. When our character is in conflict, then we dig deep and decide who we are and who we want to become; we reach for principles, motivation, and values; we realize that our choices define us, that we become what we choose. To help us through these trying decisions, we can turn to Marcus Aurelius, Roman emperor, warrior, and philosopher. He tells us to perform each action as if it were our last. Similarly, Ignatius of Loyola, soldier and founder of the Jesuits, tells us to imagine ourselves on our deathbed and then choose as if the choice were the last event in our life.

In cases of character conflict, once the objective analyses are finished and we have concluded that waiting longer will not clarify the problem, then we can "push" the decision by focusing on the positive side and then, when we are able, decide quickly so as not to prolong the pain of conflicting choice. If we struggle in conflict and win, if we make the good choice, we are molding our character and subsequent choices will be less difficult.

Changing Criteria: Putting on the Gloves

Jennifer used to buy gloves for price, warmth, and color. One winter her wrists were cold, so she bought longer gloves. Then she read about the insulating power of Thinsulate and she bought a pair filled with this material. But they slipped on her steering wheel, so she searched out a nonslip variety. Her original list of three criteria grew to six: price, warmth, color, length, material, and grip. With time, our criteria will change and became firmer.

Feelings: A Boost Toward Decision

Sometimes our feelings can give us that extra thrust toward a decision. Many people make decisions not knowing that their feelings are driving their thoughts. If, however, we are highly aware of our feelings, if we are aware of how they act as barriers and can mislead us, if we are honest with ourselves and know ourselves reasonably well, if we give them input but not control, we can use feelings as *part* of the deciding process. They can be the extra push we need.

THINKING ACTIVITY 14.1
Feelings and Decisions

We have just suggested a rather dangerous procedure: to use feelings to assist us in deciding even though feelings often sabotage thought. At this point it might be wise to reflect back on when they have helped or hindered decisions. Which of our feelings might help us to make a sound decision? How or when can we trust them?

Imaging the Action

Another help in deciding is to form an image of ourselves doing the action. This method is similar to the systematic desensitization method of J. Wolpe, which can help us eliminate our fears. For instance, if we cannot decide to go to a stern school authority or a terrifying boss, we can visualize ourselves walking down the hallway toward the person's office. When we can do this without significant anxiety, then we can visualize ourselves knocking on the door, then walking in, and finally, saying the difficult message. It is important to be relaxed at each step before we image the next one. Imaging can prepare us for difficult decisions and actions.

Role-Playing into Reality

After we have imaged it, then we can act it out, or role-play it. Delancy Street, a community prison in San Francisco, used role-playing to change thinking. Male prisoners had to get haircuts, wear suits, and even walk "normally." They were asked to act as if they were successful, good citizens. This acting seemed to change their thinking, for their recidivism rate was quite low. About 80 percent of the role players entered society and stayed there; apparently, many became the citizens whom they role-played.

We too can draw upon the power of acting to help ourselves carry out the decision. When a decision demands change and we don't seem to have the power to decide, we may be able to role-play the action. At first we will probably feel stiff, but repetition will make it easier; consequently, it will become easier to think about acting that way routinely. Finally, we will have the strength to do what we have been role playing, and then our minds and our bodies will work together. By playing the role we can become the role.

THINKING ACTIVITY 14.2
Role-Playing

Get a group of friends together, or perhaps a group assigned in class, and brainstorm some topics that would frequently call for a decision. Try to determine the desired outcome and then act as if that were the outcome. For instance, if you wish to be positive and confident in approaching a difficult person, then *act* positive and confident while other people play the roles of the difficult person. This activity can easily be adapted to fit many situations. Continue to role-play until the role begins to feel more natural.

When to Decide

When is a big part of how. If the decision does not have to be made immediately, time and further knowledge may make the decision clearer. A president of a small college in Indiana told us that he did not like to decide quickly because time would often make the decision unnecessary. Horace, a Roman poet, wins the cunctator award: in his *Ars Poetica* he advises waiting for nine years before publishing a written work.

How long is too long? In general, the more serious the situation, the slower we should be to take action. If we are thinking about getting married, divorced, or investing our life's savings, we want a well-deliberated decision. Sometimes, however, even when the result could be catastrophic, a fast decision is needed. What if nuclear missiles are headed our way? What if a tornado is a hundred yards away? What if the oncoming car is in our lane heading toward us? What if a young child is choking and turning blue? *When* is a big part of *how*, and the answer to when is often now.

The Deciding Moment

With the problem faced and partially solved, the moment comes: "I'll do it!" As we bask in our decision, we are unaware that something has happened in our brain. About 300 milliseconds *before* we consciously knew our decision, a "PSI 300 wave" occurred. Does that mean our decision is out of our control? Fortunately, Benjamin Libet, who studies the decision wave at the University of California at San Francisco, has shown that we can stop our decision one- to two-tenths of a second before we act on it (Restak, 1979, p. 49). Perhaps our control lies as much in censoring as in deciding.

ACTION

For the most part we advocate: think first, then act. Sometimes, however, we cannot think everything through because the variables are too many and too unknown. In these cases we must use action as the test of our thought. Thomas Savery and Thomas Newcomen built the thoughts of the French physicist Denis Papin into steam pumps. Thus began the industrial revolution. The force of Papin's ideas placed into action changed our world forever.

Not all actions are so tangibly testable. Thomas More's ideal society described in *Utopia*, was never tested. However, the conceptual force of the book was tested. More compared England, a Christian society, with Utopia, a pagan society, and found England lacking. The English were shocked, and the concept of "utopia" has forever since enriched our ideological world.

Action completes thinking, but action is not the end of thought. Action gives input into the cycle of thinking-deciding-acting, leads to acting, which leads to further thinking. As we carry a decision into action, we are continually thinking about how to make it work: "A plan depends as much upon execution as it does upon concept," says Frank Herbert, in his novel *Dune* (p. 244). If we want the action to be successful, we must plan the execution. Here are some steps for developing a successful action plan:

Action Plan

1. Exactly *what* will I do?
2. *When* will I begin?
3. *Who* might help me?
4. How might I *fail?*
5. Is my plan *realistic,* achievable, measurable?
6. What *motivations,* rewards or punishments, will I set for myself in order to carry it out?

Sometimes even when our thoughts are clear and accurate and when we make the best decision possible, we still can't control the outcome. The Player King in Hamlet says, "Our thoughts are ours, their ends none of our own."

AFTER ACTION

After action comes the test of our thinking. How did the results turn out? How do we feel about ourselves? Was this a good decision or a bad decision? At this point we are just seeking objective evaluation. If our plan collapsed, we can recall that we made the best decision that we could based on what we knew then. As Scottish poet Robert Burns noted, "The best laid schemes o' mice and men gang aft agley [often go astray]." But to help ensure that our plans do work, we evaluate them after the fact. We can add a seventh step to our action plan above: when will I review the success of my plan?

If we want our action plan to have an enduring effect, we have to periodically rethink, return to the premises, adjust the plan, and remotivate ourselves. And remember, while staying objective in our evaluation we can also stay

---

THINKING ACTIVITY 14.3
An Action Plan for Improving Thinking

Because we are near the end of this book, this is a good time to apply this chapter to your own thinking. First, make a decision about what you want to do to develop your thinking ability in the future. If you find this difficult, call upon the techniques you have learned in this chapter. Once you have made the decision, write out the steps in your action plan, following the questions listed above. Be sure to add a date by which you will evaluate the success of your thinking plan. You may wish to share the results of your decision with others.

positive: we can look on the rain as refreshing or depressing; we can look on college as a prison of the body or a freedom of the mind.

SUMMARY

In this chapter we have seen that the complete thinker is also the decider and the doer. We have found that our other thinking bases prepare us to decide; we have learned to set goals, consider alternatives, and estimate probable outcomes; we have learned to follow up decisions with an action plan; and we learned the following specific ways to help us decide: firm our facts, face our fears, call on our character and our feelings, and image and role play the action. We have found that timing is part of the decision, and that after the decision and action we can judge it, adjust it, and set action plans to continue effective thinking and acting.

DECISION AND ACTION CHALLENGES

1. Think of a decision that you have been putting off. What are some of the factors in your delay? Do you need more information before you decide? What are the consequences of deciding wrongly? Of not deciding? Can you think through the process on paper and make the decision?

2. A woman in her late thirties wanted to get married and have children. She had passed up several opportunities and was afraid her options were running out. Two men wanted to marry her: one man was fun but would make a poor father; the other was dull but would make a good father. She could marry one, the other, or neither. How would you choose if you were in the woman's place?

3. Although some of us wish ourselves so lucky, how would you choose a partner if you loved two persons and they both wanted you?

4. Does the deciding process described in this chapter work in affairs of the heart? What are the qualities you would like in your ideal mate? List them in order of importance.

5. Should you smile at a stranger? How do you make this decision? Why might you hesitate?

6. Decision: Sexual relations? Safe sex? How do you decide?

7. Decisions usually have a downside. What is the downside of deciding you want to be rich?

8. In the movie *Sophie's Choice,* the heroine, in a Nazi concentration camp is forced to choose one of her two children to be executed. How would you have decided in that position?

9. *The Underground Man* by Dostoyevski shows us one of the most turgid, twisted, convoluted, densest, brightest minds in literature. Read part 1 of this short novel to understand how too much thinking can overload the mind's circuit.

10. Has excessive self-consciousness (thinking about oneself too much) ever made it difficult for you to speak or act? Have you ever thought yourself into a knot? How did you cut through that knot and act?

11. Does new knowledge change old decisions? Studies have shown that swimming after eating does not cause drowning, yet people from an older generation have difficulty entering the water after eating.

12. What is the meaning of the saying: "I do and I understand"?

13. Is not deciding really deciding?

14. As we choose, we choose ourselves. What does this statement mean and how accurate is it?

15. What do common expressions such as "Put your money where your mouth is," "He's a blowhard" and "She talks a good line" say about our attitude toward action?

16. Image the action: Select a difficult decision you have to make and picture yourself gradually, in steps, getting closer to doing it.

17. Try out the advice of Marcus Aurelius and Ignatius of Loyola. First, select a difficult choice you have to make. Then, imagine that you are dying today and that this is the last choice you will make, and then choose. Did you gain some perspective on your choice?

18. Besides giving us the confidence to decide, role playing can help us prepare for a difficult situation. Role-play a meeting with the dean of students, or role-play asking for a date from someone who might turn you down. Practice with another person or in front of a mirror.

19. Could a flip of a coin ever be a useful way to make a decision? Could even a very important decision be settled on a flip?

20. Montaigne wore a medallion with the inscription *Je m'abstiens* ("I restrain myself"). How necessary is restraint for making decisions?

21. If you wish to engage one of the greatest issues of philosophy, religion, and science, you can ask the questions: Can I really decide? Am I really free?

22. "There is nothing good or bad but thinking makes it so." Does this thought from Hamlet vitiate the worth of decision? How can we draw power from this thought?

23. How can you apply the decision-making process to decisions made in groups? What parts would be the same? What parts different? What else would you need to add?

15

The Challenge to Go on Thinking

When Robert Peary the American explorer, asked his Eskimo guide what he was thinking, the guide replied: "I do not think. I have plenty of meat."

Thinking does not stop with the end of a book or the end of a course. As long as we live we think, but *how* we think will be our choice. If we choose, we can probe the reaches of the unfolding universe, we can explore the intricacies of the mind, we can carve our thoughts into written words, and we can speak our thoughts with persuasive force. By our thinking and by our choices and actions, we will define ourselves.

Let's think about our future thinking. How wide will we range? How deep will we plunge? How well will we build?

How wide? Philosopher José Ortega y Gasset says that many things fail to interest us because they don't find enough surfaces in our mind on which to live. We have to expand our mind so that more themes—more of life—can find a place within.

How wide will we cast our senses to feed our mind? What is the sensual milieu in which we will place ourselves? What are the sights and sounds that we will seek out or reject? What physical weaknesses might distort our sensing, and what personal barriers might warp our perceptions? What strengths will focus and magnify them? And how can we select, increase, clarify, and intensify the myriad streams of sensual data that impact our sensory receptors and settle in our mind?

> ***Think About It:*** *The above paragraph asks us to think about the deluge of sensual data that inundates us by chance, by default, and by choice. Spending time in self-reflection, in discussion, and in writing increases our understanding of the sensory world and helps form and solidify the sensing patterns that best nourish our minds. Throughout this chapter, pause after each question and think about the possibilities for enlarging your own thinking.*

How far will we let our creativity roam? How hard will we strive to break the lock of habit? How long will we prod the problem and seek the solution? How often will we break the crust of custom and begin the dance of creativity? How much will we trust ourselves to reform and blend old things, ideas, and structures into new inventions, thoughts, and organizations?

With what words will we stock our mind? What books will we read? What movies will we watch? With whom will we talk? How long will we wrestle with our written words? Will we crack our clichés and recast them? Will we search for better metaphors to carry our meaning?

Breadth without depth would leave us shallow. If we had to choose only one of these dimensions, would it be "better to know something about everything than to know all about one thing" (Pascal, 1958, p. 10)? To what extent can we have both?

How deep will we plunge? As we stand on the precipice of our personal barriers and look down, will we recognize our enculturation and ego defenses? Will we listen to our feelings when they inspire us and transcend them when they do not? Will we admit our prejudices and fears? Will we struggle against our biases and reach toward objectivity? Will we admit when we're wrong? Will we read and research to gain the deep knowledge that we need in certain chosen areas? Will we struggle not to win but to understand and express our best thinking?

Breadth and depth interrelate. Our deep areas make no sense isolated from the broader context of the world. Our depth will be greatly aided by breadth. New ideas for our deep interests will come from the cross-fertilization of our wide interests.

No matter how wide or deep our knowledge, its use will be in our thinking. *How well will we build?* How will we work to develop effective thinking patterns in our mind? How will we link our ideas together? How tight will we keep our lines of logic? How will we combine our thoughts into newness? How persuasively will we present our thoughts? By effort and by choice we can change old thinking habits and adopt powerful thinking patterns to develop what Montaigne calls a "well-formed intellect." How will we form that intellect?

• • •

Thinking is not an island separated from the rest of our human nature. It does not exist in isolation from our feelings, intuitions, or dreams. It is only one part of us, yet an essential part in all of us. From poet and artist to mathematician and philospher, from musician and designer to scientist and engineer, better thinking will tend toward a better life.

The human species has used its thinking marvelously, but it still knows very little about so very much, asking today many of the same questions that were asked by minds thousands of years ago. Great thinking can unlock many doors, but there may be some that it cannot open. Yet how wondrous is the thinker: "How noble in reason, how infinite in faculties . . . in apprehension how like a god."

Appendix:
Propositional Logic

Propositional logic, also called sentential logic, is concerned with the determination of the truth value of sentences. Because the effectiveness of any argument depends on the truthfulness of its assumptions, an understanding of propositional logic can help us determine the validity and soundness of arguments.

Propositional logic is concerned with compound sentences, that is, sentences made up of two or more simple sentences. Specifically, sentential logic is concerned with how the meaning of sentence connectives like "and," "or," "if, . . . then," and "if and only if, . . . then" affect the truthfulness of the compound sentence.

Let's begin with a compound sentence that uses the "and" connective: "Sue is smart and Mark is strong." According to propositional logic, the truthfulness of this sentence depends on the truthfulness of each of the two simple sentences within it. In other words, if it is true that Sue is smart and it is also true that Mark is strong, then the sentence "Sue is smart and Mark is strong" is true. However, if either of the simple sentences within the compound sentence is false, then the entire compound sentence is false. Thus, if Sue is smart but Mark is actually weak, then the sentence "Sue is smart and Mark is strong" is false. Bear in mind that propositional logic is concerned only with the use of "and" as a conjunction between simple sentences, not as a link in a chain such as, "The house was old, unsightly, and covered with moss."

The following truth table for the connective "and" summarizes the conditions in which compound sentences using this connective are true or false. The letters P and Q stand for the two simple sentences joined by the connective "and." T and F stand for true and false. Thus, the first row of the truth table (*) would read, "If P is true and Q is true, then the sentence P and Q is true."

P	Q		P and Q
*T	T		T
T	F		F
F	T		F
F	F		F

The connective "or" used in disjunctive sentences and disjunctive syllogisms is a little more interesting because it can have two different meanings. The *inclusive* "or" really means "and/or," whereas the *exclusive* "or" means that only one alternative can be true. Consider the following sentence: "Abraham went to church or he stopped at the grocery store." In the inclusive sense of "or," Abraham could have stopped at church or the grocery store or both, and the sentence would be true. But in the exclusive sense of "or," the sentence means that he could have done only one and not the other. Thus, whether the sentence "Abraham went to church or he stopped at the grocery store" is true depends on the sense in which we use "or." The following truth table for the connective "or" summarizes the conditions in which disjunctive sentences are true or false. Notice that there is one set of conditions (*) that produces different truth values for the exclusive and inclusive meanings of "or."

P	Q		P or Q (inclusive)	P or Q exclusive)
*T	T		T	F
T	F		T	T
F	T		T	T
F	F		F	F

The last connectives we'll look at are found in two variations of if-then statements, often called hypothetical statements, which appear in hypothetical syllogisms. In the first variation, "If P, then Q" or "If the sun comes out (P), it will be warm (Q)," the sentence is true if Q follows P. However, in propositional logic the sentence is also true if P and Q do not occur, that is, if the sun did not come out and if it did not get warm. This is because the fact that P does not occur does not render false the relation "If P, then Q." Also, if P does not occur and Q does, the sentence is true, for we did not say "If and only if P, . . . " With respect to the example above, if the sun does not come out (P is false) but it becomes warm nonetheless (Q is true) this fact is still compatible with and does not negate the statement "If the sun comes out, it will be warm." If, however, the statement was "If and only if the sun comes out (P), then it will be warm (Q)," then we could not have it be warm (Q is true) without the sun (P is false) without the sentence being false. Note that if-then statements are addressing a logical connection between two elements, not a causal one. Thus, "If P, then Q" does not imply that P causes Q.

The table below summarizes the truth values of if-then sentences. Notice the one difference in truth value (*) for "if" and "if and only if" statements.

P	Q		If P, then Q	If and only if P then Q
T	T		T	T
T	F		F	F
*F	T		T	F
F	F		T	T

References

Adler, T. (1993a, May). Nicotine gives mixed results on learning and performance. *APA Monitor*, p. 14.

Adler, T. (1993b, May). Nicotine withdrawal effects impair cognitive processing. *APA Monitor*, p. 17.

Aristotle (1954). *Rhetoric and Poetics*. New York: Random House.

Averill, J. (1982). *Anger and Aggression: An Essay on Emotion*. New York: Springer-Verlag.

Bacon, F. (1965). In S. Warhaft (Ed.), *Bacon: A Selection of His Works*. New York: Odyssey Press. (Original work published 1625).

Baddeley, A. (1990). *Human Memory: Theory and Practice*. Boston: Allyn and Bacon.

Bailey, W. (1990). Murder, capital punishment, and television: Execution publicity and homicide rates. *American Sociological Review, 55,* 628–633.

Barker, Keith. (1998). Magic bullets, slate, and stradavarius; analogies, research, and policy making. *Phi Delta Kappan, 79,* 402–406.

Barron, F., & Harrington, D. M. (1981). Creativity, intelligence, and personality. *Annual Review of Psychology, 32,* 439–476.

Beck, A., Rush, J., Shaw, B., & Emery, G. (1979). *Cognitive Therapy of Depression*. New York: Guilford Press.

Beck, A. T. (1976). *Cognitive Therapy and the Emotional Disorders*. New York: International Universities Press.

Bevan, W. (1991). Contemporary psychology: A tour inside the onion. *American Psychologist, 46,* 475–483.

Bochner, S., & Insko, C. A. (1966). Communicator discrepancy, source credibility, and opinion change. *Journal of Personality and Social Psychology, 4,* 614–621.

Bor, J. (1900, May 4). Brain cells kept alive in lab. *Chicago Sun Times*, p. 3.

Bower, B. (1993, January). Warning: Cigarettes may be hazardous to your thoughts. *Science News*, pp. 46–47.

Bradley, G. (1978). Self-serving biases in the attribution process: A reexamination of the fact or fiction question. *Journal of Personality and Social Psychology, 36,* 56–71.

Bronowski, J. (1956). *Science and Human Values.* New York: Harper and Brothers.

Carmichael, L., Hogan, H. P., & Walter, A. A. (1932). An experimental study of the effect of language on the reproduction of visually perceived form. *Journal of Experimental Psychology, 15,* 73–86.

Confucius (1938). *The Analects* (A. Waley, Trans.). New York: Vintage Books.

Craighead, W. E. (1984). Affective disorders—unipolar. In S. M. Turner & M. Hersen (Eds.), *Adult Psychopathology: A Behavioral Perspective.* New York: John Wiley.

Crowther, J. G. (1969). *A Short History of Science.* London: Methuen Educational Ltd.

Damasio, A., & Damasio, H. (1992, September). Brain and language. *Scientific American,* pp. 89–95.

Dewey, J. (1910). *The Influence of Darwin on Philosophy and Other Essays in Contemporary Thought.* New York: Henry Holt and Co.

Dewey, J. (1922). *Human Nature and Conduct: An Introduction to Social Psychology.* New York: Holt and Co.

Dunker, K. (1945). On problem solving. *Psychological Monographs, 58,* 270.

Eddington, A. (1985). Defense of mysticism. In K. Wilbur (Ed.), *Quantum Questions: Mystical Writings of the World's Great Physicists* (pp. 194–208). Boston: Shambhala.

Emerson, R. W. (1918). "To J. W." In *Complete Poetical Works of Ralph Waldo Emerson.* New York: Houghton Mifflin. (Original work published 1867)

Ferris, W. P. (1998). "Fear, Stress, and Second-Guessing in Leadership Decision Making." *Journal of Management Education, 22,* 26–49.

Festinger, L., & Carlsmith, J. (1959). Cognitive consequences of forced compliance. *Journal of Abnormal and Social Psychology, 58,* 203–210.

Forrest, G. (1978). *The Diagnosis and Treatment of Alcoholism.* Springfield, IL: Charles C. Thomas.

Freedman, J. L., & Fraser, S. C. (1966). Compliance without pressure: The foot-in-the-door technique. *Journal of Personality and Social Psychology, 4,* 195–202.

Gagnon, M., Dartiques, J., Letenneur, L., & Barberger, G. (1990). Identification des facteurs de risque de la maldie d'alzheimer: Resultats preliminaires du programme de recherche PAQUID. *Psychologie Medicale, 22,* 1248–1251.

Gleick, J. (1987). *Chaos: Making a New Science.* New York: Viking.

Goldstein, E. (1992). *Confabulation: Creating False Memories, Destroying Families.* Boca Raton, FL: SIRS, Inc.

Goldstein, J. (1976). *The Experience of Insight: A Natural Unfolding.* Santa Cruz, CA: Unity Press.

Good news, bad news: Driving improves but many still fat, lazy. (1991, July 19). *Racine Journal Times,* p. 7a.

Greenough, W. (1988). In J. Heminway (producer & director), *The Mind: Aging* [Film]. Alexandria, VA: PBS Video.

Grinspoon, L., & Bakalar, J. (1985). Drug dependence: Nonnarcotic agents. In H. Kaplan & B. Sadock (Eds.), *Comprehensive Textbook of Psychiatry* (Vol. 4, pp. 1003–1015). Baltimore: Williams and Wilkins.

Haber, R. (1970, May). How we remember what we see. *Scientific American,* pp. 104–112.

Hebert, F. (1987). *Dune.* New York: Ace Books.

Horne, J. (1985). Sleep function, with particular reference to sleep deprivation. *Annals of Clinical Research, 17* (5), 199–208.

Hurt, F. (1998). "Achieving Creativity: Four Critical Steps." *Direct Marketing, 60* 40–44.

Janis, I. (1982). Decision making under stress. In L. Goldberger & S. Breznitz (Eds.), *Handbook of Stress: Theoretical and Clinical Aspects.* New York: Free Press.

Jessel, D., & Moir, A. (1991). *Brain Sex.* New York: Carol Publishing Group.

Johnson, A. (1992). *Human Arrangements: An Introduction to Sociology* (3rd ed.). New York: Harcourt.

Jung, C. G. (1964). Approaching the unconscious. In C. G. Jung (Ed.), *Man and His Symbols.* Garden City, NY: Doubleday.

Jung, C. G. (1969). A psychological approach to the dogma of the trinity. In W. McGuire & R. F. C. Hull (Eds.), *The Collected Works of C. G. Jung* (Vol. 11, pp. 108–200). Princeton, NJ: Princeton University Press. (Original work published 1948)

Jung, C. G. (1969). The stages of life. In W. McGuire & R. F. C. Hull (Eds.), *The Collected Works of C. G. Jung* (Vol. 8, pp. 387–415). Princeton, NJ: Princeton University Press. (Original work published 1939)

Jung, C. G. (1977). In W. McGuire & R. F. C. Hull (Eds.), C. G. *Jung Speaking.* Princeton NJ: Princeton University Press. (Original work published 1957)

Jung, C. G. (1983). *The Essential Jung.* Princeton, NJ: Princeton University Press.

Kant, I. (1955). *Fundamental Principles of the Metaphysic of Ethics* (10th ed.) (T. K. Abbott, Trans.). New York: Longmans, Green. (Original work published 1786)

Landers, A. (1984, November 4). Is tenderness enough? *Racine Journal Times,* p. 4c.

Landers, A. (1985, January 14). 90,000 respond on sex. *Racine Journal Times,* p. 2c.

Landers, A. (1985, January 15). More replies in sex poll. *Racine Journal Times,* p. 3c.

Landfield, P., Cadwallader, L., & Vinsant, S. (1988). Quantitative changes in hippocampal structure following long-term exposure to Δ^9-tetrahydrocannabinol: possible mediation by glucocorticoid systems. *Brain Research, 443,* 47–62.

Lederer, R. (1989). *Crazy English.* New York: Pocket Books.

Lewinsohn, P., Steinmetz, J., Larson, D., & Franklin, J. (1981). Depression-related cognitions: Antecedent or consequence. *Journal of Abnormal Psychology, 90,* 212–219.

Lewsinsohn, P., Steinmetz, J., Larson, D., & Franklin, J. (1981). Depression-related cognitions: Antecedent or consequence. *Journal of Abnormal Psychology, 90,* 212–219.

Li, D., Wu, Z., Shao, D., & Liu, S. (1991). The relationship of sleep to learning and memory. *International Journal of Mental Health, 20,* 41–47.

Maier, N. (1931). Reasoning in humans: The solution of a problem and its appearance in consciousness. *Journal of Comparative Psychology, 12,* 181–194.

Marien, M. (1998). The information revolution may not benefit society. In P. Winters and M. Williams (Eds.), *The Information Revolution: Opposing Viewpoints.* San Diego: Greenhaven.

Maslow, A. (1954). *Motivation and Personality.* New York: Harper and Brothers.

Maslow, A. (1966). *The Psychology of Science.* New York: Harper and Row.

Miranda, J., & Persons, J. (1988). Dysfunctional attitudes are mood-state dependent. *Journal of Abnormal Psychology, 97,* 76–79.

Montaigne, M. de (1967). *Essays.* Baltimore: Penguin Books.

Mullen, B., Johnson, C., & Salas, E. (1991). Productivity loss in brainstorming groups: A meta-analytic integration. *Basic and Applied Social Psychology, 12,* 3–23.

Nease, J. (1995, September 21). AT&T-NCR combo just didn't compute. *Racine Journal Times,* p. 4B.

Newbold, G. (1990). Capital punishment in New Zealand: An experiment that failed. *Deviant Behavior, 11,* 155–174.

Nisbett, R., & Cohen, D. (1996). *Culture of Honor.* Boulder, CO: Westview.

Pascal, B. (1958). *Pensees.* (W. F. Trotter, Trans.). New York: E. P. Dutton.

Penn, W. (1906). *Fruits of Solitude: Reflections and Maxims Relating to the Conduct of Human Life.* Chicago: Lakeside Press. (Original work published 1797)

Penrose, R. (1989). *The Emperor's New Mind.* New York: Oxford University Press.

Peters, T. (1987). *Thriving on Chaos: Handbook for a Management Revolution.* New York: Knopf.

Pope, H. G. Jr., & Yurgelun-Todd, D. (1996). The residual cognitive effects of heavy marijuana use in college students. *Journal of the American Medical Association, 275* (7), 521–527.

Puner, H. (1947). *Freud: His Life and His Mind.* New York: Howell, Soskin.

Quintillian. (1961). *Institutio Oratoria* (H. E. Butler, Trans.). Cambridge: Harvard University Press.

Rahula, W. (1974). *What the Buddha Taught.* New York: Grove Press.

Ramo, J. (1997, May 12). The prince of San Mateo. *Time,* p. 58.

Regan, D., & Totten, J. (1975). Empathy and attribution: Turning observers into actors. *Journal of Personality and Social Psychology, 32* (5), pp. 851–856.

Restak, R. (1979). *The Brain.* Garden City, NY: Doubleday.

Restak, R. (1991). *The Brain Has a Mind of Its Own.* New York: Harmony Books.

Rosenhan, D. L. (1973). On being sane in insane places. *Science, 179,* 250–258.

Rosenthal, R. (1966). *Experimenter Effects in Behavioral Research.* New York: Appleton-Century-Crofts.

Sapirstein, G., & Kirsch, I. (1996, August). *Listening to Prozac but hearing placebo.* A presentation at the 104th annual convention of the American Psychological Association, Toronto, Canada.

Schneidman, E. (1985). *Definition of Suicide.* New York: John Wiley.

Selected Poems of Emily Dickinson (Modern Library). (1924). New York: Random House.

Senzaki, N., & Reps, P. (Trans.). (1957). "Zen stories." In P. Reps (Ed.), *Zen Flesh, Zen Bones.* Rutland, VT: Charles Tuttle.

Shakespeare, W. (1970). *The Complete Works.* Baltimore: Penguin Books.

Silver, Brian. (1998). *The Ascent of Science.* New York: Oxford.

Skinner, B. F. (1953). *Science and Human Behavior.* New York: Free Press.

Skinner, B. F. (1976) *Walden Two.* New York: MacMillan.

Smith, C., & Lapp, L. (1991). Increases in number of REMs and REM density in humans following an intensive learning period. *Sleep, 14,* 325–330.

Spurgeon, C. (1966). *Shakespeare's Imagery.* Cambridge, England: Cambridge University Press.

Stein, P., & Motta, R. (1992). Effects of aerobic and nonaerobic exercise on depression and self-concept. *Perceptual and Motor Skills, 74,* 79–89.

Sutherland, S. (1989). *The International Dictionary of Psychology.* New York: Continuum.

Tavris, C. (1982). *Anger: The Misunderstood Emotion.* New York: Simon and Schuster.

Tinklenberg, J., Darley, C., Roth, W., Pfefferbaum, A., & Kopell, B. (1978). Marijuana effects on associations to novel stimuli. *Journal of Nervous and Mental Disease, 166,* 362–364.

Toffler, A. (1970). *Future Shock.* New York: Random House.

Vaillant, G., & Perry, J. C. (1985). Personality disorders. In H. Kaplan & B. Sadock (Eds.), *Comprehensive Textbook of Psychiatry* (Vol. 4, pp. 958–986). Baltimore: Williams and Wilkins.

Von Franz, M.-L. (1964). The process of individuation. In C. G. Jung (Ed.), *Man and His Symbols.* Garden City, NY: Doubleday.

Wassil-Grimm, C. (1995). *Diagnosis for Disaster: The Devastating Truth About False Memory Syndrome.* New York: Overlook.

Watson, B. (1968). *The Complete Works of Chuang Tzu.* New York: Columbia University Press.

Wheeler, D. (1991, July 3). U.S. has barred grants to 6 scientists in past 2 years: 174 allegations of misconduct examined in new integrity effort. *Chronicle of Higher Education,* pp. A1, A6, A7.

Wordsworth, W. (1993). Preface to *Lyrical Ballads.* In M. H. Abrams (Ed.), *The Norton Anthology of English Literature,* (Vol. 2). New York: W. W. Norton (Originally published, 1802)

Zuckerman, M. (1979). Attribution of success and failure revisited: Or the motivational bias is alive and well in attribution theory. *Journal of Personality, 47,* 245–287.

Index

Abusing language:
  ignoring the question, 247
  suggestion, 246–47
  withholding quantification, 246
Accommodation, 27–28. *See also* schemata
Action:
  completes thinking, 288
  evaluating, 288–90
  importance of, 280
  plan of, 289
  and self-definition, xxi
Actor-observer bias, 25
Ad hominem argument, 244–45, 246, 248
  legitimacy of, 245
Adler, A., 59
Affirming the consequent. *See* reasoning
  fallacies
Affirming a nonexclusive disjunct, 168
Alcohol:
  effects on thinking, 59
  Korsakoff's syndrome and vitamin B, 59
All-or-nothing fallacy. *See* Either/or fallacy
American beliefs, 15
Amphetamines, effects on thinking and social
  functioning, 60
Analogical argument, 179–81
Analogical order. *See* order
Analogies. *See also* Order
  and analogical order, 128–29
  Chuang Tzu's, 180–81
  and clustering, 128
  and evaluating thinking, 276
  false, 185
  good, 180
  and inductive arguments, 177, 179
  and metaphor, 82
  and prioritizing, 128–29
  and proof, 180
Analyzing, and organization, 126–27
Anger:
  Aristotle, 29, 31
  and assertiveness, 30
  causes, 29
  and cognitive restructuring, 31
  dealing with, 30–31
  Jesus, 31
  Plato, 29
  and problem solving, 258–59
  reason, ally of, 29
  and self, 21

thinking, effects on, 29–30, 42
ventilating, effects of, 30
Anselm, "I doubt . . . ," 2
Anticipation. *See* Preliminary evaluation
Appeal:
  to Authority, 187–88
    and Christian Church, 196–97
    in persuasion, 227–28
    vs. scientific method, 196–97
  bandwagon, 189
  to fear, 242–43
  to ignorance, 189–90
  to pity, 242
  to pride, 244
  to tradition, 188–89
Aquinas, T., 44
  refuting opponents, 238
  senses and mind, 44
  structural clarity, 133
Archimedes, 117
  and King's crown, 107
Arguments. *See also* Deductive thinking, Inductive
    thinking, Syllogism
  ad hominem, 244–45, 246, 248
  analogical, 179–81
  attacking, 174–75
  between couples, and hasty generaliza-
    tion, 183
  deductive, and inductively derived premises,
    176, 179
  inductive, disputing, 176–77
  inductive, sound, 177
  sound, 177. *See also* Sound argument
  straw man, 246
  Summa, 2
  valid and invalid, 141, 142, 162
    testing, 142–46
  validity and propositional logic, 295
Aristotle, 273
  analogical order, 129
  on anger, 31
  on anger and reason, 29, 31
  on chronological order, 128
  golden mean, 274
  and Locke, 45
  on metaphor, 82, 108
  nothing new, 274–275
  on persuasion, 226, 227, 229
  rational animals, 97, 230
  "stir emotions," 230

Aristotle (*cont.*)
  and syllogism, 1
  "thinking animals," 3
Assertiveness, resisting persuasion, 241
Assimilation, and schemata, 27–28
Attitudes, and cognitive consistency, 36–38
Attribution, 24–25
  and psychological health, 24
Attribution error, 25
Audience. *See* Writing, Persuasion
Aurelius, Marcus
  and deciding, 285–86
  imagining advice, 291
Authority. *See* Reasoning fallacies, appeal to
  authority
Averill, 29, 30

Bacon, F.:
  idols of mind/cave, 79
  on words, 87, 92
Baddeley, A., 70
Bailey, W., 256
Bakalar, J., 60
Balance theory, 37–38
Bandwagon appeal, 189
Bare attention, 54
Barker, K., 96
Barriers to thinking. *See* Personal Barriers
Barron, F., 255
Beck, A., 32, 35
  overgeneralization, 32, 35
Begging the question. *See* Circular reasoning
Beliefs:
  American, 15
  and feelings, 98
Berkeley, G., only perceptions, 2
Bevan, W., on experimenter bias, 213
Biased return. *See also* Unbiased return
  Ann Landers survey, 219
Biases, self-serving, 25–26
Bible, and appeal to authority, 187
Black and white fallacy. *See* Either/or fallacy
Black and white thinking. *See* Polarized
  thinking
Blank slate. *See* tabula rasa
Bloom, Benjamin, 270
Bochner, S., 28
Bor, and scientific method, 196
Bower, B., 59
Bradley, G., 24
Brain, 56–75 (Chapter 4). *See also* Thinking,
  Metaphor, Synapse
  absorbing thoughts, 49
  and alcohol, 59
  and better thinking, 62–63
  cortex, 3, 57–58, 97
  creating reality, 79
  definition of thinking, 5–6, 76
  development, 62–63
  innate structures, 119–20

  and language, 85
  limitations of, 63–64
  as muscle, xxi
  mystery, 5, 56
  neuron connections, 57
  neurotransmitters, xxii, 58
  number of neurons, 57
  and nutrition, 58–59
  requirements for proper functioning, 73
  and senses, 44–45
  and sensory data, 120
  vs. mind, 64–65
  weight, 97
  words per minute, 7
Brainstorming, 112
  in evaluating thinking, 277
Breadth and Depth of thinking, 293
Brecht, Bertolt, *Caucasian Chalk Circle,* 278
Brevity:
  and evaluation, 276
  and Voltaire, 276
Bronowski, J., evaluating, 270
Burke, J., 7
Burns, R., 289
Bushnell, N., on taking action, 280
Byron, Lord, "tis to create . . . ," 9

Cadwallader, L., 60
Capital punishment, 255–56
Carlsmith, J., 36
Carmichael, L., 66
Case studies, 220–21
  and Carl Jung, 220
  generalization problem, 220, 223
  and Sigmund Freud, 220
Cases of Fraud, 216
Catastrophizing, 35
Categorical propositions. *See* Propositions
Caucasian Chalk Circle, 278
Causal order. *See* Order
Causal thinking, error in, 183–84
Cause and effect:
  contributory cause, 182
  correlational designs, 210, 223
  determining direction of, 210
  establishing in science, 207
  and evaluating thinking, 277
  four types, 181–82
  and human freedom, 204
  and inductive thinking, 181
  necessary cause, 181
  and problem solving, 253–54
  and scientific thinking, 194
  sufficient and necessary cause, 182
  sufficient cause, 181–82
Centrality of Thinking, 6
Cerebral cortex, 3, 57–58. *See also* Brain and language, 77
Cernan, C. W., genius and simplicity, 272
Cervantes, M., forewarned, 239

Chance, and research results, 211–13
Changing Criteria: Putting on the
  Gloves, 286
Chaos, 133
Chaos, and order, 119
Chaos theory, 262
  and causal order, 133
Chaotic systems, 262
Character, and deciding, 281, 285–86
Chomsky, N., innate ideas, 45, 77
Christ:
  Confucius and Kant, 228
  and metaphor, 108
Chronological order. *See* Order
Chuang Tzu, and metaphor, 108
Chuang Tzu's Analogies, 180–81
Cicero, 2
Circular reasoning, 172, 190
Clearly Embarrassing, 91
Clichés, 91, 93–94, 293
  avoiding, 49, 94
Clustering, 125–26
Cocaine, effects on thinking, 60
Cognitive consistency, 36–38
  and thinking, 42
Cognitive dissonance, 36–38
  and rationalization, 36
Cognitive therapy:
  and feelings, 100
  and anger, 31
Coleridge, S., organization, 119
Communication. *See also* Dialogue, Language,
    Listening, Persuasion, Writing
  healthy climate for, 258–59
  as thinking, 5–6
Comparison group, selection of, 208–9
Components, identifying, 256–57
Composition. *See* Writing
Composition fallacy, 185–86
Compound sentences. *See* Propositional logic
Conclusions:
  in inductive reasoning, 175–77
  in soft deductions, 151–52
Confucius, and metaphor, 108
Confucius, Christ, and Kant, 228
Connotations, 87–89
Conscious selection method, 103
Context, of word, 90–91
Contributory cause, 182
Control group:
  defined, 207
  selection of, 208–9
Controlled experiments:
  defined, 207
  and ethical problems, 210–11
  vs. correlational designs, 208–9
Conversions of propositions, 168–71
  hypothetical, 170
  particular, 169–73
  universal, 169

Copernicus, N., 47, 53
  and Catholic Church, 196–97
  and extravagant hypothesis, 184
Copernicus and Galileo, 197
Corax of Syracuse, rhetorician, 1
Correlation, and problem solving, 253, 256
Correlational designs, 208–11
  cause and effect problem, 223
  ethics and practicality, 210, 223
  hidden variable problem, 209, 222–23
  limitations, 222–23
  and prediction, 223
  problems of, 209–11, 222–23
  value of, 210–11
  vs. controlled experiments, 208–9
Cortex. *See* Cerebral Cortex
Cost-benefit analysis, 262
Craighead, W., 33
Creating a Healthy Communication Climate, 258–59
Creative thinking. *See* creativity
Creativity, 107–18 (Chapter 7)
  and capability, 114
  coaxing, 114–17
  conditions of, 111–12
  crucial to critical thinking, 107
  define, 108
  and desire, 114
  Edisonian effort, 114–16
  and evaluation, 117, 270, 276–77
  and fear, 111, 282
  fermentation and insight, 116
  inhibitors to, 111–12
  kinds of, 110
  and Leonardo da Vinci, 117
  and metaphor, 108–9
  prepcreation, 115–16
  and problem solving, 255, 259, 268
  a study on, 110
  and talent, 110
  as thinking base, 107
  variety of, 110–11
  who can be creative, 110–11
Crick, F., 83
  DNA, 273
Crime:
  and capital punishment, 255–56
  variables correlating with, 256
Critical Reading Before We Sleep, 61–62
Crowther, J., 197

Damasio, A., 77
Damasio, H., 77
Dante, A., and metaphor, 108
da Vinci, Leonardo:
  and creativity, 117
  and the Greeks, 2
Death of Ivan Ilych, 161
Decision, 280–91 (Chapter 14)
  and action, 288–89
  alternative, 281

Decision (*cont.*)
  Marcus Aurelius on, 285–86
  barriers to, 282–84
  changing criteria, 286
  and character, 281, 285–86
  and courage, 284
  criteria, 285–86
  difficult, 285–86
  and fear, 281, 282, 284
  and feelings, 281, 286
  and goals, 281, 282
  Ignatius of Loyola on, 286
  and imaging, 281, 286–87
  importance of, 280–81
  information overload, 283
  and knowledge, 281, 282, 285
  and motivation, 283–84, 285
  and probability, 281, 282
  pros and cons, 284–85
  and role playing, 281, 287
  and stress, 38–39
  thinking bases, 281
  thinking too much, 283
  three-step process, 281–82
  and timing, 287–88
  and values, 281, 282, 283
Deductive reasoning. *See* Deductive Thinking
Deductive thinking, 134–75. *See also* Arguments,
    Logic, Syllogism
  conclusions in soft deductions, 151–53
  conclusions of vs. inductive, 175, 176
  defined, 134
  and order, 123
  and soft deductions, 151–53
  vs. inductive, 175–76
Defense mechanisms. *See* Ego-defenses
Definition/defining, 87
  and problem solving, 252–53
Dementia, and intellectual activity, 63
Demosthenes, self-deceit, 24
Denial, 22
  and psychological health, 24
Denying the antecedent, 165–66
Depression, 32–34
  and amphetamines, 60
  causes of, 32, 33
  coping with, 33–34
  decision-making, 33, 34
  effects on thinking, 32, 33, 35, 42
  and exercise, 33
  and irrational beliefs, 32–34
  resolving, 33–34
Descartes, R.:
  bent oar, 47, 48
  "I think, therefore . . . ," 2
  use mind well, 2
Desensitization, 286
Determinism:
  contradiction with responsibility, 204
  defined, 202

  as foundation in science, 202–5
  and human beings, 202–4
  and indeterminists, 203–4
  macrocosm vs. microcosm, 202
  and probability, 203, 205, 222
  Skinner on, 201, 204
Determinism and Probability, 205
Dewey, J., religious emotions, 15
Dewey vs. Truman, telephone survey, 220
Dialogue:
  and evaluation, 270, 271–72
  and thinking, xxii, xxiv, 9–10
Dichotomous thinking. *See* Polarized thinking
Dickinson, Emily, poem, 62
Disjunctive syllogism. *See* Syllogism
Dissonance. *See* cognitive consistency
Distribution of terms. *See* Syllogism
Door-in-the-face technique, 240, 248
Dostoevski, F.:
  prisoner of thinking, 283
  Underground Man, 283, 291
Doyle, A. C., working backwards, 265
Dreams:
  deprivation effects, 61
  and intellectual activity, 61
  and learning, 61
Dune, 288
Dunker, K., 260
Durant, W.:
  man occasionally rational, 13
  on reason, 134

Eddington, A., on proof, 205
Edison, T.:
  and creativity, 108, 114
  genius, 114
Edisonian effort, 114
Ego-defenses, 22–23
  and challenge to think, 293
  defined, 22
  denial, 22
  projection, 22–23
  and psychological health, 24
  rationalization, 23, 36, 214, 230
  and self-concept, 42
Einstein, A., 56:
  challenged world view, 207
  imagination and knowledge, 107
  merger of energy and matter, 82
  and problem solving, 255
  theory of relativity, 189, 273
Either/or fallacy, 172–74
Either/or propositions. *See also* Syllogisms, disjunctive
  disjunctive syllogism, 167–68
  fallacy of, 168. *See also* Either/or fallacy
  mistakes in, 168
Elements, order of, 121–22
Eliot, T. S.:
  indecision, 281
  objective correlative, 103

Ellison, L., 3
Emerson, R. W., life too short, 41
Emotional Mansion, 129–30
Emotions. *See* Feelings, Passion
Empathy:
  reducing actor-observer bias, 25
  reducing anger, 31
Empiricism:
  and philosophy, 196
  and science, 222
  and scientific method, 196, 198. *See also* Operational definition, 199
Enculturation, 13–19
  and challenge to think, 293
  and evaluating thinking, 275
  of Freud, 14
  of Jung, 14
  prejudices and values, 42
  religion and, 15–16
  sources, 14–15
  southerners vs. northerners, 14
English:
  pitfalls and limitations, 91–94
  power and importance, 85–91
  sloppy, 87
Enthymemes, 147–49
Equivocation, 160–62
  and *Death of Ivan Ilych,* 161
Erroneous attacks:
  ad hominem argument, 244–45, 248
  attacking a straw man, 246, 248
Ethics:
  and controlled vs. correlational designs, 210–11
  and persuasion, 227, 228
  and problem solving, 263
Eubonics, 95
Evaluation, 270–79 (Chapter 13)
  and action plan, 289
  and analogies, 276
  balance, 274
  brainstorming, 277
  and brevity, 276
  Caucasian Chalk Circle, 278
  cause and effect analysis, 277
  and chronology, 274–75
  completeness, 274
  and creativity, 117, 270, 276–77
    through dialogue, 270, 271–72
  and enculturation, 275
  and feelings, 276
  imitation and expansion, 273
  and inductive thinking, 277
  and language, 270, 276, 277
  and logic, 270, 277
  and memory, 270, 275, 277
  and metaphor, 276–77
  monologue, critical, 272
  nouns and verbs, 276
  and organization, 270, 277
  and perceptions, 275

personal barriers, 275
perspective, 274
and predictability, 273–74
and probability, 279
and reasoning fallacies, 277
and senses, 270, 275
simplicity and complexity, 272–73
starbursting, 277
stereotypes, 275
and stress, 275
systematic nature of, 270–71
and thinking bases, 270, 275–77
word order, 276
Expectations, and schemata, 27–28
Experiment. *See* Controlled experiments, Scientific method
Experimental group:
  defined, 207
  selection of, 208–9
Experimenter bias, 213–15, 223
  defined, 213–14
  Rosenhan study, 214
  Rosenthal study, 214
Experts, relying on, 187
Extravagant hypothesis, 184–85
  and pseudoscience, 221

Fallacies. *See* Reasoning fallacies
Fallacy of composition, 185–86
Fallacy of division. *See* Reasoning fallacies
False analogy, 185. *See also* Analogical argument
False authority. *See* Reasoning fallacies, appeal to authority
False dilemma. *See* Either/or fallacy
False disjunct, 168
Fears:
  challenge to think, 293
  creative thinking, 282
  decision-making, 282, 284
Feelings (Emotions), 29–35. *See also* Passion, Tone, Chapter 6: Feelings,
  American family, 99
  anger, 29–31
  as beliefs, 98
  business community, 98, 104
  challenge to think, 293
  Church's attitude toward, 98–99
  and decisions, 286
  depression, 32–34
  enhanced thought, 97, 105
  and evaluating, 270, 275, 276
  and five thinking errors, 35
  maligned by society, 98
  negative effects on thinking, 29–35
  negative feelings, awareness of, 104
  passion, 31–32
  and persuasion, 230–31
  and prejudices, 98
  and reason, 13, 230
  and religion, 15–16

Feelings (*cont.*)
and root elements, 99
shaping them, 100
speech fluency, 101–2
and tone, 100–101
toward audience, 103–4
toward topic, 103–4
as values, 98
vs. thinking, 97
words exciting, 88
and writing, 102
Festinger, L., 36
Five thinking errors, 35
Five W's, 122, 124, 132
Flame words, 88
Foot-in-the-door technique, 239–40
Forgetting, 68–70
causes of, 69–70
and cramming, 69
cues, 70
interference theory, 69
repression, 69
Forrest, G., on denial, 22
Four figures of syllogisms, 138, 139–40
Four-terms fallacy, 159–60
Fraser, S., 239
Fraud, cases of , 216
Freedman, J., 239
Freedom:
Maslow on, 203, 204
and prediction, 203
Skinner on, 201, 204
Free will. *See* Indeterminists, Determinism
Freud:
enculturation of, 14
on rational creatures, 230
on rational inquiry, 214
unconscious mind, 273
Frost, R., pathless wood, 38

Gagnon, M., 63
Galileo, G., 53
Catholic Church, 196–97
Copernicus, 197
scientific method, 194
Gasset, J., things fail to interest, 292
Generalization:
case-study, 220, 223
hasty, 182–83
and inductive thinking, 182
limitations of, 210–11
problems of, 223
reasonable vs. hasty, 183
and representative sample, 219, 220
Generalizations and abstractions overused, 91–92
Genesis (Book of), appeal to fear, 242
Gleick, J., 133
Goals and deciding, 281, 282
Goldstein, E., 68

Goldstein, J., 54
Greenough, W., 63
Grinspoon, L., 60

Haber, R., 69
Hamilton, A., on passion, 43
Hamlet, 283, 289, 291
Harrington, D., 255
Hasty generalization. *See* Reasoning fallacies
Hearing, 49. *See also* Listening, Senses,
sensitivity
Hegel, G., history, 2
Henry, P., liberty or death, 104
Herbert, F.:
on action, 288
thought (vs. action) is real thing, xxi
Hidden variables (third variables), 209,
222–23
High Specificity, 92
Hollow Men, 103
Homer:
and metaphor, 108
sing to me, 102
Horne, J., 61
Human behavior. *See* Prediction
Hume, D.:
and skepticism, 2
and sound argument, 177
Hypothesis. *See also* Extravagant hypothesis
defined, 194
formulation, and scientific method, 195
testing of, 195
untested, 196
and pseudoscience, 221
Hypothetical syllogism. *See* Syllogism

Idea of Self, 20
Ideas, innate, 45
Idols of the cave, 79
Idols of the mind, 79
"If and only if . . . ," 165, 166
If/then statements. *See also* Syllogism,
hypothetical
and hypotheses, 194
Ignatius of Loyola:
and deciding, 286
imaging advice, 291
Ignoring the question, 247
Illicit major, 156–58
Illicit minor, 158–59
Illicit process, defined, 156
Illogicalities and English language, 93
Imaging, and deciding, 281, 286–87. *See also* Pre-
liminary evaluation
Imagining. *See* Imaging
Imitation, and evaluation, 273
Importance of Agreed Meaning, 161–62
Indeterminists, 203
Inductive reasoning. *See* Inductive thinking

Inductive reasoning fallacies, 182–86
Inductive thinking, 175–86
 and causation, 181–82
 conclusions of, 175–76, 177
 conclusions of vs. deductive, 176, 177
 defined, 175
 and evaluating thinking, 277
 and generalization, 182
 Hume, David, 177
 and order, 123
 and probability, 175, 176, 177
 and science, 176
 soundness of, 177, 182
 vs. deductive, 175, 190
Information:
 gathering, 255–56
 moderately discrepant, 28
 sources of, 257–58
Innate ideas, 1, 45, 119
Insko, C., 28
Inspiration method, 102
Interference theory, 69
Inuits, 78–79
Invalid conversions, 170. *See also* Valid conversions, 168–71
Investing time (manipulative tactic),
 241–42, 248
Irrational ideas/thinking. *See also* Ego-defenses,
 Reasoning fallacies
 and depression, 32–35, 42
 five kinds, 35
 and stress, 35, 42. *See also* Stress,
 38–40

James, William:
 and emotions, 29
 on rational creatures, 230
 on rational inquiry, 214
Janis, I., 38
Jefferson, T., 98
Johnson, A., 172
Johnson, C., 112
Jung, C. G., 22, 61
 archetypes, 119–20
 enculturation, 14
 and Freud, 14
 innate ideas, 45
 on problems, 252
 projection, 22
 on rational creatures, 230
 on rational inquiry, 214
 self, owning up to totality of, 24
 shadow, 26

Kant, I., 63
 Confucius and Christ, 228
 and problem solving, 255
 space, time, and the mind, 119
Keller, H., 78

Keynes, J. M., on Newton's problem solving, 260
Kirsch, I., 215
Knowledge:
 challenge to think, 293
 and deciding, 281, 282–83
 explosion of, 193–94
 and persuasion, 227–28
 and problem solving, 255–56, 257–58
Korsakoff's syndrome, 59

Landers, Ann, 219
 survey, 219
 biased return, 219
Landfield, P., 60
Language, 76–96 (Chapter 5). *See also* Nouns
 and Verbs, Wittgenstein, Words
 abusing, 246–47
 and cerebral cortex, 77
 changing, 89
 clarity of, 91
 clichés, 49, 93–94
 and communication, 5–6
 connotation, 87–89
 as container of thought, 94
 context, 76, 90–91
 to create, 114
 decline of England, 80
 distortion, 79–81
 euphemisms, 80–81
 and evaluating, 270, 276
 idols of the mind, 79
 illogical, 93
 innate vs. learned, 77
 Keller, Helen, 78
 lawyers and lawmakers, 84
 limitations of, 4, 84–85
 meaning, 76, 85–86
 and memory, 85
 as metaphor, 83–84
 perception, affecting, 78–79, 86
 redundancies, 92–93
 shackles thinking, 80–81
 sloppy, 87
 and society, 79–81
 as "software," 77
 structuring power of, 78–79, 94
 and thinking, 76, 77
 universalizing power, 78, 84, 94
 universal terms, 78, 84
 Whorf hypothesis, 78–79
 word order, 76, 89–90
Lao Tzu, on knowledge, 228
Lapp, L., 61
Lawmakers and Lawyers, 84
Learning, marijuana's effects on, 60
Leonardo da Vinci, 117
Letting Go, 21
Lewinsohn, P., 32
Li, D., 61

Listening, 49–52
  asking questions, 51
  how to, 50–51
  and memory, 51
  organizing thoughts, 51
  paraphrasing, 51
  posture, 51
  power of, 50. *See also* Hearing, Senses, sensitivity of
  read the body, 51
  reasons for, 50
  summarizing ideas, 51
  and thinking, 45
  tone of speech, 51
  value and needs, understanding, 51
Loaded Words, 258
Locke, J., 98
  tabula rasa (blank slate), 2, 45
Logic, 134–92 (Chapter 9). *See also* Arguments, Deductive thinking, Inductive thinking, Logical thinking, Syllogism
  challenge to think, 293
  deductive, 134–75, 190
  and evaluating, 270, 277
  fallacies. *See* Reasoning fallacies
  inductive, 175–90
  and order, 123
  and persuasion, 230
  propositional, 295–97
  sentential, 295–97
  syllogism. *See* Syllogism
  truth tables, 295–97
Logical fallacies. *See* Reasoning fallacies
Logical necessity:
  and inductive argument, 175, 181
Logical reasoning. *See* Logic, Logical thinking, Syllogism
Logical rules for syllogisms, 162
Logical thinking. *See also* Logic
  as heart of critical thinking, 134
  and nicotine, 59
  and stress, 38
Lowballing, 240–41, 248
Luther, Martin, on Galileo, 197
Lytton, Lord, self-deception, 23

Maier, N., 260
Major premise. *See* Syllogism
Major term. *See* Syllogism
Malapropism, 87
Manipulation, 227. *See also* Manipulative tactics, Persuasion
Manipulative tactics:
  appeal to fear, 242–43
  appeal to pity, 242
  appeal to pride, 244
  door-in-the-face technique, 240, 248
  foot-in-the-door technique, 239–40, 242, 248
  investing time, 241–42, 248
  lowballing, 240–41, 248

Marien, M., 194
marijuana, effects of, 60
Marshall, J., 270
Marx, K., 2
Maslow, A.:
  goal of science, and human predictability, 204
  novel solutions, 251
  prediction of human behavior, 203
  problem solving, 251
  seeing what we need to see, 24
Meaning. *See also* Equivocation
  agreed, importance of, 161–62
  language, 76, 85–86
Meditation, 58. *See also* Bare attention
  and stress management, 41
Memory. *See also* Forgetting
  changing nature of, 66–68, 73
  of childhood, 66
  dream deprivation, 61
  episodic, 67
  and evaluating, 270, 275
  and hypnosis, 68
  improving, 70–72
  and language, 85
  long-term, 68
  and marijuana, 60
  meaningfulness, 66–67, 70, 71
  mnemonic techniques, 71–72
  mystery of, 56
  and nicotine, 59
  and order, 124
  and practice, 71
  recall vs. recognition, 69
  and repetition, 71
  semantic, 67
  short-term, 68
  and stress, 38, 39
  and thinking, 65–66
Mendeleev, D., periodic table, 121–22, 273
Mental orders. *See* order
Metaphor:
  for the brain, 83
  challenge to think, 293
  controls thinking and knowledge, 82–84
  creativity, 108–9, 117
  creativity and evaluation, 276–77
  defined, 82, 108
  Einstein's, 83
  and euphemisms, 81
  and language, 82–84, 108
  and law, 84
  limitations of, 84
  secret of the universe, 84
  and Shakespeare, 109
  and understanding, heart of, 109
Metaphysics, and science, 222
Middle term. *See* Syllogism
Milton, J., 82

Mind. *See also* Brain
  structures reality, 63–64, 79
  vs. brain, 64–65
Mind/body problem, 64–65
Minor premise. *See* Syllogism
Minor term. *See* Syllogism
Miranda, J., 32
Misthinking, 10
Mnemonics, 71–72
Modus poems syllogism, 164
Modus poems tollens syllogism, 167
Modus tolendo poems syllogism, 167
Modus tollens syllogism, 165
Monet, C., 48
Montaigne, M.:
  decision, ideal, 280–81
  intellect, well-formed, 293
  medal: "What do I know," 2
  and metaphor, 108
  the mind, 79
  restraint, 291
  on simplicity, 272–73
  thinking as child, 276
Montesquieu, C., 98
Moore, G. E., on questions, 112
More, T., *Utopia,* 288
Motivation:
  and deciding, 283–84, 285
  experimenter bias, 214–15
Motivation mountain, 234, 235
Motives, and deciding, 263–84
Motta, R., 33
Mullen, B., 112
Multiple syllogisms, 148–50
Myth of Genius, 255
Myth of Perfection, 254

Napoleon, and steamship, 10
Narration, 128. *See also* Writing
National Rifle Association, 215
Natural/mental orders, 120–22
Nease, J., 19
Necessary and sufficient cause. *See* Sufficient and
  necessary cause
Necessary cause, 181, 182
Needs, and problem solving, 257. *See also* Persuasion, values and needs
Neurons, defined, 57. *See also* Brain
Neurotransmitter, xxii, 58
Newbold, G., 256
Newcomen, T., and action, 288
Newman, J. H.:
  structural clarity, 133
  thought and speech, 9
Newton, I., lines of force, 5
Nicotine:
  effects on learning and memory, 59
  effects on logical reasoning, 59
  effects on problem solving, 59

Nine-dot problem, 254
Nouns and verbs, 90
Nutrition, and stress management, 41–42

Objective correlative, 103
Observation:
  casual, 195
  as domain of science, 196, 199
  as empirical world, 198
  Galileo and Copernicus, 197
  and inductive reasoning, 175–76, 177
  and operational definition, 198, 217
  and philosophy, 196
  scientific method, step of, 194
Ockham's razor, 2
  defined, 184
  and evaluation, 273
Omaguas, 78
Operational definition, 198–99, 217
  debated, 199
  defined, 198
Order, 119–33 (Chapter 8). *See also* Organizing
  alphabetical, 122
  analogical, 120, 128–30
    and Aristotle, 129
    and clustering, 128
    effectiveness of, 130
    as natural and mental order, 128
  analogy, seminal structural, 129–30
  arbitrary, 122, 123, 132
  causal, 121, 127
  causal, and chaos theory, 133
  chronological, 120–21, 128, 131
    and Aristotle, 128
    and Pascal, 128
    and pilots, 121
    and writing, 128
  domestic, 133
  of elements, 121–22
  five W's, 122, 124, 132
  logical, 122, 123, 132
  logical and five W's, 122
  and memory, 124
  mental, 122–24
  mental vs. natural, 122
  and mind, 119–20
  and narration, 128
  natural, 120–22
  origins, 119–20
  prioritizing and analogies, 128
  scientific, 122–23
  and scientific method, 124
  and thinking, 122, 124
  topical, 120, 131
  using, 127–31
Organizing. *See also* Order
  analyzing, 126–27
  clustering,125–26
  and evaluating, 270, 277

Organizing (*cont.*)
and prioritizing, 127
steps in, 124–27
and writing, xiv
Orwell, G., 80
Other Attribution Errors, 25
"Ought" from an "is," 189
Overgeneralization, 32, 35
Owning Up To Our Dark Side, 26

Papin, D., and action, 288
Pascal, B.:
on balance, 274
breadth vs. depth, 293
and chronological order, 128
on feelings and reasoning, 99, 105
and persuasion, 231, 236, 248
Thoughts, 2
Passion. *See also* Feelings
defined, 31
and depression, 32
effects on thinking, 31–32, 42
Peary, R., Eskimo guide, 292
Penn, W., passion as fever, 31
Penrose, R., 63–64
Perceptions, 45. *See also* Senses
and evaluating thinking, 275
and schemata, 27–28
Periodic table, and predictability, 273
Perry, J. C., 23
Personal barriers, 13–43 (Chapter 2)
anger:
causes, 29
negative effects on communication and problem solving, 258–59
negative effects on thinking, 29–30, 42
and better thinking, 13, 15, 42
defense mechanisms. *See* Personal barriers, denial, projection, rationalization
denial, 22
depression, 32–34, 42
emotions. *See also* Personal barriers, passion
negative effects on thinking, 15,
29–33, 35
religious, 15–16
and prejudice, 230
and thinking errors, 35
enculturation, 13–19, 42, 275, 293
and evaluation, 275
expectations and schemata, 27–28
passion, 31–32, 42. *See also* Personal barriers,
emotions
projection, 22–23
and psychological health, 24
rationalization, 23, 36, 214, 230
schema, 27–28
self-concept, 19–21, 42
self-serving bias, 20, 24–26, 42
transcending, 42

Personalization, 35
Persons, 32
Persuasion, 226–50 (Chapter 11)
abuse of language, 246–47
adjusting goals, 234
Aristotle, 226, 227, 229, 230
asking for the response, 238–39, 247
assertiveness, 241
and audience, 231–34, 236, 247
and biases, 228–29, 230, 236
and challenge to think, 293
credibility, 236
deceitful, 239–47
defined, 226
demographics, 232
and education, 229, 232
emotional appeal, 230–31
emotions, 230–31, 247
erroneous attacks, 244–46
ethical vs. deceitful, 239
ethics of, 227, 228
first impression, 236
goal of, 234, 238
and honesty, 228
knowledge, 227–28, 232
likability, 229
and logic, 230, 239
manipulative tactics, 239–44
motivation, 229, 235, 242
motivation mountain, 235
needs, 230, 232–33
objectivity, 228
organizing for, 234–39
position, acknowledging, 236
as presumptuous, 227
purpose, 229
rationale, 238
and rationalization, 230
and rational/logical thinking, 230
root elements, 230–31, 234, 238
values, 230, 232–33, 234, 236
values and needs, 232–33, 234
and writing. *See* Writing
Peters, T., 133
Philosophical Investigations, 77
Philosophy. *See also* Logic, Determinism
and empiricism, 196
vs. scientific method, 196
Pinter, H., past and memory, 65
Placebo, 215
Placebo effect, 215
Plato, 273
on anger and reason, 29
and feelings, 102
innate ideas,1, 45, 119
and medieval thinkers, 2
Poetic impression, 110–11
Polarized thinking, 35
Politics and the English Language, 80

Pope, A.:
  be not first nor last, 89, 278
  on change, 89
  passion and reason, 31
  on pride, 244
Post hoc ergo propter hoc, 183–84
Prediction:
  and chaos, 262
  and correlation, 223
  of human behavior, 203, 205, 221
  and periodic table, 273
  and problem solving, 260–62
  unfulfilled, and pseudoscience, 221–22
  and verification, 195
Prejudices:
  beliefs and emotions, 230
  and challenge to think, 293
  enculturation, 14, 42
  feelings, 98, 99
  and persuasion, 234
Preliminary evaluation, 260–62
  anticipation, problems in, 261–62
  and trial and error, 265
  and working backwards, 265
Premature closure, 38
Premises. *See* Propositions
Pride, and evaluating thinking, 275
Prioritizing, and organization, 127, 128
Probability:
  and decision-making, 281
  and determinism, 205, 223
  and evaluation, 279
  exaggeration of in persuasion, 242–43
Problems. *See also* Problem Solving
  action vs. thinking, 251
  causes, looking for, 253–54, 267
  components of, 256–57
  defining, 252–53, 267
  human relationships, 252–53, 257
  kinds of, 251
  nine-dot, 254
  solutions. *See* Solutions, Problem solving
  without a cause, 254
Problem solving, 251–69 (Chapter 12). *See also*
    Problems, solutions
  and anger, 258–59
  anticipating potential problems, 267
  barriers:
    removing, 254–55, 268
    status, 258
  cause and effect, 253
  causes, searching for, 253–54, 267
  as challenge, 267
  and chaos, 262
  checking facts, 266
  coinciding variables, 253
  and communication, 257, 258–59
  components, 261, 166
    identifying, 256

compromising, 266
cost-benefit analysis, 262
creative thinking, 255, 259, 260
deadlines, 266
defined, 251
defining problems, 252–53, 267
effectiveness, 263
empathy, 266
ethics, 263
evaluating solutions, 267
five-step process, 251–52
as fun, 267
gathering information, 255–58, 268
goals, 251, 264–65
human component, 262
human relationships, 263
information, sources of, 257–58, 268
intelligence, 255
loaded words, 258
myth of genius, 255
myth of perfection, 254
nicotine effects, 59
preliminary evaluation, 260–62, 265
pros and cons, 260, 262–64
and reflection, 267
reliability, 263
reversibility, 263
risks of, 263, 265
self-esteem, 254
and stress, 38
subgoal analysis, 264–65
timeliness, 263
tips, 266–67
transcending conventions, 259
trial and error, 265, 268
values, 263
wild card variables, 261
Projection, 22–23
  defined, 22
  and denial, 22
  and psychological health, 24
Proof, 205–7, 223
  and Einstein's theory, 206–7
  and persuasion (Aristotle), 229
Propositional logic, 295–97
Propositions. *See also* Syllogisms, premises
  affirmative, and categorical, 135
  affirmative, and rules for syllogisms, 162
  categorical, defined, 135
  conversion of, 168–71, 190
  hypothetical, conversion of, 170
  inductively derived, 176
  kinds of, 137–38
  particular:
    converting, 169–70
    defined, 137–38
    distribution properties of, 155–56
    meaning of, 137–38
    negative, 155–56

Propositions (*cont.*)
  rules for syllogisms, 162
  positive, 155
  rules for syllogisms, 162
  singular, 138
    distribution of terms, 156
  universal, 137
    converting, 168–69
    defined, 137
    distribution properties, 155
    forms of, 137
    meaning of, 137
    negative, 155
    positive, 155
    rules for syllogisms, 162
Pros and Cons:
  assessing, 260, 262–64
  and deciding, 284–85
Pseudoscience, 221–22
  defined, 221, 222, 224
  examples of, 221
  hypotheses, untested, 221
  power and mystery, 222, 223
  vs. science, 221
Psychological health, and personal barriers, 24
Ptolemy, C., and extravagant hypothesis, 184–85
Puritanism, 98

Quark/lepton theory, 274
Quintilian, M., 2
  feelings and eloquence, 101

Racine, J., violence and reason, 29
Rahula, W., idea of self, 20
Ramo, J., 3
Rationalism, 98
Rationality. *See* reason
Rationalization, 23, 214
  and cognitive dissonance, 36
  and persuasion, 230
Reality. *See* Brain, creating reality, limited ability
Reason:
  and anger, 29–31
  and changes, 121
  and feelings, 13, 99. *See also* Emotional influ-
    ences, 29–35; and Chapter 6: Feelings
  human capacity for, 42
Reasoning. *See* Reason, Deductive thinking, In-
    ductive thinking
Reasoning fallacies:
  ad hominem, 244–45, 248
  affirming the consequent, 166
    and converting a hypothetical, 170
  affirming a nonexclusive disjunct, 168
  appeal to authority, 187–88
    and the Bible, 187
  appeal to ignorance, 189–90
  appeal to tradition, 188–89
  bandwagon appeal, 189

circular reasoning, 172, 190
composition fallacy, 185–86
deductive fallacies (informal), 171–74
denying the antecedent, 165–66
either/or, 172–74
equivocation, 160–62
and evaluating thinking, 277
extravagant hypothesis, 184–85
fallacy of composition, 185–86
fallacy of division, 171–72
  vs. universal propositions, 171
false analogy, 185. *See also* Analogical argument,
    179–81
four-terms fallacy, 159–60
hasty generalization, 182–83
  and arguments between couples, 183
  and selective attention, 183
illicit process:
  illicit major, 156–58
  illicit minor, 158–59
inductive fallacies (informal) 182–86
invalid conversion, 169–71
post hoc ergo propter hoc, 183–84
reductio ad absurdum, 174–75
  and persuasion, 230
slippery slope, 186
  and human relationships, 186
  and stereotypes, 183
straw man argument, 246, 248
undistributed middle, 154–56
  rule for, 162
Recall vs. recognition, 69
Recollection method, 103
Reductio ad absurdum. *See* Reasoning fallacies
Redundancies, 92–93
Rejections on minor grounds, 263
Religion:
  and crime, 255–56
  and enculturation, 15–16
  and persuasion, 234
  and pseudoscience, 221
  and science, 196, 197, 199
  and thinking, 14, 15–16, 197
Replication of research, 212–13
  scientific method, and verification,
    195–96, 212
Representative sample, 211–12
  and Ann Landers' survey, 219
  and surveys, 218
Repression, 69. *See also* Forgetting
  and psychological health, 24
Reps, P., 27
Replication. *See* Scientific method, replication
Republic, 102
Research methods, kinds of, 222
Restak, R., 59
Right word, and clear thinking, 87
Role playing, and deciding, 281, 287
Root elements, 230, 234, 238

Rosenhan, D., and experimenter bias, 214
Rosenthal, J., 9
Rosenthal, R., 214
Rousseau, J., on feeling and thinking, 97
Rules for the Categorical Syllogism, 162

Sagan, C., on astrology and astronomy, 193
Salas, E., 112
Sampling error, and chance, 187
Sapirstein, G., 215
Savery, T., and action, 288
Scheible, Arnold, brain as muscle, xxi
Schemata (schema):
  and accommodation, 27, 28
  and assimilation, 27, 28
  defined, 27
  and expectations, 27
  moderately discrepant information, 28
  and stereotype, 27–28
Schneidman, E., 33
Schopenhauer, A., on rational
  creatures, 230
Science, 193–225 (Chapter 10). *See also* Scientific
  method
  and abortion, 200
  deterministic assumptions of, 222
  deterministic foundation, 201–5
  domain of, 196, 199–201, 222
  domain of observation, 196
  empirical nature, 198–200
  and hypotheses, 194–95, 222
  and inductive reasoning, 176
  limitations, 222, 223
  and metaphysics, 222
  operational definition of variables,
    198–99
  probability vs. determinism, 222
  and religion, 196, 197, 199
  value of, 223
  and values questions, 200, 201, 222
  vs. philosophy and appeal to
    authority, 196
  vs. pseudoscience, 221–22
Scientific literature, amount of, 193–94
Scientific method, 193–95. *See also* Science
  cause and effect, 194
  and Christian Church, 196, 197
  experimentation and data collection, 194
  four steps, 194–95
  and hypotheses, 194
  as mental order, 122–23, 124
  and observation, 194, 199–200. *See also*
    Observation
  replication, 195, 212, 222
  systematic observation, 194
  validation and evaluating thinking, 271
  verification, 195–96
  vs. appeal to authority, 196–97
  vs. philosophy, 196

  vs. pseudoscience, 221–22
  without testing, 271
Scientific thinking. *See also* Science, Scientific
  thinking
  and cause and effect, 194
  and hypotheses, 194
Selective abstraction, 35
Selective attention, and hasty generalization, 183
Self, 19, 20, 21
Self-concept, 19–21
  and defensive thinking, 42
  defined, 19
Self-serving bias, 20, 24–26, 42
  attributions, 24, 25
  defined, 24
  and psychological health, 24
  and self-concept, 42
Seminal structural analogy, 129–30
Seneca, L., on anger, 29
Senses, 44–55 (Chapter 3)
  and the brain, 120
  deception of, 45, 47
  and evaluating, 270, 275
  limitations of, 63
  sensitivity (power of), 45, 48
  sharpening, 48–49
  and thinking, 44, 45, 47, 292
Sentential logic. *See* Propositional logic
Senzaki, N., 27
Shadow, Jung's, 26
Shakespeare, W., 1, 47, 163
  on actions, 280
  on alcohol, 58
  on brevity, 276
  on completeness, 274
  creativity, 109
  deception of the face, 53
  metaphor:
    center of literature, 273
    master of, 109
    word order, 96
Significance, 211–13, 223
Significance level, 212, 223
  two standards of, 212
Silver, B., 187
Simplicity, 272–73
Sizeable Effects, 213
Skinner, B. F.:
  on determinism and free will, 201, 204
  on prediction, 261
Sleep, 61–62
Slippery slope argument, 186
Smith, C., 61
Smith, H., brain and mind, 56
Social science:
  assumptions, 202
    contradictions of, 203–4
    of determinism, 202–5
  limited by free will, 204

Socrates:
  know thyself, 229
  unexamined life, 1
Socratic method, 113–14
Soft deductions, 151–54
  validity of, 153
  vs. classic syllogisms, 151
Solomon, King, 270
Solutions:
  evaluating and modifying, 267
  generating, 255–59, 268
  good vs. perfect, 254
  imperfect, 254, 263
  long-term and uncertainty of, 261–62
  perfect, 254
  and problem definition, 252–54
  rejections on minor grounds, 263
  selecting, 260–67
  and stress, 38
Some Common American Beliefs, 15
Sound argument:
  deductive, 141, 177
  Hume, David, 177
  inductive, 177
Spurgeon, C., on metaphor, 83–84
Starbursting, 112–14
  in evaluating thinking, 277
  vs. Socratic method, 113
State of the Nation Survey, 217–18
Status barriers, and problem solving/
    communication, 258
Stein, P., 33
Stems and affixes, 86–87
Stereotypes, 27–28
  assumptions of, 28
  defined, 27
  and enculturation, 14
  and evaluating thinking, 275
  and hasty generalization, 183
  and problem solving, 259
  and schemata, 27
  sources of, 27
Stimulants, 60
Stoicism, 98
Straw man argument, 246
Stress, 38–42
  effects on thinking, 38–39, 42
  and deciding, 38–39
  defined, 38
  and disease, 38, 39–40
  and evaluating thinking, 275
  and irrational ideas, 41, 42
  and judgment, 38
  and logical thinking, 37
  management. *See* Stress management
  and meaning, 41
  perceiving alternatives, 38–39
  preoccupation with ideas, 38, 39

problem solving, 38
signs and symptoms, 39–40
sources of, 38
Stress management, 40–42
  managing body's response, 41–42
  removing the source, 40–41
  three categories, 40
Structural requirements for syllogisms, 162
Structure. *See* Order
Subgoal analysis, 264–65
Sufficient and necessary cause, 182
Sufficient cause, 181–82
Suggestion, 246–47
Sumner, W. G., 172
Surveys, 216–20
  advantages, 217
  Ann Landers, 219
  anonymity, 217
  biased questions, 217
  defined, 216
  and honesty, 217
  representative sample, 217
  State of the Nation Survey, 217–18
  unbiased returns, 217–18
  unscientific surveys, 219–20
  validity, conditions for, 217
Sutherland, S., definition of pseudoscience, 224
Syllogism. *See also* Propositions, Deductive
    thinking
  categorical, 135–50, 154–63
    conclusion as premise, 148–50
    conclusion, truth of, 141
    defined, 135
    reasoning errors in, 154–62
    rules for, 162
  classic vs. soft deductions, 151
  deductive logic, basic form of, 134
  diagram of parts, 137
  disjunctive, 167–68
    affirmation/denial (modus pollens tollens), 167
    denial/affirmation (modus tollendo
      pollens), 167
    and either/or fallacy, 172
    and equivocation, 161
    modus pollens tollens, 167–68
    modus tollendo pollens, 167
    reasoning error in, 168
  distribution of terms, 154–56
    defined, 155
    and particular propositions, 155–56
    rules for, 162
    and singular proposition, 156
    and universal propositions, 155
  and enthymeme, 147–49
  in everyday life, 147–50. *See also* Soft deduc-
    tions, 151–54
  figures of, 138, 139–40
  hypothetical, 163–66

defined, 163–64
major premise of, 164
mixed, 164
modus pollens, 164, 166
modus tollens, 164–65
negative (modus tollens), 164–65
positive (modus pollens), 164, 166
reasoning errors in, 165–66
kinds of, 135
logical rules, 162
major premise, 135, 137
defined, 135
major term:
defined, 135, 137
and distribution error, 156–58
and figures, 138
middle term
defined, 136, 137
and distribution, 154–56
and figures, 138
rules for syllogisms, 162
minor premise:
connections between minor and major
term, 136
defined, 136, 137
minor term:
defined, 136, 137
and distribution error, 158–59
and figures, 138
modus pollens, 164, 166
modus pollens tollens, 167–68
modus tollens, 164–65
modus tollendo pollens, 167
multiple, 148–50
parts of, 136–37
predicate, defined, 136
premises:
inductively derived, 176
more than two, 148–50
and rules for syllogisms, 162
truth vs. validity, 141
reasoning errors in:
categorical, 154–62
disjunctive, 168
hypothetical, 165–66
structural requirements, 162
terms, number of, 162
undistributed middle, 154–56
logical rules for, 162
universal propositions, 137
rule, 162
valid, defined, 141
validity and truth of conclusion, 141, 148, 172
Synapse:
defined, 58
and drug effects, 60
and environmental stimulation, 62–63
Syrus, Publilius, on questions, 247

Tabula rasa, (blank slate), 45, 53
brain metaphor, 83
Tavris, C., 30
Tennyson, A., 4
Tertullian, Q., 12
Testing. *See* Evaluation
Thinker, noble like a god, 294
Thinking:
and action, xxi, 280, 288
assumptions of this text, xxiv
and the brain, 57–65. *See also* Brain
and brain's limitations, 63–64
breadth vs. depth, 293
centrality of, 6
and choices, 4, 5
as communicating, 5–6
cultural legacy, 1–2
definition, xxii, 5–6, 76
and dialogue, xxii, xxiv, 9–10
and drugs, 59–60
environmental stimulation, 62–63
evaluating, 271–77. *See also* Evaluation
importance of, 2–5, 10
and language, 76, 77, 276. *See also* Language
life without, 4–5
and memory, 65. *See also* Memory
needs and wants drive thinking, 91, 99
not isolated island, 294
and nutrition, 41–42, 58–59
only one part of us, 294
and orders, 124. *See also* Order
as possibility, 4
right word, 87
and religion, 14
and schemata, 27–28, 42
sharpening through senses, 53. *See also* Senses
testing. *See* Thinking, evaluating
as undivided, xxiii
unexpressed, 6
what we are, xxi
and writing, xxii
Thinking animals, 3
Thinking bases, xxiii-xxiv, 270
and creativity, 111
and deciding, 281, 284
as means of evaluating, 275–77
Thinking errors, 35
Third variable (hidden variable), 209, 210, 222
Third variable problem, 209
Thoughts:
accumulation of, 4–5
combination of, 5
Thriving on Chaos, 133
Time, investing, 241–42, 248
Timing, and deciding, 281, 287–88
Tinklenberg, J., 60
Toffler, A., 193
Tolstoy, L., *The Death of Ivan Ilych,* 161

Tone:
  and communication, 104
  defined, 101
  and feelings, 100–101
  and listening, 51
  and writing, 101
Topical order, 120, 131
Tractatus, 77
Transcending conventions, 259, 260
Trial and error, 260, 265, 268
Truth tables, 295–97
Truth value. *See* Propositional Logic
Truth vs. validity, 141

Unbiased return:
  defined, 217
  and surveys, 217–19
Underground Man, 283, 291
Undistributed middle. *See* Reasoning fallacies
Universal propositions. *See* Propositions
Utopia, 288

Vaillant, G., 23
Validating thinking. *See* Evaluation
Valid conversions, 168–71
Validity:
  of case-study generalization, 220
  and conclusion, 141
  of generalization, 223
  and surveys, 217
  and syllogisms, 141
  and truth of premises, 141
Values:
  and deciding, 281, 282, 283, 285
  and enculturation, 42
  and feelings, 98
  and persuasion, 230, 232–34, 236
  and science, 222
  and worth of problem solutions, 263
Values and needs:
  and persuasion, 232–34
  table, 233
Variables, 211–13
  coinciding, 253
  defining, and experimenter bias, 214
  operational definitions. *See* Operational
    definitions
  subjectivity of interpretation, 214
  wildcard, 261
Venn diagrams, 142–46
Verification. *See also* Evaluation
  and prediction, 195
  and replication, 195
Vincent, S., 60
Violent crime, 255–56
Vitamin B, 59
Voltaire, on brevity, 276
Von Franz, M. L., and the shadow, 26

Warhaft, 87
Wassil-Grimm, 68
Watson, J., 77
  DNA, 273
What Social Classes Owe to Each Other, 172
Wheeler, D., cases of Fraud, 216
Whorf, B., 2, 78
Wildcard variables, anticipating and problem solving, 261
Withholding quantification, 246
Wittgenstein, L., 2
  dualistic theory, 77
  language and life, 4, 76
  limits of language, 4
  unity of thought and language, 77
Wolpe, J., desensitization, 286
Wordiness, 92
Word order:
  and evaluating thinking, 276
  and Shakespeare, 96
Words. *See also* Nouns and Verbs, Language
  Bacon on, 87
  connotation of, 87–89
  context, 90–91
  definitions of, 87
  excite emotions, 88
  flame, 88
  malapropism, 87
  meanings, 85–86, 161–62
  order and meaning, 89–90
  precision of, 87
  right one, 87
  stems and affixes, 86–87
Wordsworth, W.:
  blank slate idea, 53
  formula for writing poems, 103
Working backwards, 260, 265–66
Writing. *See also* Language, Metaphor, Words
  analogical development, 128–30
  audience, 103–4, 231–34
  brevity, 276. *See also* Wordiness
  chronological development, 128
  clarity, 91, 124
  clichés, 49, 93–94
  connotations, 87–88
  context, 76, 90–91
  creativity, xxiii. *See also* Creativity
  definitions, 87
  descriptive papers, 53, 54–55, 129–31
  euphemisms, 81
  examples, using, 92
  feeling, xxiii, 102. *See also* Feelings
  invention. *See* Creativity
  journalistic order, 122, 124, 132
  mirror of the mind, xxii, 6–8, 10
  narration, 128
  nouns and verbs, 90
  organization, xxiii, 124–31. *See also* Order

persuasion, xxiii, 234–39. *See also* Persuasion
purpose, 229
and sensing, xxiii. *See also* Senses
and thinking, xxii, 6–9
tone, 101

topics. *See* Creativity
wordiness, 92
word order, 76, 89–90

Zuckerman, M., 24